VIEWS IN REVIEW

VIEWS IN REVIEW

POLITICS AND CULTURE

IN THE STATE OF

THE JEWS

AVISHAI MARGALIT

FARRAR · STRAUS · GIROUX · NEW YORK

Farrar, Straus and Giroux
19 Union Square West, New York 10003

Copyright © 1998 by Avishai Margalit
All rights reserved
Distributed in Canada by Douglas & McIntyre Ltd.
Printed in the United States of America
Designed by Abby Kagan
First edition, 1998

Library of Congress Cataloging-in-Publication Data
Margalit, Avishai, 1939–
   Views in review : politics and culture in the state of the Jews /
by Avishai Margalit.—1st ed.
      p.   cm.
   ISBN 0-374-24941-5 (alk. paper)
      1. Israel—Politics and government.   2. National characteristics,
Israeli.   3. Statemen—Israel—Biography.   4. Berlin, Isaiah, Sir.
I. Title.
DS126.5.M326   1998
956.94—dc21   *98-26382*

Grateful acknowledgment is made to The New York Review of Books *who published versions of many of these essays; also, to* The New Republic *for permission to reprint portions of "The Philosopher of Sympathy."*

IN MEMORY OF MY PARENTS,

MOSHE AND MIRIAM,

founding father and mother of my story

CONTENTS

PREFACE

ISRAEL IS NOT ONLY A PLACE BUT ALSO AN OBSESSION. IT MAKES A
total claim on those who are under its spell. With the poet I may say
that mad Israel hurt me into politics; that is, it made me obsessed if
not possessed with the politics of the place. Or that is how I feel on
some gloomy occasions. On other occasions, I relish Israeli politics in
spite or because of their mad intensity.

I was raised in a political home. We had politics for breakfast, for
lunch, and for supper. By politics I mean *politics*: not just political
ideas and ideals but also news of infighting and intrigues. If ideas
were our butter, what makes politicians tick was our bread. Our keen
interest was in the schemers, not only in the dreamers. Then, being
trained and becoming a trainer in philosophy drew me to the dreamers, though I never lost interest in the schemers. This book is about
both.

Over the years I have been writing about Israel and the Israelis, I have been fortunate to have Robert Silvers as my editor at *The New York Review of Books*. He constantly demanded of me facts, arguments, and plain words rather than puns, parables, and pundit's pronouncements. I may not always have been up to his demands, but I tried to be. His ability to immerse himself in another person's prose I find uncanny, and I am very grateful to him.

I am also grateful to Leon Wieseltier for his informed comments on my essay on Isaiah Berlin, which first appeared in *The New Republic*, and portions of which appear here.

Elisabeth Sifton, who suggested the ways in which I might arrange my essays in a book—not in the chronological order in which they were written but by their inner logic—was a constant source of help, encouragement, generosity, and good judgment. Over the years Naomi Goldblum has helped me put my writing in proper shape, for which I thank her.

Edna Ullmann-Margalit is my closest friend and closest critic of all my essays. No acknowledgment can do justice to her contribution to them. I only wish I knew how to express fully my gratitude for her support.

A.M.

JERUSALEM, AUGUST 1998

VIEWS IN REVIEW

INTRODUCTION

EVERY FOUR YEARS ISRAEL HOLDS SPORTS COMPETITIONS FOR JEW-
ish athletes from all over the world. This is the Jewish olympics—
the Maccabiah. Since it is a Jewish olympics there is a bit of a discount
on the notion of an athlete—even bridge players are considered athletes. The idea of the Maccabiah originated in the late 1920s, and
after the first Maccabiah many of the athletes and their companions
remained as illegal immigrants in what was then Palestine. One of
them was my mother.

In July 1997 the Maccabiah took place in Tel Aviv. A bridge was
built across the Yarkon River for the athletes to march across on their
way to the opening ceremony in the stadium. During this ceremony,
as the sky was streaked with fireworks and the President of Israel sat
with the Prime Minister in their box, while the Australian delegation
was marching across the bridge, it collapsed like a pile of matchsticks,
the marchers were tossed into the stinking, poisonous waters of the

Yarkon, and five of them lost their lives. An investigating committee set up later determined that it had collapsed as the result of "general systems failure"—that is, everyone involved in building it was responsible for the calamity.

At first glance this is nothing more than an embarrassing story about an organizational and engineering failure that ended in death —a tragic story, but not a tragedy. Yet on the very night of the event the collapse of the bridge was turned into an allegory. Even I, "as a philosopher," was asked to "reflect" in the media about the meaning of this event. A philosopher, in the Israeli media, is a person who is expected to have opinions about everything in general and about nothing in particular. From one talk show to the next the symbolic meaning of the collapsed bridge swelled. "What does it say about us? What does it say about our existence? What does it say about Israel?"

I tell the little story of the collapsed bridge, even though it is almost a "non-event" compared with many of the accidents and catastrophes that Israelis endure, because I detect a general trend in it: the tendency to describe and think about Israel in allegories. Nothing is what it is; everything is something else. This allegorical depiction of Israel is like a "general systems failure" disease—all of us who write and talk about Israel are infected with it.

In the present book I have collected essays that I wrote about Israel over quite a few years. They deal mainly with politics and the connection between politics and culture in Israel. In a certain sense they are essays in social criticism. But basically they are a sometimes desperate effort on my part to understand rather than to criticize the society I live in, a society which my parents played a part in founding and whose future, I hope, my children will share. Putting them all together has forced me to think about the way I and others write about Israel. By way of introducing them, I am presenting these thoughts both as background and as "stage directions" for reading on.

Writing for people who are not members of my community in a language which is not mine has advantages, apart from the obvious disadvantages. One advantage is that I have been forced to be explicit about issues familiar to all Israelis. Writing about matters familiar to the members of one's own community allows one to make do with lazy and cozy hints, an implicit kind of writing that is full of nuances but often based on the incorrect assumption that we all understand the obvious points. More often than not, the obvious is not obvious at all.

The subject matter of many of the essays is history: both the recent history of Israel and the events that preceded the establishment of the state fifty years ago. There are two reasons for this. First, history is obviously important when one tries to explain what is happening in the present as well as what can be hoped for and what should be feared in the future. Second, the concepts of justice which are adhered to by those involved in the tensions and conflicts within Israeli society and between Israel and its neighbors are historical concepts. They depend on answers to questions such as who was here first, who did what to whom and why. As a result, historical arguments are central—probably too central—in Israel and the Middle East.

Let us return to the bridge over the river Yarkon and ask what explains the tendency to write allegorically about Israel. At first glance it seems simple. Israel is the Holy Land whose every hill and stream is part of a sacred history and a sacred geography—an exposed mythological nerve. Sacred histories and geographies are made out of symbols rather than events, and therefore are fertile ground for allegories. The inspired historian Johan Huizinga claimed that in the Middle Ages people could not look at red and white roses blossoming among the thorns without transforming the flowers into tortured saints and virgins among their tormentors. This medieval way of thinking, in which symbolic associations replace the linking of causes with effects, is still prevalent in the Holy Land.

But the simplicity of this explanation is misleading. In a serious sense the modern Jewish settlements in Palestine, from the late nineteenth century until the establishment of the state of Israel, only barely overlapped the Jewish people's historical homeland; they were, in fact, at a distance from the symbolic regions of the "Holy Land." Take the example of the river Yarkon—in the Hebrew consciousness the antithesis of the Jordan River—and the city of Tel Aviv on its banks. The biblical Jordan River belongs to an enchanted world, with the Israelites' crossing of it on their way to the Promised Land deemed analogous in its miraculousness to their crossing of the Red Sea. The Psalmist writes, "The sea saw it, and fled, Jordan was driven back" (Psalms 114:3). The prophet Elijah struck the Jordan with his mantle and divided it in two (II Kings 2:8) just as Moses divided the Red Sea, then crossed the river with his disciple Elisha. Elisha, for his part, managed to cause the iron head of an ax, which had fallen off the wooden handle and landed in the Jordan, to float on the water. For Christians, Elijah and Elisha are prefigurations of another pair on the enchanted river Jordan—John the Baptist and Jesus. In contrast, the Yarkon River belongs entirely to the secular, nonenchanted world. The only mention of it in the Bible is as a river that runs to Jaffa. If the Jordan River is the hero, the Yarkon River is the antihero.

Jabotinsky's militant, maximalist form of Zionism had a slogan: "The Jordan River has two banks; this one's ours, and the other one, too." The import of this slogan today is that the "Greater Israel" over which some Jews are demanding domination should also include the area that is now in the Kingdom of Jordan. When they wanted to ridicule less maximalist types of Zionists, whom they called "defeatist," the militants satirically ascribed to them the slogan "The Yarkon has two banks," meaning they were willing to make do with a smaller Israel, a mere enclave in the Tel Aviv area.

When the Israelites crossed the Jordan on their way to the Land of Canaan, they came from the east. They settled on the hills of the Jordan's west bank, the same West Bank where Palestinians now live. They had almost no presence on the Mediterranean coast, where, in the western part of Canaan, on the banks of the Yarkon, lived the Philistines, a "sea people." The biblical Land of Israel, the Jewish people's "historic homeland"—the one saturated with symbolic meanings—is virtually unconnected to the land of the Philistines on the banks of the Yarkon. Yet the Zionist immigrations to Palestine, like those of the Philistines to Canaan, were from the west, from lands across the Mediterranean, and the Zionists settled mainly in the Philistine region, along the Mediterranean coast, nowhere near the Jordan. Even now, 80 percent of the Jewish population of Israel lives along the Mediterranean coast at a safe distance from their historic homeland.

The Zionist settlers chose this particular area for a number of reasons, mostly having to do with the availability of land there. But one thing is very clear: they did not choose to settle in any of the four holy cities—Jerusalem, Safed, Tiberias, and Hebron and in general avoided the symbolic regions of the Land of Israel. It is hard to believe that this was for only or even mainly economic reasons. The truth is, these symbolic regions both attracted and repulsed them at the same time. On the one hand, they had sufficient attractive force to bring the Zionist settlers to Palestine rather than Uganda, which was once suggested as a place for Jews to settle. On the other hand, they had enough repulsive force so that the Zionists, wanting a new beginning, preferred to settle near but not in them. There was no symbolic fundamentalism in the Zionist settlement of Palestine. The ideological stance that insisted Jews must literally live in the symbolic regions took hold mainly after the Six-Day War in 1967 or, more precisely, after the Yom Kippur War in 1973. Until then living nearby was good enough.

Just as the Yarkon is the antithesis of the Jordan, so Tel Aviv is the antithesis of Jerusalem. Present-day Tel Aviv is an entirely secular city that has nothing to do with sacred geography and has no sacred history—indeed, no history at all. The only Tel Aviv in the Bible was a Babylonian city on the banks of the Chebar River mentioned by the prophet Ezekiel. But even West Jerusalem, in which I have lived all my life, began to be built only in the late nineteenth century. This did not stop Jews from calling it, well before 1967, the eternal capital of the Jewish people. If the Jerusalem of my childhood was sufficiently close to the "Holy of Holies," Tel Aviv was not symbolically near anything. It was built on golden sand, not on symbols.

Gershom Scholem claimed that it is impossible to create a Jewish existence free of heavy symbolism because of the very nature of the Hebrew language. Hebrew has been used as a holy language for too many generations for us to be able to slough off its symbolic aspects, he claims. When Israeli children play hide-and-seek they declare the game over by saying, "The vessels are broken and no one is playing." This apparently innocent interjection uses an expression, "the vessels are broken," which is a foundational expression in Jewish mysticism

—an equivalent in the cosmogony of the Kabbala to the Big Bang in modern cosmology. As a native Israeli I can attest that Israeli children are able to play hide-and-seek without kabbalistic allusions. They are not alluding to anything, any more than English-speaking children playing cops and robbers and shouting "Bang bang!" are alluding to the Big Bang theory. And this is not only true of children. Israeli adults are able to fornicate, drink beer, and enjoy brass bands just like Danes, for instance, without any symbolic mantle covering their language. The tendency to use symbolism excessively is more prevalent among writers about Israel than among the people they write about.

But another tendency associated with allegorical writing does indeed infect both commentators and ordinary Israelis—the tendency to see everything as a symptom. The collapse of the bridge was perceived as a symptom of the gap between Israel's pretensions to be a technological power and the reality in which a structure whose construction should have been presumed safe nevertheless collapsed. This symptom reveals a deep anxiety in the Israeli consciousness—the fear that everything we do is a *khaltura*. *Khaltura* is the Israeli word for moonlighting. It comes from Russian, apparently from the name of a revolutionary named Khalturin whose every attempt at assassination ended in grotesque amateurish failure. Many Israelis, in my impression, fear that Israeli culture, the child of the Zionist revolution, is a culture of *khaltura*—of amateurs dressed up as professionals. Amateurs have the charm of spontaneity and an ability to improvise, and they sometimes even attain amazing achievements. But these achievements are sporadic, and the drop-offs in performance can be great and painful. Professionalism raises the general level of performance.

The idea of amateurism arouses existential anxiety because Israel's security doctrine is based on a belief that it has a "qualitative edge" over its hostile neighbors, a qualitative edge that is supposed to inhere in "islands of professionalism" such as the elite units in Israel's army and the air force, as well as in its advanced industries. When two helicopters of the Israeli Air Force collide on their way to Lebanon and seventy-five soldiers are killed, or when Israel's best naval commando unit fails in an operation in Lebanon, or when Mossad agents embarrassingly bungle an attempted assassination in Amman, the event triggers anxiety that Israel's qualitative edge has eroded. Given Israel's long record of violent conflicts with its neighbors, this existential anxiety heightens a hypochondriac tendency to find diagnostic symptoms for the "Israeli situation" everywhere, even in the collapse of the bridge. My own use of the story of the bridge may attest to this tendency.

People write about Israel in clichés. But, then, people write about every country and every issue in clichés. Many clichés are written about Israel because so much is written about Israel. For a long time Israel was the third-greatest newsmaking country in the world, after the United States and the Soviet Union. The need to avoid clichés leads writers to make desperate attempts to find "interesting angles" for describing Israeli reality. They resort to writing about Israel in paradoxes, which has itself become a sophisticated cliché. Once upon a time, in our age of innocence, there were cute paradoxes: it was a country where mothers learned their mother tongue from their children; or—the mother of all clichés—the native Israeli was called a Sabra, from the word for prickly pear, which is thorny on the outside and sweet on the inside, a cliché that gives all clichés a bad name. Nowadays the paradoxes are based on striking contrasts between the "old" and the "new," on "historical ironies" in which every action leads to results opposite to those intended by the agents, and on other kinds of backward somersaults that are supposed to present Israel as more exotic than it already is.

One finds the tendencies to write allegorically, symptomatically, and paradoxically about Israel among all writers about this country, including myself. But it is always difficult to write simply, directly, and informatively, especially where Israel is concerned. These are problems not of style but of content, and the content involves mainly the underlying concept of Israel's history.

Zhou Enlai was once asked whether the French Revolution was a good or a bad thing. "Too soon to tell," answered the aged leader. This is a long view. From an equally long perspective the question of whether or not the "Zionist revolution" in Jewish history succeeded surely does not yet have an answer. Yet we have an understandable, if illusory, wish to get a prompt answer to questions that can truly be answered only in the long run. But in the long run, as Keynes remarked, we shall all be dead.

THE ESSAYS COLLECTED here discuss leading figures in Israeli history, problems of the Israeli polity, matters of Israeli culture and ideology. I have the impression that there is a clear dividing line between the historical consciousness of the political leaders I have written about—Sharon, Shamir, Peres, Rabin, Netanyahu, Barak— and that of the writers of the books I also discuss (excluding, of course, the books written by the leaders themselves). To use Nietzsche's terminology, the line is that between the monumental and the critical approach to history.

Nietzsche distinguishes three human situations: acting, respecting others, and suffering. Monumental history is associated with the acting hero. People who create this type of history are in situations of great conflict and need heroes from the past to identify with. In the face of difficulties and obstacles, these past heroes demonstrate that the difficulties are temporary and that once they are overcome there is greatness to be attained. David Ben-Gurion, first Prime Minister of Israel, served as a monumental hero for political leaders like Rabin, Peres, and Sharon. The Maccabiah ceremony begins with a torch relay, in which the torch is handed on from Modi'in, the place where the Maccabees' revolt against the Greeks broke out in the second century B.C.E., until it reaches Tel Aviv. The monumental approach sees history as a relay in which the historical heroes are the torchbearers. In Ben-Gurion's monumental perspective his predecessors were Moses, who took the Israelites out of Egypt and handed the torch to Joshua, who conquered the Land of Canaan and handed the torch to rulers who handed it on to King David, and then to Judas Maccabaeus, who rebelled against the Greeks and established the Hasmonean Kingdom; the torch was then handed on to Bar Kokhba, who rebelled against the Romans, but then it was extinguished for two millennia, until finally it was rekindled by Ben-Gurion himself.

Critical history, on the other hand, is a response to moral distress. It attempts to settle accounts with the past, indeed to serve up indictments against the past. Critical historians select facts about the past the way prosecuting attorneys do: to make a convincing case against the accused. They consider themselves the exact opposite of antiquarian and monumental historians. And the monumental and critical approaches clash not only over what happened but also over what might have happened instead. Israeli historians who take the critical view stress the opportunities that were missed—for saving Jews during the Holocaust, for making peace with the Arabs at various junctures, for establishing a more just socialist society or an open liberal one. (Sometimes the two types switch. Critical historians, who in principle underplay the importance of individual will in shaping history, nevertheless blame the heroes for various failures, as if life had been subject to their will. And monumental historians, who supposedly give decisive weight to the will of leaders, tend to present those leaders' cruel decisions as a manifestation of the inevitable course of history.)

Both monumental and critical histories of Zionism are largely reactions to its pretensions of having brought about a revolution in Jewish life. The state of Israel is the product of an ideology whose standard-bearers considered themselves revolutionaries. The combination of ideology and revolution on the one hand gives rise to monumental history, and on the other invites a sharply critical view. Indeed, the very use of the word "revolution" is suspect because every historical event that people want to invest with drama and importance is given the honorific title "revolution." "Revolution" is especially suspect in the case of Zionism, for Zionism does not fit the stereotype of a revolution at all. Many of the early Western European Zionists were more like Victorian philanthropists than revolutionaries. And the Zionist movement in its early stages was so full of idle chatter it could not be seriously considered revolutionary. Just looking at the photographs of the representatives at the First Zionist Congress, mummified in their stiff collars and black frock coats, is enough to suggest that the combination of "Zionism" and "revolution" is as oxymoronic as "cold fire." In fact, most of these early Zionists were philanthropists who considered the "Jewish problem" to be not their own personal problem but rather the problem of their poor relatives in Eastern

Europe, to the solution of which they had to contribute something.

The Hebrew author S. Y. Agnon, a Nobel laureate and a committed but ironic Zionist, wrote a story in which an implicit comparison is made between a group of Zionists who travel to a Galician town and a Bundist socialist who happens to be on the same train on his way to the same town to meet his fiancée. (The Bund was a radical Jewish socialist movement that in prerevolutionary Russia was at least as large as the Communist Party.) The day they arrive there is a pogrom against the Jews in that town. The Bundist, who rushes to their defense, is arrested by the police, and his shackled hands are bleeding. At that very moment the Zionist leader arrives, carrying a bouquet of roses he has received at a Zionist banquet. The Bundist turns out to be the true revolutionary who is willing to sacrifice himself. His hands are red with his own blood while the Zionist's hands are red with roses. Agnon suspected that only socialists were capable of total devotion whereas Zionists were destined to hold ceremonies.

Nevertheless I believe that the Zionist movement at its practical level, putting its ideas into action, had true revolutionary zest and great willingness to endure personal sacrifice, no less than the Bund. This Zionism considered the "Jewish problem" its own problem and aspired to revolution in the deep sense of the word—what Nietzsche calls a "reevaluation of all values." Practical Zionism tried to promote a radical transformation of values in Jewish life, not a mere change —even if a fundamental one—in the social order in which Jews might find a solution to their problem. But it did not aspire to be revolutionary in the sense of violent action. The French Revolution, which was very bloody indeed, has become a paradigm for revolutions in general, and the trait of violence has taken over the concept of revolution to the point where they are generally conflated. But I believe that violence is linked with revolution only correlatively, not essentially.

The Zionist revolution was not violent among the Jews themselves. The number of political assassinations that have occurred in a century of Zionism—including the terrible murder of Yitzhak Rabin—is minuscule. Perhaps the assassination of Rabin was a turning point, and maybe there will be violent clashes in the future between those who consider themselves sane Zionists and messianic Zionists. But the Zionist revolution was a velvet revolution as far as violence among Jews is concerned. Nevertheless, it has had very violent effects—in the bloody clashes that its efforts to realize its goals have brought about between Jews and Arabs.

I ascribe great significance to the Zionists' revolutionary aspiration to change traditional Jewish values, both as an active historical force and as a criterion for evaluating their achievement. Turning Jewish values around means changing the Jewish people's viewpoint on how Jews should live their lives, as a collective and as individuals. This is much more radical than to criticize actual events in the light of accepted values.

For many centuries exilic Jews harshly judged events in their own lives on the basis of traditional religious values. The idea that they were in exile meant that theirs was not the sort of life they thought they ought to be living, which could come about only through miraculous redemption. The Zionists' critique of Jewish life in the Diaspora, which has come to be known as the "Negation of the Exile," blamed traditional Jewish values for preserving this negative attitude toward exilic life; Zionists claimed that in insisting that change could occur only through divine intervention, not through political action, the old Jewish values prevented change. The Negation of the Exile was often quite vitriolic, with clear anti-Semitic overtones. The exilic Jews were seen as flawed, ill with a sort of spiritual sickness that required moral correction.

The Zionist inversion of values also transformed the notion of the ideal Jew from a rabbinical scholar to a pioneer who would both till the land and fight. Socialists spoke of tilling the land, while bourgeois Jews wanted to own it. Both were considered to be turning values around from the situation of Jews in exile who, in most Western countries, were forbidden to own land and were thus disconnected from nature. Tilling the land would heal the Jewish people in general and individual Jews in particular, would transform them from being parasites to being producers. Working the land in particular and doing manual labor in general were considered paradigms of productive work that should replace the "parasitic" traditional Jewish occupations of trader and middleman. The turnaround of values would "invert the pyramid" of Jewish occupations, so that the broad base would consist of farmers and manual laborers.

This Zionist aspiration had very concrete historical consequences. In order to work the land, you have to have land. And if tilling the land was such a central element in the Zionist value system, then land must be acquired for Jewish settlers in Palestine and Jews must work this land themselves. This apparently innocent, pastoral aim contained the seeds of the clash between Jews and Palestinian Arabs. For this was land where the Palestinians lived, and tilling this land was what they did.

The various trends of Zionism differed in how large a turnaround they demanded of Jews. Menachem Begin's militant Zionism, which is being continued by Benjamin Netanyahu's party, demanded solely a change in attitude toward military power. It sees the Jews as having lost their pride during centuries of exile because of lack of power, so the restoration of Jewish power, including military power, is thus not merely of instrumental value for realizing the goal of a Jewish state in the Land of Israel, but of major educational significance for molding a "generous and cruel race." This form of Zionism is minimalist in the degree of value change it advocates but maximalist in its claims on real estate.

The Zionism of the Labor movement, which was and is dominant in practical Zionism, had, on the other hand, far-reaching expectations about an extensive transvaluation of all Jewish values. Its demands are aristocratic, in a way, and lead to elitist haughtiness, though the Labor Zionists' patronizing elitism was not mere *Mayflower* snobbery—it had a clear ideological basis. Eventually it led to the Labor movement's alienation from many of Israel's so-called Oriental Jews, and this has had severe effects on Israeli politics. And it was one of many causes that led to the even more tragic alienation between Jews in Palestine and the Jews who remained in Europe; the Holocaust gave this a horrific twist.

BEFORE THE MODERN era, Jewish history had already gone through a crucial turnaround of values, old enough to be judged even by Zhou

Enlai's standards: what I shall call the transition from biblical to rabbinical Judaism. This was accomplished by a bold, extensive interpretative enterprise that changed the way Jews understood many biblical figures. For example, the biblical patriarch Jacob—whose adopted name, "Israel," later became the name of the Jewish state—was transformed from a shepherd and a sort of nomadic Bedouin patriarch into a rabbinical Torah scholar. Where the Bible says that he was a "tent dweller," for instance, new homiletic interpretations turned him into a dweller in a metaphorical tent called "the tent of the Torah," no less than a house of learning in which Jacob studies the Torah all his life. This was not the usual case of an artistic anachronism intended to bring a biblical figure closer to the reader, as in the seventeenth-century painter Claude Lorrain's encounter between Jacob and Laban in the shade of leafy trees in a landscape of water and Alpine mountains. Rather, the new interpretation was based on a fundamental turnaround of values, in which actual shepherds become metaphorical ones, the Torah scholar was placed at the top of the value scale, and the violent battles described in the Bible were explained as verbal debates about issues of law in the house of learning. In this value inversion there was no place for a civic value like courage, which was replaced by extreme devotion. Martyrs no longer died in acts of ultimate courage but in acts of ultimate devotion.

The rabbis presented this turnaround of values as a precise continuation of the old ways, devoid of change. It remains an open question whether the rabbinical commentators were aware of the value inversion they perpetrated. I believe they understood it very well, but this is not the point here. What is important for our purposes is that a radical turnaround of values can take place without any pretensions and perhaps even without the awareness of its occurrence. In this case, the explicit goal was exactly the opposite of what in fact occurred: the rabbis declared their complete loyalty to the preservation of values. The "phonetic fanaticism" of the rabbinical literature did not allow even the slightest deviation from the biblical passages being interpreted, after all. Secular Zionism, in contrast, required an explicit transformation of Jewish values, sometimes blatantly and intentionally distorting traditional expressions. For example, there is a biblical commandment to declare the unity of God twice every day, using the formula in Deuteronomy 6:4, "Hear O Israel, the Lord is our God, the Lord is One." At the Maccabiah ceremonies in the 1930s, however, when the torchbearer arrived at the stadium, he would declare, "Hear O Israel, our fate is One Israel."

Thus a turnaround in values can occur with or without explicit declarations. But declarations can also occur without values actually having changed. Did Zionism actually bring about an inversion of Jewish values? Zionism undoubtedly transformed Jewish life dramatically: it led to the establishment of an independent state for the Jewish people. But did this also change what Jews think about what the good life is for the Jewish people in general and for individual Jews, too? Obviously there has been a revolutionary transformation in modern Jewish life, and it includes an essential change in values, but not the declared Zionist one.

Until the modern age European Jews constituted one of the many groups within Europe's feudal society. The Jewish associations were religious communities with broad autonomy to conduct their internal affairs. Occasionally they flourished, but generally they were discriminated against and even persecuted. But it would be a grave error to think that their lives were devoid of politics. There was a complex, sophisticated Jewish politics whose purpose was to safeguard the rights of the Jewish corporations. The fact that Jewish diplomats were called "pleaders" does not mean that Jewish diplomacy did not exist.

Zionism has prided itself not only for returning the Jewish people to its historic homeland but also for bringing the Jews back to history: this metaphor of "return" is both pretentious and misleading. The Jews were not passive objects of persecution, lacking effective political will. Jewish communities achieved political gains for their members, some of which were impressive in comparison with the achievements of other medieval associations. These gains were extracted by economic rather than military power, but this does not mean that Jews are excluded from history. The idea that Jews appeared on the "stage" of history in the first act as players with swords, that they were taken offstage in the second act when their swords were broken, and that the Viennese Zionist playwright Theodor Herzl returned them to the footlights in the third act with guns—this is a farce. The Jews were always part of history.

In the modern era in Europe, with the breakdown of the structure of the medieval associations and with the centralization of authority, the autonomy of the Jewish communities was seriously damaged. All subjects, or citizens, were to be integrated into the nation. The integration of the Jews is the name of a problem, not of a solution. In many countries liberals, particularly, believed that the way to integrate Jews into civil society was to "improve" them, morally as well as aesthetically. They were expected to wear modern clothes and speak the national language without a Yiddish accent. Sometimes integration required conversion, especially as a condition for a civil service post, a professorship, a staff position in a hospital. The demand that the Jews "improve" themselves was also shared by secular, educated Jews who aspired to assimilate into the general society. Yet, ironically, it was precisely those Jews who underwent such "improvements" and managed this integration—often with dizzying success as economic and cultural competitors in the urban middle class—who brought modern anti-Semitism upon themselves and their fellow Jews. (One form of it is based on the notion that modern Jews, who compete with Gentiles in their new respectable guise, are more dangerous than old-fashioned Jews. This sort of anti-Semitism views Jews as flawed in their essence because of their "race," rather than solely or mainly because of their religion. The philosopher Sidney Morgenbesser once asked his students to list three events in the modern age that could not be explained as due to the rise of the middle class. This kind of modern anti-Semitism would not appear on the list.)

My description of European Jewish life is obviously schematic. The forces attracting people to the traditional Jewish community and those repelling them from it were very complex. For many Jews it was not a matter of choosing between the old club of the Jewish community or the new club of the civil society, but of drifting. "Leaving the ghetto" was not necessarily undertaken in order to lose one's Jewish identity, to assimilate into the larger community as quickly as possible. The accusation that Jewish intellectuals intentionally denied their Jewish identity in order to assimilate is more polemical than historical. European and, later, American Jews had to find their place in a changing world, as everyone did, for everyone had to respond to the new conditions—urbanization, industrialization, worker mobility, social mobility, expanding markets, extensive division of labor, widespread education, and accelerated secularization. Jews may have been more affected than others around them because the changes were most intense in the cities, where most of them lived. (In Warsaw and Odessa in the late nineteenth century, for example, more than 30 percent of the inhabitants were Jews, whereas in the population as a whole they represented only 4 percent.) And it was modernization, which began in western Europe and spread eastward, that led to the most profound changes in the lives of Jews, many of whom adopted values, ideologies, and lifestyles appropriate to the new age that, for lack of a better term, I shall call "modernist."

If modernism was a revolution, the Jews were its avant-garde. They did not wait for Zionism to transform their values. Indeed, Zionism, imbued as it was and is with nationalist romanticism, was perhaps the least modern ideology of those espoused by Jews who had left the ghetto. Even the Zionist battle cry for a revolution in the traditional occupations of Jews was essentially antimodernist, for the Jewish communities in the Diaspora had occupational structures that fit economically developed societies much better than did the agrarian fantasy at the heart of the Zionist dream.

Sometimes a loss of old values is associated with nostalgia and sentimental sadness. And sometimes this nostalgia has the power to adapt an old value to a new reality. An example is in the history of the word *mensch*. In the shtetl being a *mensch* meant being someone capable of compassion and sympathy for people, singly or in groups, who were in distress. The early Jewish immigrants to the United States and some people of my parents' generation in Palestine gave this word a new meaning: it came to express a person who exemplified the obligation of adopting a policy of defending minorities and the oppressed—not so much out of ideology but because "you have to be a *mensch*." But the aggressiveness that Israel introduced into Jewish life destroyed this ideal. Even the nostalgia for being a *mensch*, in the old-fashioned sense, is not what it used to be.

Another example is the idea that one must act with *sechel*. In Hebrew this word means "intellect" or "reason," but when it was adapted into Yiddish—with the pronunciation "seychel"—it acquired new connotations. One of them is "good sense," a good realistic sense of judgment; another is "common sense," which implies suspicion of theories and doctrines, irony and skepticism about what one can expect of people. In addition, *sechel* shows in a forgiving, humorous attitude toward human weakness and, perhaps most important, in an infinite willingness to make the compromises that "life demands." In Mapai, the leading political party of the Labor movement, quite a few people had *sechel*, and this was not held against them. Levi Eshkol, for example, "the great compromiser," who succeeded Ben-Gurion as Prime Minister, was generally acknowledged to have a great deal of *sechel*. The story has it that when asked, "Tea or coffee?" he would answer, "Half of each." This story became a symbol of Mapai compromise. Pinhas Sapir, Eshkol's Finance Secretary, was also a person with *sechel*. These practical Mapai men were very far from having either a monumental or a critical view of Jewish history. Another person with a supreme degree of *sechel* was Chaim Weizmann, Israel's first President. Weizmann was not in the Labor movement, but he became an ally, partly because he believed Labor had people with *sechel*. Weizmann couldn't imagine that the Jews could have a state without *sechel*. He was wrong.

The Mapainiks I've mentioned were the Mensheviks of the Zionist revolution. If there was one thing none of them believed in, it was the idea that human beings can be changed. They considered Menachem Begin and his Herut faction as lacking in *sechel* (except for Yohanan Bader). The Zionist revolution's Lenin, Ben-Gurion, also did not believe one could change the values of the Jewish immigrants to Israel, but he considered them a transitional generation, like the Israelites who wandered in the desert for forty years after leaving Egypt so that their children could enter the Promised Land with the mentality of free people. He believed that the immigrants' children would undergo the hoped-for turnaround in values, and he intended to bring this about whether or not they wanted it.

If Jewish values were transformed without Zionism, as part of the great thrust of modernization, why do I place so much stress on the Zionist aspiration to turn Jewish values around? Because Zionism aspired to effect this transformation of Jews *within their own state*. This aspiration went far beyond the task, already difficult enough, of establishing a state for Jewish people in their historic homeland. It demanded political expression of the profound social and mental change in the way Jews should and would live—as individuals and as a Jewish collective. The philosopher Yeshayahu Leibowitz, a most critical Zionist himself, described Zionism in very minimalist terms: Zionism, he said, wanted a state for the Jewish people because Jews were sick and tired of living under Gentile rule. As with many of his claims, you can't be sure whether this was meant to be a factual description or a prescriptive explanation of what he thought should have been Zionism's aim. My own claim, which I make as a factual description, is that the Zionism of the Labor movement aspired to far more than that. It was to be an internal Jewish transformation, not one based on an external ideology. Although even non-Marxist wings of the Labor movement called themselves socialist, they based their transformational hopes not on international socialism, but, rather, on secular variations of the biblical theme of the "chosen people." The exemplary Jewish community of an independent state had to preserve the old idea of chosenness. To be sure, not everyone said, as Ben-Gurion did, that Israel must be a "light unto the nations." Many said Israel should simply be a normal state, like the better of the Gentile nations. But the intensity with which the demand for normality was stated made even this idea somewhat abnormal.

I CLAIM THAT much of the criticism of Israel, both internal and external, is directed at its pretensions rather than its reality. Pretension breeds criticism.

There is a sense in which Zionism's pretension to turn Jewish values around failed even before anyone tried to bring it about: The European Jews who were supposed to be the subjects of the revolution were murdered in the Holocaust, and the other Jews whom Israel then recruited to take their place did not necessarily want to transform their values. Let me spell this out.

During the nineteenth century, Jews experienced a dramatic demographic shift. In 1800 there were about 2.5 million Jews in the world,

80 percent of them in Europe. By mid-century the number of European Jews had increased to 5 million. The global total increased dramatically in the twentieth century—13.5 million on the eve of World War I and 16.5 million on the eve of World War II. In 1913, 5.5 million of the 13.5 million Jews lived in tsarist Russia, another 2.5 in the Austro-Hungarian Empire; in the United States, where Jews had numbered only 250,000 in 1890, the Jewish population, swollen by an unprecedented immigration, reached about 3.5 million. Only 8 percent of the Jews in the world at that time were Oriental, or Sephardic.

The people who spoke for the Zionist movement always spoke of the Jewish people as a whole, but Zionism as a solution to the "Jewish problem"—a label for a host of problems—was intended for European Jews, more precisely for East and Central European Jews. Oriental Jews were almost beyond the Zionist horizon: they were a small minority of Jews, they were culturally and geographically remote, and they did not speak Yiddish, the shared language of European Jews. But the murder of 6 million European Jews in the Holocaust changed the Jewish demographic map and, with it, the configuration of Jews who were potential citizens of the future Jewish state.

At present 80 percent of Israel's roughly 5 million residents are Jews, and half of them are Oriental Jews. The story of the Oriental Jews is complicated. Before the birth of Israel, there were Zionist movements in Iraq, Egypt, even Tunisia, Algeria, and Morocco; but as a rule they were apolitical and semi-messianic; they certainly did not promote a change of values. On the contrary, the Middle Eastern and North African Jews considered value change an act of extreme disloyalty to their parents, families, and communities, and they experienced the changes imposed on them when they arrived in Israel as coercive and patronizing. Just as Peter the Great's "modernizing" act of forcing Russian boyars to shave off their beards was perceived as tyrannical, so Israel's forcing Yemenite boys to cut off their long curly sidelocks—at the time of the great immigration of Yemenite Jews to Israel in the 1950s—became a symbol of coercive tyranny in the name of "modernization."

Nietzsche wrote that values cannot be refuted, only frozen. The values of the Oriental Jews in Israel were frozen, but now they are thawing out—a very important and powerful cultural and political fact. Naturally, Jewish immigrants to Israel from Islamic countries, like those from Europe, underwent many extreme transformations in their lives, but I am interested here not in actual life changes but in changes in one's view of how one ought to live. At present the slogan about "returning to the ancient glory," used by the Oriental Jews' strongest political party, is gaining ground, and this is quite openly a battle cry against the Zionist ideal of transformed values.

One book I discuss in an essay here is entitled *The Tragedy of Zionism.* The tragedy of Zionism for me (and this is different from what that book's author meant) is that the European Jews who should have been Zionism's revolutionaries were murdered or, if they managed to escape the Holocaust, were trapped in the straitjacket of Communist regimes hostile to Zionism. Of course, all or even most European Jews had not been Zionist—far from it; and true, after the destruction of European Jewry the contrasts between Zionists and non-Zionists were muted and opposition to Zionism faded. But even when Zionists had encountered harsh, consistent opposition among their fellow Jews, they were still candidates for revolution. The revolution came too late.

MY CENTRAL CLAIM here is that the Zionist aspiration for a revolution in values invites both a monumental perspective and a sharply critical one. The question is not whether these two perspectives are psychologically plausible: obviously a declared yet unfulfilled pretension, like a hot-air balloon, provokes us to stick a pin in it. For example, Israel has pretensions to foster a cultural and scientific renaissance among Jews. Yet while German Jews before World War II won many Nobel Prizes in the sciences, no Israeli scientist has been a Nobel laureate. Similarly, although Zionism was supposed to have changed the Jewish attitude toward the body—as the Maccabiah suggests—it was Mark Spitz, a skinny "exilic" member of the American delegation to the Maccabiah, who went on to win seven Olympic gold medals, while Israeli athletes so far have won only one silver medal, in women's judo. But these are just annoying pinpricks.

What drives a sword rather than a pin into Israel's pretensions is the claim that in all of Jewish history there has never been such a parasitic community, so dependent on donations from elsewhere, as modern Israel. What happened to Zionism's moral revolution in values? The Labor movement used to say, It is easy to be moral when you have no power—you have the morality of the victim, which is what Jews in exile had, a "spiritual" morality that did not have the responsibility that comes with power—but we shall establish a society with military power, and we shall be capable of violent undertakings but have a different attitude toward them; we shall act morally even in using force; there will be no unnecessary violence but violence only for defense and never offense; we shall engage in war only when we have no choice, when war is imposed on us; and we shall not fight any wars whose purpose is to further the interests of the Jewish state by violent means. This is why Israel's army is called the Israel Defence Forces (IDF).

Nowadays this credo sounds hollow. After the Lebanon War in 1982, which Begin expressly called a war of choice, it was forgotten that the pretensions expressed in this credo had existed in the Labor movement throughout its many years of hegemony—in the pre-state Jewish settlement in Palestine as well as later in the state of Israel. They attract flames of criticism, not merely pinpricks of annoyance. The Zionist doctrine of Israel's "purity of arms" must confront all the war horrors committed by the armed forces of the Jewish settlement in Palestine—the Haganah, the Irgun, and the Lehi—as well as by the IDF after 1948. And consider Israel's wars one by one: were they wars of choice or no choice? The list begins with the Sinai, or Suez, campaign in 1956, when Israel joined the collusion between France and Great Britain to make war on Egypt. It continues with the Six-Day War of 1967, which Egypt did indeed blatantly provoke but which, it can be argued, might have been avoided. And so on.

It is easy to recognize these flames of criticism, and I saw them often in the books I have written about in these essays. The question I want to ask is not whether Israeli deeds invite or justify such moral criticism but whether the very aspirations of Israel and of the Jewish settlement in Palestine justify this holy fury. After all, the worst thing one can say about ungrounded moral pretensions is that they involve hypocrisy. Hypocrisy resulting from pretensions is a nasty, irritating trait, but it is in my view minor in comparison with cruelty and humiliation.

I have reservations about critical history, for it gives exaggerated weight to its denunciation of hypocrisy, seeing it as the vice of all vices, because, it is claimed, integrity can coexist with many vices but not with hypocrisy. Hannah Arendt, writing about revolution, claimed that crime and criminals make us wonder about radical evil, but only hypocrisy is rotten to the core. This comment seems adolescent to me, as do many other remarks made against hypocrisy in the name of sincerity. My own view is that there are two possible ways of looking at hypocrisy: either the hypocrite is self-deceived and is unaware of his hypocrisy, in which case the cause of his lack of integrity is his self-deception; or he is aware of his hypocrisy and is using it for his own ends, in which case he is no different from any other cheat or pretender, and is preserving whatever integrity he has under his false mask. No, there is no need to make the world safe for hypocrisy, and no need to make it a mortal sin either.

I do not feel comfortable with monumental history either, for it is often not history but mythology. Even if you are critical of Israel, you can recognize that its establishment was an amazing social and political success story. When Herzl wrote *The Jewish State*, only a few tens of thousand Jews lived in Palestine, and while he was writing the book, he would test himself from time to time by solving arithmetical problems, to prove to himself that he was not losing his mind. Then, only fifty years after the First Zionist Congress, the Zionist movement succeeded in establishing an independent state. A poor community of 650,000 Jews then more than doubled itself in four years (mainly through immigration), managed to make forgotten and almost lost Hebrew its official and literary language (spoken by all these new immigrants), and became a major military power. This is a fantastic story, which can be perceived as an ignoble political success story or as a noble ethical failure, but one cannot but be impressed by it, just as one cannot ignore its painful darker side—the expulsion of the Palestinians from their land and their oppression under Israeli occupation. The story of Israel must be told as a complex problematic rather than as a monumental saga.

BOTH THE MONUMENTAL and the critical kinds of historiography are "in the service of life," as Nietzsche put it. What about history in the service of truth? Shouldn't we study history in order to find out what really happened, not in the service of life but in an attempt to understand the past and the present? Not an attempt to praise or blame, but to understand?

I have no suicidal desire to enter into the debate about whether history can be written objectively. The issue has been discussed with great intensity in the controversy between the "old" and the "new" historians in Israel, a debate in which Tom Segev, another author I write about here, is a participant. In his view the controversy is not between "old" and "new" historians but between old mythmakers and new historians, for he believes that Israeli historiography began only recently, when relevant archives were first opened for public scrutiny. I don't think that's the important distinction, since the "old historians," given their closeness to people in power, could always gain access to archives even when they were officially "closed." In my opinion, the division lies elsewhere—between the "old" antiquarian tendencies and the "new" critical approaches. But both these approaches are histories in the service of life, to use Nietzsche's terms.

Some of the participants in the debate, especially on the critical side, are postmodernists who believe that there is no such thing as history in the service of truth, that all history is in the service of life. For them the critical question is "Whose life?" They direct their criticism at what they fashionably call the "Zionist meta-narrative," which they say is the purportedly authoritative version of Israeli history told by the Ashkenazi elite. They claim that many stories should be told from many different points of view: that of the Palestinian Arab citizens of Israel, of Palestinians under Israeli rule who are not citizens, of Oriental Jews, of non-Zionist ultra-Orthodox Jews, of women—people at the periphery of Israeli society. In short, there are many perspectives on Israeli history. The dominant one—from which

Israel is seen as an idealistic, Zionist, Ashkenazi society surrounded by enemies, absorbing new immigrants and taking them through an accelerated modernization process—is at best only one of them; at worst it perpetuates the hegemony of an elite served by "old" historians and sociologists. Here postmodernism becomes a post-Zionist ideology.

The debate has been fruitful, for it has opened up a discussion about new ways of understanding history and society—in spite of all the buzzwords like "discourse," "narrative," "subtext," "code," "social construction," appearing in it with irritating frequency. There really is something to be learned about different versions of the truth concerning Israel. Be the authors' motive "oedipal," a desire to "murder" the founding fathers of Israel, or antiquarian, an uncritical internalization of the founding fathers as the nation's "superego," many true, thoughtful insights are achieved. Still, I believe in the possibility of history not in the service of life—life of the brother or life of the other—but in the service of truth. We do not need the perspective that Zhou Enlai wanted, but we do need a greater distance than historians have today.

Let us focus on only one historical issue directly relevant to political life in Israel—namely, the use of historical analogies. Historical understanding is based on judgments of similarity among peoples and events, just as the law is based on precedents, and to call different events revolutions, for example, is to judge what is similar about them. Similarity is based on a ratio of shared to distinctive features, and our judgments depend on the relative weights we assign to various features. (For example, I assign more weight to value change and less to violence in calling Zionism revolutionary.) But history has no natural phenomena; revolution, unlike radium, is not a natural phenomenon. So when a set of historical events is described as a "revolution," these events do not become a homogeneous group for which general laws can be formulated, as one can for radium. And judgments about historical similarity and difference are not objective or scientific. They vary from one historian to the next, from one historical period to the next, and no facts can decide between them. With laws of nature, different scientists' classification of things into kinds, such as radium or rabbits, can be judged by their explanatory and, in particular, their predictive power. But this has no analogue in history: there are no such laws and no worthwhile predictions in history.

Historicism denies not only the existence of historical laws but the possibility of historical analogy. Each event or hero is unique and can be understood only in the chronological sequence in which it occurs. In one sense many Jewish historians have been historicists solely with respect to Jewish history, claiming that historical analogies are good only for Gentiles. For them, as for Tolstoy, all happy families are alike but every unhappy family is unhappy in its own way: the Gentiles are all happy, but the Jews are unhappy in their own unique way. This caricature of Jewish historicism captures a characteristic line of thought in Jewish and Israeli culture: a deep distaste for making historical analogies between Jews and Gentiles. In current debates in Israel it is acceptable to compare present-day Jews with Jews of the Second Temple period but unacceptable to compare Israel, say, with other fifty-year-old states such as India. The only analogy that the political right in Israel permits is the one that compares every Israeli compromise in which Israel gives up something to the Munich agreement; every "surrender" reminds them of Neville Chamberlain's umbrella.

One barrier to comparing Israel with other countries and societies is a linguistic one: there is no "immigration" to Israel, but only *aliyah*—namely, "going up," rising, in a spiritual sense. *Aliyah* is more akin to spiritual pilgrimage than to ordinary immigration. Yet one way to understand Israel is, quite obviously, to compare it with other immigrant societies.

The barriers historicism erects against comparing Israel with Gentile nations is related to the monumental view of Jewish history. But even the critics are not always helpful, since they focus on the discrepancy between ideological aspiration and reality, and compare the actual state of affairs in Israel not with the actual situation in other countries but with "theoretical models." For example, critical historians often claim that Israel is a militaristic state—in comparison not with, say, Tojo's Japan or Tito's Yugoslavia, but with models of militaristic society. This is like a hypochondriac reading about the symptoms of a disease and finding them in himself. "Models" of militaristic societies are not like billiard-ball models of a kinetic theory of molecules; they are vague, general, and simplistic; like horoscopes, they fit whatever we want them to. To understand Israel's history and society better, we need careful comparisons with other actual societies.

There is also the question of which Israel is being compared. There is the "smaller Israel" of 1948–67, which existed within the Green Line, as it was called, for nineteen years. And there is the "Greater Israel" that conquered the West Bank from Jordan and the Golan Heights from Syria and the Gaza Strip from Egypt, which has been in existence for thirty years. The Israeli regime today can be described as a democratic one that still exists within the Green Line, with the addition of territories under military occupation being held temporarily for the purpose of negotiation. Alternatively, it can be described as a regime that rules the entire area of Greater Israel, with the temporary nature of the military occupation being in doubt. Meron Benvenisti, two of whose books I consider in these essays, is the leading exponent of the view that Israel must now be judged within the geographic setting of Greater Israel, and that its regime is similar to the "democracy of masters" in ancient Athens—where the masters are Israeli citizens and the Palestinians are the helots. In this picture, the Oslo Accords did not change the situation substantially. And lastly, Israel can be described vaguely, as an entity without geographic or social borders, since it purports to be the homeland of the entire Jewish people.

History is also a branch of rhetoric. Historians debate as to the most appropriate way to write it: as a drama, as a story narrated by either an omniscient author or a participant, or, rejecting these "literary" forms, as a reasoned argument. Many of the critical books I discuss here seem to me to be like indictments in a legal drama.

If Israel is living a legal drama, where do I fit in? I am neither Israel's prosecuting attorney nor its defense attorney. I am certainly not its judge. The only role I can seriously consider is that of a witness. But what sort of witness? I am not a state witness. I belong to Israeli society as an engaged citizen, but in no way can I provide inside information in return for immunity from prosecution. I am not an expert witness, because I am not an expert. I am not a moral witness in the sense that, say, Anna Akhmatova was in Stalin's Russia ("I stand here as a witness for the simple people who survived from those times and places"), and I have no special moral standing—I am neither persecuted nor a sufferer. I am not even an eyewitness to much of what I write about; I am a witness mostly through listening and reading.

But I really do not like the role of witness at all. I do not like the idea of describing Israel through an explicit or implicit legal drama. I see myself in a different guise, in the role of an anthropologist's native informant, a member of the tribe who tells the anthropologists about the tribal customs and, especially, about its language. A native informant is not a measuring device: I am not a seismograph recording social earthquakes. But I do have opinions about them, and I do have worries about the direction in which the tribe is going. I do not hide my opinions or worries in what I report. My worries are increasing and my opinions are becoming more extreme because my tribe is now in bad hands.

I HAVE LEFT the essays more or less as they originally appeared, and I have indicated the time of their original composition; but I have added to each a short introductory or concluding update. I chose to present them this way because, as a native informant, I was asked more than once to predict the future—for example, to guess the results of an upcoming election—and I wished to show how I did that. I am not ashamed of my record in predicting a future which is now history, for my essays are not dramas or even narratives. I consider them extended postcards from Israel. Someone who writes postcards, says the philosopher Richard Rorty, is exempt from Hegel's problem of how to end the book. I am indeed exempt from this problem, and I am even more clearly exempt from Hegel's monumental problem of how to end history.

1

EHUD BARAK AND THE PENANCE OF THE LABOR PARTY

APRIL 1998

SOMEWHERE IN THE SOUTH OF ISRAEL, FAR FROM TEL AVIV BUT NOT very far from Gaza, lies the poor sleepy town of Netivot. Netivot was established in 1957 as a "development town," and nearly all its reluctant early residents were new immigrants to Israel from Morocco and Tunisia. Nearby is another development town, Ofakim, which recently made headlines in Israel for its record unemployment figures. Established in 1955, it, too, is inhabited mostly by immigrants from Morocco and Tunisia. In Israel's first direct election for Prime Minister, in 1996, the results for Netivot were very clear: 86 percent for the Likud candidate Benjamin Netanyahu, 11 percent for the Labor Party candidate, Shimon Peres, running after the assassination several months earlier of his Labor rival and colleague, Prime Minister Yitzhak Rabin. Ofakim's results were similar: 74 percent for Netanyahu, 24 percent for Peres.

The two towns exemplify something about Israel that hasn't got much attention during this fiftieth anniversary year: the largest community of immigrants is made up of Jews from non-European countries—from the Orient as Israelis say—who are relatively poor, have low social status, often live far from the main cities, consider themselves religious or "traditional," and have become a major political force by solidly voting for the right. They come mostly from North Africa (the Maghreb), mostly from Morocco, and until the immigration from the former U.S.S.R. in the 1990s, they were the largest Jewish subgroup in Israel. Ever since Menachem Begin's rise to power in 1977, with his first election as head of the Likud Party, the Oriental Jews have increased in power and significance.

In 1997, a year and a half after Rabin was assassinated and a year after Labor had lost the election, the Labor Party held its convention not, as usual, in an affluent section of Tel Aviv but in Netivot. To be sure, not all of Tel Aviv's citizens are affluent and of European origin. Israel's periphery begins in the city's southern neighborhoods. In north Tel Aviv, Peres won 70 percent of the votes as opposed to Netanyahu's 30 percent, whereas in the Oriental semi-slums in the south of the city Netanyahu received 80 percent to Peres's 20 percent. (Altogether Peres took Tel Aviv with a 10 percent margin.) Still, it was a novel, unexpected gesture when Labor had its convention not on its home ground in Tel Aviv but on the arid soil of Netivot. The name Netivot is both symbolic and ironic. It means "paths," in a reference to Proverbs 3:17, "All its paths [*netivot*] are peace." For Labor, it is a new idea that the paths to peace with the Arabs go through the Oriental Jewish town of Netivot.

At the June 1997 convention, Ehud Barak, who had succeeded Peres as leader of the Labor Party, delivered an important opening speech in which he begged forgiveness, on behalf of the Labor movement, of the Oriental immigrants. He said that while Labor should be proud of its momentous role in founding the state of Israel and "the ingathering of the exiles," "we must admit to ourselves" that new immigrants had been channeled directly to development towns like Netivot, and in this absorption process "the inner fabric of communal life was torn. Indeed, sometimes even the intimate fabric of family life was torn. Much suffering was inflicted on the immigrants, and this suffering was etched in their hearts as well as in the hearts of their children and grandchildren. There was no malice on the part of those responsible for bringing the immigrants here—on the contrary, there was much goodwill—but pain was inflicted nevertheless. In acknowledgment of this suffering and pain, and out of identification with the sufferers and their descendants, I hereby ask forgiveness in my own name and in the name of the historical Labor movement."

The writings of the Church make a careful distinction between two types of repentance, attrition and contrition, the difference between them being in the motive. Attrition is repentance out of fear (of punishment), while contrition is repentance out of love (of God). The issue is whether attrition, or penance out of fear, is worthwhile. Political repentance is always an act of attrition, and Barak fears the wrath of the Oriental community at the ballot box. But political repentance may be valuable, whatever the motive, so long as it does not come easily. The angry response of veteran Labor Party members to Barak's address is enough to show that his asking for forgiveness was not an easy task. And Barak expressed regret for the right reason. Labor's sin was the mortal sin of pride; its attitude toward the Oriental immigrants was one of insufferable superiority. Shlomo Zemach, a childhood friend of David Ben-Gurion and a thoroughly free spirit in his own right, recounts in his diaries that on May 28, 1963, he met the then Minister of Education, Zalman Aranne. Aranne expressed exasperation with the Oriental children, saying that their "understanding and ability" were "dull." Zemach was taken aback. "That is a racist theory," he said, to which Aranne responded, "Facts are facts."

The facts about Aranne himself are confusing. He did more than anyone in Israel to help in the education of Oriental children, and yet, like his contemporaries in the Labor leadership, he viewed them as inferior. The Labor leaders differed among themselves as to whether this inferiority was cultural or constitutional. Ben-Gurion, as usual, had a biblical view of the matter. He compared the Oriental immigrants to Israelites who had come out of the "House of Slavery" in Egypt (read: Morocco) and wandered in the desert with Moses (read: Ben-Gurion) for forty years. But he expected their descendants, who were not exposed to the "slave mentality" of Arab culture, to be different. Needless to say, for the Labor leaders only Ashkenazi Jews had "culture"; Oriental Jews had, at best, a "heritage." Barak was right: Labor had sinned more in its attitude toward the Orientals than in its deeds.

EHUD BARAK WAS chief of staff of the Israeli Army until 1995 and he is the most decorated warrior in the history of the Israeli Army, having received five marks of distinction, which are greatly admired in Israeli society. His main claim to fame is as the extolled commander of Israel's most prestigious commando unit, the one that became famous in the operation to rescue the hostages at Entebbe in 1976. Barak's commando unit, which the fighters in it call The Unit and the general public calls the Sayeret Matkal, is a powerful symbol of elitism among Israeli youth. The stereotype of a member of this unit is an Ashkenazi kibbutznik, an Israeli of European descent who has grown up on a kibbutz or in another form of cooperative farming settlement, the *moshav*.*

In that opening address to the Labor Party, Barak made a telling reference to The Unit, claiming that its founders were not youngsters brought up on the kibbutz, but, rather, Oriental boys who had arrived in Israel in the 1950s and had never gotten credit for forming the Sayeret Matkal. And, indeed, it is true that when Barak joined the army in 1959, the Sayeret Matkal was an Arabized unit in military intelligence—with its soldiers sometimes disguised as Arabs—and most of them were chosen from the Oriental communities because of their appearance and their knowledge of colloquial Arabic. The young Barak looked like a Jordanian crown prince, short and sporting a big mustache. He was recommended to the Sayeret Matkal by an Oriental boy who had been a boarder in Barak's kibbutz and was serving in The Unit at that time.

But later the Sayeret Matkal underwent a significant change, be-

---

*You can meet this ideal type of fighter in The Unit in (Colonel) Moshe "Muki" Betser's autobiography, *Secret Soldier* (New York, 1996).

coming a top fighting commando unit, in addition to an intelligence one. And Barak perhaps more than anyone else was responsible for this change. As an elite commando unit, the Sayeret Matkal attracted young kibbutzniks as well as city-bred Ashkenazi youngsters from "good families." Among those who joined it was Benjamin Netanyahu, called "Bibi." Later his older brother, Jonathan ("Yoni"), and his younger brother, Iddo, joined as well. Barak was Bibi's commander, and Bibi greatly admired him. Even now, with the intense rivalry between them, the imprints of Barak on Bibi are still quite noticeable, and one gets the impression that Bibi is constantly in need of Barak's approval.

One can hardly exaggerate the mystique of The Unit in Israel. It is as important to understand it as to appreciate the role of Oxford in British society or of Harvard in American history. The image of The Unit has been associated with four attributes: kibbutz upbringing, Ashkenazi background, elitism, and adherence to the Labor movement. Barak exemplifies all four, and this image hounds him politically. How the combination of these four attributes emerged, and what it has to do with the Oriental communities, is a story worth telling.

The most prestigious military unit in Israel's War of Independence in 1948 was the Palmach (a Hebrew acronym for "assault companies"). It was the striking force of the Haganah, the Labor movement's underground. Among the Palmach's commanding officers were Yigal Allon, Moshe Dayan, Yitzhak Rabin, and Haim Bar-Lev, all of whom later became leading figures in the Labor Party. The Palmach fighters came from the kibbutz movement and the socialist youth movements associated with it. The Marxist influence in the kibbutz movement frightened Ben-Gurion, who regarded it as a direct threat to his Mapai Party. Thus one of his first moves at the end of the War of Independence was to disband the Palmach, a move that was bound to alienate the youth of the kibbutz movement from the army.

When Dayan became chief of staff in 1953, he totally changed the kibbutz and *moshav* youngsters' attitude toward the army. He appointed Ariel Sharon as brigadier of the paratroopers. This paratroop brigade carried out all the "retaliation assaults" of the 1950s—that is, the retaliatory raids against villages in neighboring Arab countries that were suspected of sheltering Palestinian attackers. The paratroopers became a great attraction for kibbutz youngsters, who then made the army their arena of excellence, becoming, in effect, the serving gentry of Israel. During these years young kibbutzniks did not take matriculation exams, which serve as an entrance ticket for higher education in Israel, but instead excelled as officers in combat units, as pilots, or as fighters in commando units. Having endured the spartan way of life in the kibbutz, being inured from childhood to hard, demanding physical work in the fields, familiar with the precomputer technology of maintaining and repairing agricultural machines, and pumped with motivation by the kibbutz society—all this made the youngsters matchless soldiers.

When Oriental Jewish youngsters encountered the kibbutzniks in the army they saw them as soldiers in the Prussian Army may have perceived the Junkers—as able but supercilious. However, this wasn't the only encounter that Oriental Jews had with the kibbutz. Many of those who had immigrated to Israel in the 1950s and early 1960s and been dispersed to small towns lived far away from the cities but close to the kibbutzim, where as wage laborers they met the native-born Israelis. They found the kibbutzniks cold, haughty, and exclusive; the kibbutzniks found them primitive, prickly, and violent. The kibbutz standard of living was not very high, but the kibbutz gardens looked ravishing in contrast to the shadeless shabbiness of the immigrant towns. The grass in the neighboring kibbutz looked especially green, and the immigrant youngsters were especially green-eyed when they peered at the kibbutz swimming pools.

Menachem Begin won his first election in 1977 with a demagogic campaign using a very effective image that captured these feelings of the Oriental immigrants, contrasting "the kibbutz millionaires in their swimming pools" to the working people in the neighboring development towns. The Labor movement had run Israel for its first thirty years, from 1948 to 1977, and it had run the Jewish community in Palestine—the Yishuv—for twenty years before the establishment of the state. During most of that half-century Begin was in the opposition, and the party he headed—the Herut (Freedom) Party, which later became a principal component of Likud, now headed by

Netanyahu—was perceived by Labor as a pariah party. The Herut leaders were almost all Ashkenazi Jews—in fact, the most Ashkenazi of the Ashkenazim, that is, Polish Jews—but between Begin and the Oriental Jewish communities there was the bond of being outcasts. And Begin became the voice—the roar—of all those who felt insulted and rejected by the Labor movement. His hatred was their hatred. Begin won his next election, in 1981, by sending Israeli pilots to destroy an Iraqi nuclear reactor; the pilots in that mission were mostly boys who had been brought up in the kibbutz swimming pools.

Begin thus succeeded in transcending the great divide between the Ashkenazim and the Orientals by becoming the paradigmatic Jew. For many Moroccan Jews, Begin was an honorary Moroccan Jew; others saw him as a Moroccan through and through. The Ashkenazim associated with him received instant indulgence from the Orientals and were absolved of all Ashkenazi sins. By being the enemy of their enemy, they became the Orientals' friends. In this way Bibi Netanyahu, although born in Rehavia, a famously elite academic neighborhood of Jerusalem, having attended what at the time was considered a very elitist school there, and then having served in The Unit, managed to escape Barak's destiny. By belonging to Begin's party, Netanyahu is perceived as being part of the coalition of the insulted.

Netanyahu's lack of credibility has become a public cliché in Israel, but on one important issue he is utterly genuine: he radiates an intense, Nixonian hatred of what he calls "the elites." When thinkers such as Pareto, Mosca, and Michels or C. Wright Mills wrote about "the elite," what they had in mind was a minority power elite that controls important aspects of a society. The Labor establishment in Israel lost that power a long time ago, but it retains a power that really matters—the power to insult. The Labor elite is more of a prestige elite than a power elite.

Barak's task as the new head of the Labor Party is formidable: to overcome the deep-seated resentment about the current situation in Israel felt by many but mainly by Oriental Jews. I use the term "resentment" advisedly. Resentment, unlike raw hatred, is a moral emotion, a feeling of indignation about what is perceived as a past wrong. The challenge to Barak in overcoming this resentment is not only to regain political and governmental power but also to convince the Oriental Jews that peace with the Arabs is not merely for the Ashkenazi and the affluent but for all Israel. It is not so much peace with the Arabs that Israel's Oriental Jews oppose as, rather, the culture of peace as it is promoted by the left. The Oriental Jews feel threatened not only by Palestinian terror but also by Peres' slogan of "the New Middle East," in which they fear they will not have a place. So the challenge to Barak is not merely political but also cultural, which makes it very tough indeed.

EHUD BARAK WAS born Ehud Brog in 1942 at Kibbutz Mishmar Hasharon, about thirty miles from Tel Aviv. His father, Israel, was born in Lithuania. When the father was six months old, his parents were murdered in a pogrom, and he was raised by his grandmother, who moved to the Ukraine. In 1930 Israel immigrated to Palestine and enrolled at the Hebrew University of Jerusalem. Two years later he and nine friends jointly founded a kibbutz. The kibbutz is a very demanding form of life, and founding one, like founding a monastery, is an outstanding ideological act. But there is a sense in which Mishmar Hasharon was not an "ideological kibbutz." It belonged to Zionism's mainstream Mapai movement, which described itself as an advocate of "practical" socialism, with the stress on "practical"—that is, on plain common sense. There is actually nothing plain or commonsensical about a kibbutz, but calling it "practical" meant avoiding the doctrinal posturing that was typical of the Marxist stream in the kibbutz movement. The Mapai viewed Marxist talk of class conflict in Palestine as idle chatter at best and idealistic nonsense at worst.

Thus, although Barak was raised in a kibbutz, he was not raised as an ideologue. He considers himself in the center, "because that is where the real solutions are." I am not sure what "the center" means in Israel—it may well be imaginary, like the equator—but it is where Barak naturally belongs.

What singled out Barak as a child on the kibbutz was the fact that he took advanced-level piano lessons in Tel Aviv. He must have been good at it, since a recital of his was favorably reviewed in the paper. He wasn't particularly good at the more usual activities of kibbutz youngsters—namely, sports—rather surprising in a person later known for being a commando officer.

In 1973, at the outbreak of the October War, Barak and Netanyahu took the same flight from New York back to Israel, Barak coming from Stanford and Netanyahu from MIT, where they were students. Barak went on to lead an improvised tank unit in that war. With his scientific and technological bent—he was studying physics, mathematics, and systems analysis—he mastered the art of the tank to a degree unknown among infantry-trained soldiers. His promotion to general was rapid—he received this rank in 1981 at the age of thirty-nine, from then Defense Minister Ariel Sharon. Ten years later, after serving as head of military intelligence, as commander of the Central Command, and as deputy chief of the General Staff for four years, during the *intifada*, he was appointed chief of the General Staff—that is, commander of the Israeli Army.

That Barak did a superb job as commander of the Sayeret Matkal has never been in dispute. He did well in all his military posts, but not indisputably so. The main controversy is about how good a chief of staff he was. It is hard to evaluate his success because he had to meet the utterly unrealistic expectation of revolutionizing the army, of making it "small and smart." It is hellishly difficult to reform a conservative institution like an army, and in Israel since the October War it has become even harder to succeed, because the army has lost its mystique. But whatever disputes there may be about Barak's success in the army, he very thoroughly impressed at least one informed judge of military affairs—Yitzhak Rabin.

An army officer with political aspirations is judged not only by the degree of his success but also by how many skeletons are hidden in his army kit bag, for in politics these skeletons tend to pop out. Barak has the shadow of a skeleton in his kit bag from when he was chief of staff, and this shadow now hovers over him. According to "foreign sources," the Israeli Army in 1992 was planning to use a missile to make an attempt on Saddam Hussein's life. The plan was tried out by The Unit and demonstrated to the high command. During the exercise a missile was fired by mistake, killing five soldiers and wounding four others; one of the wounded later accused Barak of standing idly by and not attending to the wounded and claimed that Barak left the scene of the accident in his helicopter before all the wounded had been taken to the hospital. It turned out that the wounded had actually been treated promptly and efficiently by well-trained medics in the area—it had been no business of Barak's to attend to the wounded in any case—and he apparently had not left the scene before the wounded were evacuated. Thus it seems that Barak behaved rationally under the circumstances but did not show compassion. But since this is exactly the problem that his image suffers from, it was only exacerbated by the incident.

Barak was a very politically minded chief of staff. The Labor Party waited eagerly for his release from the army so that he could join its leadership. In 1995 Barak was appointed Minister of the Interior in Rabin's government, and after Rabin's assassination in 1996 Peres appointed him Foreign Minister. Peres kept the prestigious Defense Ministry for himself so that the glow of the office would shine on him when he ran for Prime Minister against Netanyahu. The outrageous terrorist bombing perpetrated in Jerusalem in August 1995 by the extremist Islamic group Hamas turned this glow into drab. There is a feeling that if Peres had given the Defense Ministry to Barak he would have done better in the subsequent election. After Peres' defeat, Barak was the first to put his act together, winning the leadership of the Labor Party quite easily in a four-way race, with 51 percent of the vote.

Another contender in that race, Shlomo Ben-Ami, who received 15 percent of the vote, was particularly impressive for both his vision and his articulation of it. Ben-Ami, a professor of history, is an expert on modern Spain who served with distinction as Israel's ambassador there. He was born in Tangiers, the free city of Spanish Morocco, and experienced the traumatic immigration of the 1950s to Israel as a boy. Ben-Ami married into an illustrious Ashkenazi kibbutz family while Barak married into an illustrious Sephardi family in Tiberias. The option of dissolving the "ethnic gap" between Ashkenazi and Oriental Jews not by politics but by intermarriage looked promising for a while. But the rate of intermarriage, which rose from 7 percent in the 1950s to 24 percent in the 1980s, stopped there. It does not seem promising any more.

The ethnic gap remains and needs to be dealt with. It is preferable to view it in terms of education than in terms of economic indicators, since the largely Ashkenazi immigration from the former Soviet Union in the 1980s confounds the economic picture. Only 4 percent of Israeli-born Jews of Oriental background obtain a higher education, as opposed to 15 percent of those of Ashkenazi background. Four times as many Ashkenazi as Sephardic Jews have academic and scientific jobs, and among those born in Israel the ratio is six to one in favor of the Ashkenazim.

Ben-Ami is painfully aware of this ethnic gap. However, he and the head of the Histadrut, the General Federation of Labor, Amir Peretz, also a Moroccan Jew, stress the class gap more than the ethnic gap. Ben-Ami argues—I believe rightly—that Labor cannot win elections in Israel by focusing on the issue of peace. Labor must broaden its agenda and become once again a social democratic party which addresses noncondescendingly the worries about education, employment, and health among the resentful constituencies. It must also, in Ben-Ami's view, dim the blatant secular glare that has estranged "traditional" Oriental Jews—those who are religious in a cultural sense without being strictly observant—from the Labor Party. His take on the political issues is supported by a thorough, sound analysis written for the Labor Party by Shevach Weiss, a member of the Knesset and a professor of political science.*

Barak co-opted Ben-Ami for his team, but it remains to be seen whether he will make a difference. I think he should. In a week when newspaper headlines in Israel were dominated by growing unemployment, especially in the development towns, Barak did well in the polls, receiving 46 percent to Netanyahu's 23 percent; in a week when peace, or rather the lack of it, dominated the headlines—the week when Netanyahu spent time with Clinton, just before the Monica Lewinsky affair broke—he tied with Netanyahu (41 percent for each of them).

---

*Analysis of the Results of the Elections for the Fourteenth Knesset and for the Prime Minister (in Hebrew, 1996).

Shimon Peres used to say that polls should be treated like eau de Cologne—sniffed but not swallowed. Yet Peres himself was the first to swallow them. Barak does not—he is clearheaded enough to know that when election time comes around the vote will once again be very close and will be decided to a large extent by the Oriental constituents.

I HAVE BEEN discussing the conflict between different types of Jews in Israel using the terms "Oriental" and "Ashkenazi." But are these the right words to describe this ethnic and class conflict? There is a linguistic problem. The set of contrasting terms that is usually used in Israel is Ashkenazi and Sephardi, biblical place names whose meaning was changed in the Middle Ages, "Ashkenaz" being used as the name for Germany and "Sepharad" for Spain. The name "Ashkenazi" is now used for descendants of Jews in medieval Germany and France. Many of these Jews immigrated to various Slavic countries in late medieval times, and many of their descendants immigrated to the United States in the last century, so that at present the largest community of Ashkenazi Jews is in the United States. Thus "Ashkenazi" remains a reasonably good term for these Jews. But "Sephardi" is not so good a term for Israel's Oriental Jews, as most of them have nothing to do with the descendants of Jews expelled from Spain in the year Columbus discovered America. The reason Israelis use "Sephardi" as a contrast to "Ashkenazi" is basically due to the contrasting religious customs of the two groups, for which these terms have been used for centuries. As a description of the ethnic roots of each, however, the terms are misleading.

Another pair of contrasting terms used in Hebrew is "Westerners" and "Easterners." There is a good deal of irony here, since "Easterners" refers to Jews of the Maghreb, a word meaning "west," denoting the western part of the Islamic Empire (that is, all of North Africa). The term "Westerners," on the other hand, is used to refer to Jews from Eastern Europe, leading to even more linguistic confusion. I have therefore decided to stick with the most prevalent terms in the literature—"Ashkenazi" and "Oriental." In any case, a social conflict, like a rose, remains a solid conflict whatever name is used.

On the eve of World War II an estimated 90 percent of the Jews in the world were Ashkenazi. There was only the most tenuous contact between Ashkenazi and Oriental Jewry at that time. Oriental Jews were barely on the periphery of awareness for Jews in Eastern and Central Europe, where Zionism was strongest. (One exception to this benighted neglect was the concern of French Jews for Oriental Jews. In 1860 French Jews formed the first modern organization for promoting Jewish solidarity, the Alliance Israélite Universelle, with the motto "All Jews are comrades." What triggered the establishment of the Alliance was the involvement of some French Jewish notables in the Damascus blood libel affair, which occurred in 1840: when a Capuchin friar who lived in Damascus was murdered, together with his servant, the Capuchins accused the Jews in the city of perpetrating this crime in order to obtain their alleged ritual requirement of blood for the Passover Seder. This renewed incident of the ancient Christian blood libels against Jews led Jews in France to realize that there was a need for an organization to protect Jews everywhere against anti-Semitism. The Alliance was particularly good at creating an effective Francophonic school system in territories then imperially controlled by France, notably the Maghreb. I believe that the Alliance was by far the most important institution for Jews there, for the Zionist movement, although it professed to speak on behalf of all Jews everywhere, did hardly anything for them.) And in the Jewish community in Palestine, Oriental Jews were then only 10–15 percent of the population.

The Holocaust changed the demography of the Jewish people and greatly increased the proportion of Oriental Jews. In Israel this change was dramatic: the fraction of Oriental Jews rose to nearly one-half during the first massive wave of immigration in 1948–51, which more than doubled the Jewish population of Israel; out of 700,000 newcomers, about half were Oriental Jews. In the second wave of immigration, 1955–57, and the third one, 1961–64, most of the newcomers came from Morocco.

Conventional wisdom about the origin of the Oriental resentment against the Labor Party traces it back to the first wave of immigration in 1948–51, when immigrants lived in appalling conditions in transition camps *(ma'abarot)*, essentially shantytowns. There was massive unemployment, and those who did find jobs could only get meaning-less ones in ad hoc public works paying very low wages. Worst of all, the veteran Ashkenazi of the Labor Party were unbearably patronizing to the newcomers, as proverbially manifested by the government's humiliating policy of forcing them to be disinfected with DDT. These "sins" against the new immigrants are generally considered to be at the origin of the Oriental resentment against Labor.

I do not believe this is the principal explanation for it. It is im-portant to distinguish between the various phases of the mass immi-gration to Israel in the 1950s: the first phase, in which the newcomers lived in the transition camps, and the second, when they were trans-ferred to development towns such as Netivot and Ofakim, where con-ditions were considerably better. Yet I believe that the main source of the immigrants' resentment can be traced to this second phase. What lends support to my claim is the different attitudes of Moroccan Jews and Iraqi Jews toward the Labor party. Iraqi Jews were the largest subgroup of Oriental newcomers in the first immigration wave, while the Moroccans arrived in the second and third waves. Yet the Iraqi Jews' resentment of Labor is by no means as great as the Mo-roccans'. If one judges by their votes, one sample shows that 57 percent of the Iraqi Jews voted Likud as compared with 73 percent of the Moroccans. Also, there is a notable representation of Iraqi Jews in the Labor leadership and a conspicuous absence of Moroccans.*

My own explanation for the relentless Moroccan resentment against Labor involves housing. The transition camps, to which the Iraqi Jews were mainly sent, were temporary; they lingered on as wretched slums until the mid-1960s but then disappeared completely, and their in-habitants moved into the center of the country. The development towns, where the Moroccan Jews mainly live, are permanent, cutoff enclaves that can promise only shabby lives with shabby prospects. (The difference between the market price for an apartment in a de-velopment town and one in central Israel is so great that residents of the development towns have little prospect of ever being able to move.)

*Eliezer Ben-Rafael and Stephen Sharot, *Ethnicity, Religion and Class in Israeli Society* (Cambridge, Eng., 1991), p. 287.

There is another community whose deep resentment against Labor does in fact go back to the transition camps, however. This is the community of Yemenite Jews. What troubled them in the transition camps was not the hardship of life—they were quite accustomed to hardship in the Yemen (more so than, say, Jews from Baghdad, who had a much higher living standard). But nearly all of them believe that hundreds of Yemenite babies were snatched from their families in the 1950s and handed over for adoption to Ashkenazi families—mostly in the kibbutzim but also outside Israel. Moreover, they believe that this was done systematically with the knowledge, if not active participation, of state organs—hospitals, the Ministry of the Interior, the police, and the courts, all of which were run by the Labor Party.

Jews from Yemen had first immigrated to Palestine at the same time as the early Zionists came from Eastern Europe, beginning in 1882. Just before the establishment of the state of Israel there were 35,000 Yemenite Jews in Palestine, forming perhaps its largest Oriental community. Then, between December 1948 and September 1950, nearly 50,000 Jews were brought to Israel from Yemen in what was poetically described as Operation Magic Carpet—namely, by plane. These Yemenites in Palestine were not hostile to Labor. (The Sephardic community in Jerusalem, which adopted the first Yemenite newcomers, treated them very badly indeed.) And the Labor pioneers considered the Yemenites more attractive than other Oriental Jews: they spoke beautiful Hebrew and were docile and ascetically thin. If Arab laborers in a Jewish settlement earned 10 beshlik (a Turkish coin) a day for digging, and Ashkenazi pioneers were paid 15 beshlik for the same work, the Yemenites were in between, at 12½ beshlik. They were considered "natural laborers," as the expression went. But the immigration of 1948–50 changed the situation, and the Yemenites no longer accepted being taken for granted by Israel's Labor establishment. What caused the change was the story of the kidnapped babies.

Recently there was an outbreak of Yemenite violence headed by a cult leader named Uzi Meshulam, a self-proclaimed rabbi who has been clamoring for an investigation of the case. One of his spokesmen, an Ashkenazi and a former student of mine, before the outbreak of the violence presented me with what he believed to be compelling evidence of the alleged kidnapping. I was not convinced. I believe that the hold the alleged kidnapping has on the Yemenite community goes back to Yemen's highlands, which were occupied by the Zaydi sect, a zealots' group with a program of extensive forced conversions of Jewish orphans to Islam. Indeed the hunt for Jewish orphans in Yemen over the last two centuries was one of the main reasons that Jews emigrated. But what I believe is immaterial; what matters is that the Yemenite community in Israel believes this appalling thing actually happened.

The fact that Yigal Amir, the murderer of Yitzhak Rabin, comes from the Yemenite community is no accident. Amir claims he killed Rabin to prevent the Oslo Accords from being implemented, but the motive (not the reason) for his hatred of Rabin was aggravated by this grudge about the kidnapped babies, of which Amir was well aware.

Still, the experience of the transition camps has, overall, helped to shape a shared Oriental Jewish sense of what Israel is like, a shared "identity," even, which the immigrants to Israel from Islamic countries did not originally perceive themselves as sharing. In the 1960s I worked for six years as an instructor in a youth village for immigrant children, mostly from the Maghreb. I vividly remember the mother of a Tunisian youngster who moved to Paris herself but sent her son to Israel. On a visit to the village one day, she discovered to her horror that her son had an Iraqi girlfriend. She demanded that I break up the relationship because, she claimed, "our people" (Tunisian Jews) had nothing in common with "those people" (Iraqi Jews). So the shared Oriental identity is a consequence of Israeli experiences, and it is partly a negative identity—a way of distinguishing oneself from the Ashkenazim of the Labor Party and their "Arab-loving" fellow travelers in the peace camp. The transition-camp experiences became a shared myth of origin for the "Oriental identity": "We all went through the humiliating ritual of the DDT applications."

IN HIS LABOR PARTY address, Barak also touched upon another serious problem in the Moroccan community—namely, the disintegration of the family and of the community as a whole. But this problem has been caused not merely by mistakes made by the Labor Party. In order to understand its causes, we must go back to what happened in the Maghreb before the establishment of the state of Israel. Talking about Jews from the Maghreb as if they were a single group hides the significant differences among them, including the differences in how long and how deeply they were influenced by the French protectorate. The French protectorate in Algeria began in 1830; in Morocco it began officially in 1912, though in actuality not until 1935; in Tunisia it was in 1881.

This difference is reflected in the trend of emigration of Jews from these countries. In the years when 75 percent of Morocco's Jews emigrated to Israel, 75 percent of Algeria's Jews went to France. In Tunisia 50 percent went to France and 50 percent to Israel. One thing is clear: the more urban, better skilled, and more secular they were, the more they tended to emigrate to France (sometimes with a stopover in Israel). But the tendency to explain everything that happened to Maghreb Jews in Israel as a function of negative selection—that is, because the least able went to Israel—is misleading. A study done in the 1970s of sets of brothers, one of whom ended up in France and the other in Israel,* showed that those in France did better in their occupations and incomes than those who went to Israel; the deep-seated belief among Moroccan Jews that they are discriminated against in Israel has some basis, for social inequities as well as inequalities in skill and education put Moroccans at the bottom of the Israeli ladder. Still, there was some negative selection in the immigration to Israel, as those better qualified for a place in a modern economy went to France. Moroccan Jews were less qualified than Algerian ones in this respect because the French influence on Jewish education in Morocco had been relatively short-lived.

Jews in much of the Maghreb, like Jews in Europe, tended to be found not in the countryside but in the towns. The Jewish quarter

---

*Michael Inbar and Haim Adler, *Ethnic Integration in Israel: A Comparative Case Study of Moroccan Brothers Who Settled in France and in Israel* (New Brunswick, N.J., 1977), p. 144.

(*mellah*) of every North African town is usually one of the oldest. In Fez, for example, the Jewish quarter of the old city, al-Funduk al-Yahūdi, goes back to its very foundation in the eighth century, and in the sixteenth century a Hebrew printing house flourished there. But many, if not most, of the Jews in Morocco lived in the countryside, in the Atlas region, and moved to the *mellahs* only when the French took over. One city they moved to in great numbers was Casablanca, and a common nickname for Moroccans in Israel in the 1950s was "Casa." And many of the bad things that Moroccan Jews in Israel said had happened to them in Israel—and that Barak, too, attributed to the same cause—had already happened when Jews from the Atlas moved to a marginal existence in Morocco's cities. Some old-timers did fabulously well as enterprising merchants but these Jews tended to stay in Morocco (creating the illusion among many immigrants to Israel that they could have done just as well if they, too, had stayed).

Jews in the Maghreb led a shadowy social existence, especially in the cities, accepted by neither the French nor the Muslims. The perceptive novels of Albert Memmi, a Tunisian Jew, give the reader a clear sense of the Jews' ambiguous status, especially those who received a French education.* Despite all the problems, Israel could give the North African Jews a better feeling of being at home than either the Maghreb or France. In the above-mentioned study of sets of brothers, those in Israel reported being better integrated into society (for example, they had more friends outside their own community) than those who went to France. And although the North African community is overrepresented in Israeli prisons, it is also heavily represented in the police force. In fact, the stereotype of a policeman in Israel is a North African, much like the old stereotype of the Irish policeman in the northeastern United States. And like the Irish in America, North Africans are heavily represented in Israeli politics.

PERES LOST THE election in 1996 by fewer than 30,000 votes; but he lost by 10 percent of the vote within the Jewish population, and only

---

*See, notably, *Pillar of Salt* (1952; English translation 1991) and *Agar* (1955; English translation 1984).

the massive support of Arabs (94 percent of the Arab vote) narrowed his margin of defeat. In a democratic regime a vote is a vote: that is what children are taught in school, at least in some schools. But that is not what you are taught on the Israeli street. If Peres had *won* by an edge of only 30,000 votes, the right would have merely substituted his name in the poisonous campaign it had already waged under the slogan of "Rabin, you have no mandate"—meaning that the Labor Party doesn't have a majority among Jews. Indeed, the campaign of the right against the Oslo Accords, the interim agreement with the Palestinians, concluded in 1993, has been meant to delegitimize the Arab vote in Israel. If we add to this the fact that the hard core of the right, the ultra-Orthodox community, in which Netanyahu received 95 percent of the vote, does not think much of democracy anyway (they consider it to be good for Gentiles, not Jews), then we can see that Barak's task is not limited to tipping 15,000 votes from one side to the other. If Barak wants to continue with the "peace process" as a process that will truly lead to peace—and not, as it is for Netanyahu, as one that is a substitute for peace—he needs to convince the Oriental Jews. That is, he must increase support of the Labor Party among Oriental Jews by at least 5 percent.

Opposition to the Oslo Accords in Israel is correlated mainly with religion and age. The more religious and the younger you are, the more likely you are to oppose Oslo. Among Oriental Jews there is a predominance of all the characteristics that typify opposition to Oslo —low level of education, young average age, and religiosity. And when these variables are factored out, ethnic origin as such is not a significant indicator of opposition to the accords.* The opposition, I believe, is actually not so much to the accords themselves as to those who made them.

In the last election, it seems, the state of Israel's economy made little difference to Oriental voters. The economy had boomed under Rabin's prime ministership, in 1992–96. In 1995, for instance, its growth rate of 7 percent was the highest among Western nations. Unemployment was reduced from its peak of 11 percent in 1991,

---

*Tamar Herman and Ephraim Yaar, "Is There a Mandate for Peace?," in Dan Caspi (ed.), *Communication and Democracy in Israel* (Jerusalem, 1997).

under Shamir, to 6 percent in 1995. The Labor government had changed Israel's priorities, and instead of channeling money to settlements in the West Bank, had given it to development towns and to education (the education budget almost doubled). But all this made little impression on the Oriental voters. Does this mean that the state of the economy will not affect the next elections either? I doubt it. There is, I believe, an asymmetry between booms and bad times. In Israel you are not given credit for economic success under your government, but you lose points for a bad economic situation. Israel today is in a recession (a very slow growth rate with a sharp decline in investments) but not a depression (a negative growth rate). The unemployment rate is steadily rising, especially in the development towns. If the number of unemployed reaches 200,000—and this might actually happen—Netanyahu will be in trouble with Oriental Jews.

So Netanyahu may lose. But can Barak win? A poem of Goethe's describes a quiet scholar returning from a party. "How was it?" he is asked. "If they were books," he answers, "I should not read them." I presented some friends of mine with this "Goethe test" and asked them, "If Israeli politicians were books, which of them would you read?" They mentioned Moshe Dayan, more reluctantly Ariel Sharon. Then they stopped. "What about Barak?" I asked. "If he were a booklet," answered one sharp friend. Then I presented them with an inverse Turing test, asking them, "If Israeli politicians were computer programs, which of them would you choose?" Here Barak won hands down. Barak is indeed perceived by many people as an elaborate computer, precise and good at calculating many steps ahead. But he is seen as lacking the stormy spontaneity, the wild inner freedom, and the lack of inhibitions of a Moshe Dayan or an Arik Sharon. Still, the issue here is choosing a Prime Minister, not a literary hero. Dayan and Sharon did not make it to the top. There was something self-destructive in both of them.

Barak does not lack human texture and inner complexity, but he finds it hard to express them. The metaphor that hounds Barak most does indeed come from the world of computers: he is said to be "Bibi-compatible." Netanyahu is no Barak, just as Dan Quayle is no Kennedy. But there must be some similarity between Barak and Netanyahu that evokes this metaphor. First of all, they both entered an established party as an outsider and became its head. Both of them did this by radiating the image of a winner in contrast to the old loser (Shamir in Bibi's case, Peres in Barak's case). Both stride forward relentlessly, motivated by boundless ambition. *The Economist* had Netanyahu on its cover with the caption "A Serial Bungler." That is exactly what Barak thinks of Netanyahu: someone utterly incompetent in running Israel. But he admires Netanyahu as a campaigner running for office. And Netanyahu is constantly running. There are no more political leaders who believe in permanent revolution, but there are quite a few postmodern political leaders who are permanent campaigners. For them a political campaign is not an instrument for attaining office—instead, the office is an instrument for running an even better campaign. The campaign is the goal. Barak, unlike Netanyahu, is not such a permanent campaigner. In fact, so far he has shown himself to be not much of a campaigner at all. He is made for being in office, not running for it. He does not radiate warmth or populist charisma. He is brilliant, but in the way a graduate student can be brilliant, not in a politically relevant sense.

Barak is an obsessive analyzer. Ask him what time it is, quips Ofer Shelach, one of Israel's most astute political commentators, and you'll get an informed explanation of how a watch works.* And he is a fast learner. He has already improved in his television appearances, and he may eventually become good at them. But that's all style; what about content? I believe that Barak is truly committed to reaching an agreement with Syria, even though the price would be to give up the Golan Heights. I believe that he is committed to concluding a permanent agreement with the Palestinians on terms that can be acceptable to both sides, although I don't know what these terms are. He may also be a social democrat, if it will help him gain power.

The biblical prophetess Deborah famously said to her general, "Arise, Barak!" (Judges 5:12). So far the modern Barak has not risen enough with the Oriental Jews. They are the key to his rise or fall.

---

*Ofer Shelach wrote an informed and perceptive profile of Barak in *Ma'ariv* (April 21 and 25, 1997, in Hebrew).

2

THE RISE OF THE
ULTRA-ORTHODOX

NOVEMBER 1989

WHAT PEOPLE TALK ABOUT IN ISRAEL SEEMS MOSTLY TO BE DETER-
mined by what they saw the evening before on Israel's only television
network. In October 1988, just before the general elections, people
were startled to see, in the center of the television screen, a man in
a long, regal, ottoman robe, a tall turban on his head, and John
Belushi-style dark glasses that contrasted with his full silvery beard.
He was flanked by motionless men in black, all with black beards.
The man in the center started murmuring, and the other men repeated in unison what he said. This was, it turned out, an established
ritual performed by the former Sephardic chief rabbi, now the spiritual head of the Sephardic ultra-Orthodox party (Shas), which was to
do unexpectedly well in the October elections, receiving 6 out of 120
seats in the parliament. On national television, the chief rabbi, Ovadia

Yosef, so that his devout followers could vote for Shas, was freeing them from the holy vows they had previously taken which had bound them to rabbis from rival parties. He was cleansing his followers and cursing his enemies in religious incantation.

For me and for other secular Israelis who had never before seen anything like this on Israeli television, the television screen was a Wellsian time machine tuned to a remote medieval station. The producer of the broadcast, Uri Zohar, once the most popular comedian and film director in Israel, a kind of left-wing Jerry Lewis, had some years ago converted to become a born-again Jew and has since become an ultra-Orthodox rabbi. Whatever else he may now do, he is not trying to be funny.

Such religious broadcasts affected the results in the elections; so did the "charisma" of the various rabbis who appealed for votes. But their charisma was exaggerated. It does not by itself explain why the vote for the three ultra-Orthodox parties—Shas, the Aguda, and The Flag of the Torah—doubled since the last election in 1984, giving the three more than 11 percent of the vote. These religious parties got more votes because they created formidable educational and welfare institutions during the last few years. Their political power is no accident, and the charisma that counts has become, as Max Weber put it, "routinized": that is, the appeal of these parties derives from their religious activities, and not from the personality of one octogenarian rabbi or another.

The election results came as a complete surprise. None of the opinion polls had predicted the strength of the ultra-Orthodox parties. The pollsters had seen the signs of it but had dismissed them as sampling errors. "We didn't see it because we didn't know it," said one of the pollsters, memorably.

The ultra-Orthodox parties together have 13 seats out of 120 in the current Knesset, compared with 6 previously. Since the two major parties, Likud and Labor, have roughly the same strength (40 and 39 seats, respectively), the increase in ultra-Orthodox political power has raised the possibility that Israel could be governed by a narrow coalition composed of the Likud, the religious parties, and other parties on the right of the Likud—practically all of them committed to Israel's permanent control of the West Bank. Prime Minister Yitzhak Shamir seemed for a while last autumn to favor such a narrow coalition but he avoided it, for reasons I will discuss later. It nevertheless remains a possibility.

Of the three ultra-Orthodox parties the Sephardic party (Shas), composed almost entirely of Oriental Jews largely from North Africa, won six seats, the Hasidic party (Aguda) five seats, and the Lithuanian party (The Flag of the Torah or *Degel Hatorah*) has two. Aguda and The Flag of the Torah reflect the division in the Orthodox Jewish community that goes back to the conflict in eighteenth-century Eastern Europe between the emerging popular movement of Hasidism, with its emphasis on ecstatic worship, and Jews of the elitist "Lithuanian" group—so called because of its origins in Vilna and its vicinity—that stressed the traditional scholarly study of the Torah and the Talmud.

In addition to these ultra-Orthodox parties—"ultra" because they oppose virtually everything to do with modern life—two separate religious parties that are Zionist, not ultra-Orthodox, took part in the election. The National Religious Party (NRP) ended up with five seats (one more than in the previous election). The NRP has become intensely nationalistic, exerting pressure on the Shamir government to support more settlements on the West Bank and to tolerate increasing vigilantism. Many settlers, however, including members of the Gush Emunim, the first group within the NRP that settled on the West Bank, have broken with the NRP and now work for even more extremist right-wing parties, such as Tehiya ("Rebirth" or "Renaissance"), which, without quite saying so, favors the expulsion of Palestinians from Greater Israel. A new, small, and dovish modern Orthodox party (Meymad) failed to gain even a single seat in the Knesset.

The success of the ultra-Orthodox parties produced an uproar in the secular press, including cartoons caricaturing the Orthodox Jews that were reminiscent of *Der Stürmer*. A well-known artist, a sculptor who writes regularly for a popular daily paper, wrote, "When you see [the ultra-Orthodox] you understand why there was a Holocaust and why Jews are hated." The ultra-Orthodox leaders replied by once more attacking the concept of Zionism, whose goal of a secular Jewish homeland they have always opposed, not only because it prematurely sought the return to the Holy Land that they believe should be brought about only by the Messiah, but because of Zionism's practical consequences earlier in the century. In the words of an editorial in *Hamodia*, the newspaper of one of the ultra-Orthodox parties, "it was Zionism"—by provoking British restrictions on entry into Palestine —"that prevented many Jews like us from immigrating to the Land of Israel and thus caused their death in the Nazi gas chambers."

Secular Jews often call the members of ultra-Orthodox groups the "blacks," referring to the black clothes they habitually wear. In fact, the label "blacks" has undergone several transformations in Israel. When the Likud rose to power for the first time in 1977, many secular Ashkenazi Israelis, who derive from Europe, felt that the "blacks"— that is, the Oriental, or Sephardic, Jews, who made this victory possible by their support for Menachem Begin—had stolen the country from them. Today secular Orientals join the Ashkenazis in their feeling that the religious "blacks" are stealing their country. And Ashkenazis and Orientals alike, in growing numbers, feel scorn for, and fear of, the "real blacks"—namely, Palestinian Arabs.

THE TERM "ULTRA-ORTHODOX" is misleading. True, these religious groups are particularly fervent in their practice of Orthodox Judaism. But they are different from modern Orthodox Jews—who make up about half of Israel's approximately 550,000 adult religious Jews— since in addition to rejecting Zionism, they reject practically anything to do with modern life and modern values. The Hebrew expression is not "ultra-Orthodox" but rather *haredim*, which literally means "tremblers," a word derived from the verse "Hear the word of the Lord, ye that tremble at his word" (Isaiah 66:5).

The religious community in Israel is predominantly Orthodox: the very small groups of Reform and Conservative Jews, which are mostly from the United States, have no influence on Israeli life. The modern Orthodox Jews differ from the ultra-Orthodox in being willing to take part in worldly activities, whether at work or at school or at home, that are not directly related to religion. In the schools to which they send their children, "secular studies" like science, technology, literature, and history are taught much as they are in the secular schools. Most modern Orthodox high school graduates seek professional careers, for example in medicine and engineering, rather than religious vocations. In the schools of the ultra-Orthodox, by contrast, young men can pursue only "sacred studies" (although girls are being taught some secular subjects, such as foreign languages and some science— "the wonders of creation"—and literature). Many modern Orthodox students attend Israeli universities, but ultra-Orthodox ones go only to the rabbinical academies, called yeshivas.

The ultra-Orthodox and the modern Orthodox are roughly equal in their numbers of followers—perhaps between 250,000 and 300,000 adult Israelis belong to each—but they are not equal so far as political power is concerned, since many modern Orthodox split their vote among nonreligious parties. Most religious Sephardis who are not ultra-Orthodox, for example, vote for the Likud and not for the National Religious Party.

To say, as the press does, that the elections in the fall and winter of 1988–89 showed the "rise of religious fundamentalism" in Israel is also misleading if one does not distinguish between biblical fundamentalism, which takes the words of the Old Testament literally, and talmudic fundamentalism, which means observing the Jewish laws covering all aspects of family and public life that have accumulated over three thousand years. It is a long tradition: according to the Jewish calendar, it is half as old as time. The *haredim* essentially espouse talmudic fundamentalism, although on occasion they also expound biblical fundamentalism. In a broadcast on behalf of the Sephardic religious party Shas, for example, its leader, a handsome man with Omar Sharif eyes, said excitedly that one simple Sephardic woman kissing the Torah is worth more than fifty professors who say that man evolved from the ape. In the same vein, a *haredi* member of the Knesset tried, some months ago, to prevent the award by the Israeli parliament of the prestigious Wolf Prize in physics to Stephen Hawking because his big bang theory contradicts Genesis.

But the most important characteristic of the *haredim* is halakhic fundamentalism, which holds that in private and communal matters Jews must follow the views of recognized authorities on Halakha— that is, the ritual law and civil law contained in the rabbinical literature, as well as the decrees, ordinances, customs, and mores that were not canonized, and were therefore transmitted mainly through oral tradition.

To follow Halakha strictly is to have religion intervene in every aspect of human life, including the most private and the most trivial. Instructions are provided for everything from putting on one's shoes in the morning (first left, then right) to performing the highly important ritual of phylacteries (*tefilin*), the two small black boxes containing scriptural passages that are attached to leather strips that one winds around the left hand and the head, and wears during morning services, as a reminder of God's unity (much as a young man in love will tie a woman's handkerchief around his wrist to be reminded of her). A ritual hand washing and a benediction must take place before one eats a piece of bread, and another blessing must be said afterward. Hardly any of the actions one takes can be "spontaneous"; they are all mediated by regulations. The justification for such pervasive religious intervention in everyday life is Halakha as interpreted by the rabbinical authorities of the day. Its purpose is to create a holy community, and this, according to the biblical covenant, is the vocation of the Jewish people in the world. The source of the authority for Halakha itself is, in some sense, God or revelation; but in what sense and with what relation to the sacred Scripture are matters of extensive debate.

Various Israeli ultra-Orthodox groups, moreover, complicate the halakhic regulations by adding their own restrictions. The Hasidic rabbi of Gur, who carries on the traditions of a long line of rabbis from the Polish town of Gur, for example, has issued a set of thirty-nine restrictive rules concerning conjugal sexual relations. They prohibit the man from kissing the body of the woman and require that the bedroom be completely dark and that the couple be covered by a blanket from head to toe. These regulations were in fact sharply criticized by one of the more venerable rabbinical authorities, the "Stapler" rabbi, who condemned any man who does not try to satisfy his wife sexually.

On the whole the ultra-Orthodox are obsessed with sexual morality. Little girls are taught from an early age that they are dangerous sexual objects. They are prohibited, for example, from singing in front of anyone except the members of their immediate family, because even their voices are considered sexual organs.

WHAT IS THE attraction of the ultra-Orthodox way of life, especially for the secular Israelis who are "born again" and join one of the ultra-Orthodox groups as adults? Part of the appeal is the absolute clarity regarding what is allowed and what is forbidden. Members of ultra-Orthodox groups are at least partly released from having to make the decisions that are such a source of anxiety for the rest of us. Marriages are largely fixed by marriage brokers; apart from a rabbinical vocation no secular jobs have high status and there are no "careers" that are approved of. Even such decisions as whether or not to have an operation and which doctor to go to are referred to the rabbi. To live in a world so dense with rules and obligations can give one a sense of purpose: the ultra-Orthodox believe that by their efforts to follow Halakha they are helping to establish a holy community.

The ultra-Orthodox communities themselves are closed and protected worlds that give their members a feeling of belonging, a sense that they are among people who look after one another. The ultra-Orthodox Jews tend to cluster together in the religious neighborhoods in Israel's cities, although a few live in enclaves cut off from the rest of the *haredi* community. When family members become sick or die, or in other times of crisis, one is never alone. The modern habit of ceaseless shopping is frowned on, and conspicuous consumption is forbidden. Some communities impose restrictions on the size of apartments, and on how much can be spent to improve the bathrooms and kitchens. On the other hand, the ultra-Orthodox are willing to pay for an impressively organized social welfare system in which neither the sick nor the orphaned have to worry about being cared for.

Another source of attraction of the *haredi* life, and not necessarily for intellectuals, is the study of classical rabbinical texts, whether in small groups or in formal classes or individual readings. The problems dealt with in these sessions are very like legal case studies. For example, how to divide a garment between two claimants, one of whom claims all of it and the other only half: this leads to discussions of complicated problems of distributive justice.

If the life of the devout as I have described it sounds like a communitarian paradise, from a secular, individualistic perspective it may seem a kind of hell, in which the warmth and sense of community of the ultra-Orthodox way of life become oppressive meddling. There is little respect for privacy or for distinctive individual activity among the ultra-Orthodox. The person who is different, or deviant, risks bigotry and harassment.

The bonds of communal life are further strengthened by the deep loyalty and affection accorded the spiritual leader. The underside of such feeling is unrelenting hatred between rival religious communities and their leaders, particularly between the Hasidic Jews who support the Aguda Party and the other ultra-Orthodox groups. The hatred can turn to violence, but it is usually expressed on walls and billboards, in the Chinese style. Indeed it was these communal rivalries, more than animosity toward the secular parties, that impelled the differing ultra-Orthodox political groups to campaign all the more energetically in the recent elections and to come out to vote in greater numbers.

Since in the Jewish view religion concerns not just a person's conduct but the life of the community, the ultra-Orthodox want to mold all public life in Israel in such a way as not to violate Halakha. This means closing down not only all public transportation and all businesses on the Sabbath, but all forms of entertainment, including television, as well.

THE TWO MAIN factions of the *haredi* community—the Hasidic and the Lithuanian—are both equally committed to Halakha. Originating in Eastern Europe among Ashkenazi Jews, both factions in Israel now include Sephardic Jews as well. However, very few Sephardim have been drawn to Hasidism: most of the ultra-Orthodox Sephardis accept the religious authority of Lithuanian leaders.

The Hasidim derive from the popular pietist movement founded in Eastern Europe during the eighteenth century in opposition to the conventional practice of restricting talmudic learning to a small elite. It emphasized the importance of religious devotion and intense prayer by all Jews in the community. The early egalitarianism of the movement soon gave way to more authoritarian practices. Today Hasidic communities in Israel and elsewhere (for instance in Brooklyn or Antwerp) are each organized around the figure of the *zaddik*, traditionally referred to by the acronym *admor* (standing for "our lord, teacher, and master"), who is the apex of a Hasidic court community of elders and scholars, men thought to be particularly wise and devout. The *admor* is perceived as endowed with a special spiritual power enabling him to communicate with the divine more directly and effectively than others in the community of believers. He thus functions as a mediator between his community and God.

The central value of religious life for the Hasidim is that of *Devekuth*, or being one with God. This attachment is not predominantly intellectual, but instead stresses inner feelings, as typically expressed in ecstatic prayer, which, to the Hasidim, is a higher expression of the authentic religious life than the study of the Torah and Talmud. The various Hasidic courts give different weight to the study of sacred texts, on the one hand, and, on the other, to the attainment of supreme religious experience; but they all place less emphasis on Torah study than the Lithuanians do. The Hasidic *admor*, his court, and the community are conceived as a single organic entity, and the yeshiva school for studying the Torah and Talmud is only one of its components.

Of the many Hasidic *admors* some are grand old men in rags who lost their congregations in the Holocaust. But the two most important in Israeli politics are the *admor* of Gur, who is old and ill, in charge of a large and obedient Hasidic community that lives mostly in Jerusalem and Bnei-Brak; and the eighty-seven-year-old *admor* of Lubavitch, Menachem Schneerson, the head of an international group of perhaps 100,000 Jews or more based in Crown Heights, Brooklyn, where he lives. From there millions of dollars have been sent to support the Lubavitch community in Israel. (The name derives from the village in Russia where the sect originated.) Schneerson's influence on the last Israeli general elections became notorious when it was reported that he had instructed his followers in various European cities who hold Israeli passports to return to Israel to vote for the Hasidic Aguda and offered to pay their way. The Lubavitchers believe that the "Greater Land of Israel" must stay in Israeli hands.

The other main Ashkenazi *haredi* community, the Lithuanians, derive their name from the fact that the opposition to the growing Hasidic movement in Eastern Europe during the eighteenth century arose in Lithuania, where the towering figure of Rabbi Elijah ben-Solomon, the Gaon (genius) of Vilna, became the most formidable critic of Hasidism. Traditionally, the enemies of the Hasidim were referred to as the Opponents (*Mitnaggedim*). However, since the rivalry has somewhat slackened, the more neutral word "Lithuanians" is now more widely used.

The central value in the religious life of the Lithuanians is the study of the Torah and the Talmud and the vast literature of exegesis that has accumulated over many generations. Unmarried men study at the yeshiva, married men at the *kolel*. The entire community devotes itself to maintaining these institutions and supporting the men attending them, who are supposed to remain fully absorbed in their task. A *talmid chacham*—a rabbinical scholar who excels in his studies—is at the top of the Lithuanian social hierarchy and enjoys the highest prestige. This position may bring material benefits, especially in marriage. The promising rabbinical scholar has a good chance of marrying the daughter of a well-to-do family, which then supports the couple while he continues his studies. In less affluent Lithuanian families, it is often the wife who must make a living for the family, and it is always the wife who shoulders the entire burden of housekeeping and raising children.

Usually there are many children. *Haredi* couples, whether Lithuanian or Hasidic, marry early: 70 percent of the women marry before they are twenty (90 percent before twenty-two); 90 percent of the men marry before twenty-four, and they are subject to the commandment to procreate. Women are brought up to prepare themselves for the task of serving their scholar husbands. The wife's sacrifice is considerable, since her husband is away from home at his studies all day, and it is not uncommon for *haredi* families to have from six to ten children.

The leaders of the Lithuanian ultra-Orthodox community in Israel are selected entirely according to their distinction in religious study. Thus the head of the largest and most prestigious Lithuanian yeshiva, the ninety-two-year-old Rabbi Eliezer Shach, is also the leader of all the Israeli Lithuanians—even when it comes to questions such as whether the party representing the Lithuanian community should join a coalition government and under what conditions. His authority is strengthened by the fact that most ultra-Orthodox Sephardic Jews also regard him as their spiritual leader, together with their Sephardic Rabbi Ovadia Yosef. This means that the leaders of both the Ashkenazi Lithuanian party, The Flag of the Torah, and the Sephardic party, Shas, obey Rabbi Shach's orders. The Lithuanians' attitude toward the state of Israel derives from their faith in the Torah: for them, the secular Zionist state is based on heresy. However, over the years they have moderated their criticism, and, while remaining anti-Zionist, they now support the government in return for generous subsidies for their educational institutions.

The recent elections revived the historic rivalry between the Hasidim and the Lithuanians. The long-standing and implacable hostility between the Hasidic *admor* of Lubavitch and the Lithuanian leader caused the followers of each patriarch—Schneerson's followers in the Aguda Party and Shach's in the Flag of the Torah and Shas parties—to denounce the other's bitterly. Shach suspects, rightly, that the Lubavitcher *rebbe* has messianic aspirations—that he might encourage his followers to see him as the divine redeemer of Israel and the world. He sees in him a potential danger similar to the threat posed to the Jews in the seventeenth century by the false messiah Shabbetai Zevi.

Each of the two Ashkenazi *haredi* communities has developed impressive institutions in Jerusalem, Bnei-Brak (near Tel Aviv), and other cities. These include an educational system, subsidized housing, and elaborate arrangements for matchmaking, for celebrating family and communal events, for funeral services, for providing kosher food, and much more. The social structure of both communities resembles that of institutional feudalism without a feudal bureaucracy; but the members of the Hasidic communities are much more like serfs than are those in the Lithuanian sects.

The large *haredi* families have a low standard of living, contrary to the fantasy of some secular Israelis that they are enormously rich. The overwhelmingly religious nature of their education does not prepare most of them to hold even modestly paying jobs, and the *haredi* male tends to enter the job market relatively late, if at all. Still, the *haredi* welfare and other services I have mentioned are more expensive than those provided by the richest secular communities. They are made possible by an efficient system of soliciting voluntary contributions, especially from Jews abroad, which amounts to a tax to redistribute wealth to the poor. In recent years the *haredi* communities have, through sophisticated political lobbying, won an increasing share of support from the state in the form of subsidies and tax breaks. Here *haredi* society, otherwise so self-sufficient, impinges politically on the rest of Israel.

Until recently, the most striking aspect of the *haredi* for most secular Israelis has been the spectacle of people determined to carry on the pre-Enlightenment life of Eastern European Jewish communities of the eighteenth century and earlier, whether in the somber clothes that they wear, or the Yiddish they use in everyday speech, or in their efforts to impose on the entire country laws restricting activity on the Sabbath. Lately, however, the quite different groups of ultra-Orthodox Sephardi have become highly visible for the first time.

The Sephardic *haredi* community originated in the great waves of immigration to Israel from North African and other Arab countries during the 1950s and 1960s. Many of the immigrant families, clinging to their own Orthodox culture, shunned the secularism of the Israeli educational system and instead enrolled their children in the existing ultra-Orthodox educational institutions. These institutions exercised so great an influence over their children that some grotesquely adopted Eastern European manners, including a Yiddish pronunciation of many Hebrew expressions. As these Sephardic children have grown up under the influence of Ashkenazi Orthodoxy, the Sephardic religious community in Israel has undergone a transformation. It is becoming more fanatical and more concerned with setting religious standards, such as imposing strict rules for the behavior of young women. It is becoming less like the traditional Sephardic Jews from cities like Fez, who tend to be fairly easygoing about customs and doctrinal matters, and more like Eastern European Jews, who have traditionally tended more toward religious fanaticism during their long war against the Enlightenment.

THE EMERGENCE OF Sephardic ultra-Orthodoxy in Israel must thus be seen as part of the reconstruction of the European Ashkenazi ultra-Orthodox communities after the Holocaust. The wretched survivors of these communities, who arrived in Israel during and after the war, were in no condition to undergo a rebirth and renewal. During the 1950s, fewer than two thousand students were enrolled in ultra-Orthodox yeshivas in Israel: the community was thought of as old and dying. At that time, in 1952, a famous "summit meeting" took place between David Ben-Gurion, the political leader of secular Israel, and Rabbi Karelitz (known as the "Hazon Ish"), the highest rabbinical authority of the time and the spiritual leader of the Lithuanian community. In the eyes of the Orthodox, this meeting assumed cosmic significance, somewhat resembling the legendary meeting, reported in the Talmud, between Alexander the Great and the high priest Shimon the Zaddik. Discussing the clash between secular and religious communities in Israel, the rabbi is reported to have told Ben-Gurion that when two carts meet head-on on a narrow bridge, clearly the empty one should give the right-of-way to the laden one—"laden" referred here to Jewish tradition, "empty" to the secular who have thrown the load off their cart.

As the years went by, many of the older Israeli Zionists of Ben-Gurion's generation, who in their youth had rebelled against their tradition and their religious past, and had become thoroughly secular, started to feel that the cart they were riding in was indeed empty. This generation proved particularly vulnerable to pressure from the religious community to be "more Jewish." They did not themselves become Orthodox but they were willing to be more tolerant of the rabbis, conceding, as some put it, that "a little bit of *Yiddishkeit* will do no harm." The religious community at that time seemed tame, more an object of nostalgia than a threat. In 1978 the government of

Menachem Begin made its largest concession to the rabbis when it agreed to a wholesale exemption of yeshiva students from military service.

To be exempt from military service in Israel is a serious matter. No society, perhaps in all history, has imposed on its citizens a longer compulsory military service: at least three years' regular service for men (it is usually extended) and two for women, and then a month or more per year of reserve duty for men up to the age of fifty-five —not counting the more extensive periods of active service during Israel's five major wars, including the *intifada*, the uprising by Palestinian Arabs living on the West Bank in 1987–88. The draft exemption is not the only cause of the growth of the ultra-Orthodox community in Israel, but it is an important one. During the years after it was adopted, the number of yeshiva students increased dramatically. Today there are more of them in Israel—estimated at between 30,000 and 40,000—than there ever were in Eastern Europe.

During the 1960s and 1970s, not only did the yeshivas significantly increase their recruits but entire Hasidic dynasties, which had lost almost all their members in Europe, were revived. As they expanded, the yeshivas, mainly the Lithuanian ones, began to absorb boys of Oriental extraction, especially from families in the poor ultra-Orthodox neighborhoods. The more gifted Oriental boys were drawn to the yeshiva world not only because it offered them a prestigious way to carry on studies while exempt from the draft but also because their own communities, unlike those of the Eastern European Zionists, retained a favorable view of religious tradition. In this way a *haredi* elite began to form among the Sephardis, who adopted the Lithuanian rabbis as their rabbinical authority.

The Sephardis, however, were ambivalent toward the Ashkenazi type of ultra-Orthodoxy that was expressed in the Lithuanian yeshivas. Many Sephardis felt humiliated because they were usually considered second-rate students, less sharp-witted than the Lithuanians; but they developed virtually unbounded admiration for the great masters of Halakha who headed the yeshivas. The insults by Ashkenazis were particularly resented when it came to politics. Sephardis felt ignored by the Ashkenazi leaders in the strongest *haredi* political party, the Aguda, which was then controlled by a combination of Hasidic and Lithuanian leaders who allowed them no representation. They decided to act. With the blessing of Rabbi Shach, they formed, in 1984, their own political party, Shas, and did well in the elections that year, gaining three seats in the Knesset. Thus Sephardic ultra-Orthodoxy became a political force in Israeli society.

The increasing numbers of Sephardic ultra-Orthodox became evident in the 1988 elections, when Shas won 4.7 percent of the vote, largely as a result of its diligent efforts to create the network of communal institutions it calls To the Fountain (*El Hama'ayan*); this provides needy Sephardic families with free comprehensive education and social welfare service, and most of its costs are covered by the state.

Not all the ultra-Orthodox Sephardim, however, have joined forces with the Lithuanians. Consider, for example, a Sephardic *zaddik*, the son of the late Abu-Hazira, a holy man of the North African community, who was once a notorious criminal and now thrives on selling expensive bottles of "holy" water to barren women. He has joined the Aguda Party of the Lubavitcher Hasidim, whom the Lithuanians detest, in the hope that he could establish under their auspices a regal Hasidic court at the palace he recently built for himself in a backward township in the Negev desert. Both the Likud leader Yitzhak Shamir and the Labor leader Shimon Peres made pilgrimages there before the elections in the hope of ingratiating themselves with a part of the North African community, but unsuccessfully. The alignment between the Sephardic practitioner of black magic and the Lubavitcher Hasidim held fast.

ONE MORE ULTRA-ORTHODOX community needs to be mentioned— the ultra-ultra-Orthodox community, which traditionally rejects all forms of participation in the Israeli political system and still rejects the state of Israel as sinful and heretical. This is the so-called Haredi Congregation, which boycotts the state, its elections, and some of its monetary benefits (such as monthly checks for child allowance paid by the national insurance). Its otherworldly religious standards once had a considerable influence, especially in making the ultra-Orthodox groups that take part in politics defensive about their own degree of religious purity. Today, however; this extremist community is in decline, mainly because its increasing willingness to accept state funds has dulled its moral authority.

The Haredi Congregation, concentrated mainly in ghettolike neighborhoods (in Meah Shearim in Jerusalem) and Bnei-Brak, consists of two factions: "Jerusalemites"—those who have lived in Jerusalem for many generations—and a few Hasidic groups, the most important of which is the Satmar community (which originated in Romania, moved to Hungary, and today has its center in Williamsburg, Brooklyn). It also includes the militant Hasidic community of Toldot Aaron, which has been the main force behind the so-called Sabbath Wars, the violent attempts to close theaters and other entertainments on the Sabbath, and the much-publicized demonstrations against the archaeologists working to uncover the foundations of the City of David. The phenomenon of children throwing stones began not with the *intifada*, but with *haredi* children stoning cars driving on the Sabbath. Those in Israel now calling for shooting Palestinian children who throw stones, arguing that the stones are deadly weapons, would of course never dare to propose shooting the *haredi* children. They are, after all, Jewish, and in Israel this is the difference that makes the difference.

ALL FACTIONS OF *haredim* reject modern life. This is one of its main conflicts with the Zionist movement, since Zionism was in essence a Jewish response to modern ways of thinking and living, and its leaders emphasized both their secularism and their commitments to science and political nationalism. Zionism claimed to provide an alternative to assimilation and to the loss of Jewish identity, while, at the same time, enabling Jews to emerge from the ghetto and to live free of religious restriction. To the ultra-Orthodox, by contrast, secularism, political nationalism, and to a certain extent science, too, are a direct threat to the religious way of life.

Nor can the ultra-Orthodox accept Zionism so long as the central political authority in Israel is not subject to Halakha but presumes to replace it. Secular education offends them because it threatens the traditional institutions of Torah study. Even such basic assumptions of modern life as the claim of moral autonomy for the individual are unacceptable to them because ultra-Orthodox society is predicated upon the authority of tradition and of Halakha. The ultra-Orthodox see a deep connection between the evils of modernism and the clothes people wear, and for them an especially weighty cause is the struggle against modern women's fashions. Recently the ultra-Orthodox have been claiming that secular modern life is responsible for the drug problem, and that every member of modern society is a potential drug addict. This view attracts adherents in Sephardic neighborhoods in Israel, where drug addiction is a problem. In these neighborhoods, one could say religion comes between opium and the people.

The ultra-Orthodox tend to speak dismissively of the National Religious Party, which has undergone many transformations. Up until the June 1967 war its religiosity had no special intensity and was entirely compatible with conventional bourgeois life. In matters of foreign policy, it was moderate. During the 1950s it objected, for example, to some of the military raids into Jordan and the Sinai that Ben-Gurion ordered. After 1967 its younger members became more and more intense about religious observance and at the same time increasingly nationalistic. Following the dramatic October War of 1973, the group known as Gush Emunim was formed within the party and became the avant-garde of the settlers moving into the West Bank.

Gush Emunim numbers about 5,000 settlers, who are popular among the students in Israel's religious high schools and modern yeshivas. Its leaders and principal activists are for the most part graduates of the Merkaz Harav yeshiva in Jerusalem, dominated by the spiritual influence of the late Rabbi Zvi Yehuda Kook. Gush Emunim differs crucially from the ultra-Orthodox in giving strong religious significance both to the history of the conflict over the Land of Israel and to the occupied territories. The theology of Gush Emunim is one of messianism without a messiah. Its followers believe that history is inexorably moving toward messianic days, or a state of redemption, even though their scheme ignores the persona of the messiah himself.

The founding of the state of Israel in 1948, and the conquest of the historic parts of the Land of Israel in 1967, are for them events of the utmost religious importance, since they reveal the overall divine scheme of redemption.

However, Gush Emunim is better understood as a political and not as a religious phenomenon. In the Israeli political spectrum its members occupy the ultra-right-wing position (after all, they organized and defended the terrorist Jewish underground exposed several years ago), while at the same time they have no close relations with the ultra-Orthodox camp.

The younger generation in the National Religious Party itself, however, have started to become closer to the ultra-Orthodox in religious matters. Some of the young men are attending *haredi*-style yeshivas, and many married women are covering their heads. Yet, in spite of their growing religious extremism, they also want to show that they can deal with modern life, and they make a point of combining Orthodox religious practices with knowledge of science. In their television broadcasts during the election campaign, the NRP took care to show their youngsters wearing knitted yarmulkas and sitting by computer consoles. The ultra-Orthodox show them in black hats, blowing the shofar.

WHEN MENACHEM BEGIN came to power in 1977, the NRP had twelve seats in the Knesset, the most it has ever received, and the party became part of Begin's coalition government. Today, it has only five members. The total number of religious party deputies has thus not changed much from election to election, but the NRP has lost while the ultra-Orthodox camp has gained.

The religious parties, whether modern or ultra-Orthodox, oppose any manifestation of Jewish religious pluralism in Israel. They want complete monopoly of Orthodoxy over all religious life in Israel, and they are still determined to push through the Knesset the notorious law by which the only converts who can qualify as Jews under the Law of Return are those who have undergone Orthodox conversion. This is the infamous "Who Is a Jew" law, whose purpose, in effect, is to deprive the Conservative and Reform denominations of Judaism of their legitimacy.

The same proposed law was an important factor in Prime Minister Shamir's decision last autumn to form a broad coalition government with Labor, rather than a narrow government with the religious parties, although for a while he misled the religious parties into thinking they might be part of a narrow coalition. Were Shamir to yield to the pressure from the religious parties and to commit himself to passing the law they wanted, he feared that he would antagonize Israel's Jewish supporters in the United States. He believes that the organized American Jewish community will swallow just about every toad he might feed it—except for a law that it feels will undermine their legitimacy as Jews.

The religious parties are not satisfied with the monopoly they have over marriage and divorce among Jews. In order to show that the state has no authority over Halakha, they now want to abolish the right of citizens to appeal to the Supreme Court regarding decisions of the rabbinical courts. Abolishing the appeals would be a far-reaching step toward undermining the legitimacy of Israel's judiciary and legislature.

Very little can be expected of ultra-Orthodox politics with respect to a peace settlement with the Palestinians. The *haredi* community is concentrated around its communal institutions, as I have emphasized, especially their yeshivas and other institutions of learning, and this basic fact determines the character of its politics. Their highest priority is to ensure the flow of state funds to build up and maintain their own institutions; national political questions are of secondary importance. That is why the *haredim* will always try to find a place in the ruling coalition—it is the best way to obtain money. And the Likud will always be able to offer them more than Labor can.

In order to form a coalition of its own, Labor needs, in addition to at least some of the religious parties, the support of the small parties on the left. And these are not willing to pay a high price in order to take part in a coalition with the religious parties, Orthodox or ultra-Orthodox. "For the sake of peace I'm willing to wear a *streimel*" (the Hasidic fur hat), the maverick politician Ezer Weizman joked during the coalition negotiations. That is, in order to gain the support of the religious parties, he is willing to pay nearly any price. However, Shulamit Aloni, the militant secular leader of the Civil Rights Party, would never say she was willing to wear a *sheitel*—the head covering of the *haredi* women—partly because she doubts a coalition with the religious parties will improve the prospects of peace.

The Likud has traditionally taken a more favorable view of religion than Labor, and it is freer of the strong secular commitments that have always characterized the Labor Party. In principle, only the Likud could form a narrow coalition with both the religious parties and the extreme right. This is the basic premise of Israeli politics—though not a premise for Shimon Peres—and this is what makes the Likud the ruling party. Because it knows that the Likud can form a narrow coalition government if it wants to, Labor has agreed to be the Likud's junior partner.

TOWARD PALESTINIANS, ALL the religious parties share roughly the same cast of mind. They see Arabs in general, and the Palestinians in particular, as wholly alien—goys who are particularly menacing because of their proximity. When it comes to formulated political opinions, however, the Lithuanians of The Flag of the Torah are doves. Its spiritual and political leaders and its voters as well say they are willing to exchange land for peace. But they have only two seats in the Knesset, and their attitude must be understood as expressing prudence rather than a moral position. Zionism for them means a commitment to territorial greed and military adventurism that can only bring harm to the Jews, and it sharply contrasts with their own ascetic idea of Judaism as based on study of the Torah.

Unlike the nationalists of the NRP, they have no interest in Greater Israel, and indeed they fear that claims to more land will provoke hostility among the nations of the world. Their anti-Zionism has therefore encouraged their political moderation. However, in spite of all this, they believe their schools and other institutions must come first; their responsibility to the rest of Israeli society is of secondary, if not of marginal, importance. This is why they are willing to join a right-wing nationalist government if the price is right.

Shas, the Sephardic *haredi* party, is divided in political matters. Its spiritual leaders tend to have political views close to those of the Lithuanians, but its voters, many of whom still feel the hostility to Arabs that is characteristic of North African Jews, tend to favor Likud positions, particularly those of Ariel Sharon, and in some cases the extreme views of Rabbi Kahane, whose main followers are poor young Sephardis and who has no support from any of the *haredi* leaders. Shas continues to defer to the spiritual authority of the Lithuanian Rabbi Shach—the same rabbi who, at the time of the Lebanon War in 1983, referred to General Sharon as a *"rodef"*—that is, a wanton murderer who under talmudic law could legitimately be killed without trial. Still, in view of the political feelings of its constituents, Shas will not break its political ties with Sharon.

In the coalition government, one of the two members from Shas is the Minister of the Interior, Rabbi Arieh Deri, the youngest and perhaps most intelligent of the current ministers. Recently, Deri, together with the Sephardic leader Rabbi Ovadia Yosef, was invited by President Hosni Mubarak to visit Egypt. They told their host that saving Jewish lives took precedence over the commandment of holding on to Greater Israel. Deri is certainly someone to watch in the coming months or years. Perhaps if there is a change in the deadlock of Israeli politics, it will come from him.

As for the Hasidic ultra-Orthodox party, the Aguda, its views, heavily influenced by those of the Brooklyn Lubavitcher *rebbe*, are those of the extreme right wing. In Israel this means a commitment to holding on to all of Greater Israel and a willingness to enter into a direct and explicit conflict with the United States over doing so. The more "moderate" right wingers in the Aguda are those who, despite their commitment to Greater Israel, will do anything to avoid a confrontation with the American government. For them, too, however, the primary aim of the party is to increase the prosperity of the Hasidic communities that support it. So the Aguda, too, extracts the highest possible price for supporting the Likud, and, although it is still angry with Shamir for bluffing during the coalition negotiations, it will stick with him.

The politics of the NRP come down to biblical nationalism. Most of its leaders nowadays are extreme right-wing (although some are more moderate), and its constituency is by and large extremist. Ideologically its supporters favor the idea of "the unity of the nation"; that is, given the chance, they would favor a broad, national unity coalition government over a narrow coalition, even a right-wing one.

Currently, the only chance for movement toward peace in the Middle East is President Mubarak's proposal to have Israelis and Palestinians meet in Cairo for preliminary negotiations. The Palestinian delegation would include, in addition to representatives from the occupied territories, two Palestinians who were expelled from Israel and who are members of the PLO. Shamir objects to their being included, but Yitzhak Rabin accepts it. The cabinet decision of October 6 was to turn down Mubarak's invitation to Cairo. This disagreement between the Likud and the cabinet decision has once again raised the possibility of a narrow government headed by Labor and shared with the religious parties.

To form such a coalition Labor would have to yield to all the demands of the religious parties in matters of religious law and additional funds, in exchange for support of a political settlement with the Palestinians: a government of *Strimenl* and peace. The chances for such a development are, I believe, extremely small. In the end, what is unacceptable to Shamir will not come to pass. However, what would be acceptable to Shamir depends to a considerable extent on what President George Bush and Secretary of State James Baker tell him he has to accept. The catch, unfortunately, is that what Baker and Bush will tell Shamir to accept depends to a considerable extent on what they believe Shamir is willing to accept.

The Israel of 1998 is celebrating its Jubilee while in the grip of a Kulturkampf. The two sides in this conflict are the Orthodox Jews—especially the ultra-Orthodox—and the secular Jews, and it is a conflict that many Israelis find as menacing as the one between Jews and Arabs.

Significant changes have taken place in the religious camp since I wrote this essay a decade ago. For one thing, it has increased its electoral power from 13 percent in the 1992 elections, which brought the Labor Party leader Yitzhak Rabin to power, to 19.5 percent in the 1996 elec-

tions, which Benjamin Netanyahu won with the backing of 98 percent of the ultra-Orthodox. This change in electoral power is due partly to a change in the Israeli electoral system, but it also reflects an ideological shift. Ultra-Orthodox Jews, almost without exception, define themselves as belonging to the right, while 80 percent of religious Jews in general thus define themselves and only 22 percent of Jews who consider themselves secularists say that they belong to the right. There is no need to be a footnudnik and further document the obvious: all polls and studies that have been conducted in Israel attest more or less to these findings. Also since I wrote my essay, the Hasidic Rebbe of Lubavitch, Menachem Schneerson, died, although this fact itself is very much in dispute among his followers. Yet if his messianic nature is still in dispute, his political-messianic message is not in dispute at all: not an inch of the holy land of Israel should be given up to the Palestinians. The Habad community with or without the Rebbe is going to remain the core of Israel's political right.

What does belonging to the right mean in Israel today? Among other things, it means that only 9 percent of the ultra-Orthodox support the Oslo Accords between Israel and the Palestinians, as compared with 56 percent of secular Jews. In one survey, 86 percent of the ultra-Orthodox did not accept the proposition that Palestinians want peace with Israel; in contrast, 70 percent of the secularists agreed with this proposition. Two converging trends can be discerned in the religious camp, then: the ultra-Orthodox are becoming more and more nationalistic, developing a non-Zionistic jingoism; whereas ultranationalists of the modern Orthodox variety are veering more and more toward ultra-Orthodoxy in the religious sense.

The old notion that the non-Zionist ultra-Orthodox in Israel were, on religious grounds, politically moderate in their attitude toward the Arabs no longer holds water. Moreover, the ultra-Orthodox no longer join up with the political right for merely tactical reasons (to extract more money for their community), but, on the contrary, have become its hard core. A few of their rabbis still retain the old stance of political moderation with regard to Arabs, but the constituency is far out to the right.

To be sure, this ideological shift has its economic causes. The ultra-

Orthodox community is by now utterly dependent on state funds. More than 60 percent of its men are voluntarily out of work. They are so heavily subsidized by the state as rabbinical scholars that it doesn't make economic sense for them to take low-paying jobs, and they don't have the training to get high-paying ones. The average number of children an Orthodox woman has during her lifetime is seven, which is three times the average for Israeli women in general. A family of six children with unemployed parents receives the equivalent of $2,000 a month tax-free from the state, which is above the average income for an Israeli family. But, then, the ultra-Orthodox family is far above the average size of the ordinary Israeli family, and so they remain poor nonetheless.

A community so heavily dependent on the state cannot afford to antagonize its economic benefactor. So, instead of attacking Zionism as such for spreading heresy among Jews, it directs its attacks against "the left" as the bearer of all Zionist sins. The ultra-Orthodox perceive the nonreligious right as still being "Jewish" but in a childish way. (Much use is made of the talmudic expression "a child in captivity" to denote a person who is nonreligious due to ignorance rather than willful denial.) They see the right as people "with their heart in the right place," while the left is made up of sinister "Arab lovers."

Both versions of Orthodoxy—the modern and the ultra—are determined to impose the Orthodox monopoly on religion in Israel, if necessary by law. Orthodox rabbis are the only ones entrusted with performing marriages and divorces, conversion and burials. The idea is to prevent Reform and Conservative Jews from breaking the Orthodox hold on religion in Israel.

The synagogue that secular Israeli Jews don't go to is an Orthodox one. Therefore they have been fairly indifferent to the plight of Reform and Conservative Jews. But recently this secularist attitude towards religious pluralism has been gradually changing. More and more secularists are now siding with Reform and Conservative groups in their struggle for recognition in Israel.

But the main change among the secularists with regard to the ultra-Orthodox community has been in the type of criticism directed at it. In the past secular Israelis focused on the fact that the ultra-Orthodox, although sharing the benefits of Israeli citizenship, do not serve in the army and do not carry a share in the heavy burden of Israel's security. Now, however, the criticism has been extended and it also includes an older Zionist theme: that the ultra-Orthodox community consists of economic parasites who live on "Israeli taxpayers' money."

3

FROM RUSSIA
WITHOUT MUCH LOVE

JUNE 1991

MANY IMMIGRANTS WHO ARRIVED IN ISRAEL FROM THE SOVIET UN-
ion in 1990 came off the plane carrying dogs in their arms. This
seemed odd, since Jews are not noted for their friendliness to dogs.
An enterprising journalist soon reported that the immigrants were
trying to take with them out of Russia anything they could sell in
Israel. There weren't any carpets left, but they had heard that well-
to-do young Israelis in Tel Aviv were buying dogs as pets.

The immigrants arriving toward the end of the year were given
instructions at the airport for using gas masks, but Saddam Hussein
had, in effect, done them a favor by distracting the attention of Arab
countries from the huge immigration of Jews to Israel and concen-
trating their attention on the Gulf. With few Arab protests, about
200,000 immigrants arrived in Israel during the year, including

183,000 from the Soviet Union. Just before the fighting started in the Gulf War, the rate of immigration swiftly rose. In December alone 36,000 immigrants arrived in Israel. When the war began this rate was cut in half, and in February only 3,000 immigrants came from the Soviet Union.

The Soviet Jews said they were waiting to see what happened. Now they are starting to emigrate once more, and 200,000 more Jews are expected to arrive during 1991. If this trend continues, as many as a million Jews will leave the U.S.S.R. for Israel during the next few years. Since Israel's current population is only about four million, adding a million people would radically change Israeli life—it is as if the United States were to absorb the entire population of Italy within five years.

The immigration of Soviet Jews to Israel is closely linked with the possibility of their immigration to the United States. During the 1970s and 1980s, about 350,000 Jews left the Soviet Union with Israeli visas, but when they reached Vienna many changed their destination and went to the United States. Indeed, during the late 1980s, about 85 percent of them went to the United States.

The main organization dealing with the immigration to Israel is the Jewish Agency, which is an unofficial arm of the Israeli government. That many of the Soviet emigrants during those years wanted to go to the United States brought into play two other Jewish organizations dealing with immigration: HIAS (the Hebrew Immigrant Aid Society) and the American-Jewish Joint Distribution Committee (JDC), both independent of Israel. HIAS dealt with the immigration of those who wanted to go to the United States, especially with the paperwork required for getting immigration visas from Washington; the Joint provided Soviet immigrants in Europe with food, clothing, housing, and education while they waited to go to the United States, Israel, or other countries. The Jewish Agency, on the other hand, gave help only to those who wanted to continue on to Israel. The JDC made an agreement with the United States government by which the latter would pay the expenses of each person who was later accepted as an immigrant to the United States.

Soviet Jews went by rail or plane to Vienna, since there were no direct flights to Israel at that time. In Vienna a Jewish Agency representative collected their passports and asked each one where he or she wanted to go. The usual answer was "to the States," and the people who gave this answer were transferred to the care of the JDC, which sent them to Viennese hotels and their files to HIAS. Anyone who wanted to go to another country, for example Germany, went directly to that country's embassy in Vienna.

Then, with Gorbachev's rise to power after 1985, the stream of emigrants increased enormously. In order to keep down the costs of waiting in Vienna, an expensive city, the emigrants were transferred to working-class resort cities in southern Italy, particularly Ladispoli. This created a bottleneck, and a request was made to increase the staff of the American immigration office. This request was granted, and the staff was increased to a maximum of two hundred employees.

Three serious controversies soon developed. The first was a disagreement between the Israeli government, speaking through the Jewish Agency, and the Jewish organizations outside Israel. The Jewish Agency claimed that the emigrants "belonged to Israel" since they had left the Soviet Union with Israeli visas. In the United States, some American Jews supported the Zionist principle of "the centrality of Israel in Jewish life," while others upheld the liberal principle of giving each emigrant freedom of choice.

The second controversy was between Israel and the United States, again with the Israelis claiming that the emigrants "belonged" to them. The third was on the question of increasing the American immigration quota. During the 1970s and early 1980s, Jewish immigrants from the U.S.S.R. to the United States were accepted as part of the quota allotted to Soviet refugees. But with Gorbachev the quota was no longer sufficient, and the question was whether to increase it. At the same time, organizations of Asian immigrants (mainly from Vietnam and Cambodia) were also demanding an increase in their quotas.

The Israeli government did not want the quota to be increased but hesitated to say so publicly, since there was considerable support among American Jews for the principle of giving emigrants the freedom to choose whether to go to Israel or elsewhere. Strong pressure by Jewish organizations on the Reagan administration led to a considerable expansion of the category of immigrant "parolees"—that is, immigrants who cannot become citizens or receive government support, but who have the right to work if their guarantors accept responsibility for them. Expanding this category placed a heavy financial burden on American Jews, and some American Jewish organizations tended for this reason to direct the immigrants to Israel.

American law requires that immigrants who enter the United States as refugees prove (1) that they are persecuted for their politics or religion in their country of origin; and (2) that no other country is willing to accept them. HIAS gave the Soviet emigrants help in showing that the first condition was fulfilled. Since Israel was eager to accept them the refugees could not satisfy the second condition, but the Reagan administration chose to ignore this fact.

After negotiations in 1989, Secretary of State George Shultz and Foreign Minister Eduard Shevardnadze reached an agreement in October to allow direct immigration from the Soviet Union to the United States. The paperwork could now be taken care of in Moscow; those who did not directly apply for immigration to the United States had to go to Israel, and they could fly there directly. No doubt a large number of those who apply to Israel rather than to the United States do so because the American quota for Soviet immigrants is limited and the Jewish applicants now have many competitors. They are also aware that however much they would prefer to live in New York or California, Israel does not want the U.S. quotas for Soviet Jews to be raised, and American Jewish organizations are not on the whole asking for it either. Once the immigrants arrive in Israel their preferences are not so clear. A poll of a representative sample in April by the Dahaf Institute asked, "In which country do you think you would get along better?" Forty-six percent said Israel, 11 percent said the United States, and 40 percent said there was no difference between the two.

BEFORE AND AFTER Saddam Hussein's Scud missiles in January, the main topic of conversation here in Israel has been the Russian immigrants. In order to absorb a million immigrants Israel needs, according to the most conservative estimates, an additional $20 billion (at 1990 prices) during the next five years to provide for basic necessities such as food, housing, and medical care and also, mainly, for investment that will create jobs. Commercial banks in the United States and Europe would have to put up a large part of that money, and they will not do so unless the loans are guaranteed by the U.S. government. Two questions are being asked: one in public—will the United States supply the money and guarantees required? The other in private—will the United States exact any political price for these guarantees? If Israel can't borrow $25 billion during five years, it will be faced with an extremely severe economic and social crisis.

The immigration to Israel could therefore change the meaning of the phrase "pressure on Israel." Israel, as the country receiving the most U.S. aid, has had $3 billion a year in economic and military assistance since 1973, and "pressure on Israel" used to mean the threat of reducing this sum. In fact, this is no threat at all, since the political influence of the Israeli lobby and its American Jewish supporters in Congress and elsewhere has been powerful enough to ensure that the $3 billion was paid annually. Now Israel's need for an additional $25 billion makes it, at least potentially, more vulnerable to American pressure than ever before, especially during lean times in the United States.

This could be the political significance of the Soviet immigration for Bush's "New Order" in the Middle East, if there is to be one. Whatever happens, however, the effects on Israel will be dramatic. Israel, still in some respects a Third World country, will be absorbing much of the educated elite of a superpower. While only 0.6 percent of employed Israelis have degrees in the natural sciences, people with such degrees make up 7.1 percent of the immigrants. That is, there are proportionately twelve times as many people with degrees in the natural sciences among the immigrants as among the Israelis. There are also thirteen times as many engineers and architects, four times as many technicians, and nearly six times as many doctors. The proportion of skilled and unskilled manual workers is much smaller than it is among Israelis.

Some of these statistics may be misleading. A good many people who got on the plane to Israel as, say, Mr. Rabinowitz, may get off as Dr. Rabinowitz, and some immigrants probably managed to add several years of university studies in a few hours on the plane. Aside from forgeries, it is very difficult to evaluate Soviet university degrees by Western standards. For several years Israel has been giving qualifying examinations to doctors from abroad (while exempting doctors from the United States and Canada, where the standards are considered high). Among the Russian doctors who took these examinations in 1990, 70 percent failed. Only 15 percent of those who passed managed to do so without taking a special course. The Russians complain that the examiners are unfairly giving them failing grades to protect the interests of the local doctors' guilds. The Israeli examiners claim that the exams are easy and point out that 65 percent of the doctors coming from Argentina, as well as 75 percent of those from Western Europe, passed the test without a preparatory course. Still, medicine and the biological sciences do not have high status in the Soviet Union, and the prestige of doctors there is lower than in the West—much lower than that of physicists, for example.

The various Israeli employers I have talked to have conflicting views. Some of them are immensely impressed by the education, skills, and seriousness of the immigrants; others have only contempt for them, and claim they stumble when dealing with modern technology. But most economists agree with Michael Bruno, governor of the Bank of Israel, that successfully absorbing a million Soviet immigrants would mean that Israel's "human capital"—the economic value of the workforce, of which education is a component—will double.

The Soviet immigrants have enormous advantages over Israelis in education. About 40 percent of the immigrants have had between thirteen and fifteen years of schooling, in contrast to 15 percent of Israelis. Sixteen percent of the immigrants went to school for more than sixteen years. Israeli universities estimate that 2 percent of the Soviet immigrants—four thousand people—are qualified to teach in universities. Among them are enough mathematicians to fill several times as many mathematics departments as Israel now has. And those who are yet to arrive are thought to be more talented and qualified, since people who have more to lose have been in less of a hurry to leave. A colleague at the Hebrew University, who is from the previous generation of Soviet immigrants, said to me recently, "The mathematicians who left for Israel are the ones they would wrap in paper bags in Russia. Some of the ones they wrap in cellophane went to Princeton and MIT. Most of the best mathematicians are still in the Russian academies."

FEW ISRAELIS REALLY know the immigrants, yet they talk ceaselessly about what they are like, and much of what one hears is predictable. Before they arrived, it would have been rare to find an Israeli computer programmer who wrote or even could recite poetry. No one is surprised that the Soviet immigrants are much more likely to do so. As one would expect, they are also deeply suspicious of anything that smacks of ideology, especially socialism. I heard from a teacher that an immigrant boy complained to him that instead of being taught mathematics in school he was being taught "Leninism." The boy, it turned out, was referring to compulsory Bible lessons: for him the Bible is part of Israel's official ideology, not part of its culture, and any official ideology for him is "Leninism."

During the 1930s, Israel also had a wave of immigrants that were much more highly qualified than the rest of the Jewish population: the settlers who were fleeing Hitler. As with the Soviet Jews now, many among the German immigrants then were not Zionists, and their cultural and professional qualifications were impressive. They were thought to be amazingly competent and responsible, but the settlers from Eastern Europe tended to see them as humorless, soulless, psychologically blinkered, and unable to comprehend suffering. The prevailing attitude toward today's Russian Jews is different. Far from perceiving them as machinelike, people talk about their "Russian soul."

But such images are, after all, largely based on the fictions people create. The facts show that the Soviet immigrants are older than Israelis as a whole, with fewer children and young people among them. The median age of the immigrants is thirty-two, of the Israelis, twenty-seven. Infants and children under five make up 12 percent of the Israeli population but only 8 percent of the immigrants. Thirty-four percent of the immigrants have only one child, as opposed to 21 percent among Israelis. The average Soviet immigrant family consists of three people. They are, on the whole, mature, well educated, professional people with small families. Many are fluent in English and accomplished in mathematics.

The immigrants are called "Russian immigrants," although in 1990, 59,000 arrived from the Ukraine (including 12,000 from Kiev), 23,000 from White Russia, 26,000 from the Central Asian cities such as Tashkent, and only 45,000 from Russia itself (15,000 from Leningrad, 10,000 from Moscow). During the 1970s a far greater proportion of immigrants came from the Baltic republics, and many of them could remember Jewish life free of Soviet rule. Hardly any such people are among the current arrivals. They are products of the Communist regime, even though most of them were never Communists, and very few could be called even "cynical Communists"—that is, those who, for career reasons, have their names on the lists of government posts that are open only to Party members: the *nomenklatura*.

There is a nasty racist edge to the questions Israelis raise about the Soviet Jews: Do they "look Jewish"? Are they in fact Jews? The nineteenth-century British psychologist Francis Galton invented a technique for constructing a collective portrait of particular groups by putting one picture on top of another and, by mapping the common points, arriving at a "typical" group member. Many Israelis have constructed such a mental picture of the numerous immigrants who appear on television screens here almost every evening.

The older immigrants "look Jewish" to the Israelis, but then old people often look Jewish. The traditional stereotype of a Jew is an old person. The young immigrants tend to look Russian—with snub noses, high cheekbones, wide Slavic faces among the women, fair hair, light complexions, and even steely blue eyes instead of the "suffering" brown eyes of the Jewish stereotype. In general, to Israelis the Soviet immigrants look like Gentiles. Many Israeli Jews of European origin (Ashkenazis) say, "Great, they'll improve the race, the next generation won't look so Sephardi," while a Sephardi told me, "They are even more Ashkenazi than the Ashkenazis. Real Christians, it's frightening." That the Russian immigration will change Israelis not only culturally but also physiognomically is felt to be a source of hope by the Ashkenazis and of fear by the Sephardis. People are often embarrassed at first to speak about such feelings but they tend to emerge as one talks. In the Israelis' attitudes toward the many Soviet Jews who don't look Jewish, one may detect an erotic ambivalence toward the beautiful Gentile.

The Israeli minister responsible for immigrants when they arrive is Rabbi Yitzhak Peretz, a representative of Shas, the Sephardi ultra-Orthodox party. His office provides them with the government's "absorption basket," including a mortgage for buying an apartment, a school for learning Hebrew, and temporary housing. Peretz has acquired a reputation for being one of the most incompetent ministers in Israel's history. He has not even managed to rent an office in any of the cities in which there are thousands of immigrants, and the facilities for looking after them are in a chaotic state.

Peretz also caused a stir when he said that a third of Soviet immigrants are not Jewish. Some people thought that this was an attempt to distract public attention from his incompetence, but Peretz was mostly concerned not to offend two of the most powerful communities in Israel, the ultra-Orthodox and the Sephardis, each of which is uneasy about the Soviet immigration. The immigrants are entirely non-Sephardi and very secular—that is, they are seldom religious, and hardly ever ultra-Orthodox.

The storm that greeted Peretz's statement soon subsided. Speaking against immigration in Israel is like speaking against motherhood, and the Sephardis who openly did so—one of their local leaders even wrote a letter to Gorbachev asking him to stop Jews from leaving— were severely criticized. Some Sephardi Israelis of Moroccan origin then invited the new immigrants to an Oriental feast, as if making a grand conciliatory gesture. Still, when stories and pictures of a revival of the Russian Orthodox Church in Israel began to appear—including pictures of people alleged to be immigrants receiving incense from bearded Russian Orthodox priests—Peretz's claim that one third of the arrivals are not Jewish was strengthened in the public mind.

Soviet Jews are officially those who identify themselves as Jews when they fill in the box labeled "*national'nost*" in the Soviet census. This does not mean "nationality"; the closest approximation in English might be "ethnic group." Since being a Jew in the Soviet Union is no great honor and until quite recently had many disadvantages, some Jews undoubtedly "converted" when they responded to the census. Those who listed themselves as Jews may be taken to consider themselves Jews, but since there is a high proportion of mixed marriages among the Soviet Jews, a great many spouses and children are prepared to consider themselves Jewish even though, according to Jewish religious law, they are not Jews because their mothers are not Jewish. The proportion of such non-Jews may be a third, as Peretz declared, or it may be half or more. No one knows, and aside from Orthodox Jews no one wants to know.

On the whole, however, these secular Russian immigrants have a clear interest—both personal and collective—in a secular Israel in which they will not have to conform to religious laws they don't believe in. The theological situation was summed up by a mining engineer I talked to from the Ukraine: "God is something very nice for parasites. Working people have no time for him. My husband and I are working people." This could become an important political fact, since their secularism could lead the immigrants to oppose the Orthodox parties and also the parties of the right that depend on them for support and make many concessions to them.

THE FIGHT FOR the "Jewish souls" of the immigrants is very intense. The Immigrant Absorption Ministry has indeed failed dramatically to help arriving immigrants, but the ultra-Orthodox officials who run it are much more concerned with what it calls their "spiritual absorption." To learn Hebrew the immigrants are sent mainly to schools run by the Orthodox, where they are subject to incessant religious missionary activity. The men and boys are required to wear skullcaps, and the women and girls are required to dress in accordance with Orthodox custom—long-sleeved dresses, no slacks or short skirts, etc. This indoctrination is called *Yiddishkeit* and one often hears from Orthodox spokesmen that *Yiddishkeit* never hurt anyone.

This Passover the Absorption Ministry distributed specially printed Passover Haggadahs with a Russian translation for the immigrants. One of the passages in the Haggadah is a fable of four types of sons, among them a wise son and an evil son. In the ministry's Haggadah the illustration of the wise son is of an Orthodox man with a full beard and a large black skullcap, while the evil son, a clean-shaven young executive without a hat, is portrayed as a secular Jew. The ministry's spiritual concern, moreover, is not only for the living but also for the dead. Before an immigrant killed in a traffic accident could be buried in a Jewish grave, a circumcision was performed on the corpse. (This necrophilic item was reported on the back pages of the Israeli press but became a central item on Soviet television.)

My own impression is that the Soviet Jews are fairly immune to indoctrination not only in traditional religion but also in civil religion. On the first day of Secretary Baker's recent visit to Jerusalem, an Arab murdered four women. Seeing a band of Russian musicians playing outdoors near the center of Jerusalem, an angry woman approached them and asked them to stop. "This is not a time to be happy, now is a time of national mourning in Israel," she shouted at them. The trumpeter stopped playing and said in broken Hebrew, "Here in Israel not communism. Here capitalism, here freedom"—and they went on playing all the more loudly.

Israel's left-wing parties hope that such irreverent immigrants will be so opposed to religious legislation that they will not support Israel's government, which is both right-wing nationalist and clerical. But to deduce the new immigrants' future voting patterns from their secularism itself requires a leap of faith. I was able to see a privately conducted survey of the views of the immigrants in 1990 by a reliable public opinion expert. One clear and striking finding was that the immigrants' political views are even more hawkish than those of most of the rest of the Jewish population in Israel. More than half the respondents said that Israel should keep all the occupied territories, even if Israel were guaranteed adequate security arrangements and, in exchange for giving up the territories, could live in peace with the Arabs. By contrast, more than half of other Israeli Jews expressed the opinion that Israel should be willing to give up at least part of the territories in return for a secure peace. About 85 percent of the immigrants believe that the Arabs could, and should, be expelled from both Israel and the occupied territories. Among Israeli Jews, by comparison, about 70 percent believe that it is desirable to expel the Arabs, while 15 percent believe that it is politically feasible. Moreover, about a quarter of the Israeli Jews think that it is necessary to speak to the PLO, while only 2 percent of the immigrants think so.

A colleague of mine, a professor from Russia who is active among the immigrants on behalf of the Labor Party, tried to explain their views to me. The immigrants come from the wide expanses of Russia to this tiny country, he said; and then Israel's left-wing politicians tell claustrophobic Russians that even this country, for all its tiny size, must be divided. This seems a lunatic notion to them. And since they come from a country where entire nations have been transferred from place to place, the idea of transfer doesn't seem terrible to them.

HOW SUCH POLITICAL views will be expressed politically is not yet clear. Most immigrants who replied to the poll I earlier cited— 70 percent—had not yet decided which party they would support, but among the 30 percent who had decided, a clear majority favored the Likud over the Labor Alignment. When the same immigrants were asked for their views of Israeli leaders, 11 percent had a "very favorable" opinion of Ariel Sharon, and 35 percent a "somewhat favorable" view; 8 percent had a "very favorable" view of Prime Minister Shamir, and 43 percent were "somewhat favorable." Not even 1 percent had a "very favorable" view of Shimon Peres, and only 15 percent were "somewhat favorable" to him. Mikhail Gorbachev is as popular as Shamir among the immigrants, and both of them are more popular than Yitzhak Rabin.

One of the participants in this popularity contest is the famous refusenik Natan Sharansky. He is as popular as Boris Yeltsin, with 7 percent having a "very favorable" view of him and 35 percent "somewhat favorable." The immigrants have no recognized leader, but Sharansky is perhaps the best known, and one hears rumors that he is quietly organizing a political party. Ideologically it would probably tend to the right. In a poll conducted by the Tazpit survey organization, 53 percent of the immigrants said they would vote for a purely Russian list for the Knesset.

If a "Russian list" is established, this, in my view, could be all to the good. Even if its supporters are hawks, its representatives will have to concern themselves with the interests of immigrants generally. This means that the Russian list will have to be pro-American in some degree, since the only hope for obtaining enough money to absorb the immigrants is from the United States. This could blunt the claws of the hawks among them.

The prevailing view of the Israeli press is that if elections were to take place in Israel tomorrow, the right-wing parties would be strengthened, particularly by the support of Soviet immigrants. On the other hand, it is difficult to predict how the immigrants would vote in the future if, as could well happen, a social and economic catastrophe occurs partly as a result of the immigration and the government is held responsible. In such circumstances the Soviet immigrants could not expect much sympathy. In a poll of Israeli Jews taken by the Dahaf survey organization 63 percent said that they are not willing to lower their standard of living for the immigrants, while 34 percent are willing to do so.

Clearly Ashkenazi and Sephardic Jews have very different attitudes toward the immigrants. Before the present immigration Israel had a slight majority of Sephardis, with a large majority of them in the younger age groups, a fact which seemed to ensure a heavily Sephardic Israel. The Russian immigration will now increase the proportion of Ashkenazis, much to the dismay of the Sephardis. The newspaper *Hadashot* on April 24, 1991, quoted a Likud member of the Knesset who is the mayor of one of the development towns established in Israel during the 1950s to absorb the mass immigrations that still have huge Sephardic majorities: "I am beginning to hear new tunes," he said. Some of the mayors of development towns are afraid. They say that because of the Soviet immigration, the Sephardis will have to go back to their previously low status as second-class Israeli citizens. The same Knesset member quoted a colleague: "The immigration will destroy the prospects of young leaders that were coming up in the development towns during the 1970s and 1980s; they will all be replaced by Yasha, Grisha, and Misha."

The immigrants themselves speak with contempt for "Asiatics"— their name for Sephardis. An immigrant couple I know was offered a place in a development town not far from Jerusalem which is mostly populated by Sephardis. "I want to live near you Europeans," the wife said to me, "and not near the Asiatics in that town." A Russian immigrant taxi driver who had somehow arrived in Israel via New York defined a Sephardi to an American visitor as "a Hebrew-speaking Puerto Rican." When the Soviet immigrants I have talked with use the word "Asia" to refer to the Sephardic Jews, the word stands for dirt, lack of culture and hygiene, and shouting in the streets.

THE GOVERNMENT IS seeking to direct Soviet immigrants to the north as part of programs for the "Judaization" of the Galilee region, where a large concentration of Israeli Arabs live. So far, 32 percent of the immigrants live in the north, while only 22 percent of Israeli Jews live there. The government has always wanted to change the "demographic balance" between Jews and Arabs in the Galilee, partly out of fear that the concentration of Arabs there will someday lead to their demand for autonomy, or for the separation of the Galilee from Israel and its annexation by one of the Arab states bordering on it (Jordan, Syria, or a possible future Palestinian state).

If large numbers of Soviet Jews are to be installed in the Galilee, the government might expropriate Arab land on which to settle them; there have already been attempts to expropriate land from the Arabs near Nazareth. Arabs both inside and outside Israel almost unanimously oppose the immigration but Israeli Arabs most of all, since they understandably fear that the settlement of the Russian Jews will occur at their expense.

A far more serious issue concerns the effect of the immigration on settlements in the occupied territories, which are intended by the right wing to block any future political agreement in which Israel would give up territories for peace. The Israeli government promised the

United States and the Soviet Union that it would not send the immigrants directly to settlements on the West Bank and the Gaza Strip. But if pressure of the immigration raises the cost of buying or renting apartments in Israel and Israelis therefore are impelled to move to the heavily subsidized apartments in the territories, then it doesn't matter who the settlers are. The Housing Ministry's current plans are to build 24,000 new housing units for 90,000 people in the territories. Last year the Housing Ministry, which is run by Sharon, spent $700 million there on new construction.

The Bush administration has said that the question of settling immigrants in the territories is a test of the good faith of the Israeli government. Sharon, for his part, has been provocatively settling them in the West Bank in order to create tension between the Bush administration and Shamir. But all this is a mere sideshow. Indirectly or directly, the immigration will increase the settlement of Jews in the territories, and this is undeniably the policy of the Israeli government.

For all their numbers the immigrants, with the seriousness of their problems in finding jobs and housing, are strangely isolated in Israel. They sometimes seem to be living in a cultural space station detached from Israel's gravity and connected to signals coming from the home station in Russia—a kind of Jewish Soyuz. They work hard at learning Hebrew, but for them Hebrew is merely an instrument for getting along at work. Their preferred language remains Russian. Michael Gendlev, a poet and doctor who emigrated to Israel in 1977, writes in the liberal-left journal *Politika* that until the latest Soviet immigration about two hundred Soviet Jews who call themselves writers and poets had come to Israel, of whom he estimates that twenty to thirty are not hacks. During 1990, another four hundred registered writers arrived, some of them more reputable; today there are more than thirty Russian-language periodicals in Israel.

Some Ashkenazi Israelis long for closer relations with the new immigrants, and arrange meetings with them in which they try to create rapport, for example by singing songs of socialist youth movements of the 1940s and 1950s. They forget that some of the songs are Stalinist compositions about the heroic Red Army for example, one about General Semyen Budenny, a comrade of Stalin's. The immigrants cringe with embarrassment.

That the Soviet immigrants are having severe difficulties making a living is evident. Israelis see them collecting unsold vegetables thrown away at the market, and they hear stories about suicides among them. A few days ago I left my house and saw a young man sitting on the nearby railway tracks. Two women were trying to persuade him to get out of danger. The young man was silent. I heard one of the women say, "He's certainly a Russian—they have nothing to live for." As it turned out, the young man was not a Russian, but the fact that this was the first explanation that crossed the woman's mind was not surprising. The next morning I saw the following headline in the *Dvar* newspaper of May 1: "Immigrant Student Hangs Self; His Wife Attempts Suicide Immediately Afterward." A family friend was quoted as saying: "Igor missed Russia and it was hard for him in Israel." Not far from where I live, a street that used to be quiet at night is frequented by dozens of Russian prostitutes. "These women were not prostitutes in the Soviet Union," a Russian friend tells me. "Poverty is driving them onto the streets."

Israel has absorbed mass immigrations before; between 1949 and 1973 the gross national product grew by 10 percent each year; but after the Yom Kippur War this growth came to a standstill. As a result of that war Israel more than doubled the size of its army, and its defense expenditures fluctuate between a quarter and a third of GNP. The financing of defense by inflation got out of hand, and during the 1982 Lebanon War it led to hyperinflation of Latin American proportions.

Finding jobs for the new immigrants would require renewed growth in the economy, but the present right-wing government will not do what Ben-Gurion did in the 1950s, when he limited the defense budget to 8 percent of GNP in order to absorb the mass immigration. The risks of war and civil strife in Israel are so high that foreign and Israeli entrepreneurs will not take the chance of investing in Israel unless they have guarantees that their money will be protected. The Shamir administration refuses even to try to negotiate a political agreement that would make Israel attractive to investment, and in Israel today there are no significant internal sources of investment.

Whatever economic policy is adopted—whether the free market, Gosplan, or "the Israeli method" of allocating funds to entrepreneurs close to politicians in power—outside investment will be necessary for growth that can lead to employment.

Loans will be needed to provide for housing. Ariel Sharon, as Housing Minister, controls $4.5 billion for construction and is in charge of distributing government land to contractors. He thus wields enormous political leverage. If he succeeds, he will become a strong candidate to take over as Premier from Shamir. If he fails, it could be the end of his career. So far he has been failing. One newspaper headline called him "a bulldozer with a motorcycle engine," because 25,000 new immigrants per month require at least 6,000 new housing units per month, and so far fewer than half that number are being built. In December 1990, when 36,000 immigrants arrived, construction began on only 2,600 apartments.

The only government that could be expected to provide the required sums for housing as well as other needed investments is that of the United States, whether directly, in the form of grants, or indirectly, as a guarantor for loans from private banks. Will the United States do so if the Israelis continue to resist any negotiation with the Arabs? Most of the immigrants in the poll I mentioned earlier (about 70 percent) believe that the Soviet immigration will work against the interests of the Arabs, and only 10 percent believe that it will have a positive effect on the Arabs' well-being. On the face of it, the Soviet immigration is indeed bad news for the Arabs, and thus for an Arab-Israeli agreement. Shamir has twice declared that "a Greater Israel" is necessary to accommodate the immense new immigration, and that the new immigrants will keep in office the right-wing bloc that rejects any territorial compromises. (Defense Minister Moshe Arens says, "The last one to use the formula 'peace for territory' was Hitler.") Since the immigration will directly and indirectly expand the settlements in the occupied territories, more possibilities for trading land for peace are closed off.

On the other hand, the Soviet immigration can also serve as the best instrument the United States has had so far for bringing Israel to a peace agreement. The current right-wing Zionist dilemma is not one of "territories vs. peace" but of "territories vs. immigration." Absorbing immigration and consolidating the Jewish settlement in Israel are the two central Zionist values. But the Israeli right wing will be faced with a difficult decision if the United States provides support for the immigration only if Israel gives up territory as part of an agreement with the Arabs. (The recent rescue of Ethiopian Jews was impressive and moving testimony to the strength of the commitment of the Israeli government and public to Jewish immigration, without regard to economic or social consequences. No one asked whether the Ethiopians were educated—they are not—or whether they were white.)

American pressure could take two different forms: holding back the economic aid and loan guarantees needed to absorb the immigrants, or increasing the U.S. immigration quotas for Soviet and Israeli Jews. Financial pressure is perhaps more likely and would in any case be more effective in the short run.

American spokesmen like to say they rule out "pressure" on Israel, but in fact only the word "pressure" is ruled out. It can be called "reassessment." When Baker recently met with Palestinians in Jerusalem, they understood him to say, in effect, forget about the possibility that the President will put economic pressure on Israel. The grants are given by Congress and Israel again has extensive support there. But Baker's own record shows that this claim is only partially correct. The administration has much room for maneuver in distributing the funds appropriated by Congress and it could cause Israel grave problems even if Congress votes for aid to Israel. Baker underlined this in 1989 when he stalled for a year in giving Israel a guarantee for a loan of $400 million to help settle the immigrants. This is, after all, only pocket money in comparison to the $10 billion in grants and guarantees Israel intends to request in September.

I have heard it argued that the same factors that make Israel vulnerable to pressure—unemployment, lack of housing, etc.—also lead to pressure within the United States, particularly by Jewish organizations, to help the unfortunate Jews coming out of the Soviet Union. Just as public opinion forced the President to help the Kurds, it may also force him to help Israel if the situation of the Soviet immigrants becomes more visibly pathetic. But the immigrants obviously do not lack medicine, blankets, or temporary shelter. The credits and loan guarantees that are needed for economic development involve abstract transactions that may not easily lend themselves to emotional campaigns. It is too early to say whether the newest condemnation by both Baker and Bush of increasing West Bank settlements as an obstacle to peace means that the United States intends to bring serious pressure on Israel. What is clear is that the administration is in a stronger position to do so than any American government in many years. The prospect for peace is still one of hope against hope, rather than of hope abandoned.

I open the newspaper to the sports section in July 1998. In the middle of the page there is a table giving Israeli statistics. These records are much improved from the time I myself was on the field (triple jump). Half the names are Russian: this is one reason why these records are so much better, and this is typical in many walks of life and fields of expertise in Israel today.

In five years (1990–95) Israel got for free some 30,000 teachers, 14,000 professionals in the arts and media, and 14,000 scientists. For a country with just over 5 million people, these are staggering numbers. The economic boom in Israel during Rabin's era, as well as Israel's successful entrance into the high-tech global markets, is not unrelated to the Russian immigration.

Unlike the emigrations to Israel from the Soviet Union in the 1970s, which came mostly from the peripheral republics, two-thirds of those who arrived in the 1990s came from the Slavonic heartland, about 150,000 of them from the three major cities of Moscow, St. Petersburg, and Kiev. These are highly sophisticated urban people. Also, whereas the Soviet immigrants in the 1970s consisted mostly of Jews whose Jewishness had some content, the later Jews of the Russian immigration were mainly "passport Jews," Jews with a negative Jewish identity: that is, having been designated as Jews in the Soviet census, these people knew only what they were not: not Russians, not Ukrainians, etc. They seemed and felt very similar to their neighbors but their passports made them different. As it happens, negative identity is also their story in Israel.

Nahum Barnea, a leading journalist in Israel, once said, half tongue-

in-cheek—but only half—that in Israel there is a contest between two identities determined through negation: your Jewish identity is determined according to how much of an anti-Arab you are; and your Israeli identity is determined according to how much of an anti-Orthodox you are. The negative identity of "the Jew" nourishes the right, the negative identity of "the Israeli" nourishes the left. According to this criterion, it seems that there are more "Jews" in Israel than "Israelis."

What made possible the absorption of the recent Russian immigration (more than a third of whom are not even "passport Jews," unless one counts forged passports as well) is the fact that they soon developed a strong "Jewish" identity. All polls reveal that they are the ones who mistrust Arabs the most. And even though one would have expected these Russian immigrants to be "Israelis" according to the negative definition above, it turns out that they are more (negative) Jews than (negative) Israelis, and tend to be more on the right than on the left. In 1992 Russians helped to bring Rabin to power, in a protest vote against the government of Shamir. But in 1996 a newly formed Russian party did very well in the election (seven seats in the fragmented Israeli parliament of 120), and has become an important element in Netanyahu's right-wing coalition.

The liberal left seems to have lost hope of ever reaching out successfully to the culturally self-segregated Russian community. This is a terrible mistake, I believe. In the long run, the right is an unstable coalition of cultural ghettos: the ultra-Orthodox Ashkenazi ghetto, the ultra-Orthodox Sephardi ghetto, the ghetto of settlers and their sympathizers, the ghetto of Oriental Jews on Israel's periphery, and now the Russian ghetto. All these communities compete for limited and dwindling government resources and are ideologically strange bedfellows anyway. I believe that in the long run the Russians will break away from this coalition, for their aspiration—or at least their children's aspiration—is to join the secular Ashkenazi middle class, but on their own terms. Culturally, and now politically, they feel strong enough to negotiate the terms of entrance. My fear is, however, that in the long run there will be very little left to negotiate.

4

THE USES OF THE
HOLOCAUST IN ISRAEL

I believe that the Holocaust was a unique event in human history in an important sense: unique because it combined humiliation and destruction. Although neither component is unique, the combination is. The Nazis wanted to humiliate homosexuals but not necessarily to destroy them, and they wanted to destroy Gypsies but not necessarily to humiliate them. To the Jews they wanted to do both, and they did. In this respect the Nazis' radical anti-Semitism deviated from the traditional Christian anti-Semitism, which aimed to humiliate the Jewish religion and thus the "stiff-necked" Jews, for the Church needed humiliated Jews to remain alive as a sign of their defeated religion. Eventually, according to Church doctrine, they would recognize the "True Israel," the Israel of the spirit—namely, Christianity.

The Jews have had a long history, and extensive experience of traditional anti-Semitism, against which they have devised quite effective survival tactics. And they have survived. But Nazism was something radically new. There was nothing they could have done to be prepared for it. For one thing, there was no way to negotiate with the Nazis. It is thus unsurprising that both Jews under Nazi rule and those elsewhere did not know how to cope with it. I am not sure that we would want anyone to lead their lives in preparation for the "worst possible case" when this really is the worst.

The pre-state Yishuv did not know how to cope with Nazism either. There was nothing they could do effectively to deal with such a menace. Their failure was, as it were, a verbal one: the lack of any expression of an organized sense of solidarity with the Jews of Europe. The book I discuss in this essay did not deal with what people like my parents felt about their families being destroyed in Europe while they lived in a place of relative safety in Palestine—in fact, they were devastated. It discussed mainly the institutional reaction of Jews in Palestine to the Holocaust as reflected in documents of the period.

FEBRUARY 1994

IN SEPTEMBER 1942, MORDECAI SHENHABI, A MEMBER OF A KIBBUTZ in Palestine and former delegate to several Zionist conferences, suggested to leaders of the Jewish National Fund that they set up a memorial for Jews killed in Europe in the 1940s with the name Yad Vashem—roughly, "a memorial and a remembrance." That September, of course, most of the people who were to become victims of the Holocaust were still alive. But the incident, which is reported in Tom Segev's book *The Seventh Million: The Israelis and the Holocaust* (1993), suggests that the destruction of European Jewry was being treated by many Jews in Palestine as an event in the past, at a time when it had only just begun to occur.

Remembering the Holocaust with ceremonies and rituals has become central to the civic religion of Jews in Israel, and their attitudes toward the Holocaust have become a part of their identity as Israelis. Segev's book is the first to examine the deep influence of the Holocaust on the history of the state of Israel, from its establishment in 1948 and the subsequent mass immigration of the early 1950s to the

Six-Day War in 1967 and the development of Israel's nuclear capacity.

Segev has reconstructed much of his fascinating history from newspaper stories, many of them long forgotten, and these give a sense of immediacy to a period usually hidden behind a thick curtain of rhetoric. But Segev also offers various judgments of his own, many of them implied, some bound to be irritating. The book's subtitle, *The Israelis and the Holocaust*, is itself misleading. Israelis have existed only since the state of Israel was established, and the book's early chapters deal not with the state but with the Yishuv, the organized Jewish community in Palestine before 1948. This distinction is not mere pedantry, in view of the misguided tendency to see the pre-state of the Yishuv as a version of the state of Israel. It is important to remember that the Jewish population of Palestine at the time of the Holocaust consisted of fewer than a half million people living among a hostile population of more than a million Arabs, all under British rule. The Arab rebellion against the British in the late 1930s was in large part a protest against the Zionist settlement; and since Arab leaders sympathized with Nazi Germany, it was plausible to suspect that they would join in the Nazi war effort.

The British, for their part, in an attempt to appease the Arabs and prevent another rebellion that would impede the war against Hitler, closed Palestine's ports to Jewish refugees from Europe. And until late 1942 and the British victory in the battle of El Alamein, Jews in Palestine were justifiably fearful that Rommel's army in North Africa would conquer Palestine and occupy it. With Palestine at the periphery of the British Empire and under severe military censorship, the Yishuv was very far from being a sovereign state.

The limitations of the Yishuv community are described far more clearly by Dina Porat in her book *Trapped Leadership* than by Segev. Porat, however, claims that the Zionist settlers felt removed from the events taking place in Europe, and did not feel obliged to respond to appeals for help or to react in any other way to the Holocaust. I believe, with Segev, that the problem was precisely the opposite. Like many other liberation fighters, the principal Zionist leaders—David Ben-Gurion, Moshe Shertok (later Sharett), Golda Myerson (later Meir), and Berl Katznelson—had an exaggerated sense of their own power, an illusion sustained by the need to show that they were capable of running a state. They even, in some cases, accepted responsibility for not having saved European Jews when it is very doubtful whether they could have done anything at all. In other words, they invited the criticism that they did not do enough to save the Jews of Europe.

Segev fails to describe the response to the Holocaust of the non-Zionist *haredim*, or ultra-Orthodox Jews. The ultra-Orthodox did not experience any crisis of faith or of theology when confronted with the absolute evil of the Holocaust. Their conception of current events is not historical but is based on typology: they interpret current events according to the ways these events reflect the models of the past. For the ultra-Orthodox, the Nazis were prefigured by the Amalekites— the ancient people who were the first to fight the Israelites in the desert and thus became the prototypical evil anti-Semites (see Exodus 17:8–16); and the Holocaust followed the biblical pattern of the destruction of the Temple.

The ultra-Orthodox response to the Holocaust was directed, then, not at God for having allowed the Jews to be murdered but at the Zionists. Their dangerous rebellion against the Gentiles, they argued, had helped to cause the Holocaust. Since anti-Semitism (in its typological formulation, "Esau hates Jacob") is a fact, the Jews' only chance of survival, in the ultra-Orthodox view, is through acceptance of Gentile rule. Zionism, by aspiring to establish a state without waiting for the advent of the Messiah, was a form of rebellion that only enhanced anti-Semitism's radical and vicious forms. According to the prominent Orthodox rabbi Moshe Scheinfeld, "What the heads of Zionism inflicted on European Jewry during World War II [could not] be described as other than killing in the proper sense of the word." The Zionist leaders, he said, were "the criminals of the Holocaust who contributed their part to the destruction."*

The second complaint of the ultra-Orthodox was that the Zionists

---

*Cited by Dina Porat, in "Amalek's Accomplices Blaming Zionism for the Holocaust: Anti-Zionist Ultra-Orthodoxy in Israel during the 1980s," *Journal of Contemporary History*, Vol. 27 (1992), p. 698.

acted shamefully during the Holocaust. Instead of working to save the Jews of Europe, they concentrated on establishing a heretical Zionist state in the Holy Land. In the few instances when the Zionists in power were able to save some Jews, they discriminated against the ultra-Orthodox who were not Zionists. Segev himself agrees with the latter criticism of the Zionist Yishuv as "Palestinocentric."

There is a strange dialectic between secular Zionist and Orthodox responses to the Holocaust. In late December 1942 the Zionist organizations in Palestine proclaimed a month of mourning in solidarity with the Jewish victims in Europe, three days of which were designated as days of fasting and lamentation, including mourning processions headed by rabbis carrying Torah scrolls. These are traditional Orthodox Jewish ritual responses to public catastrophes, and many leftist Zionists flinched at this religious expression of mourning. But they did not have their own means of expressing it: two thousand years of Jewish martyrdom had given Orthodox Jewry an edge when it came to expressing grief. Even the secular newspapers used the biblical style of lamentation in their reactions to the extermination: "Cry, Jerusalem," said an editorial in the newspaper *Dvar*, "for the fallen of your exile; shout, Zion: save your sons and daughters, be refuge to my children and little ones."

The traditional forms of lamentation encouraged a sense of distance from the catastrophe, however, as if the grief expressed were in response to the destruction of the Temple and not the persecution by the Gestapo. The mourning rituals also suggested that although this catastrophe was of greater proportions than any in the past, it did not differ from them in kind. The traditional Orthodox Jewish responses to disaster were, in general, highly ambivalent: on the one hand, they would say, the current affliction is the most terrible that has ever occurred; on the other, the Jewish people have already survived many such calamities. This traditional Jewish reaction prevented people from seeing the Holocaust as something both horrific and unique.

In my view there was very little the Yishuv could have done to save the Jews of Europe. But there still remains the question whether Zionist leaders failed to express solidarity with those who were being exterminated in Europe. The Israeli poet Haim Guri once asked Antek

Zuckerman, one of the leaders of the Warsaw Ghetto uprising, what would have happened if the Yishuv had sent 500 fighters into the ghetto by parachute. Zuckerman answered that 490 would have been killed by antiaircraft fire; the other ten would have landed, but no one would have known what to do with them, and they, too, would have eventually been killed. What the Polish Jews needed was not 500 men but one messenger. "They needed a single man to bring them a good word from the land of Israel," an expression of solidarity, Haim Guri said. "Only one man—and he never came."

Why did the Zionists in Palestine fail, on the whole, to express strong solidarity with their brothers and sisters in Europe? The reasons were ideological and not merely psychological. Zionism was a revolution in Jewish life, and the Jewish tradition of lamenting collective persecution, which Zionism considered a poor substitute for action, was one of the cultural tendencies they wanted to reform. At the time of the Holocaust, Ben-Gurion did not believe it possible to do anything practical to save the Jews of Europe and what was not practical did not interest him. His first concern was to mobilize world Jewry for the task of establishing a Jewish state. He and the other leaders of the Labor movement rejected protest that was merely expressive and not directed at specific political goals. They identified such sentiments not only with the religious tradition but also with the followers of Jabotinsky on the revisionist right, which they perceived as trapped in grandiose nationalistic rhetoric and incapable of effective action. Thus on the one occasion when there was a real need for expressive politics—because no other form of politics was possible—the Zionist movement largely failed.

The Zionists saw traditional reactions to disaster as the passive response of a group without political will; it was only one step to an accusation, which first appeared during the Holocaust itself and later became a recurring motif in Israeli public life, that the Diaspora Jews went to their death "like sheep to the slaughter" instead of dying "a hero's death." This patronizing attitude toward the Jews in Europe was based in part on the fact that most of the leaders of the Warsaw Ghetto uprising were members of socialist Zionist youth movements. To the people in the Yishuv their uprising seemed to illustrate what their own response to Nazi persecution would have been. This contempt for those who did not mount such an uprising and who were "led like sheep to the slaughter" was one reason why survivors who arrived in Palestine and later in Israel were often ashamed to talk about their experience.

Furthermore, many in the Yishuv felt that the Holocaust had resulted in a kind of negative selection: "I believe that those who lived were the ones who survived because they were egotistic and took care of themselves first," said a Zionist official, David Shaltiel, who later became a general in the Israeli War of Independence.

Segev severely, and rightly, criticizes this attitude, citing some of the appalling pronouncements that were prevalent in the Yishuv. In June 1942, for example, Yitzhak Gruenbaum, who had been one of the leaders of Polish Jews before his immigration to Palestine, told the Jewish Agency that the problem with Polish Jews in the exile was that they preferred "the life of a dog over an honorable death." Little did he know that his own son Eliezer was serving as a kapo in Buchenwald at the time. That among all the millions of Soviet soldiers who were captured by the Nazis, many of whom died in captivity under horrifying conditions, not one serious rebellion broke out did not cause the left to think twice about their characterization of the Jews as "beaten dogs."

Zionists in Palestine also felt estranged from European Jewry because they were then in the midst of an unprecedented economic boom. British Army forces stationed in the Middle East were buying everything from food and clothes to antitank roadblocks in Palestine, and the soldiers spent their leaves in Tel Aviv, Haifa, and Jerusalem. Cafés and restaurants were full, and the atmosphere in the normally ascetic Jewish community was more that of a holiday resort than of a population in mourning.

What was known about the Holocaust in the Yishuv? The information about the killings was available and was published, although not always with the prominence it deserved, and the accusation that the Yishuv leaders censored the reports from Europe is nonsense. Belief and denial, however, could paradoxically exist at the same time. Thus, for example, Apolinari Hartglass, a Zionist activist who had immigrated from Poland and was a member of the Rescue Committee for European Jewry, was the first to speak soberly and accurately about the systematic extermination of millions of Jews in the Nazi-occupied countries, of whom he believed only a few tens of thousands would manage to survive. "They are exterminating the population in Poland mercilessly and with sly cruelty," he said, on the basis of reports he heard in 1940. But when refugees arriving from Poland in 1942 confirmed his fears in grim detail, he said to one of them, "If I believed everything you're saying, I'd kill myself." The evidence tempts one to say that many in the Yishuv knew about the extermination and yet did not believe it.

SEGEV DEVOTES A THIRD of his book to the ways the Holocaust has been dealt with in Israel, particularly in the three important trials that have taken place in Israel since the establishment of the state. Both Adolf Eichmann's trial in 1961 and John Demjanjuk's in the late 1980s were explicitly considered "show trials," whose declared purpose was to "educate the youth" who had not been "there." Even the trial in the mid-1950s of Israel Kastner for collaborating with the Germans in Hungary had some aspects of a "show trial."

Segev dismisses the Demjanjuk trial, which he covered for *Ha'aretz*, as an "educational failure." Once the key question at the trial became one of identification—that is, whether or not John Demjanjuk was "Ivan the Terrible," the sadistic murderer of Treblinka—the trial deteriorated into a series of technical disputes about the type of paper and staples used in identity cards issued to the Ukrainian guards at the Trawniki training garrison and so on. The court determined that Demjanjuk was beyond a reasonable doubt Ivan the Terrible of Treblinka, but an appeal to the Supreme Court overturned the verdict when new evidence from the former Soviet Union strongly suggested that Demjanjuk had been a camp guard but was not Ivan the Terrible. Neither the conviction nor its reversal had much effect in Israel.

By contrast, Eichmann's trial, which took place after he was captured by the Mossad in Argentina and brought to Israel in 1960, had enormous educational impact. Native-born Israelis were exposed to the details of the Holocaust for the first time, and with all the drama inherent in a courtroom trial. Not only did the trial help to change the image of Holocaust victims as sheep or beaten dogs, it also finally broke the barrier of silence between Holocaust survivors and Israelis who had not been in Europe during the war. Many Israelis began to listen attentively to the survivors' stories, and the survivors discovered they had an important story to tell.

Some of those outside Israel viewed the Eichmann trial from the perspective of Hannah Arendt's reports in *The New Yorker* and her subsequent book (which has not been published in Hebrew to this day). Arendt's reporting infuriated many Israelis. Segev does not defend Arendt's judgmental tone when she writes disparagingly about the Jewish Councils, but he agrees with her criticism of the ways the Holocaust was appropriated by Zionists and later by Israel, as if all Holocaust victims had been Zionists on their way to Israel. Israel does not necessarily have the right to speak on behalf of European Jews since in fact only a small number of European Jews were Zionists. (I believe, however, that Arendt's assertions about the "banality of evil" are misguided. She fails to make the important distinction between those who instigate evil and those who simply comply with it. Goebbels was anything but banal. Eichmann was a borderline case.)

Kastner's trial is little known outside Israel, but it caused some Israelis to arrive at a more negative assessment of the Yishuv's leaders during the Holocaust. A Zionist Jewish leader who had headed the Rescue Committee set up to save Jews in Hungary, Kastner was found guilty of collaborating with the Nazis, particularly in the negotiations with Nazi officials that allowed him to select 600 of the 1,685 Jews who escaped on a "VIP train" to Switzerland in 1944. Among them were various members of his own family and inhabitants of his hometown. The presiding judge, Benjamin Halevy, condemned him severely: "In accepting the offer, K. sold his soul to the devil."

Dr. Moshe Keren, *Ha'aretz*'s judicial commentator at the time of the trial, wrote, "One of the many astonishing things in the opinion is that the judge explicitly admits that there was no hope of organizing a Jewish resistance at that point in the war. . . . If that is the case, what does he want, for God's sake?" The Supreme Court exonerated

Kastner of all guilt on appeal. Not only had he not sold his soul to the devil, but, in the court's opinion, he had done all he should and could have done "at every juncture." In March 1957, several months before the Supreme Court reached its decision, Kastner was murdered under circumstances that remain mysterious. The murderers came from the lunatic fringe of the right, but their leader had worked, until fifteen months before the murder, for Israel's Security Service.

Kastner was a member of Ben-Gurion's Labor Party and one of its candidates for the Knesset. The demagogic lawyer Shmuel Tamir, an extreme right-wing opponent of Ben-Gurion and his party (and later Minister of Justice in Begin's administration), used the trial to attack the government, and Judge Halevy, later a member of the Knesset in Begin's party, did nothing to restrain his accusations in court. Tamir's idea, according to Segev, was to present the Yishuv leadership at the time of the Holocaust essentially as an offshore Jewish Council—a *Judenrat*—with Kastner as its representative in Hungary. With supreme arrogance Tamir told a witness who had served on Kastner's committee, "While your comrades collaborated with the British and you with the Nazis, we were out fighting to save Jews." In Tamir's view, the Yishuv leaders, like the *Judenrat* in Budapest, were not the proud rebels they should have been, but a group of meddlers and cowards who betrayed the virtues of Jewish dignity and pride.

This nasty, patronizing judgment was still current in Israel during the 1950s. It was tempered, however, by more humane appeals to public opinion, such as Ben-Gurion's: "The Jews who lived in safety during the time of Hitler," he said, "cannot judge their brothers who were burned or slaughtered or who were saved." Parliamentary elections took place shortly after Judge Halevy's original statement was made public, and his talk of a "pact with the devil" had an important part in election propaganda. Begin's party doubled its strength, while Ben-Gurion's party suffered its worst decline until Begin was elected Prime Minister in 1977.

MENACHEM BEGIN'S ROLE as the great dramatist of the Holocaust in Israeli politics did not begin with Kastner's trial. In 1951 the Israelis negotiated with Konrad Adenauer's government for payments of reparations both to Nazi victims and to the state of Israel as the refuge of Holocaust survivors. Segev provides an excellent account of the talks that led to the agreement ratified by the Knesset in January 1952. In the months before the Knesset debate, Begin had become severely depressed; he felt that he had come to the end of his political career and was considering returning to his previous career as a lawyer. A vicious debate over German reparations with Ben-Gurion—whom he called "the tiny despot and great maniac"—was just what he needed to get him back into public life.

Begin had already arrived in Palestine before the extermination was at its worst, but, as Segev points out, he always gave one the impression of having come from "there." (He claimed that he saw with his own eyes his parents murdered by the Nazis while they were standing by a river reddened with the blood of the five hundred Jewish inhabitants of his town. His own sister said this was a tall tale and that he was away from home when his parents were killed.) Begin chose to lead the opposition to the reparations in what was the stormiest parliamentary debate ever to take place in Israel. At a demonstration that ended in a violent attack on the Knesset, Begin was reported to have said of his plan supporting such behavior against the reparations, "Today I will give the order—yes!" Another version quotes him as saying, "Today I will give the order—blood!" He was suspended from the Knesset for three months. Ben-Gurion won the debate and Israel agreed to accept reparations.

But Begin established the Holocaust as a permanent concern of Israeli politics, not only for the Ashkenazi Jews from Germany and Eastern Europe but for the Oriental Jews, many of them from North Africa. He used it in the most manipulative way for his own political purposes. Writing to President Ronald Reagan in 1982, he claimed that destroying Yasir Arafat's headquarters in Beirut made him feel as if he had sent the Israeli Defense Forces to Berlin to eliminate Hitler in his bunker. Amos Oz responded in an article in *Yediot Aharonot*, "Hitler is already dead, my dear Prime Minister," adding, "Again and again, Mr. Begin, you reveal to the public eye a strange urge to resuscitate Hitler in order to kill him every day anew in the guise of terrorists." Ben-Gurion, for his part, wanted to base the new Jewish identity on the experience of building a new society and a sovereign Jewish state, not on the worship of the dead. Underlying the debate between Ben-Gurion and Begin was the primary question of the meaning of the Holocaust for Jews in Israel—especially how to remember it and how to perpetuate its memory. Segev devotes his last chapter, in which he describes a visit to Auschwitz and other former concentration camps in Poland, to the theme of memory, "the struggle to shape the past."

IT IS IMPORTANT in any discussion of the Holocaust to separate two questions which have become dangerously conflated: First, how are we to remember the Holocaust and keep its memory alive? And second, what are we to learn from it? To the second question, the nationalistic response encourages the use of military force; a nation that has undergone a Holocaust, so the argument goes, has the right to do anything to prevent such a situation from occurring again. And, the argument continues, pervasive Arab anti-Semitism should make us see that it could happen again. The humanistic response—that of Segev and other Israeli radical liberals—argues that the sort of genocidal racism that made the Holocaust possible can occur in any society. Racism must therefore be fought everywhere, including in Israel. The Holocaust obliges Jews to fight the kind of hatred from which it arose and get rid of the kinds of conditions that engender Nazi behavior. It follows from this line of thought that Israelis should end the military occupation of Arab land and stop believing that they are "moral" simply because they are Jews.

Attempts have been made to combine the two approaches into one common "Zionist lesson." Segev recalls asking the head of Yad Vashem, Yitzhak Arad, about what we should have learned from the Holocaust.

Arad, very cautiously, said that he assumed that over the years a national consensus had developed in Israel, largely independent of party affiliation. Everyone agrees that the Holocaust teaches what awaits a nation in exile that has no state of its own; had Israel been established before the Nazis came to power, the murder of the Jews could not have been possible.

I myself believe that if there is one sure way to trivialize the Holocaust, it is by extracting "lessons" from it. The Holocaust was carried out by human beings, some of them banal and some not. It was not simply an act of monsters but the result of a monstrous ideology. The combination of circumstances that produced this industrialized murder was unique, however, and because of this, there is no ideological lesson to be learned from it. The Jews were not prepared for a Holocaust because it is not possible to be prepared for a Holocaust. If anything, Jews were psychologically more prepared for affliction than most other nations—but not for this sort of catastrophe. But to say there is no ideological "lesson" to learn from the Holocaust does not mean that people's lives should not be affected by it. It should prompt us to change, but such a change is not a didactic matter, to be achieved by one lesson of the Holocaust or another.

The question of remembrance remains important. We must remember not only the death chambers but also the rich complexity of Jewish life in Europe which died in them. Zionists resist reviving the memory of the life they rebelled against, but remembering the Holocaust requires a reevaluation of Zionist criticisms of the Jewish world that was destroyed. As for the form of remembrance, the only appropriate way to perpetuate the memory of the Holocaust is through meticulous documentation and mastery of facts. In the case of the Holocaust, the devil is in the details.

5

PROPHETS WITH HONOR: BUBER AND LEIBOWITZ

NOVEMBER 1993

EARLY THIS YEAR A NINETY-YEAR-OLD MAN WAS DRIVING ISRAEL crazy. In January, Yeshayahu Leibowitz was declared the winner of the Israel Prize, which is awarded by the Minister of Education in a formal ceremony on Independence Day to honor an Israeli citizen for his life's work. The winners are usually highly respected Israelis whose activities are not controversial. Leibowitz is different. According to the judges, the prize was awarded to him partly because he has been a "rebuker at the gates." In biblical times the courts of law were located at the city gates, and a "rebuker at the gates" was a person who defended the rights of the oppressed. The expression came to mean a social critic with religious inspiration, practically synonymous with a prophet.

However, as the prophet Amos said, "They hate him that rebuketh in the gate" (Amos 5:10). Yitzhak Shamir had an immediate comment: "The very decision to award the Israel Prize to Leibowitz disgusts me." Yitzhak Rabin inquired at a cabinet meeting whether the prize committee's decision could be changed. The answer was no: the prize had been awarded by an independent, nongovernmental committee. Embarrassingly for Rabin, it turned out that on the committee was a former general who had been the chief intelligence officer on Rabin's own staff.

But at the same time an appeal was made to the Supreme Court to cancel the award because Leibowitz urges Israeli soldiers to refuse to do military service in the occupied territories. The cabinet spent an hour and a half discussing the award to Leibowitz, and Rabin and most of the ministers in his government announced that they would not attend the ceremony at which the prize would be given. Leibowitz, for his part, said that the actions of the Israeli Army's undercover units in the occupied territories were no different from those of the Muslim group Hamas. At last Leibowitz announced that he would relieve the government of the burden of giving him the prize.

Isaiah Berlin—who, like Leibowitz, was born in Riga—has called Leibowitz the "conscience of Israel," yet very few outside of Israel have heard of him. The recent English translation of his collected articles provides a useful introduction to his work.* Leibowitz writes marvelously clear Hebrew, heir to the crystalline language of Maimonides and the editor of the Mishnah. It is very far from the broken Hebrew of the rabbinical period. The English translation is precise and responsible, although it cannot convey the power of the original.

In contrast to the Israel Prize award that never took place, the Hebrew University, in 1958, held a grand ceremony in honor of Martin Buber's eightieth birthday. David Ben-Gurion came and sat in the first row to show his respect for Buber, to whom he sent birthday greetings as "a friend, an admirer, and an opponent." Ben-Gurion was neither a friend nor an admirer—only an opponent. But Buber, in

---

Judaism, Human Values, and the Jewish State, edited by Eliezer Goldman, translated by Eliezer Goldman, Yoram Navon, Zvi Jacobson, Gershon Levi, and Raphael Levy (Cambridge, Mass., 1993).

contrast to Leibowitz, was a very polite critic of the Israeli establishment. If Rabin had Ben-Gurion's sense of history, he would have
understood, as De Gaulle once said of Sartre, that "Leibowitz is also
Israel." In Israel, Buber and Leibowitz have both acquired the ambiguous status of "prophets." It is worth comparing them and considering how the half-serious, half-mocking title of "prophet" applies to
each of them.

Buber believed that his life was exemplified in his writings, and
he never encouraged anyone to write his biography while he lived.
Perhaps he expected that his many letters would be edited and published to reveal a "life in letters," and, indeed, an impressive collection
of Buber's letters has recently appeared, with a useful introductory
biographical sketch by Grete Schaeder. "The bare facts of Buber's
biography can be quickly stated," she writes, for "his life was not
marked by many external developments."*

I'm not sure she is right. It is true that Buber was married to the
same woman for more than sixty years, and that he spent most of his
life at his desk. But he was active in the Zionist movement from its
beginnings in Central Europe. He lived and worked under the Nazi
regime almost until the "last possible moment" (1938). He moved
from Vienna, where he was born in 1878, to Galicia, then a part of
Poland under Austrian rule, then to Germany, and, in 1938, to Palestine. But I agree that the impression one gets of Buber's life—an
impression that is only strengthened by reading his latest biography
—is that Buber succeeded in living a sheltered life even when in
hostile surroundings.†

Buber's parents were divorced when he was three years old, and
he was separated from his mother. When he finally saw her again
after many years, he felt that something was missing in their longed-
for meeting. This "encounter that never was" with his mother was
an important experience for him and a source of his longing for what

---

The Letters of Martin Buber: A Life of Dialogue, edited by Nahum N. Glatzer and Paul
Mendes-Flohr, translated by Richard and Clara Winston and Harry Zohn (New York,
1993).

†*Encounter on the Narrow Ridge: A Life of Martin Buber*, by Maurice Friedman (New
York, 1993).

he called a "significant encounter." Until the age of fourteen, Buber lived with his grandfather Solomon, a patrician Jew who owned an estate in Galicia and was a scholar and a great collector of Jewish manuscripts. He then went to Lvov to live with his father, an immensely rich Polish Jew, and studied in a Polish *Gymnasium*. At eighteen he went to Vienna, where he tried to combine university studies with his Zionist activities, but after a year of "study and thought" in Florence, instead of following the career in academic life that had been expected of him, he became an editor in a Berlin publishing house. For ten years, until 1916, he lived in Berlin and then, until he left for Palestine in 1938, he lived in the little town of Heppenheim, near Frankfurt. At the same time he became the director of Jewish adult education programs under the Nazi regime. In Jerusalem, Buber was professor of sociology at the Hebrew University until his retirement. He died in 1965.

Leibowitz came to Palestine by a somewhat different route. Born in Riga in 1903 to a religious family, he acquired a religious education at home while studying at the local *Gymnasium*. When he was sixteen he emigrated with his family to Berlin, where he studied chemistry and philosophy at the university, and received a doctor's degree. Leibowitz served as assistant to the noted biochemist Karl Neuberg, and in 1928 he began the medical studies in Cologne that led to his medical degree in 1934. He left for Jerusalem later that year to become a professor at the Hebrew University, where he has taught chemistry, biology, neuropsychology, and the history and philosophy of science. Although he has retired he continues to teach philosophy of science to this very day.

Both Leibowitz and Buber mastered an exceptional range of knowledge and have been willing to make their learning available not only to students but to adults in lectures, courses, and informal seminars. Buber became well known among German Jews to a large extent because of his popular lectures, and much the same could be said about Leibowitz's reputation among the educated classes in Israel. Leibowitz served brilliantly as the chief editor of the *Hebrew Encyclopedia* and wrote many of its entries on science and philosophy, including "Bernard, Claude" and "Ben-Gurion, David."

On the first page of his biography of Buber, Friedman writes, "It was Buber's beard that made many speak of him as a biblical prophet." (I remember how surprised I was to see the beardless prophet Habakkuk in Donatello's group statue of prophets, *Lo Zuccone*.) Yet, of course, it was not so much his beard that made people see Buber as a prophet as his "spirituality," his sublime Zarathustra-style rhetoric full of biblical imagery, and his criticism of society from a religious perspective—all these, combined with a particularly photogenic beard, created the prophetic image.

Yet Buber "the prophet" aroused deep suspicion in Israel. A prophet is a person who takes risks, and Buber was unjustly perceived as spoiled, a spiritual dandy. His collection of ties could compete with Imelda Marcos' collection of shoes. Buber had close friends who were also compared to prophets—Gustav Landauer, who was murdered by right-wing extremists after the failure of the 1919 "German revolution" in Munich, and Franz Rosenzweig, the tortured religious thinker, who suffered from total paralysis. But these men were exempt from the suspicions that clung to Buber, including the harshest accusation of all—that Buber, when speaking to his people, kept looking out of the corner of his eye to see what impression he was making on the goyim. When a literary critic compared Buber to Jeremiah, another critic immediately attacked him: "How can you compare the spontaneous Jeremiah to the cerebral Buber, who always seems to look around after writing a beautiful line as if to say, 'Look how beautifully I write'?" By "cerebral" this critic apparently meant "calculating."

YESHAYAHU LEIBOWITZ IS often called a prophet in Israel, mostly a prophet of wrath. He has the sharp ascetic face of Savonarola and a tall, thin, monkish body. (A French movie about Leibowitz was entitled *No One Is a Prophet in His Own Country: Nul n'est prophète en son pays*, but this is nonsense: Leibowitz is very much a local prophet.) The image of Leibowitz as a prophet is sustained by his fierceness, and his fearlessness, as a social critic who writes from a religious viewpoint, by his dramatic ability to make his audience confront a fateful "either-or" decision, and by his razor-sharp rhetoric, which is combined with the humor of a stand-up comedian. *Either* we get out of the occupied territories, he would say, *or* we meet our moral downfall. *Either* we create a Jewish state that observes the Torah *or* we become a nation that has no connection with historical Judaism. Leibowitz is capable of supreme moral provocation. He used the expression "Judeo-Nazis" to describe the mentality of some of Israel's right-wing politicians—words no one else in Israel would dare use. After the Six-Day War, when the Wailing Wall became the site of many national festivities, he called it the "Disco Wall."

Leibowitz is not impressed by the record of prophecy in Israel, for, in his opinion, "all the prophets that arose in Israel did not succeed in reforming even one soul." The period of the prophets in Israel was the peak of idol worship. For Leibowitz, the Jewish law, Halakha, rather than prophecy, is the secret of Jewish survival through two millennia of life in the Diaspora.

Halakha is the normative part of the Jewish religion, which has been compiled during the last two thousand years, mainly in the Talmud and the commentaries on it. Buber, for his part, sees the success of Halakha as the catastrophe of Judaism: "The strength of Judaism was not held down from without, but also from within by the despotism of the Law, which is to say, by a mistaken, disfigured, distorted religious tradition."

Thus it is not prophecy but their view of Halakha that divides Leibowitz from Buber. For Leibowitz, Halakha is the most appropriate expression of man's attitude toward God. For him, religious awareness cannot be formulated meaningfully in words; it is an attitude toward the world, which places God at the center of life. Obeying Halakha with its many rules governing every aspect of daily life is the supreme act of human choice that comes from the need to worship God. It is not meant to fulfill any other sort of human need. It is a free expression of the belief that the purpose of worshipping God is to place God at the center of the world.

Leibowitz says that Gershom Scholem, the foremost scholar of Jewish mysticism, once told him, "You believe in the Law and not in God." The philosopher Ernst Simon, a friend and student of Buber's, said that Leibowitz "observes the Torah commandments in order to irritate God." What he meant is that Leibowitz so carefully avoids giving reasons for observing the religious law that it seems as if the only reason left is that he wants to irritate God by doing so. Buber was not an observant Jew, but Leibowitz, who sees the essence of historical Judaism in the worship of God according to Halakha, scrupulously observes its many commandments.

Leibowitz is prepared to accept Scholem's remark that he believes in the Law, but for him this is the only meaning of the expression "I believe in God." Belief for Leibowitz is accepting the obligation to worship God according to Halakha rather than believing some propositions about God. Moreover, in his view the word "God" has meaning only in the phrase "worshipping God," as if this were a single word, "Godworshipping," in which "God" has no independent meaning. It is as if we said that "home" has a meaning only in the word "homework." Leibowitz believes that metaphysical talk about divinity has no meaning. In this respect he is a radical positivist: the only meaning the concept of God can have is to be found in "worshipping God"—a description of an activity.

What remains difficult, of course, is the inevitable question: At whom is all this activity directed? Why are we to believe that an Old Testament personal God is there, worshipped by Jews observing the Law? Leibowitz cannot extricate himself from the basic difficulty posed by this question, and he does not try. He characterizes Judaism only descriptively, as a historical phenomenon, and normatively, as a way of life centered on the observance of the commandments.

As one might expect, Buber and Leibowitz differ over the texts they consider central to Judaism. In contrast to Leibowitz, whose hero is Maimonides, for Buber the Bible is central, and he is himself one of its most interesting modern commentators. This can be seen from his and Franz Rosenzweig's translation of the Bible into German, as well as from his own many books about the Bible, among them *The Kingship of God* (1932), *The Prophetic Faith* (1942), *Abraham the Seer* (1955), and *Moses* (1964).

Buber and Rosenzweig dealt extensively both in lectures and in articles with the methodological problems of translating the Bible into German. In 1936 their essays were collected into an impressive volume that bore the Teutonic title *Scripture and Its Germanizations* (*Die Schrift and Ihre Verdeutschung*).* The translators rightly say in their preface that the key ideas of Buber and Rosenzweig with respect to the Bible—its unity, its stress on a linked series of messages, its grounding in oral recitation, and the importance of repetitive patterns of kernel words—are all present in this volume. Buber returned to the original Hebrew meanings of the words, using literal translations that had become corrupted by being invested with theological significance. Thus, for example, instead of the usual German translation of the Hebrew word *Qorban* as *Opfer*—sacrifice—Buber used the word *Darnahung*, which preserves the Hebrew root of "coming near." Bringing a sacrifice is a way of coming nearer to God. (This interpretation is based on Buber's sensitive reading of the story about Korah in Numbers 16, where one can see a connection between holiness, bringing sacrifices, and coming near.)

AMONG ALL THE different leaders in the Bible—patriarch, lawgiver, prophet, judge, king, wise man—Buber chose to emphasize the suffering prophet, who was for him more important than the king-messiah figure of David. The tradition of rabbinical Judaism, to which Leibowitz belongs, brought the prophet down from his high station; leadership through inspiration is hard to reconcile with the religious authority based on the exegesis of texts. Protestant thought revived interest in prophecy, and this brought Buber close to Protestantism.

At the center of Buber's world, alongside the Bible, are the Hasidic writings that emerged in Eastern Europe, especially in Poland and Ukraine in the eighteenth century. About this literature, as well as about the kabbalistic literature underlying it and the extensive research that has been done on it, Leibowitz might at best be prepared to say what has been attributed to the great Talmud scholar Saul Lieberman: "Nonsense is nonsense, but the history of nonsense is scholarship."

---

*Scripture and Translation, translated by Lawrence Rosenwald and Everett Fox (Bloomington, Ind., 1994).

To many readers Buber is primarily the Buber of Hasidic stories. A typical example is the story called "The Signature."

When Rabbi Menahem (Mendel of Vitebsk) wrote letters from the Land of Israel he always signed himself: "He who is truly humble."

The rabbi of Rizhyn was once asked, "If Rabbi Menahem were really humble, how could he call himself so?"

"He was so humble," said the rabbi of Rizhyn, "that just because humility dwelt within him, he no longer regarded it as a virtue."*

Leibowitz, echoing the judgment of Scholem and his followers, accuses Buber of "kitsch" and of "fabricating" Hasidic writings. He finds the tales sentimental and fuzzy in their meaning. But Buber's interest in Hasidism was not only religious but nationalist—like the interest that the Brothers Grimm had when they collected fairy tales as part of the German national cultural revival. Buber's critics agree that he had vast knowledge of Hasidic literature, but claim that he shifted attention away from the more than one thousand works of philosophical thought in the Hasidic literature in favor of the Hasidic tales, creating the impression that Hasidism is a sort of Zen Judaism, with the stories of rabbis comparable to the profound but obscure stories of the Zen masters.

No doubt Buber was sometimes attracted to the "vast, vague and sentimental," but there is also some truth in a remark of the novelist S. Y. Agnon, who briefly helped Buber to collect Hasidic stories, that Buber managed to turn "provincial anecdotes into universal legends," the price for this achievement being the "improvement" of the stories. Buber was faced with the typical translator's dilemma of whether to be faithful to the texts or to make them more attractive, and he chose to make them more attractive. He saw Hasidism as a movement that renewed Judaism's interest in the "here and now"—a religious trend that sanctified everyday experience and overcame the sterility of end-

*Martin Buber, *Tales of the Hassidim: The Early Masters* (New York, 1947), p. 180.

less scholarly disputation over the texts. He therefore believed that Hasidism should serve as a model for Zionism, as a redemptive movement with spiritual significance. Only by imparting religious significance to the Zionist enterprise would it be possible to prevent it from degenerating into just another "national liberation movement."

Scholem, by contrast, saw Hasidism as a "quietistic" movement, a religious trend in which the worship of God involves the abandonment of the ego, the annihilation of the human will. In Scholem's view Hasidism is not the sanctification of the everyday but just the opposite: it is a gnostic attempt to remove "divine sparks" from concrete experiences in order to return them to their harmonic divine source. It is not the individual of the "here and now" that is the central idea of redemption in Hasidism, as Buber thought, but the gnostic denial of the individual's will and selfhood.

For Buber the essence of Judaism is not commandments but the Jewish people's unique encounter with God, which is magnificently documented in the Bible. The message of the Jewish people is neither monotheism nor any other sort of theology but the discovery that one can speak to God. Both Buber and Leibowitz are antitheological theologians, opposed to metaphysical justifications of religion. For Leibowitz such justifications have no cognitive meaning—there is no way to verify or refute religious claims. Buber's distaste for religious metaphysics is existential: God is not a triangle—you pray to Him, you don't prove theorems about Him. And you most certainly don't pray to Him with St. Anselm's prayer, asking God to give you the strength to prove His existence.

Buber describes an encounter he had in Berlin with the aged, influential pastor Wilhelm Hechler. After several hours of conversation Hechler was suspicious of Buber and before they parted asked him directly, "Do you believe in God?" Buber tried to reassure Hechler that he did, but the answer he thought he ought to have given him, the answer he spent his whole life trying to articulate, came to him on the way home: "If belief in God means speaking about Him in the third person, then I don't believe in God. But if belief means being able to speak to Him in the second person, then I do believe."

Buber thought that belief is the authentic biblical belief in God, and that it was St. Paul who "Hellenized" biblical belief. Paul replaced "belief in" by "belief that," thus changing belief from encounter to a doctrine with a church. But Buber's idea that we can converse with God without having any notion (independent of the conversation itself) of who it is we are speaking with is no less dubious than Leibowitz's idea that we can worship God without having any notion (independent of the act of worship itself) of who this God is that we are worshipping.

LEIBOWITZ LOATHES CHRISTIANITY for two central reasons. The first, unoriginal, one involves the perception of Christianity as the most ancient anti-Semitic movement, which has sustained all other such movements. According to this view the source of anti-Semitism is theological, in contrast to an ordinary xenophobia based on economic or social competition. It is hatred for the "murderers of God's son." Leibowitz believes that there is a continuous line from the anti-Semitism of the Church Fathers to the Auschwitz crematoria.

His second, theological, reason for loathing Christianity is that in rebelling against Halakha as the way of worshipping God, it became the supreme expression of the idolatrous world's abuse of Judaism. For Leibowitz the contrast between Christianity and Judaism can be seen in the clash of their basic symbols: Abraham's binding of Isaac, and the crucifixion of Jesus. Abraham expressed a theocentric attitude central to Judaism: Man is willing to sacrifice his son for God. In contrast, the Christian attitude is anthropocentric: God sacrifices His son for Man. Almost any educated schoolchild in Israel could quote Leibowitz on this contrast between Judaism and Christianity, but the source of the contrast is actually Buber: "The prophetic idea of man who suffers for God's sake has here given way to that of God who suffers for the sake of man."

There is not a little irony in Leibowitz's emphasis on Abraham, in which he takes the willingness to sacrifice Isaac as the symbol of Judaism. After all, it was Paul who used the example of Abraham in his attack on rabbinical Judaism—that is, the "Pharisees." In Romans 4 and Hebrews 11, Paul described Abraham as the model of the non-Halakhic believer who was prepared to perform the supreme non-Halakhic act of sacrificing his son, in contrast to Moses, legislator of the commandments and symbol of the Halakha. Abraham is the evidence Paul gives that Man is justified by his faith, and not by Halakhic acts.

Leibowitz detests Christianity, but he tries not to hate Christians. He nevertheless detests Jewish converts to Christianity, since he sees the act of conversion as an act of ultimate betrayal of the Jewish people. He made this clear in the case of Mordechai Vanunu, a technician at Israel's nuclear reactor in Dimona, who, after he revealed information about the reactor to the British press, was kidnapped by the Mossad. Before he sold Israel's atomic secrets Vanunu had converted to Christianity in Australia. Leibowitz, who had been one of the chief opponents of Israel's nuclear program in the early 1960s, was asked to comment on the treatment of Vanunu, and he uncharacteristically refused to respond. "There is nothing to say about Vanunu," Leibowitz asserted, "since he's a traitor. He converted to Christianity."

In the long tradition of harsh, bitter, public disputations between Jews and Christians, the last one to take place in Germany—in 1933—was between Buber and the pastor Schmidt. Buber's defense of Judaism and the Jews is one of the proudest and most moving documents in the history of Christian-Jewish debate. He said:

I live not far from the city of Worms, to which I am bound by the tradition of my forefathers, and from time to time I go there. When I go, I first go to the cathedral. It is a visible harmony of members, a totality in which no part deviates from perfection. . . . Then I go over to the Jewish cemetery consisting of crooked, cracked, shapeless, random stones. . . . The dust is there, no matter how thinly scattered. There lies the corporeality of man. . . . I have stood there, have been united with the dust, and through it with the Patriarchs. That is a memory of the transaction with God which is given to all Jews. From this the perfection of the Christian house of God cannot separate me, nothing can separate me from the sacred history of Israel.

Even Buber's stand in this debate did not quiet the suspicion among the Zionist settlers that he was always trying to please the goyim.

BUBER'S FAME IS based primarily on his religious thought. Yet it is my impression that his ultimate concern was not encounter with God but encounter with people. It is not so much God himself that is the center of his concern as the kingdom of God. Buber sees the kingdom of God as a society founded on "I-You" rather than "I-It" relationships. The English translation of the book's German title, *Ich und Du*, changed the everyday word "Du" (the familiar form of "you") into the sublime word "Thou." This led to a skewed interpretation of Buber, as if the only thing he intended to talk about was the human relationship with the divine.

Buber arrived in Palestine in 1938 and taught at the Hebrew University until his retirement in 1950. He did not teach theology but served first as professor of social philosophy and then as head of the sociology department. He had been interested in the study of society ever since he was Georg Simmel's leading pupil and the editor of the important series *Gesellschaft* (*Society*).*

But he was not a sociologist in the usual sense of the word. He was interested in anthropological philosophy, which, as he understood it, is concerned with defining the nature of man by discovering the conditions and relations that make a society possible. He was interested not in the empirical conditions of any particular society, but in "social ontology"—that is, the general conditions for creating a community. The term "society" as he used it derived from traditional German sociological Romanticism, and is ambiguous between *Gesellschaft* and *Gemeinschaft*—that is, between "society" in the sense of an association

---

*A most interesting selection of his "sociological" writings has been published under the editorship of the noted sociologist S. N. Eisenstadt, who was Buber's pupil: *On Intersubjectivity and Cultural Creativity* (Chicago, 1993).

based on formal relations that serve social functions, and "society" in the sense of a community based on primary relations of immediate contact and belonging. Buber was mainly interested in society in the sense of community—*Gemeinschaft*. As he recognized, the longing for community in modern society is based to a large extent on utopian hopes, since the familiar forms of association in capitalist societies are not based on communal ties.

In Buber's work we find something odd yet familiar: utopian thought coming from a social and cultural pessimist. He is concerned with the "kingdom of God" as a supreme example of community, as opposed to the "kingdom of Man" described by sociology. For him the most thoroughgoing religious socialism is that in which the kingdom of God is an established society ruled directly by God. This would be a society in which people interpret their actions toward one another out of the awareness that they are all able to speak with God. Their discourse with God would guide their spontaneous behavior and lead to an anarchistic society founded on community relationships, which are relationships of dialogue.

Buber was influenced by Gustav Landauer to conceive of the utopian community of the kingdom of God as a society in which no one has power over another—that is, as an anarchistic community. He influenced Landauer in turn to see the anarchistic community as religious in character. Buber's "city of God" is not meant to be a theocracy of clerks ruling in the name of God, but a primary community ruled by relations of absolute mutuality. Such a society could be based on the primary relation of belonging, in the sense that one belongs to one's family regardless of one's achievements. In Buber's view, a clerical theocracy is one of the ugliest manifestations of the "city of Man," and does not belong to the "city of God."

Buber's anarchist views were anchored in Jewish sources. The key biblical phrase he uses to support his view is Gideon's response when he is offered the monarchy: "I will not rule over you, neither shall my son rule over you: the Lord shall rule over you" (Judges 8:23). Buber devoted an entire book to the biblical idea of the kingdom of God. But "Jewish sources" can be used to support virtually any political position. Leibowitz, who has an anarchist temperament but holds no anarchist views, is a Hobbesian, and he too draws on Jewish sources. For him the key phrase is the Mishnaic saying "If not for their fear of the kingdom, people would swallow one another alive" (*Ethics of the Fathers*, chapter 3). In other words, the justification for any ruling authority is the fear of war of all against all. The government has to assure the continuation of life and it is none of its business to determine what the good life is.

Buber's original thought is expressed in his "dialogic" philosophy, built on his famous work *I and Thou*. This book, too, met with deep suspicion. Ben-Gurion wrote to Buber's friend the philosopher Hugo Bergmann, who was a classmate of Kafka's and one of the founders of the Hebrew University: "Buber's 'I–Thou' is actually nothing but a double 'I.' He talks to himself—and creates a conversational partner in his imagination. . . . This may be pleasant but it is nothing more than self-deception." Ben-Gurion was considered psychologically obtuse even by his admirers, but he was astute enough to discern Buber's narcissism. Leibowitz, who fought hard against Ben-Gurion, seeing him as Israel's Bismarck, nevertheless had a view of Buber that was not far from Ben-Gurion's:

> I would say that he was a ladies' philosopher, and I say "ladies" rather than "women," since if a philosophy is good, it is equally good for men and women. But there is a type of person called "ladies," and if they start to think philosophic thoughts their philosophy cannot be taken seriously. He was not a professional philosopher, and I do not consider him of any importance, from any angle or aspect.

Here Leibowitz was expressing the opinion of many people who disparaged Buber as a philosopher. In my view they are mistaken.

BUBER'S "I–THOU" philosophy suffers greatly from having been twisted into a cliché of preachers, psychiatrists, social workers, and flower children. But if bullshit, in Harry Frankfurt's classic definition, is lack of concern with truth, then Buber cannot be accused of it. In spite of all the suspicion directed at him, Buber had something important to say in philosophy.

The first philosopher to do justice to Buber's thought was Michael Theunissen, whose penetrating book *The Other* devotes an important chapter to Buber's dialogic philosophy (1984 in English; 1977 in German). As Theunissen shows, Buber's philosophy is a response to phenomenology—that is, to the philosophical enterprise that attempts to "constitute" the world by means of consciousness. To constitute the world does not mean to create the world, but to carry out the mental act by which an object is built up in consciousness. The objects in our consciousness are an *achievement* of such activity. To constitute an object, such as a table, is not to do the carpentry work that creates the table, but to perform the mental operation that makes the table an object in consciousness. When we think, we are always thinking about *something*, whether it exists or is imaginary. What needs to be clarified is which features of our thought allow it to bring into being the objects that we think about.

The point of origin for phenomenologists is the same as Descartes's, the thinking ego. A central question here is how, among all the objects that the ego succeeds in thinking about, another person comes to be perceived not as just another object but as another subject—that is, a being who itself originates thoughts. Heidegger's contribution to the enterprise of constituting the world in general, and another person in particular, was his idea that consciousness is not the only source of constituting objects, that human activity also has a crucial part in it. Sartre and Merleau-Ponty contributed by stressing that the subject's body, as well as the body of the other, has a central place in the constitution of the self and of the other.

In considering how the subjective world is created, Buber shifted the point of origin of this subjective world. For him it is not Descartes's conscious ego or some sophisticated version of it. I would describe the point of origin with the phrase "We meet. Therefore I am." The basic element of the human world is relations rather than objects, and these relations consist of unmediated encounters. The "I" is derived from these relations. Buber attempted to characterize the basic "I–You" relation underlying all human experience and to distinguish it from the "I—It" relation. The latter is the "objective" relation to the world—that is, the relation to objects, not to subjects. Buber attempted to deduce the ontological consequences as well as the moral and political consequences of these two fundamental relations. In religion the fundamental encounter is also between I and Thou, where the Thou is now the Big Other.

Buber's shift of basic ontology also involves a shift in the way we come to know things. If for Husserl the central sense for constituting objects is vision, while Heidegger perhaps adds the sense of touch, for Buber the main sense is hearing, the sense that is vital for listening to others. Buber's reading of the Bible pays special attention to hearing and listening. Some of Buber's critics felt that he himself was not capable of a real dialogic relationship with others, and that actually he felt at home only with books, while many others have described encounters with Buber in which they noted "what a great listener" he was. My own impression is that Buber had the gestures of a good listener—gestures that are well known to psychiatrists—and include focusing the gaze on the eyes of the other, bending toward him "so that nothing should disturb us," asking questions about details that attest to the complete interest of the questioner in the person being questioned. These can be "tricks of the trade" and not necessarily a relationship of listening with immediacy and absolute mutuality. Perhaps Ben-Gurion was to some extent right in his nasty claim that Buber was capable of a dialogic relationship only with himself.

BUBER AND LEIBOWITZ are both Zionists, in the sense in which both Kropotkin and George Orwell are socialists. Leibowitz's Zionism could hardly be simpler: We are sick and tired of living under the rule of the Gentiles and the time has come for us to have our own state. No more but also no less. He does not ascribe any spiritual significance to Zionism, let alone redemptive significance, and he detests the arrogance of the desire to create a "new Jew." The goal, for him, is a political one: a state for the Jews, but a state that has purely instrumental value. Any attempt to ascribe intrinsic value to the state he considers a blatant manifestation of fascism.

In this he is mistaken. Ben-Gurion and De Gaulle, for instance, both ascribed supreme value to the state, but they were statists, not fascists. In Leibowitz's view Zionism in the state of Israel has turned the state into a goal instead of an instrument, thus leading to a fascist Israel. What distresses him most is the use made of religion in Israel. In his instructive introduction to Leibowitz's book Goldman writes: "Most disturbing for Leibowitz himself is the debasement of religion by its use as a rationalization for vicious chauvinism and fetishistic irredentism." Leibowitz would, of course, prefer that all the Jews in Israel observe the commandments, but to coerce them to do so would for him be wrong, since accepting the commandments ought to be the supreme expression of human choice.

Leibowitz denounces the attempt of secular Zionism to provide the state of Israel with a secular Jewish identity. For him this is a travesty of Judaism. A state of Israel with a secular identity would be no more closely connected to the historic Jewish nation than the modern Greece of Papandreou is to the ancient Greece of Pericles. Leibowitz believes that the task of religious Judaism is to offer the state of Israel an attractive opportunity for creating a Jewish polis. He once tried to argue that this requires adapting Halakha to the reality of sovereignty. He wanted, for example, to update Halakhic rules according to which it is forbidden to decode dispatches in the Foreign Ministry on the Sabbath, since this does not involve the saving of life, which is the only rationale for violating the Sabbath.

The demand that Halakha be adapted to the new reality of a sovereign state has disappeared from Leibowitz's writing in recent years, apparently because of his despair over Israel's religious public. His main demand is now for the absolute separation of state and religion in Israel, for he believes that only such a separation can save religion from being prostituted by a secular state that makes use of it as an ideological fig leaf. Leibowitz sees the messianic Zionism of the Gush Emunim group as a return to the darkest trend in Jewish history—the false messianism of Shabbatai Zevi, which ended in the conversion of the "messiah" to Islam. He sees the Gush Emunim rhetoric of "blood and soil," in the name of the holiness of the land, as idolatry. The combination of blood and soil is to Leibowitz, as it was to Karl Kraus, something that leads only to tetanus infection.

The roots of Buber's Zionism, in contrast to Leibowitz's, are in myth—the beginning of God's kingdom over all the nations of the earth. Buber's Zionism is a strange mixture combining the themes of nationalism, the brotherhood of man, and the connection with the earth. The connection man–soil–blood (these words are etymologically connected in Hebrew) has a symbolic meaning which Buber locates in the Bible. In Buber's view, Zionism is justified only if it leads to a renewal of Judaism within the setting of an "organic nation" that will express "human solidarity" with the Arabs who live in the Land of Israel. Humanity must be placed above the state, and one must not ascribe holiness to power politics. Zionism must create the basis for a creative community life that would be superior to that of the decadent West.

For many years the Zionist movement concealed its ultimate aim, which was the establishment of a Jewish state in the Land of Israel. In fact, until the 1942 Biltmore Plan this was not the movement's declared aim. There were, of course, factions within Zionism, inspired by Jabotinsky, that fought for declaring as a goal the creation of a Jewish state, but most Zionists believed that in order to acquire the support of the great powers this ultimate goal must be blurred. For some, concealing Zionism's ultimate aim also relieved their conscience, since they knew that a Jewish state could be achieved only through violent confrontation with the Arabs. Buber was clearly one of those whose Zionism was made possible only because its ultimate goal had been blurred; he consistently advocated a "binational state."

Leibowitz's and Buber's criticism of Israel is most telling when it comes to the "Arab question." Leibowitz's image as a prophet has been strengthened by his "prophecy" during the euphoria following the Six-Day War that Israeli colonial rule over the territories would lead to moral corruption. Leibowitz gave no credit to the "Jewish morality" that was supposed to provide moral immunity against a corrupt occupation. He insisted that the logic of the occupation would lead many of Israel's most qualified people to join the Secret Service, while only quislings would be considered good Arabs by the Israelis.

Many people remember Leibowitz's prophecy about colonial rule, but what is most interesting about it is that he took seriously, from the outset, the possibility that Israel would remain in the territories for a long time. Leibowitz's proposed solution since 1967 has been unilateral Israeli withdrawal from all the territories—the only way, he says, for Israel to save itself from moral suicide. He has never made his solution conditional on what the Arabs would do. He was prepared to assume the worst with respect to the Arabs' attitude—namely, absolute refusal to accept the existence of Israel. He nevertheless believes that his solution is the only one that can save Israel from the curse of ruling over another people. He has called for uncompromising civil disobedience against the occupation, and he urges young Israelis to refuse to do their army service in the territories.

Leibowitz does not consider the struggle between Jews and Palestinians in the Land of Israel as a clash between rights. In his view the term "rights" has meaning only in a legal setting. The struggle is rather between aspirations which each side considers legitimate. The only way to reconcile these aspirations without the destruction of both sides is by dividing the land. Concerning the recent accord between Israel and the Palestinians, Leibowitz said in an interview with his friend Michael Shashar, "It is a big step in the right direction. I must admit that I was completely wrong. I did not believe that Rabin's government would make this move. Every rational person can now see that the Palestinian state has been founded. It was the right position to advocate during the last twenty-five years. I was wrong in my judgment of Rabin's government."

Buber, too, objected to Chaim Weizmann's formula, which described the struggle between Jews and Arabs in Palestine as a clash between legitimate rights on both sides. To Buber this formula led to a "moral tie" that gave legitimacy to the use of force as a "tiebreaker." On the other hand, Buber took exception to the solution of his friend Hans Kohn, who, confronted with the Arab problem in Palestine and unable to imagine a just Zionist solution to it, left the country for the United States. Buber favored a "prophetic politics," which in his view means always doing the moral thing in the specific situation in which you find yourself, rather than basing your morality on principles and doctrines. Not only did he believe in a binational state, he was exceptional among those who favored such a state in being prepared to limit Jewish immigration to Palestine until an arrangement could be

reached with the Arabs.* Buber died in 1965, two years before the
Six-Day War, and it is a loss not to have had his views on the policies
of annexation.

Although Buber and Leibowitz are both thinkers with a particular
interest in religion, their admirers in Israel are to be found mostly
outside religious circles. It will be said of Leibowitz what Ernst Simon
once said of himself: "I cannot speak to the people I pray with, and
I cannot pray with the people I speak to." But in both cases, even
though their main audience for many years has been secular, their
force as "prophets" comes from their religiosity. Of them both one
can say: A prophet is one who saves the honor of his country, even if
the prophet has honor everywhere save in his own country.

---

*S. Y. Agnon was once standing on a Jerusalem street talking to Martin
Buber. As Buber left, Agnon was approached by a friend.*

"What were you talking about?" the friend asked Agnon.

*"Well," replied Agnon, "Buber told me that he has two insurance
policies—one to cover this and that, one to cover that and this." Agnon
paused for a moment and added, "Have you ever heard of a prophet
with two insurance policies?"*

*Buber was the object of deep but unjustified suspicion in Israel. He
was treated not so much as a false prophet but as a phony one. There
were deep prejudices with regard to his unconventional religiosity. I
remember the butcher in my childhood neighborhood in Jerusalem telling my mother, "No one will ever find me selling 'Buber-fleisch'"—he
meant nonkosher meat. I grew up in Jerusalem surrounded by such
prejudices against Buber. Some were crude and open, others subtle and
secretive, but they were there. The more Buber became "known among
the Gentiles," the less was he recognized in Israel.*

---

*The most important and penetrating Buber scholar, Paul Mendes-Flohr, has edited an
excellent collection of Buber's writings on the question of the relations between the Jews
and the Arabs, prefacing it with illuminating introductory notes. *A Land of Two Peoples:
Martin Buber on Jews and Arabs* (Oxford, 1983). This fascinating document, because of
its moral force and clearheaded criticism, will inevitably impress even people who differ
with Buber.

But the stature of Buber, an outsider in Israel, has been growing with time, and even as a philosopher he deserves a much better hearing. He had something new, though not always well developed, to say in philosophy. Between the standard philosophical positions of the first-person point of view (represented by Descartes) and the third-person point of view (represented by Hegel) he introduced the second-person point of view, the "Thou." He was not the first to do this, but he did it differently.

I was a student of Yeshayahu Leibowitz, who died in 1994 at the age of ninety-one. He made a great impression on me. Later we became colleagues. When he read this essay, he immediately summoned me to his office to discuss it. In public Leibowitz was fire and wrath, but in private he was the sweetest of men. When I entered his office he was sitting with my essay in front of him, marked with different colors of ink, which I presumed reflected the severity of my mistakes. But then, to my surprise, he broached another subject entirely—how he, Leibowitz, had been so wrong about Prime Minister Rabin. He had not expected Rabin to produce anything useful and was thus surprised by his work in bringing about the Oslo Accords.

Then he added, "I shall die soon. I don't know when, but soon. At least now Rabin's deed gives some hope to the Zionist enterprise, a hope which I had almost completely lost."

Hearing this from him, I was greatly moved. With Leibowitz's death, Israel's stature was shortened by a head.

6

PASSAGE TO
PALESTINE

SEPTEMBER 1985

DURING THE WAR WITH JAPAN, SO THE STORY GOES, AMERICAN IN-
telligence succeeded in breaking the Japanese code—all except one
adjective. This adjective would occur in sentences like "This nation
is . . . ," "That leader is not . . ." Having gathered much data, the
decoders concluded that this adjective must be "pro-Japanese." It was
only after the war, when the code books were captured and studied,
that it turned out that the adjective was "sincere." In the Israeli case,
the missing adjective in expressions like "This Arab nation is . . ." or
"That Arab leader is not . . ." would probably be interpreted, in the
light of the evidence, as "pro-Western and willing under duress to
consider the Labor Party's Jordanian solution." It would take the capture of Israeli code books to learn that the adjective is "moderate."

The use of the word "moderate" is acceptable only to one element of the Israeli regime, the Labor Party and those on its periphery. For the other ruling group, the Likud, a moderate Arab leader is by any interpretation a contradiction in terms. Were an Arab leader found who accepts the Likud position, they would find a way to disagree with him. These are days of search for Palestinian leaders who will meet the American-Israeli notion of moderation. Such people, when found, would be allowed to take part in a Jordanian-Palestinian delegation to the peace talks within the framework of the "peace process."

The timing of Moshe Ma'oz's book *Palestinian Leadership on the West Bank* might seem to be perfect.* He attempts to delineate the features of "moderate" Palestinian leaders who might be acceptable to (part of) the Israeli government as participants in a joint Jordanian-Palestinian delegation. His answer, in short, is: the mayors of the major West Bank towns. However, by the time Ma'oz finished writing his last chapter, it turned out that all but one of the mayors he deals with were no longer mayors: all were deposed, some were expelled (Muhamad Milhem and Fahd Qawasma), some were badly wounded by "nonmoderate" Jewish terrorists (Karim Khalef and Bassam Shak'a). Khalef died in the meantime, while Qawasma was murdered in Jordan by "nonmoderate" Arabs. The one exception is Elias Freij, still mayor of Bethlehem. Except for him, Ma'oz's candidates are no longer candidates.

The question of a Jordanian-Palestinian delegation is no doubt "on the agenda." But it is doubtful whether it is indeed an important question. When we hear talk of a delegation that will join the "peace process," two senses of that phrase have to be distinguished. The first is the ordinary one—a series of events and negotiations aimed at achieving a settlement between the warring parties. But there is another, more Mediterranean, sense to the notion—something more akin to a "cease-fire in Beirut" than to a "cease-fire." The peace process on this second interpretation is a game of let's pretend, in which the parties behave *as if* they were negotiating; and while some, or even all, of them are interested in a settlement, each knows very well

---

*Published in London in 1985.

that within his own camp there is a faction capable of vetoing any negotiated compromise. The participants therefore cannot pay the price of compromise—and they know it. Nevertheless, each side has its reasons to keep the game of simulation going—whether because there's no better one around, or because they need time to prepare for the next round of fighting, or whatever. Above all, each has to prove—to his own camp as well as to the opposing ones—that he has an indispensable political part to play.

Except for the many members of research institutes studying the Middle East conflict, very few people believe that any real peace process is going on now. The number of people who make their living from such "conflict research," like that of cancer research, threatens to approach the number of those who die from it.

My own suspicion is that the latest talk of the composition of the delegation that will join the peace process is talk of peace in the "as if" sense. Evidence for this I find, among other places, in the indefatigable search for "moderate" rather than for *representative* Palestinians. I should add, however, that a peace process of the simulated variety is not necessarily bad in itself. For one thing, it may postpone the shooting season. Also, unexpected things can happen. For example, one of the participants may be mistaken about the nature of the game and take it seriously. And if this happens to be Secretary of State George Shultz, then the "as if" game may turn into a real process. Even Prime Minister Shimon Peres, realizing that his term of office is soon to be over, may decide to become ambitious and take risks. But then, ambition should be made of sterner stuff than Peres', and after the fatally unpopular mistake of exchanging more than one thousand prisoners by arrangement with Ahmed Jabril's "nonmoderate" organization, Peres' space in which to maneuver was sharply reduced.

IN HIS PREFACE Ma'oz writes:

Finally I wish to indicate that while studying the subject and writing the book, I also drew upon my personal experience as an adviser on Arab Affairs to the Israeli Defence Minister Ezer Weizman and to the Coordinator for Activities in the Territories, General Danni Matt, during 1979–80. I believe that my participation in Israeli policy-making on the West Bank has not prejudiced my scholarly approach to this delicate and controversial subject. I trust that this position indeed enabled me to acquire a deeper understanding of the West Bank issue, also from the perspective of its Palestinian community. Without compromising my scientific discipline, I have pursued the study of the West Bank leadership with empathy, and this has enabled me to perceive the complexity of the problems which face them.

There is no reason not to believe him. That is, there is no reason to believe that the book Ma'oz might have written, had he not been an adviser, would in principle have been different. I am even willing to go along with him when he says that his job as an adviser made him understand better the point of view of the West Bank Palestinians. At the same time, the passage is interesting because it is symptomatic of an Israeli reality. This is a reality in which four professors of the Middle East department of Hebrew University have served as advisers to the West Bank governors, or "coordinators." (One of the four was Menachem Milson, to whom I shall return shortly.) The title of "adviser" may conceal the fact that the role itself is a powerful one, with considerable influence on life in the West Bank. And yet it is significant that, for many an academic researcher, the transition from an academic chair to a position in the military administration and then to a Middle Eastern research institute and to intelligence research is smooth and natural. In this sense Ma'oz's book reflects patterns of thoughts current in those circles of the Israeli "intelligence community" and "military administration community" that are on the outskirts of the Labor Party.

There are, however, different kinds of military governors. Ma'oz mentions his having been an adviser to General Danni Matt. I myself remember Matt as my commanding officer in the long-gone days before the occupation of the West Bank. He was then a commander of a paratroop battalion who had a legendary reputation as a military leader, and was thought by most of us to have extreme political convictions: to the right of him, it was said, there was only the Syrian desert. In the Israel of today he is close to the mainstream. This suggests that the task of finding Israeli "moderates" to form a delegation to the peace talks might not be easy.

It was Professor Colonel Menachem Milson who gave the job of adviser a particularly bad name. He is also a target for Ma'oz's criticism. For a while (between 1981 and 1982) he did have an important part to play concerning the "moderate Palestinian leadership" on the West Bank: he was determined not so much to discover it as to create it. His sense of mission significantly included his conviction that he was carrying out Labor Party policy; he also believed that he was harnessing Ariel Sharon, the Defense Minister at the time, to this policy.

The idea was this: The "Jordanian solution" of the Labor Party required "moderate" Palestinian leadership that would not demand a Palestinian state—that is to say, non-PLO leaders. This implied the uprooting of PLO influence in the West Bank. Now Milson believed that the PLO's sphere of influence was restricted to the urban intelligentsia in the West Bank. And since most of the West Bank population consists of villagers, who were held to have merely local interests limited to such questions as water, electricity, sewage, and roads, Milson was resolved to create an appropriately rural moderate leadership which would compete with the PLO and would cooperate with Israel and Jordan in finding a "solution by division" of the West Bank problem.

Milson's basic assumption concerning the urban PLO was fallacious. For one thing, the ratio of town dwellers to villagers among PLO detainees in Israeli prisons corresponds by and large to their ratio in the West Bank population.

The war Milson consequently waged against the PLO on the West Bank consisted, among other things, of harassment of any town and mayor he believed to be politically affiliated with, or leaning toward, the PLO. He also established a new organization called the Villagers' League—termed "quisling" by no less an authority than General Shlomo Gazit, the former head of military intelligence. One imme-

diate consequence of this policy was that not only the PLO but even
the Kingdom of Jordan proclaimed a death sentence on any "moderate" who joined the Villagers' League.

Sharon, who had responsibility for the occupied territories in Begin's government, of course used Milson in his own war against the
political influence of the PLO in the West Bank. But Sharon had no
need for substitutes for the PLO; his only partner for negotiations on
the future of the West Bank was Begin. Milson, however, succeeded
in out-Heroding Herod. He raised the political temperature on the
West Bank to such a level that he became a liability even for Sharon.
Milson resigned about five minutes before he was to be fired by
Sharon.

MA'OZ IS NO Milson. He is sensitive to the way people change their
views—among other things, as a result of the jobs they hold. It appears that he himself would have been willing to have Bassam Shak'a
or Karim Khalef—the two mayors who were badly wounded by Jewish terrorists—as partners for talks and negotiations. I'm not sure how
many partners he would have found within the Labor Party for these
talks. At any rate the interesting question is: Why Bassam Shak'a, but
not Yasir Arafat? After all, there are good reasons to believe that
Shak'a, as an active supporter on the West Bank of the Syrian Baath,
may be closer to the pro-Syrian—that is, less "moderate"—faction of
the PLO, not to mention that his legs were blown off by Jewish
terrorists, a circumstance that can hardly be expected to moderate his
views. Why Shak'a and not Arafat?

In the Israeli collective consciousness Yasir Arafat is the quintessential nonmoderate Palestinian. This is only indirectly linked to his
views: as I have just said, there are strong reasons to believe that he
is less "extreme" in his views than Shak'a. For my part I believe that
distinctions between "moderates" and "nonmoderates" are a matter of
style no less than of content.

Had Arafat shaved his ominous four-day beard, removed his head-
dress (thereby revealing his baldness), and dressed in the customary
shabby civilian clothes, he would have struck many Israelis as no more

menacing than a middle-level official of the tax department, a man who could be a nuisance to the not so law-abiding average Israeli citizen. And, as such, though his sponsorship of terror attacks on Israeli civilians would certainly be remembered, he would have appeared more pragmatic and "moderate" when talk of negotiations arose. But of course this is precisely the image that would have prevented him from being leader of the PLO as a combative organization. As such a leader, he needs the dark sunglasses, the uniform with pistol, and all the rest—that is, the "nonmoderate" image. And this image is what made it possible for Israeli leaders to present him not just as the "person with hair on his face" (Begin's phrase) but even as the non-person who can be taken for the devil himself. It should be mentioned, at the same time, that lately, given the increasingly visible presence of Shiites on the Middle Eastern scene, Arafat necessarily comes to be perceived as somewhat more moderate in the Israelis' eyes: the Assyrian beard, glowing eyes, and priestly black robe are rapidly becoming established as the incarnation of extremism.

The historical archetype of the nonmoderate Palestinian was Hajj Amin al-Husayni, the leader of the Palestine community in the 1930s. A famous photograph of him with Hitler certainly did not contribute any softness to his image in the eyes of the Jewish settlement at the time. His archetypal moderate Palestinian opposite was Ragheb al-Nashashibi, a former mayor of Jerusalem; Ma'oz nicely explains the difference between the two men. But he omits to mention the significant fact that in the 1930s Ben-Gurion made an attempt to meet and talk with al-Husayni, presumably believing that a settlement is required with the real enemy, not with the reasonable, "moderate" one.

A particularly interesting chapter in Ma'oz's book deals with the 1976 municipal elections on the West Bank. These elections brought to prominence the local leaders who leaned toward the PLO at the time when Shimon Peres was Israel's Defense Minister. Peres believed at the time that giving Palestinian women the right and opportunity to vote would lead to the election of more moderate (that is to say, non-PLO) leaders—a rather curious idea, coming from a man who was supposed to have learned from Ben-Gurion a lesson in political realism. As for the election results, on the one hand, Israel's leaders proudly—and rightly—claimed that there have never been more democratic elections on the West Bank; but, on the other hand, they tried to maintain at the same time that the PLO, in spite of the election results, did not represent the West Bank population. The problem was not so much the logical contradiction, but rather that the government's subsequent harassment of the elected mayors was a straightforward attempt to undo the election results.

The 1976 West Bank elections also revealed what a significant and powerful element the Communist Party had become. Its impressive leader, Bashir Barghuti, is mentioned only once in Ma'oz's book. Having served years in prison, both in Israel and in Jordan, Barghuti is in fact one of the most important behind-the-scenes leaders on the West Bank. The Communist Party has been consistently the only political force in the West Bank to recognize Israel's right to exist. However, it does not conform to the Israeli-American image of moderation because it is of course not pro-Western. It certainly could do much to thwart any Jordanian-Palestinian delegation that is formed under American auspices alone.

IF THE QUESTION Who is a moderate Palestinian leader? is perhaps not so important as it is portrayed, the following question seems of great importance indeed: Why do the Labor Party and those close to it stake all its hopes on a Jordanian rather than a Palestinian solution to the West Bank problem? I believe the answer can be found in the intelligence-military-administrative-academic establishment that is loosely attached to the periphery of the Labor alliance, and whose views in many ways are authentically represented in Ma'oz's book. The people comprising this establishment are too sober to believe that Israel needs the Jordan Valley to ensure "strategic depth" for Israel's forces in case of attack. Their thinking, to my mind, is different. Israel has been in complete control of the West Bank since the summer of 1967. The terrorist and guerrilla activities carried out there by the local population have since been relatively manageable (although it is true that eight Israelis were killed in the West Bank between April and July 1984). This state of affairs could hardly be achieved without a successful penetration of all layers of West Bank society by the Israeli secret services. My contention is that after all these years, to give up this kind of control over the West Bank is, for the establishment in question, simply too large a sacrifice.

Furthermore, the establishment presumes that Jordan's interest in this respect really overlaps Israel's, given Hashemite fears of that very same Palestinian population. The hidden agenda, then, is shared covert control of the West Bank, while Jordan might be allowed overt control of the kind suggested from time to time by King Hussein, with some thin Palestinian icing in the guise of a "confederation." As has been proved on the East Bank of the Jordan River, Jordanians are in fact masters in the art of running what one might call a "moderate" police state. They are therefore worthy partners for shared rule over the West Bank. In other words, when a member of the Labor establishment talks of Israel's "security problems" in the West Bank he is not, I maintain, primarily concerned with the Jordan River as an efficient antitank ditch roughly three meters in width. Rather, he is expressing the wish to continue to have reliable knowledge about what happens in every village and in every house on the West Bank. The search for "moderate" Palestinian leaders is, therefore, a search for leaders who would ultimately tolerate covert and joint Jordanian-Israeli control over the West Bank.

During the early 1960s Ezer Weizman—then Israel's Air Force commander in chief and later Ma'oz's boss as Defense Minister—coined the slogan "The best to the air force." He meant that the best of Israel's young people should aspire to fly planes. This in itself represented a revolutionary change of attitude in a community whose leadership kept proclaiming, even if it no longer believed it, "The best to the kibbutz (preferably in the Negev desert)." In those days Weizman was a highly nonmoderate Jewish leader; in the meantime he has become perhaps the most moderate of the present-day leaders. Immediately after the 1967 war, with prophetic sarcasm, Professor Yeshayahu Leibowitz of Hebrew University said that Israel's next slogan might seem to be "The best to the Shin Bet" ("Shin Bet" being the Hebrew acronym for Israel's secret security services). Professor

Leibowitz already saw, in a blaze of lucidity, where the Israeli raj on the West Bank was leading.

MA'OZ'S BOOK HAS very little in common with one by Tom Segev, an Israeli journalist.* Segev's book is fascinating to read, because he has a fine sense of the concrete details that reveal a country's history. He gives an account of the state of Israel in 1949, the first year after its birth, and particularly of the first Israelis, those who lived in Palestine before the state was established, as well as the newcomers. By the end of 1949 there was one new immigrant for every two preindependence settlers—and the immigrants were not just strangers but often seemed very strange indeed to the veteran Zionists.

The chapters of Segev's book follow the basic divisions in Israeli society: between Jews and Arabs, old settlers (mostly Western) and new immigrants (mostly Oriental), secular and religious groups, and, above all, the contrast between the dream and the humdrum reality. The dominant figure during this period was of course David Ben-Gurion, the Lenin of the Zionist movement. As with Lenin, Ben-Gurion's order of the day was organization, organization, and once again organization. He was also a master at setting clear goals and identifying justice with the Labor Party's latest decisions as dictated by him to the party secretariat—decisions that in Ben-Gurion's own jargon were referred to as "ethics of the prophets" and "light unto the nations."

The main story of Israel's first year is that of the great immigration, and it is told by Segev with a kind of acid compassion. The traditional Zionist movement's vision of the great immigration to Zion was limited to European Jews, more specifically Eastern European Jews. They were supposed to form the reserve army of the Zionist movement. Oriental Jews were remote from the eyes and sentiments of the Zionist leaders. After the Holocaust, however, Zionism was deprived of its natural reservoir of immigrants; Jews from east of the Elbe were now being replaced by Jews of the Orient. These were described by some

*1949—*The First Israelis* (in Hebrew, Jerusalem, 1985).

of those responsible for their absorption into Israel, all of European descent, as of "inferior human material." "The Moroccans are very wild people," Segev quotes one official as saying. And in an academic symposium during the first year, discussions were devoted to "the nature of primitiveness," and conclusions were drawn about the "mental regression" common among many Jews from Arab countries, as well as about their "retarded ego development." These were decidedly not the kind of recruits the established Jewish community in Palestine prayed for. "These may not be Jews in whose immigration we're interested, but we cannot tell them 'don't come' "—such were the words of Jacob Zrubavel, head of the Oriental Jews department of the Jewish Agency, a devout socialist.

It is indeed widely believed that the mass Oriental immigration to Israel during that time was not the outcome of a planned decision, but rather a natural consequence of the Zionist vision of the gathering of the exiles. On the other hand, it is commonly assumed that Ben-Gurion's decision to declare the establishment of the state of Israel on May 14, 1948, the last day of the British Mandate, a decision disapproved of by many other Zionist leaders, was an act of sheer will—which earned him the title of "One in His Generation." (Rabbi Yehuda Fishman, Ben-Gurion's Minister of Religion, said at the time that it was lucky Ben-Gurion was not an Orthodox Jew, or else many would take him to be the Messiah.)

I myself believe that the reverse is the case. That is to say, the mass Oriental immigration to Israel during 1949 was, in my view, the direct result of a decision by Ben-Gurion—a true act of will—while on the other hand I see the Declaration of Independence on May 14, 1948, as having merely ceremonial significance. Even if the views of those who opposed Ben-Gurion had been accepted, the invasion of Palestine by the Arab armies would have come that day anyway. The political outcome would sooner or later have been the same. King Abdullah of Jordan and King Farouk of Egypt were not so interested in the lofty words of the Declaration of Independence read out that day in the Tel Aviv museum. Each feared the other would beat him to it and gain a larger share of the Palestine pie.

Why did Ben-Gurion want mass immigration? The ideological reason, that Israel's raison d'être was the ingathering of the exiles, certainly influenced him. But Segev is also right when he claims, drawing upon a variety of evidence, that Ben-Gurion saw it as the best way to ensure Israel's military might in the long run. The new immigrants were for him a "desert generation," from whom not much could be expected. But their sons and daughters would be "real" Israelis from whom, as he was fond of saying, the first Yemenite chief of staff would emerge. Like most of his friends among the leaders of the new state, he believed that the Moroccans were savages, but unlike them he did not think that they were all that different from the rest. "I'm told many of them are thieves," he is quoted as saying. "I myself am a Polish Jew, and I doubt that there is any Jewish community with more thieves than the Polish one."

In Israel, then as later, people loved the immigration but not the immigrants themselves. The new immigrants, Segev tells us, were put behind barbed wire in the Immigration Gate camp. Israeli society today pays dearly for those early traumatic experiences of the newly arrived. But, it has to be added, the community outside the barbed wire generally was a very poor one in those days. In order to be able to absorb the huge waves of immigrants, it accepted severe austerity measures, including strict rationing, one aim of which was to ensure a minimum supply of basic commodities to all. Segev tells the story of the austerity period vividly and well. The austerity not only was an economic necessity, but also fitted the puritanical character of the people in power and their desire to govern the economy by means of administrative regulation. Liberalism, it must be remembered, was very far from the mentality of the Israeli leaders then. (The Histadrut weekly paper demanded, for example, that mediocre artists not be allowed to tour abroad, lest they ruin Israel's reputation.) And yet, as one of the newspapers at the time put it, while the previous waves of immigrants were absorbed into the existing community, the new waves starting in 1949 were absorbed alongside it.

The philosopher Martin Buber predicted serious dangers. "I'm looking for a common tradition, but I find it nowhere," he said; "I see only broken tablets." I'm not quite clear just what danger Buber was prophesying. But as early as January 1949, Zalman Aranne, the Lu-

nacharsky of the Zionist movement, was farsighted enough to predict
that the Oriental communities would form the power base of Begin's
Herut Party. (Aranne once said of himself that he realized he was
sane only on three days of the week, but the trouble was that he
didn't know which three. This prediction, however, certainly was
made on a sane day.) It took almost thirty years to happen, but in
1977 these humiliated people helped to bring Begin to power.

Segev describes the contest to gain the political allegiance of the
new immigrants, especially the attempt on the part of the ruling
Mapai Party to prevent them from falling under the influence of the
religious parties. This is significant because most of the Oriental Jews
came to Israel as religious Jews, in marked contrast to the previous
waves of secular-minded immigrants. In the end, however, Ben-
Gurion reached a compromise with the religious parties whose support
he needed to form a coalition government. In contrast to Bismarck,
he was afraid of a Kulturkampf, an all-out struggle against religious
influence. And he believed the price he would have to pay the religious parties would be lower than the price being demanded by the
left-wing Mapam, which at that time saw Soviet Russia as a "second
homeland."

Ben-Gurion was interested in getting economic aid from the United
States, and hence gave up any thought of neutrality in the Cold War
of those days. True, in Ben-Gurion's party there was talk of socialism—Golda Meir even spoke of "socialism in our time"—but what
they meant was, basically, some form of enlightened *étatisme*.

The debate over the borders of the state of Israel, as Segev describes
it, took place in 1949 and not, as is commonly supposed, during the
War of Independence of 1948. It was in 1949 that the armistice agreements with the Arab states were signed and the Green Line, the
borderline that held until June 1967, agreed upon. For the younger
generation in Israel today, the Green Line is somewhat like the
Mason-Dixon line for most Americans. The map with which the post-
1967 generation has grown up has a very different outline from the
one that prevailed between 1949 and 1967, with its famous narrow
waist near Tel Aviv.

This geographical fact is evidently useful to those in Israel who now defend the status quo of the occupation. The Green Line was already at the center of controversy in 1949, however. "Not the land but the soul was divided," Begin insisted loudly, while Mapam proposed to capture the West Bank in order to replace the Hashemite Kingdom's domination of it by "progressive" local elements who would sign a peace treaty with Israel. Ben-Gurion's position at the time was that Israel had no obligation to help establish an independent Arab state. For him the choice was between a democratic Jewish state and a binational Greater Israel; his decision in favor of the first was unequivocal.

The 1949 peace talks with Egypt and Jordan ended not with peace treaties, but only with armistice agreements. Whether or not it was then possible to achieve more in these negotiations I do not know. But I do believe that Ben-Gurion's guiding image at the time was that of the dry dock. The state of Israel, like a dry dock, could only function when the walls around it were locked, so as to enable the level—of the water in the one case, of Oriental Jews in the other—to go up. This is why a state of no peace—that is, closed borders yet no war, and therefore a continued influx of immigrants—was seen as having distinct advantages.

Segev writes that Ben-Gurion was insensitive to the human tragedy of the indigenous Arab population. He quotes him as saying, "Land with Arabs on it and land without Arabs on it are very different things." He was interested in land of the latter sort. During a staff meeting before the 1948 battle over the Arab towns of Ramle and Lydda, Ben-Gurion was asked what would be the fate of the local Arab residents. He responded, Segev writes, with a swinging gesture of his hand that was interpreted by Yitzhak Rabin, then one of the operation's commanders, as an instruction to expel the Arabs. But this was during the war. The revelations in Segev's book concern cases of expulsion that continued well into 1949. For example, the expulsion of the Arabs of Magdal—later to become Ashkelon—was carried out with Ben-Gurion's blessing. When the Haifa Arabs were concentrated into a ghetto, Ben-Gurion chose not to be informed about it. Ben-Gurion's close friend at the time, Itzhak Ben-Zvi—later President of Israel—is quoted by Segev as saying, "There are too many Arabs in

Israel." On the same occasion Ze'ev On, a member of the Knesset, said, "The landscape improved lately. I enjoy my trips now from Tel Aviv to Haifa when I see no Arabs on the way."

This mode of thinking and talking about Arabs owed much, no doubt, to a deep sense of anxiety, as well as to a desire for revenge. In the young state the Jews were convinced, and with reason, that the war, in which 1 percent of the Jewish population was killed, was imposed upon them by the Arabs. They were also fearful that the Arabs who remained within the borders of the state of Israel would become a "fifth column," since their allegiance would belong naturally to their brethren outside the borders.

Segev's story of the encounter between Jews and Arabs after the foundation of the state is a painful one. It certainly does not justify the smug history of some Labor Zionists, who are used to looking forward to the past and who describe Israel as having been born in a kind of immaculate conception, original sin starting only with the rise of Begin to power some thirty years later. The story of Israel in 1949 is, in Segev's account, a heroic story but not a pretty one.

On the face of it, the first part of this essay seems outdated. In Israel in the mid-1980s, talking to Yasir Arafat seemed as remote a notion as talking to Attila the Hun. It was the heyday of Israel's demonization of Arafat. But the Palestinian uprising, which began in December 1987, humanized Palestinians in Israeli eyes. And the less humane the conflict between Israel and the Palestinians became, the more human the Palestinians seemed.

But this is not necessarily a lasting achievement. If the Oslo Accords break down—and they well might—the Palestinians, and primarily Arafat, will regain their old place in the Israeli psyche as devils. A reversion to the situation I described in this essay is therefore not yet out of the question.

7

UNDERSTANDING THE INTIFADA

MAY 1988

FOR ITS SPECIAL ISSUE PUBLISHED ON ISRAELI INDEPENDENCE DAY in May 1987, *Koteret Rashit*, a sophisticated Israeli magazine of the liberal left, commissioned a report on daily life in the occupied territories from a talented young Israeli writer, David Grossman. Grossman was the only Israeli novelist who had previously crossed the so-called Green Line in his fiction, particularly in short stories that are set in the West Bank. An Israeli-born Ashkenazi who speaks fluent Arabic—a rare breed in Israel—Grossman took a taxi to the West Bank every day for forty days. He did not go to Gaza. This fact is not accidental. Before the recent uprising, the Gaza Strip did not exist in the minds of most Israelis, even in the mind of a writer who took it upon himself to explore the repressed zones of the Israeli national consciousness.

Koteret Rashit asked for ten thousand words, but Grossman wrote far more. The entire magazine for that week was devoted to his story. The issue's success in Israel was phenomenal. A great many educated Israelis spent the Independence Day weekend reading Grossman's article. Thus the book became a best-seller before it was published, and its success, I think, tells us something about the situation in Israel before the recent uprising.

There were those who thought that Grossman's report did no more than preach to the converted; but it did not preach, and, moreover, the converted were not so convinced. Its appeal for many Israelis was that Grossman made them feel that he had undertaken the trip to the West Bank that each of them should have taken but knew they would never take. Then, too, it gave the impression that somehow they had no more need to go there: Grossman had done it for them. And the reason why he succeeded had much to do with the descriptive and distinctly "nonpolitical" tone of his narrative.

Grossman's report projects the tone of calculated naiveté of someone who, like Cary Grant in a Hitchcock film, unexpectedly finds himself a witness to strange and sinister events and is determined to tell what he has seen and heard. The clichés of regional politics are replaced by Grossman with detailed description, in which he draws on his own family for comparisons. An old woman in Deheisha resembles his Polish grandmother; a noble, bitter Arab reminds him of his father. It's all in the family, in the mythical Family of Man.

I was not enthusiastic about Grossman's report on that Independence Day a long year ago. At the time I thought that it provided an all too convenient moral escape hatch, providing a Victorian catharsis that was philanthropic more than political. I was wary of rereading it. Whatever force it had had then, I thought, would now have vanished. But I find the book has more vitality and greater insight than I thought when I first read it in *Koteret Rashit*. True, Grossman did not predict an Arab uprising on the West Bank; he assumed that things would more or less continue as they had for almost twenty years. And yet he saw what seems to me the essential point—that the story of the occupation and of the uprising is a story of honor and humiliation. And the political conflict is a conflict between virtues and vices more than a conflict between interests.

Reading the many attempts to answer the question of what caused the Palestinian uprising that has continued over the last five months, I have myself come to think that the real question is a different one: Why didn't the uprising happen earlier? Grossman talks to Raj'a Shehade, a well-known Palestinian lawyer and human rights activist on the West Bank and the author of a moving book, *The Third Way*, on life under the occupation, and asks him, "Why is it so easy to control you? How can you explain the fact that we rule more than a million and a half Arabs, almost without feeling it?" Shehade replies:

> It takes no effort to rule a society accustomed to paternalism to the point that people do not even ask who is giving the orders. We make use of and accept authority so naturally that we do not even see the humiliation and shame it engenders.

Shehade was right to see that Israel was ruling over a society that had been used to accepting authority, even in the most intimate matters. However, like everyone else, Shehade was mistaken in believing that people who were suppressed would not feel deeply humiliated. At least the younger generation of Palestinians, born into occupation and growing up in constant friction with Israeli society, can recognize humiliation when they are subjected to it. Many in this generation work inside the state of Israel, speak Hebrew, and consequently compare themselves with Israeli young people, not with their counterparts in Damascus or Saudi Arabia.

The Palestinian uprising that began in December 1987 was directed against humiliation. Should no settlement be achieved, it will be increasingly directed against oppression; indeed it is already largely directed against oppression as well. The regulations and practices of colonial rule, when successful, are only humiliating; faced with resistance, these rules and practices become oppressive. The Israeli occupation of the last twenty years was basically humiliating, and it is now becoming severely oppressive, not just because it has become violent but because there has been a change in Israel's definition of the enemy. Until the uprising, the enemy was political: the members of the various Palestinian organizations. Now every Palestinian is an enemy.

Grossman is sensitive to how humiliation works, and the people he saw on the West Bank were willing to talk about it:

> Why do they need to humiliate me at a roadblock in front of my children, who can see how the soldiers laugh at their father and force him to get out of the car?

These words are spoken by Taher, an Arab who went immediately after the June 1967 war to a special school to study Hebrew, on the assumption that the Israelis were on the West Bank to stay. He then says to Grossman, "Sometimes you push [us] so hard that we see how scared you are." But an Israeli reserve soldier on the Jericho crossing point to Jordan tells Grossman:

> More than once I've seen a young, angry soldier use his position to humiliate an elderly and venerable man, making him run all over the place in his socks, jeer [at him] and degrade him in front of people from his village. You can only guess what that man feels about Israel after such treatment.

Taher, the Israeli reservist, and Grossman make one central point clear: The humiliation takes place in front of the people the humiliated person is close to—parents are humiliated in front of their children, local dignitaries in front of their neighbors.

There is of course nothing new in the fact that rule by an occupying power humiliates the occupied—especially at points of friction such as roadblocks set up to control people's movements, the offices that issue permits, military courts in which violators of the occupation rules are tried. However, since the Israeli government claims to assert sovereignty over the occupied territories, a real and lasting injury is added to the insult. The Israeli occupation succeeded in hurting an essential element in the Palestinian society's concept of dignity—the peasants' ownership of their land.

The chapter of Grossman's book I found most moving and at the same time most melancholy is an account of his visit to an Arab village of almost idyllic biblical beauty located in the Alfuqin Valley just outside Israel's 1948 borders. After 1948 Israel carried out attacks on the village in reprisal for raids across the border, and most of the inhabitants were forced to leave for a refugee camp on the West Bank. After the Six-Day War in 1967 it turned out that the Israelis needed the houses in the camp to resettle refugees from Gaza, and so the government allowed some of the uprooted villagers to return to their village in the Alfuqin Valley. They were given a month to rebuild the village, and they worked day and night to do so. One of the villagers Grossman spoke to compared his situation with that of those who remained behind in the refugee camp:

We now live here among real people. The people who stayed behind in Deheisha and in Jericho are miserable. They are going mad from sadness and longing for their land. They come and plead with us to give them a little garden plot. Just so they can regain a little self-respect. Something to live for. After all, it is not just land, it is everything.

For many refugees in the camps, both those under Israel's current control and those beyond it in Jordan, Syria, and Lebanon, Grossman found that "returning to the land" is taken literally. Most of them were born after 1948, but through some process of osmosis from their parents, they conceived the hope that they would return to the same villages, sometimes to the very same houses, in which their parents had lived. There may be no political solution that will satisfy the wish to return still nourished by the Palestinian refugees in the camps. The Wadi Alfuqin village cannot serve as the model for an eventual political settlement.

The uprising of the Palestinians in the territories is an act to regain their lost honor. In this respect, it is comparable to the Egyptians' crossing of the Suez Canal in October 1973. However, while in the case of the Yom Kippur War many in Israel understood that the recapture of the canal prepared the way for a settlement, that the way to Camp David was through the canal, the public attitude toward the Palestinians is different. They refuse to acknowledge the possibility that the return of the Palestinians' lost honor could contribute to a political settlement. The announced wish of the Israeli government is to restore "law and order" to the territories—which has been accurately translated: "to erase the smile from the face of Palestinian youth."

How can one explain Israel's behavior in the recent uprising? It may seem bizarre to refer to the war between the Arab *shabab* (youth) and the Israeli Army as a war of shepherds ("And there was a strife between the herdmen of Abram's cattle and the herdmen of Lot's cattle"—Genesis 13:7). After all, the Israeli shepherds have an atomic bomb. Nor is the description of the war as an intercommunal civil war adequate. Until now it has been a war between civilians of one nation and the army of the other, more similar to the strife in Algeria than to the fighting between Catholics and Protestants in Northern Ireland. Yet in one way the struggle in the territories seems like a biblical struggle: it is a battle of sticks and stones. This makes it immediately understandable to anyone watching television or reading a newspaper. It is a rudimentary struggle in which the emotions aroused are intense and immediate—hatred and rage, frustration and helplessness, the enthusiasm of solidarity and the desolation of unceasing violence. And the psychology required for understanding the situation is a Stone Age psychology.

What the daily screenings of the fighting have brought home more than anything else to an Israeli watching television is the issue of honor. Israeli television practices self-censorship these days. Even before the government started to ban television reporters from the West Bank, the violent acts of Israeli soldiers that were shown abroad every day were almost never shown here. The Israeli public sees only carefully edited scenes taken from the foreign networks—mainly the daily rituals in which young Palestinians throw stones and burn tires.

And so, one evening in March 1988, Israeli television viewers were shown the main road near Hebron, where Israeli troops had set up a roadblock. On the hill overlooking the road a group of kaffiyeh-clad youths were throwing stones at the soldiers below. Girls on the rooftops of the village were cheering the youths on. The air was heavy with showers of stones and tear-gas fumes. Into the frame of this picture entered a group of high-ranking Israeli officers who had just arrived, headed by the Central Command chief, General Mitsna. The long-legged, lean Mitsna, whose Assyrian beard is like Herzl's, began to walk up the hill. Alone, without a helmet, with a revolver: Gary Cooper at High Noon. One of the youths facing him made obscene gestures at him and moved toward him while continuing to throw stones. Another high-ranking officer from the group, short and thick-set, was now seen breaking into a run to catch the cheeky youth. He soon lost his breath. The sequence stopped at this point. We were not shown what followed. We simply saw the *shabiba* posed against the high command of the Israeli Defense Forces. All was exposed, tense. The insult to the army is felt by many Israelis to be unbearable.

Such incidents may explain why clubs have been supplied to the soldiers. Why, government spokesmen ask, is any explanation needed? After all, clubs are weapons routinely used to control riots. Remember that at the very beginning of the uprising the response of the army's officers was to fire on the rioters. Then they made mass arrests accompanied by quick mass trials; then they imposed curfews; and still later they expelled some of the "instigators." It was then that the systematic beatings started. Today all these strategies are being used, often on the same day, and hardly a day passes without some Arabs being killed.

But the sticks are only partly explained as routine weapons for riot control. What must be understood is that by using clubs, the young Israeli soldiers regain their honor, it is thought. These soldiers are eighteen and nineteen years old, an age vulnerable to masculine assertiveness. They are required daily to face crowds of stone-throwing youths of much the same age, or younger. By taking action, they are showing them who is really the stronger, who is the *real* soldier.

This is a far cry from the South Korean police with their plastic shields, their ethos of restraint, and their capacity to stand motionless through constant showers of rocks and bottles thrown by young people during the days of violent rioting in June 1987. The South Korean police force saw its honor in self-discipline. In Israel, the clubs were necessary—so it was evidently believed in government circles—to restore the soldiers' honor in the face of the challenge from Palestinians. And I mean honor, not dignity—an adolescent, macho honor.

This violent rite has torn apart Israeli society today. Israelis are divided within themselves between two extreme emotions: "fuck the Arabs" and "to hell with the territories." The first works to the advantage of people on the right, the second to the advantage of those on the left. True, the man responsible for sending the young men to break the bones of Palestinians is Labor's Defense Minister, General Yitzhak Rabin. But the greatest enthusiasm for the beatings comes from the right. The peculiar hypocrisy of the Labor leaders does not allow them to identify with young men who do the beating, only to send them to do the job.

The attempt of the last five months to crush the uprising is accompanied by two contrasting psychological processes that are taking place in Israeli society. There are, on one hand, increasingly brutal attitudes toward, and treatment of, the Arabs. At the same time the conflict has become less abstract, more human. During the past unusually long and rainy winter, for the first time since the June 1973 War, Israelis were shown, on television, Palestinians plodding through the mud of their camps. The close-ups of daily violent encounters give the Palestinians distinctive human features they never had before. Until now the faces of Arabs from the territories who worked inside the state of Israel were hidden under what the Jerusalem poet Dennis Silk refers to as "invisibility powder":

Rubbed into the skin of a million
  Ahmeds bused in from the
Territories. Into the skin, the hair,
  the kaffiyeh, the shirt.
For Arabs should be worked but
  not seen.
          (from "Vanishing Trick")

There is today a new Palestinian presence in the Israeli consciousness, a growing interest on the part of Israelis in what Palestinians think and what they want. Thus, for example, in the pages of Israeli newspapers and magazines one recently found many articles about a poem written by Mahmud Darwish, a well-known Palestinian poet.

Darwish now lives in Paris, is an active member of the PLO, and has many friends in Israel. Several Hebrew versions of the poem already exist, each with its own claims to accuracy, and daily cross-Mediterranean telephone conversations are being conducted with the poet, in which he is asked to "explain" different parts of the poem. The poem calls for the Jews to get out. (Roughly: "The time has come for you to get out / Dwell where you will but do not dwell among us.") Over the telephone Darwish explained that he meant only that Jews should leave the occupied territories. But the poem says explicitly, "Get out of our earth of our land of our sea." There is no sea on the West Bank. Darwish said he meant the port of Gaza.

Why was there such intense interest in Darwish's poem? More than a few Jews in Israel still take seriously the idea of a "national poet" as a secular prophet who would express the collective consciousness of his people. The poet, in this view, is not a "critic and entertainer" but a shaman. This may help to explain why the words of Darwish's poem have been taken here with such seriousness. But of course all of this seems bizarre—as if one needs to consult a poem in order to find out that the heartfelt wish of almost all Palestinians is for the Jews to get out of Palestine. Not all of them, though. There are certainly some Palestinians, among them perhaps even Darwish himself, who wish for a secular democratic state with the Jews—in the hope that the Jews will guarantee in that state the degree of personal freedom that the Palestinians recognize exists in Israel for Israelis and that they fear will not exist in a Palestinian state.

Be that as it may, the political question does not concern what the Palestinians wish in their hearts but what their effective demands are, the demands for which a price will have to be paid. As far as those demands are concerned, the elusive Darwish of the telephone is more relevant than the "authentic" Darwish of the poem. Political and psychological reconciliation is not a necessary condition for a political settlement, but on the other hand a political settlement can contribute significantly toward political—even if not ideological—reconciliation.

The trouble is that in the politics of honor and humiliation, it is difficult even to speak of a political settlement. It should have been obvious to those Israelis who are interested in a settlement that the

PLO is a central partner in negotiations. Even Shimon Peres, who opposes dealing with the PLO, admits that the PLO is ready for direct and immediate negotiations with Israel (although, after the killing of Abu Jihad and Syria's reconciliation with the PLO, the situation is less clear). But for most Israelis, including those who favor an agreement, the refusal to talk to the PLO has become a matter of honor —quite apart from the wish to humiliate. At the same time, for Palestinians in the occupied territories, whose uprising was not inspired by the PLO, the issue of the PLO representing them in eventual negotiations with Israel has also become a matter of honor. The Palestinians have a moral advantage here. Their right to choose their own representatives is a matter not only of pride but of self-respect.

The first thing the Israelis need to do now is to return their conflict with the Palestinians to its political dimension. In a political conflict both sides try to defend and advance their own interests, and the defense of interests requires a certain degree of rationality. In a politics of honor and humiliation there is very little rationality, and a great deal of blood.

GROSSMAN'S BOOK HAS much to do with the way the dovish left in Israel sees the Palestinian uprising. Kant distinguished between two kinds of despair: "defiant despair" and "depressed despair." People in the grip of depressed despair are paralyzed by it; in a state of defiant despair they are willing to fight against all oppression. The Palestinian uprising started when depressed despair turned into defiant despair. Grossman supplied a description of the Palestinians' depressed despair. Having read his description, many of the dovish left in Israel were able to understand the new, defiant despair. Grossman may not have changed political positions, but he has had an effect on political sensibilities.

Does this matter? The Israeli left is a marginal group in electoral strength, although it is influential as far as opinion among the Israeli elite goes—in the army, the press, the universities, and the arts. The left in Israel is hardly defined by positions on social and economic issues. It is almost entirely determined by its attitude toward the conflict with the Arabs. And, with respect to this conflict, two distinctions matter. The first, broader, distinction is between doves and hawks, which has to do with willingness or refusal to give up occupied territories. The second, narrower, distinction, between left and right, adds another element: the willingness or refusal to recognize the Palestinians, and the PLO as their representative. These distinctions are of course accompanied by an entire culture of symbols and images. The doves (or the left in the broad sense, as some would prefer) consist of Peace Now, the centrist party Shinui, and all the parties and factions to its left: a part of the Labor Party, Mapam, Shulamit Aloni's Civil Rights Party, the Progressive Party, and the Communists. The left in the narrow sense consists of many in Peace Now, many in Mapam, and the last three of these parties, as well as all the peace groups considered more radical than Peace Now (forty-six groups by the latest count).

From a different perspective, the dovish left consists mainly of Ashkenazi Sabras, who have, as foreign visitors often remark, a WASP-like self-confidence. They are entirely lacking in the traumatic fear of Arabs that characterizes the relatively new immigrants of the 1950s and their children—immigrant families who now make up well over half of the population. The left in general has little empathy with, and no sympathy for, the immigrants' fears. It is this attitude, and not just its actual political positions, that makes it unpopular in Israel. Paradoxically, however, the left is also that part of the population which has truly absorbed the fact of Israel's military might. Right-wing immigrants vacillate between a sense of megalomania about Israeli might, on the one hand, and, on the other, feelings of extreme self-pity and powerlessness. Between these extremes lies the playground of Ariel Sharon.

To both sides, young people are more important than they have been for many years, and this is especially true of Palestinian society now. It is mainly the young who are carrying on the uprising (women, too, of all ages, although much less visibly). The early days of the riots created a strong sense of solidarity among the diverse Palestinians on the West Bank and in Gaza, and they also created a feeling of intense revolutionary fervor among the young. However, as the months pass and as the measures taken by the Israeli authorities grow increasingly harsh, a "Red Guard" syndrome may be taking shape. By this I mean the ways in which young people can impose revolutionary standards that the rest of the society, especially parents who must support their families, may find difficult to accept.

There have been some signs of internal terror—for example, the murder of an Arab policeman in Jericho, meant to underscore the call for all Arab policemen in the territories to resign, as most did. Some older Palestinians say privately that such events recall to them their fears during the terror that accompanied the great Arab revolt in Palestine in 1936–39. In fact, there have not been many reprisals, and so far there is an impressive degree of Palestinian solidarity throughout the territories. If a reign of internal terror should take place, the tender age of the participants in the uprising will explain at least part of it. Young Palestinians have become keepers of the "purity of the revolution" in a society in which the uprising is also an act of liberation from traditional paternalism.

Grossman's book tells a story remarkably similar in outline to stories of classic experiments with identical twins separated at birth. Following the 1949 armistice agreement between Israel and Jordan, the Arab village of Barta'a was suddenly and arbitrarily cut into two—one half in Jordan, the other in Israel. There were even cases of families separated in this way by the Green Line. After the Six-Day War in 1967 the two halves were reunited. A villager from the Jordanian side said of his fellow villagers on the Israeli side, "They always brag about how much like the Israelis they are, yet they don't sense what the Israelis think of them. . . . I don't envy them—they don't have any pride." From the Israeli side Grossman quotes the following: "My way of thinking [comes] from here. I'm already used to this life, even to our special status among you, on this quarter-democracy you have given us. Do you think I could go now and live with them in Nablus?" This was said before the uprising. And what of today? The village of Barta'a is three kilometers from the Wadi Ara road inside the heartland of the state of Israel. It is a main road passing through a valley surrounded by Arab villages and leading to various kibbutz settlements located in the Valley of Jezreel. During the last two months there have been a few incidents in which Israeli Arab youths have thrown stones at passing traffic. For older Israelis these stones bring back the ghosts of the Arab revolt of the late 1930s. Especially powerful for them is the fear that the uprising in the territories will not halt at the Green Line. Shamir's right-wing camp is playing on these atavistic fears, using them to spread the message that this is a total war against the existence of the state of Israel within any borders whatever.

The political leaders of Israel's Arabs well understand the dangers associated with stone throwing at Wadi Ara. They are apprehensive of a violent break with the Jewish population. One Arab member of the Knesset, a member of the Labor Alignment, recently resigned in protest over Rabin's brutal policies in the territories. This suggests that the Arab votes for Labor may significantly decrease. Where those votes will go in the upcoming elections remains an open question. The Arab population in Israel makes up a voting bloc potentially larger than that of the Jewish religious parties, but its actual political power is comparatively negligible. One reason is that the Arabs vote largely for the Communist and Progressive parties, neither of them candidates for any type of coalition with the Labor Alignment. The Communists are perceived by the Jewish public as controlled by Moscow, the Progressives as close to the PLO. There is now talk of a new joint Jewish-Arab party, to the left of Labor, which would take part in Israel's party politics. But this is still just talk.

ONE OF THE most revealing stops in Grossman's tour of the West Bank is the military court in Nablus. In the occupied territories Arabs accused of crimes are tried in military courts, but justice there is neither seen nor done, and there are no courts of appeal. Grossman reports on a case—he calls it Catch 44—in which a Palestinian was charged with having contacts with terrorist organizations. He was held in custody for forty-four days awaiting trial. His lawyer was Leah Tsemel, a radical Israeli Jew and an impressive advocate. It soon became clear to everyone that the defendant had had no contact with any enemy organization. However, acquitting him would amount to a confession of error, which would be a sign of weakness. Besides, he had already been detained for forty-four days. The judge hit on a solution—he sentenced the Palestinian to the forty-four days already served, convicting him of a charge not included in the original charge sheet: unauthorized transfer of foreign currency. This was a crime for which he not only had never been charged but in fact had not committed. All he was guilty of was receiving scholarship money from Germany.

This story pales in its evil when compared to the "blitz trials" of hundreds of people, many of them children, within two days, which began soon after the uprising started. The prostitution of the law, moreover, has filtered though the Green Line into Israel as well. The former president of the Supreme Court, an honorable man, recently headed a commission appointed to investigate the procedures and conduct of Israel's security services. In its report the commission endorsed what it referred to as "moderate physical pressure"—a euphemistic expression meaning that torture is allowed for a serious purpose as distinct from torture for pleasure. For their part, the security services did not wait for the report to carry out the beatings and other practices that in some cases seem indistinguishable from torture. The report now grants to such conduct official approval of a kind never granted before.

GROSSMAN FIRST CALLED his book in Hebrew *The Yellow Time*— the time of hatred. When he was talking about the book and its proposed title to an Arab in a field dotted with yellow flowers, the man told him of the legendary yellow wind: an eastern, eschatological wind coming from the gates of hell and destroying all that is in its way. There is no hope of escaping its destructive powers. Until April, Secretary of State George Shultz's plan raised hope, especially in the Labor Party, but it now seems that Shultz's initiative is in a deep coma. The only chance for its resuscitation may come from Gorbachev's side. So with the failure of Shultz's plan the west wind may yet bring with it, as Shelley wrote, "Yellow, and black, and pale, and hectic red."

Israel's general elections will take place in November. My impression now, shared by many Israelis, as recent polls show, is that the Likud bloc is very likely to win. At any rate, it is now hard to imagine Labor forming its own government, although it may be called once again to join in a National Unity government. Three different political approaches may have emerged in Israel by then. The first is the Likud's. It would recognize a new violent order as the status quo in the territories. Maintaining the occupation will certainly be expensive, but for the Likud its price would be tolerable. In the background some who favor this approach anticipate another round of war, maybe with Syria, with the implicit promise that while it rages a great many Arabs in the territories could be expelled.

The second approach would originate from the mainstream of the Labor Party. It would come when party leaders realize that their traditional "Jordanian option" has become politically irrelevant, as Jordan itself has been making clear. The disappointment over the failure of this option would lead to a revival of Moshe Dayan's plan —that is, a unilateral withdrawal from only the densely populated parts of the West Bank (which would amount to putting the territories in a state of siege) and a unilateral evacuation of the Gaza Strip.

The third approach would possibly emerge following a radicalizing process within some circles of the Labor Party, especially if they are perceived to have done badly in the elections. This approach would call explicitly and clearly for talks with the Palestinians. Except, of course, that there is no telling whether the Palestinians will stand then where they stand now.

There will also be people, of all persuasions and in all parties, without any plan but with hope. The main hope will be that some outside power will intervene, impose a settlement, and save the region from its inhabitants. The only real hope, however, may lie in the fact that most large predictions about Israel and the Middle East have turned out to be false.

Since this essay appeared, I have written a book, The Decent Society *(published in 1996), in which I observed, "Gradually conversations I had with Palestinians during their uprising in the occupied territories, as well as conversations I had with new immigrants to Israel from the countries of the defunct Communist bloc, convinced me of the centrality of honor and humiliation in the lives of people—and, consequently, of the importance that ought to be allotted to the concepts of honor and humiliation in political thought. Thus the idea was born of the decent society as a society which does not humiliate." This essay, written at the beginning of the* intifada, *already touched on the role of humiliation in bringing about the uprising. Everything that has happened since has convinced me that the issue of honor and human dignity is at the core of the conflict between Israel and the Palestinians.*

8

IS ZIONISM A FAILURE OR A TRAGEDY?

OCTOBER 1986

IN MY YOUTH I READ A STORY ABOUT AN OLD NEWSPAPER PROOF-reader, trained in the classics, who could not stand the trivializing use by young reporters of the sublime word "tragedy." Eventually he died in a road accident, and, sure enough, the morning paper announced his death as a tragedy. Bernard Avishai calls his book *The Tragedy of Zionism*—and immediately one's attention is drawn to the question of fit between title and book. Is it a sloppy or trivial use of the notion of tragedy, or is the story of Zionism indeed a story of a fall, whose fatal inevitability and whose weighty heroes justify it?

It seems therefore a useful strategy to examine this book by the degree to which its content justifies the attribution of tragedy. Moreover, the term "tragedy," to judge from the book's prologue, might seem to have a personal meaning as well. Avishai describes his private disappointment in the realization of Zionism, when he attempted to become an Israeli and then decided not to do so. But tragedy requires heroes of weight and substance, and Avishai doesn't pretend to be writing about himself as embodying a large idea.

Avishai (né Shaicovitch) first arrived in Israel from Canada as an enthusiastic young visitor after the 1967 war. Later he "made *aliyah*"—that is, decided to emigrate—and even joined a kibbutz. There he and his wife discovered the people were strangers to them, "fine people but not our own." The birth of their first son, instead of launching them into the subtleties of purchasing disposable diapers in Israel, made them "reexamine the normative justification of Zionism." Eventually, realizing that their Sabra son was growing into a Hebrew-speaking creature who was alien to them, they packed up and went home to Canada.

Avishai's book has recently led to his being accused of disloyalty to his Zionist past and to Israel. This is a cruel and unjustified accusation. In spite of his criticism of Israel from the West, his heart is clearly in the East. Moreover, the views that led some members of the American Jewish community to refer to him as a "Jew against Zion" are the very ones that are exchanged every Friday evening among secular intelligentsia in Israel. The difference is that in Israel no one bothers to lay them out in almost four hundred closely printed pages. If Avishai is disloyal, then so are many of those living in Zion and defending its existence.

Yet Avishai's personal story is somewhat sad as he tells it, even if short of tragic:

> In calling this book *The Tragedy of Zionism*, I do not mean to suggest that Zionism is some historical misfortune. Rather, that Labor Zionism is a good revolution that long ago ran its course, that it stopped short of its liberal-democratic goals, and recent efforts to reinvigorate Zionism in Israel have only brought Israelis more misfortune.

The tragedy, then, is that of Labor Zionism; the author does not explain why he emphasizes this rather than any of the other strains that have made up Zionism. But it is clear that he regards Labor Zionism as the leading strain, as well as the most promising one, in the founding and building of the state of Israel. Hence the disappointment. The disappointment concerns the failure of Labor Zionism to fulfill its vision of establishing the state of Israel as a liberal democracy.

Avishai seems here to touch a raw wound, with Meir Kahane and his followers supplying the infection. Since Kahane's election to the Knesset in 1984 the frequency with which the word "democracy" has been heard in Israel surely exceeds by far that of its use in all previous years put together. The timing of Avishai's claim, then, seems perfect. However, in my opinion it is misleading to conceive of the challenge Kahane presents to Israeli society as a matter of democracy or even of racism. To be sure, Kahane and his followers are indeed rabid racists and pathologically antidemocratic, but the problem they present—and represent—is different: the problem is their solution to the so-called demographic problem in Israel, which is to expel the Arabs. On this point Kahane's support goes beyond the lunatic fringe that won him his parliamentary seat, and this is crucial for understanding the current Israeli scene—much more so than the issue of whether or not the state is a democracy according to Avishai's liberal theology.

Democracy, however, is a hotly debated subject in Israel today. "Democracy or Zionism?" asks the title of one of Avishai's chapters. The "or" in the question is to be taken as exclusive: *either* democracy *or* Zionism, not both. The chapter is replete with strange assertions, mostly about the liberal semantics of the Jewish heritage and of the Hebrew-speaking people: "Significantly, there was never a word for democracy in the Hebrew tradition, except for the borrowed word '*democratia.*' " The word for democracy in Hebrew is indeed borrowed. But why should that fact be any more significant than the fact that it is also borrowed in English and the languages of other democratic nations? Avishai here is like the Victorian lady who, not wanting to donate money for the translation of the Bible into Zulu, complains that the natives cannot be bothered to learn to read the Bible in the divine language of God, namely English.

Avishai's etymology does not end here. He also finds that the Israeli consciousness is influenced by the fact that the ancient word for liberty in Hebrew—*cherut*—does not carry with it connotations of personal liberty but, rather, has to do with collective liberty; while the Hebrew word for freedom—*chofesh*—is, according to him, a modern one, acquired in Europe: "Indeed, a young Israeli whose parents are from North Africa may have learned the word *'cherut'* directly from the Bible, the word *'democratia'* from resented Labor *apparatchiks* and the word *'chofesh'* from the Zionist anthem *'Ha'Tiqva.'* "

But neither the young Israeli nor Bernard Avishai nor anyone else can learn the word *cherut* directly from the Bible for the simple reason that it does not occur there. Not in *Exodus* or anywhere else. On the other hand, Israeli youth together with Avishai could find *chofesh* in the Bible—in the sense of individual freedom—that is, the freedom of the slave from his master. If anything, though, the young Israeli learns the word for freedom neither from the Bible nor from the national anthem but from the prosaic fact that school holidays are referred to in Hebrew as *chofesh*, the long summer vacation as the "big *chofesh*." This sense of freedom as vacation, as the opportunity to do as you please and in your own good time and in places other than the usual, certainly conforms to most people's concrete notion of freedom, and even precedes the notion of freedom as it figures in Avishai's liberal theology.

The Hebrew word *cherut*, in the sense of liberation from foreign domination, first appeared close to the beginning of the Christian era. Within Christianity it was given a personal meaning by St. Paul, that of liberation from the burden of the Torah. Generations later a similar notion, although with explicitly negative connotations, was used by Orthodox rabbis to describe secular Zionists as "free Jews." The founders of Zionism were liberals in the Middle European sense of the term—namely, people who aspired to be liberated from the yoke of religion. It is important to remember this: their notion of liberalism was not primarily associated with rights against the state or with civil liberties in relations with state authority. The state, indeed, was perceived as an ally, as an instrument in the struggle against religion and against the persecution of Jews on religious grounds. In the Middle European conception of liberalism that circulated among early Zionists, there was no contradiction or even tension between liberalism and statism. This is how matters stood for the first Zionists.

ZIONISM AND THE state of Israel were for a long time a junkyard for almost every European ideology. Significantly, however, liberalism in the Anglo-Saxon sense was not one of them. Today, of course, this ideology has its flag-bearers in Israel—the civil rights activist Shulamit Aloni, for example. But this is a relatively recent development. And even though Aloni came from the Labor Zionist movement, Bernard Avishai is wrong to see the liberal outlook as part of the ideology of Labor Zionism. In practice, it was the legacy of the British Mandate and, in particular, the British institutions of courts and police that injected some liberal traits into Israel.

Moreover, in the state of Israel, as well as during the period of the immigrant settlement preceding its establishment, democracy was the product of a compromise rather than a component of Zionist ideology. It was a result of the fact that the Jewish community both in the Diaspora and in Palestine has always been so fragmented that no central power could impose its will and its vision on it. This has had its own folklore, too, in the contentiousness of the Jewish character, "three Jews—four parties." The main democratic value to be absorbed by the emerging Israeli consciousness was that of intense political involvement. By comparison, American democracy, with its low proportion of voters, is seen as a democracy of apathy, not a "true" democracy. Democratic rhetoric, as part of socialist rhetoric, had its echo in Labor Zionism, but democracy was understood by Labor Zionists as "guided." There can be little doubt that the history of the state of Israel is one of increasing democratization. Israel in the time of Begin was, outside the occupied territories, more democratic than Ben-Gurion's Israel, whether we measure democracy by free expression or by free participation of citizens in public life.

Avishai rightly accuses Ben-Gurion of missing a great opportunity in not founding the state of Israel upon a constitution. That he gave up the idea of a constitution for reasons of convenience—choosing a coalition with the religious parties, which opposed a constitution, over a coalition with the left-wing Mapam, which favored it—indeed seems unpardonable. A constitution would have given Israel a legal base as a liberal democracy. I, too, believe that a constitution—especially one written in the atmosphere of goodwill prevailing when the state was established—could have worked as an effective instrument for the protection of civil liberties. But one ought not to succumb to an excessive belief in what a constitution can achieve. As if there had been no slavery in the United States under its Constitution. When a discriminatory interest of the majority against an entire segment of the population is at stake, the effectiveness of a constitution is not clear.

Like England, Israel has no constitution, but it has a number of basic laws. Avishai claims that among these basic laws are explicit discriminatory laws against Arabs, and that these are evidence that the Zionist revolution stopped short of realizing its vision of establishing a liberal-democratic state. Thus he repeats without examining it, the charge, prevalent in the American press, that the basic law of the Israeli Land Authority precludes Arabs from leasing "95 percent of cultivated Israeli land." This charge is unfounded. There is certainly discrimination against Arabs in leasing land, but it is not codified in the land law. Moreover, Avishai errs in holding that the law was passed in the first Knesset: it was passed in 1960, and was considered one of the greatest achievements of socialist Zionism in that it made most of the land in Israel the property of its entire citizenship and protected it from private ownership. In fact Begin and his cronies opposed the law in the name of free enterprise.

The charge of legal discrimination against Arabs goes back to an article in the Keren Kayemet charter (Keren Kayemet being the branch of the Jewish Agency responsible for purchasing land in Palestine), which limits the lease of Keren Kayemet land to Jews only. Keren Kayemet land now comprises 5 percent of the state land, according to one calculation, and 14 percent according to another. (The discrepancy has to do with the fact that 9 percent of the land was given to the Keren Kayemet between 1948 and 1960.) But even for this part of the land, Israeli law does not recognize the Keren Kayemet rules on leasing to Arabs—much as it does not recognize another Keren Kayemet regulation that demands that the Sabbath be observed on all its land. (This last regulation was in fact contested in court, and the Keren Kayemet lost.) The discrimination against Israeli Arabs is not in the law, then, but in the discriminatory practices of officials in charge of land administration.

However, the dialectics of the history of Israel's land policies are even more complicated. The policy of the Begin government to settle the West Bank and to channel resources from within the Green Line marking the pre-1967 border toward this end brought about the collapse of Israel's agriculture, which was until then one of Israel's most impressive successes. Many collective settlements (*moshavim*), mainly in the south, went bankrupt. Much of their land was consequently leased to Arabs, so that the extent of Arab cultivation of land in Israel today much exceeds any known in the past. The urgent problem of the Israeli Arab population today is not agricultural land but rather land for housing. It is here that Arabs are discriminated against to an appalling degree.

DEMOCRACY AS A "Zionist" issue is relatively new. The attempt to create a democratic civic religion in Israel belongs roughly to the last two years. Ever since Kahane's election to the Knesset every child in Israel has been bombarded with talk of "democracy." A prominent Israeli educator tells of visiting a classroom recently. When he asked the children what they would like to discuss, they answered in unison, "Anything but democracy." Kahane has frightened many Israelis, including those who are ideologically close to him. To the Israelis he is aesthetically repulsive, an outsider (although so were a certain Austrian, Georgian, and Corsican in their own time), but Kahane evokes comparisons that are too embarrassing, and in too explicit a manner.

The campaign against Kahanism turned into a campaign for democracy. Many organizations of good-to-medium will mobilized for voluntary work "among the youth." Democracy was given something like a numinous status in civil life. Young jingoists learned that their more blunt opinions have to be camouflaged. But when Kahane declares, "I'm only saying out loud what you are thinking," he is right. Like him, many would like to expel the Arabs. Unlike him, they do not think that football games should be banned on the Sabbath, and they do not want Halakha, the traditional religious law, to be imposed on the country. But they go along with his central creed.

Since the 1967 war the right wing in Israel has been speaking of the "Greater Israel" and the Labor Party of the "demographic problem": the former in the name of the pleasure principle, the latter in the name of the reality principle. The expression "demographic problem" is monstrous, of course. It sounds like a disturbance of ecological equilibrium as a result of an increase in the birthrate of rats. However, that today there are in Greater Israel about sixty thousand non-Jewish births annually, as against about fifty thousand Jewish births, is alarming to the Israelis. (According to the latest report presented to the government by the statistician Professor Bacchi, 43 percent of the population of Greater Israel in the year 2000 will be non-Jews.) The right wing talked for a while about the hope of a mass Jewish immigration from the Soviet Union, and then about an "awakening" among Jews in the West. But they were merely playing for time, not daring to say aloud what they realized was embarrassing to hear, that they wanted the Arabs to be expelled. "First let us settle the West Bank, then we shall see," was their expressed attitude.

Kahane in effect broke the taboo surrounding the right wing's unspoken solution to the so-called demographic problem. Following came Yuval Ne'eman, the leader of the Tehiya ("Renaissance") Party and a well-known professor of physics—a Kahane in evening dress who, at the opening of his party convention, spoke of the "resettlement" of half a million Arabs in the Arab countries surrounding Israel—a local version of the German plan to settle Jews in Madagascar. In view of this version of the expulsion of the Arabs, all the rest of the talk about "tragedy" sounds too melodramatic.

However, there is another interpretation of the "tragedy of Zionism," as Avishai presents it, and I find it even more interesting than the claim that Zionism's tragedy has to do with the failure to found in Israel a liberal democracy roughly in the American style. The Aristotelian scheme for the development of a tragic plot calls for a clear distinction between beginning, middle, and end. This sequence is preserved in Avishai's story of the fall of Labor Zionism from a laborers' society, centered on the Histadrut labor federation, to statism, and finally to the new Zionism of the Greater Israel. Moreover, the Aristotelian requirement that each stage is the necessary consequence of the preceding one is complied with: the new Zionism is a necessary development of the Ben-Gurion statism that preceded it; and the statism derived from the Histadrut society of the early Zionists. Indeed, this three-stage version of the development of Zionism is accepted by the labor movement intelligentsia today, especially as a story of decline and fall.

But there is now a great deal of cloying and idealizing nostalgia toward the Histadrut society. True, it was an impressive society in its emotional power as well as in its achievements. At the same time, however, Histadrut promoted feudal socialism on a broad scale. It was, as Avishai sometimes suggests, a federation of political groups each comprising institutions that could almost entirely encompass the domain of the individual. Schools, newspapers, sport associations, youth movements, settlement movements, social funds, enterprises, everything. Liberalism in the sense of free access to sources of information and to material resources was conspicuously absent. But oppressive ideological collectivism was present in abundance.

The idea of Zionism's tragedy can be justified, in my view, but not as Avishai's book has it. Zionism is a tragedy in the Hegelian sense —that is, in the sense of a collision between two moral forces with powerful but conflicting rights. The position of each of the conflicting parties is in itself justifiable, but the outcome is one of mutual destruction. This is the tragedy of the Zionist movement in its encounter with the Arabs in 1948. In Zionism today the tragedy is one of physical victory alongside severe moral failure.

THE BOOK THAT succeeds in conveying this failure is Meron Benvenisti's *Conflicts and Contradictions*, the ideological autobiography of a reliable and sensitive witness. A wise Irish writer, Sean MacPhiliny, said once that when a person claims that he has a solution to the problem of Northern Ireland this is a sure sign that he has not understood the problem. It seems to me that this, applied to the Israeli case, is Benvenisti's view.

Meron Benvenisti is a high priest—as well as the son of a high priest—in the Zionist rite of *moledet* in the land of Israel. *Moledet* is the Hebrew equivalent of homeland, or *Heimat*, with the connotation of one's having been born there (as in the Russian *rodina*, which seems to have been the source of inspiration for the revived biblical term). The members of the order practicing this rite were members of the youth movements of laboring Israel. An understanding of the youth movements in the Israel of those days is immeasurably more important for an understanding of Zionism than reading the texts of the founding fathers of Zionism—texts which only in the latter-day propaganda war came to have a readership.

The Israeli youth movements drew their inspiration from the *völkisch* movements in Germany and Russia. As the forests were to the German *Volk* culture and the tundras to the Russian *rodina* culture, so the Negev and Judea deserts were to Israeli *moledet* culture. Benvenisti was among the famous hike leaders of the youth movement, the son of a prominent Israel explorer and one of its first Zionist hikers. The hikes in the Negev desert had the quality of exhausting pilgrimages. I remember one such outing from my childhood with Benvenisti the leader, while we dragged after him in the intense desert heat, observing the so-called water discipline that was designed to steel the Sabra.

This homeland rite formed the Sabra, and especially the Sabra myth, more than anything else. The idea was that through those hikes in the country an attachment, not just a bond, to the land would be fostered. (The distinction is this: I have a watch I inherited from my father. It lies in the drawer, unused. I am attached to this object: it is filled with meaning for me. I also have a fountain pen. I am attached to it: it has no particular meaning for me, but I use it constantly, am used to it, and cannot do without it.) A man like Begin, for instance, has a bond to the land of Israel but no attachment to it. He does not know and never knew its landscapes, its colors, its smells. He was always a stranger to these. Even as Defense Minister he never visited the land. Benvenisti has not an abstract, symbolic bond to the land, but a deep and immediate attachment to the concrete entity called the Land of Israel.

The land to which Benvenisti is attached comprises not just the ruins of old synagogues, but Crusader and Mameluke and Ottoman ruins, too. This attachment recognizes the love that others have of the land as well. In Benvenisti's consciousness, perhaps more than in anybody else's, there is room for Palestinians. His empathy for the plight of the Arabs is altogether different from the mechanical enumeration of Israeli atrocities, and also very different from the wish of many doves to distance themselves from Arab life and withdraw to the small, beautiful Israel of yesterday, unspoiled by the Arabs.

When the Al Aqsa mosque was set fire to by an Australian maniac in 1968, Benvenisti, then deputy mayor of Jerusalem, was among the first to arrive on the scene. His first question to the Muslim guard was what had happened to the pulpit, which dated back to the time of Saladin's war against the Crusaders. The answer he received was that it had burned down. Benvenisti writes: "I, a non-Muslim infidel and a hated occupier, stood there with tears in my eyes, overwhelmed with grief." Benvenisti is very much an insider of Israeli life, even when he is a controversial figure to Israeli doves and hawks alike. When he tells us about how he left the kibbutz it sounds like the story of a monk leaving his monastery. It is a story of strong guilt feelings, worlds apart from a story about "fine people but not my own."

A large part of Benvenisti's book is devoted to the period in which he was, as a deputy mayor, responsible for East Jerusalem. During this time he was considered by everyone Teddy Kollek's certain successor as mayor of Jerusalem. It is tantalizing to think what might have happened had Benvenisti really been the heir. (The potential explosive power of two huge egos like Kollek's and Benvenisti's could blow apart more than one city hall, so the succession had no real chance from the start.) Teddy Kollek could be called Jerusalem's Fiorello La Guardia. Jerusalem is a city in which the conflicts and contradictions of Israeli society are probably more amplified and expressive than in any other place. Jews versus Arabs is only one of the conflicts. Twenty-eight percent of the city's population are ultra-Orthodox Jews, some of them fiercely militant, a community that is in open cultural confrontation with the secular community, mainly with the Ashkenazi section of it. This confrontation is violent on the Orthodox side, and full of hatred—anti-Semitic in some of its manifestations—on the secular side. An increasing number of the city's nonreligious educated young people come to see Tel Aviv as their hope for a free life. Tel Aviv's attractiveness is to be found in its "Juniah syndrome"—the hedonistic Christian enclave north of Beirut where eating, drinking, and fornicating go on while Beirut itself is burning.

Another conflict is that between Ashkenazis and Orientals. The Oriental community in Jerusalem traditionally supports the Likud; alone of the Labor leaders, Kollek has attained a majority even in this community. Kollek succeeds in keeping the city in one piece. Benvenisti seemed the only hope of maintaining Kollek's achievements in the city once Kollek retired. True, Kollek's "unified Jerusalem" is illusory in many ways. But still, Kollek makes the difference between Jerusalem and Belfast. After him, so it seems, the deluge.

Benvenisti's book makes a significant contribution to the question of democracy in Israel by radically redefining it. He believes it is a mistake to consider the West Bank a problem of foreign affairs, a matter of territories whose future will be decided in future negotiations, one way or the other, between the obvious claimants. According to Benvenisti, the occupied territories have for a long time been an internal Israeli problem. They are already inseparable from the state of Israel from the point of view of politics, economics, transportation, security, and more. In light of the fact that the occupation is now nineteen years old—exactly the length of time that Israel existed within the Green Line—the territories have to be seen as a permanent attachment to Israel. The Israeli regime, in Benvenisti's view, is not that of a democracy within the Green Line and of a colonial power outside it, but rather that of a *Herren* democracy in the Greater Israel.

This difference has political implications. It means for Benvenisti that Israeli doves have to rid themselves of the illusion that the occupation is temporary and will one day end in a single dramatic act. Since annexation has become a fact, even if it is not yet legally entrenched, the rights of Palestinians in the territories have to be fought for as much as those of Israeli Arabs who live in the Galilee region.

Benvenisti does not err with the facts, but he errs, I believe, with their interpretation. To begin with, the forces working to preserve the status quo of annexation exist within the Green Line, not in the "facts" that have been established over the past nineteen years outside it. These "facts" have, to my mind, a secondary, if not a marginal, importance. I also believe that the forces of annexation are the same ones that will be mobilized for the expulsion of the Arabs, to ensure that under no circumstances will a binational state be formed. In my view it is easier and makes better sense to struggle for the separation of the West Bank and Gaza from Israel than to struggle for liberal democracy for all the inhabitants residing in all areas of the Greater Israel. The importance of Benvenisti's challenge is that it forces the doves to relate themselves to the everyday reality of occupation, not just to an "eschatological" treaty.

Benvenisti does not propose a schematic solution. The power of this book lies in its ability to convey a sense of a living, breathing, suffering reality in the most immediate and concrete terms. It is a book that, in its more intimate sections, is truly moving, and its analytical sections succeed in revealing the deep contradictions in the attitude of Labor Zionism toward the Arabs—contradictions that have wellnigh turned it into a stylistic variant of the Likud.

Benvenisti, like Avishai, writes about the West Bank. All eyes are turned toward the West Bank, none toward Gaza (although Benvenisti recently issued a devastating report on conditions there). The Gaza Strip is a dark place, out of sight, and out of mind. In a nondemagogical description it is the Soweto of Tel Aviv. The reality of life in the strip is terrible: a population that explodes in a relatively small area—from a quarter of a million people in 1967 to half a million today; a veritable rag proletariat, of whom the lucky ones, including young Dickensian children, work in Israel in shocking conditions of exploitation, while the unlucky are left to rot in the degenerating conditions of the camps.

Prime Minister Shimon Peres has been talking lately of "Gaza first"; his hope being to reach a separate agreement with Egypt concerning the strip. The underlying assumption is that while the United States is not pressuring Israel to do anything with the territories of the West Bank, both the United States and Mubarak's Egypt are apprehensive about the future of peace with Egypt. Hence Peres' attempt to work out, with U.S. support, a plan for the autonomy of the Gaza Strip, perhaps under a trusteeship; Egypt, in return, would get increased American aid. The negotiations will be conducted by Peres during his term as Foreign Minister, after he rotates his position with Yitzhak Shamir this month. The treaty, if reached, will then be brought to the government, under the Likud premiership of Shamir. If it is turned down, the government will fall, with the United States backing Peres; if it is ratified, then Peres would take credit for it.

I myself believe that the slogan "Gaza first" is right, since it would help educate the Israeli public to come to terms with the evils of occupation. It is the wrong slogan, however, if it spearheads a drive for a solution to the Gaza problem separate from the larger solution to the problem of the occupied territories. Should Peres try to press now for separating the problem of the strip from that of the West Bank, I fear that he may find himself, like Milton's Samson, "eyeless in Gaza, at the mill with the slaves."

I took the title The Tragedy of Zionism *very seriously, perhaps too seriously. I share with Avishai—the other Avishai—the view that Zionism was a heroic endeavor. With Scott Fitzgerald I share the view: "Show me a hero and I'll write you a tragedy."*

For me the tragedy of Zionism is its so far irreconcilable clash with the Palestinians, which casts a long, dark shadow on Zionism's moral aspirations. It is a tragic conflict because it is easy for anyone with goodwill to see the moral force of the claims on both sides. Yet it is not a moral tie. The moral burden of proof is on Israel, or the embodiment of Zionism. The reason for this is not that moral demands on Jews are higher because they are on a higher moral plane but, rather, the asymmetry between the power held by Israelis and Palestinians. Having so much more power puts an added moral obligation on Israel.

9

THE MYTH OF JERUSALEM

WHEN I WAS A CHILD JERUSALEM WAS MORE LIKE A LARGE VILLAGE than a city. As in a village, there were some village idiots walking about, trailed by groups of giggling children. I particularly remember one madwoman with a gaunt, ashen face, her eyes blazing with anger and fear, who was a relative of the great mathematician Abraham Halevi Frankel. She was called "Kesher Le'echad" (tie of unity) because she preached in a babble of languages for the creation of ties of unity among people. One late afternoon I came home from school and was utterly amazed to find Kesher Le'echad sitting in the kitchen with my mother, drinking tea and eating cake. The scene didn't seem real to me. Prophets don't have tea with cake. Suddenly she got up nervously, muttered something, stood at the door and said, "We must make peace in Jerusalem *schnell, schnell*" (quickly, quickly).

Another village idiot called himself King David. He wore a black beret and had a round childish face and blue eyes expressing great innocence. As the King of Israel, he would grant us, his followers, various sections of Jerusalem. One day he decided to appoint me ruler of Mount Zion. He put his hand on my head and was about to bless me with his strange ceremony of investiture. At my side stood an Arab boy named Faras, who worked for a Greek Orthodox priest in our neighborhood.

"What about me?" asked Faras.

"He's an Arab," said one of the children.

King David thought for a moment, reconsidered, put his hand on both our heads, and appointed the two of us, his Jewish and Arab vassals, joint rulers of Mount Zion.

The question is whether it is possible and necessary to make peace *schnell, schnell* in Jerusalem, with Jews and Arabs as full partners in the ownership and administration of the city, or whether this is a solution only for children and village idiots. Any seasoned bazaar merchant—indeed, any child—will tell you that "the problem of Jerusalem" must be "left for last." Negotiations between Jews and Arabs cannot begin with a discussion about Jerusalem because this would "blow everything up." The problems are so complex that anyone who suggests a solution shows he does not understand the problem.

But I intend to suggest a solution: "Jerusalem must be one city and the capital of two states, Israel and Palestine." In 1973, several months before the Yom Kippur War, three of us, native Jerusalemites, composed a platform for a small leftist party, with the slogan "One city, capital of two states." But this view has never been popular among either Jews or Arabs. All but a small number of the Jews in Israel advocate absolute and exclusive sovereignty over all of Jerusalem. Mainstream Palestinians continue to demand an independent state, with sovereignty over East Jerusalem, which was under Jordanian rule until 1967. How could the suggestion of one city with joint Israeli-Palestinian sovereignty be a solution that is even possible?

In the talks that opened in Madrid in October 1991, Jerusalem is not being discussed. What is being discussed is something that the Israelis call "autonomy" and the Palestinians an "interim phase." But the future of Jerusalem is germane even to a temporary arrangement under which Prime Minister Shamir would grant autonomy and President Bush would promise that future negotiations would go beyond autonomy. But what kind of autonomy? The Likud government offered the Palestinians "autonomy for persons." No one knows just what this means. It is quite clear, however, that it excludes control over land and water in the territories. Israel will maintain full control over both, and therefore Israel will decide when and where to establish new settlements. The Palestinians demand "autonomy over land." This implies, at the least, a freeze both on new settlements and on adding more settlers to existing ones. According to recent public opinion polls, a majority of Israelis are willing to freeze settlements (at least during the negotiations) as long as this does not apply to East Jerusalem. (In a poll of 80,000 people by *Na'amat* and *Yediot Tikshoret*, 71 percent of Israeli citizens said that a freeze on settlements now will promote peace.)

If no distinction is made between the status of Jerusalem and that of the territories, then Shamir will have the option of breaking off negotiations at any moment, knowing that Israeli Jews will support him. He will claim that because of the Palestinians' claims to autonomy, Jews will not be able to purchase apartments in, for example, Ramat Eshkol, a Jewish neighborhood of Jerusalem that is located beyond the 1967 border. This will win him near-total support.

The problem of Jerusalem should therefore be separated from the problem of the rest of the territories. The best way to go about it is to consider Jerusalem one undivided city and to negotiate how sovereignty over it can be defined and shared. It is a solution in the sense that it would be a just settlement of the claims of both sides—and in the sense that if the two sides were somehow eventually able to accept it, then both of them would be able to make peace on the basis of it.

I BEGIN WITH the solution, but what is the problem? The problem of Jerusalem is that it is the object of a harsh, cruel, nationalistic competition between the Jews of Israel and the Palestinian Arabs. For both sides, victory in this competition means acquiring unchallenged sovereignty over the city.

What makes the problem of Jerusalem so complex is that the current nationalistic competition over the city takes place against the background of an ancient, blood-soaked religious competition among Judaism, Christianity, and Islam. To understand the depth of the nationalistic conflict one must grasp the character of the religious one. And the religious competition for Jerusalem, like the nationalistic one, is not only symbolic and metaphysical. Meron Benvenisti, in his haunting book about Jerusalem cemeteries,* writes that the Olympic Games slogan, "Higher, faster, stronger," may be appropriate to Jerusalem. Each side wants to build higher, faster, and more than its opponents. Since 1967, Jewish Jerusalem has been leading the competition, and the record of Teddy Kollek can by now be compared to the great Jerusalem builders—Solomon, Herod, Hadrian, Constantine, Suleiman the Magnificent, and Father Antonine (the Russian priest responsible for constructing Jerusalem's large Russian complex). And while the mosque minarets once rivaled in height the church steeples in the fight for the control of the Jerusalem horizon, today the clear winners are the towers of the Hilton and Sheraton hotels.

Jerusalem has always had more history than geography. King David's city, the real one, was less than twenty acres in size. It's no wonder that the first thing the King saw from his roof was Bathsheba taking a bath. In 1967 the Jerusalem municipality controlled about 10,000 acres, which grew to 27,000 acres after Israel annexed East Jerusalem. Now Ariel Sharon, as Housing Minister, wants to extend the territory of Jerusalem to include the satellite towns Maale Adumim and Betar in the occupied territories, and it is not clear that anyone can stop him.

NO ONE CAN say just why Jerusalem is where it is. The location of ancient cities is generally explained by three conditions: roads, water, and defense. But no important road runs through Jerusalem; it has

---

*Jerusalem: City of the Devil (in Hebrew, Jerusalem, 1990).

very little water, and the ancient city, even though it was built on a ridge, was not situated in a strong defensive position on the hills. It is thought that Jerusalem was founded about four thousand years ago as a city of ritual worship by the Canaanites, a view strengthened by mention in the Bible of King Melchizedek of Salem, the priest of El Elyon, as having been there. When King David captured Jerusalem and established it as his capital perhaps he did so because it had no history of Israelite worship and could be used to establish a new sacred place. In contrast to Hebron and Beth-El, moreover, it did not belong to the territory of any of the Israelite tribes and therefore could serve as a common ground for all of them. Jerusalem also has an extraterritorial status in Jewish law (although there is a controversy about this) and it belongs to all the Israelite tribes. King Solomon built the Temple in Jerusalem and concentrated all the ritual worship there, thus setting Jerusalem at the center of the national and religious consciousness of the Jewish people for all generations to come. The annoying truth about King David and King Solomon in Jerusalem, however, is that although Jerusalem is the most excavated city in the world there is not as yet a clear archaeological trace of these two illustrious kings in it.

After Solomon's death in the tenth century B.C., the kingdom was divided into the northern kingdom of Israel and the southern kingdom of Judea, with Jerusalem as the capital of the latter. In 586 B.C. Nebuchadnezzar destroyed Jerusalem and exiled many of its residents. Sixty years later, under the Persian patronage of King Cyrus, a group of Jews returned from Babylonia to rebuild the Temple and settle in Jerusalem. They built a small temple, a rather poor substitute for the magnificent one erected by Solomon. The period of Persian rule over the city ended in 333 B.C., when Jerusalem came under the rule of Alexander the Great. This marked the beginning of the city's Hellenistic period, during which the Hellenistic ruler Antiochus Epiphanes forbade Jews to worship in the Temple. In 165 B.C. the Temple was "purified" by the Maccabees after a civil war against the Hellenist Jews.

In 63 B.C. Jerusalem entered a period of Roman rule—sometimes direct, sometimes indirect. It was during this period, shortly after

Herod had rebuilt the Temple in Jerusalem as one of the most impressive structures of antiquity, that Jesus was active in the city. In A.D. 66 a Judean revolt against Roman rule broke out, and in 70 the Temple was destroyed and burned by Titus. After the great Judean revolt of 132, the emperor Hadrian conquered the city and razed it, establishing in its place a pagan Roman city called Aelia Capitolina, which Jews were forbidden to enter. In the year 313 Christianity became the state religion in Rome, and Constantine's mother started to build the Holy Sepulcher in the center of Jerusalem, turning the city into a Byzantine Christian city.

In 638 Jerusalem was taken over by a new religion—Islam. The Dome of the Rock was built on the Temple Mount. After five hundred years of exile, Jews were permitted to return and settle in Jerusalem. In 1099 Christians reconquered the city from the Muslims in the Crusade for the "liberation of the holy places." A Muslim counter-crusade in 1187—Saladin's jihad—returned the city to Muslim rule. Jerusalem flourished during the fourteenth and fifteenth centuries when it was ruled by the Mamelukes, the slave kings originally imported into the Middle East from Central Asia.

The Turks conquered Jerusalem in 1517, and its splendid city walls were built by Suleiman the Magnificent. The city remained under Turkish rule for four hundred years, until 1917, when the city was captured by General Allenby, and Jerusalem became part of the British Mandate of Palestine. The British left Palestine in 1948, and in the subsequent war between Jews and Arabs the city was divided in two: the eastern part, including the Old City, was annexed to Jordan, while the western part became the capital of the new state of Israel. In 1967 Israel conquered East Jerusalem and annexed it.

EVEN SO SKETCHY a history shows that Jerusalem, with its changes of rulers and religion, does not belong exclusively to the heritage of any one religion or any one community in the city. To establish its claims, each religion and each nation competing for the city clings to a particular sequence of events in the city's history from the Bronze Age onward and sees it as a guide to their present-day activities, while the history of others becomes for them a black hole from which not even one ray of light can escape.

One principal concept which has both undergone historical transformation and caused divisiveness is that of holiness, which is accompanied by the idea that Jerusalem is a holy city. Different ideas of holiness have given the struggle over Jerusalem its flavor of absolutism—for example, the expression that Jerusalem is Israel's "eternal" capital. The recurrent pattern is a subtle one: each religion and each national ideology started out with deep ambivalence about the city's importance; the attitude of each toward Jerusalem became one of absolute commitment only as a result of rivalry and conflict with others. The religious competition for Jerusalem and, consequently, the nationalist competition as well were sustained by the idea that the city was a holy place for various religions, an idea that requires clarification.

One day, on a school outing, we went to see a model of Jerusalem at the time of the Second Temple, including a model of the Temple itself. This model is located next to a hotel appropriately named the Holyland Hotel. After looking at the model we went down the hill on which the hotel is perched to a valley in which there was an area of high-tension electrical poles surrounded by a high fence with pictures of skulls and crossbones warning against trespassing in the enclosure. Our teacher then explained that this electrical sanctuary works on the same principle as the Temple: it is the source of light and energy for the whole city, but anyone who dares to touch its parts is electrocuted and dies. (Our teacher had apparently been reading Rudolf Otto's *Idea of the Holy*.) The holy city is indeed a place fraught with ambivalence: on the one hand, it contains a divine presence that provides it with an abundance of goodness; on the other hand, the constant danger is that defilement will alienate the divinity and threaten the city with a curse. This ambivalence between goodness and curse, love and fear, and especially purity and defilement, produces the religious tension expressed in the idea of the Temple as a place that is at once blessed and dangerous.

Biblical Jerusalem and the Temple itself were divided into areas of greater and lesser holiness, the degree of holiness reflected in the taboos applying to each. The Temple Mount was holier than the rest of Jerusalem. No one who was ritually defiled could enter it—including persons suffering from venereal discharge, women who had recently given birth or were menstruating. The Temple court is yet holier, and heathens were forbidden to enter it. The outer hall of the Temple was holier still, forbidden to anyone not of the priestly caste. Finally, the Holy of Holies, the inner part of the Temple, could be entered only by the High Priest, and only on Yom Kippur, the Day of Atonement. (There has been much controversy surrounding this system of holiness. The Judean desert sect at Qumran believed that all of Jerusalem was as holy as the Temple Mount, and that it was forbidden, for example, to have sexual relations in the city. They therefore considered the priestly Jerusalem to be a defiled and dangerous city from which it was necessary to flee to the desert.)

The concept of holiness as the exclusion of the defiled had a historical significance: people who were alien were gradually included in the category of the defiled. The presence of an outsider in the city, especially near the Temple, was "anathema" in the literal sense of the word. The author of the Psalms (79:1) says, "O God, heathens have entered Your domain, defiled Your holy temple." The Crusaders who besieged the Muslim-ruled Jerusalem adopted this verse from the Psalms as their battle cry. But the view of the alien as someone who defiles is not only something from the distant past. The British consul in Jerusalem, James Finn, reported to his Foreign Minister in England in 1848, the year of "the springtime of the nations," that a person identified as a Jew had been found in the Latin chapel on Easter. The crowd had been about to lynch him, and only the intervention of the Turkish guards saved him, after a severe beating. Finn then remarked that this incident was similar to what had occurred to a British doctor who had been caught in the Muslims' Noble Sanctuary—he, too, had been severely beaten and rescued only with difficulty. The defiling aliens have not always been rescued, especially not in our century.

While the Temple still stood, the concept of the holy place, whether Jerusalem or the Temple, as the place free of defilement came into conflict with another concept of holiness—the concept of Jerusalem as the place of pilgrimage. The Bible commands Jews to make a pilgrimage on three holidays: Passover, Pentecost, and Tabernacles. Hundreds of thousands of people used to come to Jerusalem on these occasions. Josephus Flavius writes about nearly three million pilgrims on one Passover. Even if we remove one zero, the number remains impressive. The vast Temple court in fact had enough room for three hundred thousand worshippers.

Among the pilgrims in the period before the Temple was destroyed were many who came from different foreign countries with different languages. Only thus can we understand the miracle of "speaking in tongues" which occurred on the famous Pentecost described in Acts 2. At any rate, the Temple priests accepted sacrifices as well as other presents from Gentiles, even though there were some sages— perhaps influenced by the Judean desert sect—who demanded that such sacrifices not be allowed. With such a large number of visitors, it was very difficult to make sure of everyone's purity.

Amos Elon, in his wonderful *Jerusalem: City of Mirrors* (1989), summarizes his description of the pilgrimages from all parts of the world by calling Jerusalem "a cosmopolitan city." But Jerusalem, as my friend the philosopher Sidney Morgenbesser once put it, is at the same time the most international and the least cosmopolitan city in the world. People from many different nations have always lived in Jerusalem, and in this sense it has an international flavor; but to be cosmopolitan requires that a stranger's presence should not only be tolerable but natural and welcome, and in this sense Jerusalem is not cosmopolitan in the least but sectarian in the extreme—and with a large number of sects. These sects live side by side, not together. They are each shut up in their own quarters and courtyards, sometimes behind walls and locked gates.

Jerusalem as a holy city of pilgrimages is common to all three religions, but one sense of pilgrimage is mainly the heritage of Jews and Muslims—the sense of going to Jerusalem in order to be buried there in the belief that when the dead are resurrected those buried in Jerusalem will be resurrected first. This idea is conceived so literally that grave plots on the Mount of Olives (where Robert Maxwell was recently buried) that are nearer to the Golden Gate, through which the Messiah is expected to pass, are more expensive than those further away. The nearer one is to the gate, the closer one will be to the head of the line at the time of the resurrection. At any rate, Jerusalem is surrounded by a huge necropolis, and the dead can't be ignored in any vote about Jerusalem's future.

The war between Islam and Christianity at the time of the Crusades defined Jerusalem as a holy city whose conquerors could claim that their own religion was chosen by God. At first glance it seems as though the holiness of Jerusalem for Christianity is obvious. The Christian drama of part of Jesus' life and, above all, his death and resurrection, took place in Jerusalem. The "holy archaeology" of the Byzantines also guaranteed that every biblical event has a place in the city attached to it. In holy archaeology, there are no misses. One digs and one finds. Constantine's mother, Helena, found Golgotha and the holy cross and built the Church of the Holy Sepulcher there.

However, during the Byzantine period Christians spoke more of holy places than of a holy city. The idea of the Holy Land, and to some degree of the holy city as well, came from the Crusaders. The difficulty for "learned" Christianity (as opposed to folk Christianity attached to holy relics) is the Pauline doctrine that sees the earthly Jerusalem as a Jewish Jerusalem, a Jerusalem bound to the Law ("the bondsmaid Hagar"), as opposed to the heavenly Jerusalem, a Jerusalem freed from the Law ("the lady Sarah"). This approach, based on Jesus' prophecy that no stone structure will remain whole in Jerusalem, as well as on the establishment of the Church in Rome, cast doubt on the status of Jerusalem, but the triumph of the Crusaders relieved Christianity of its ambivalence toward Jerusalem. Spirituality can be a matter of geography. When one is within reach of the earthly Jerusalem, its value rises; when one is far away from it, the heavenly Jerusalem gains more importance. The Crusaders saw themselves as vassals coming to liberate the domain of their Lord, Jesus; and with respect to Judaism, they presented themselves as the spiritual and therefore the true Israel—that is, as the legitimate heirs to Jerusalem.

Muslims, too, were ambivalent about Jerusalem's holiness, for they saw the city as a possible rival for the holy status of Mecca and Medina. According to the Koran the people who first became Muslims prayed toward Jerusalem; but the prophet tested his followers and demanded that they pray toward Mecca. The ideological basis of Jerusalem's holiness for Islam is found in the traditional interpretation of the account (in Sura 17) of the night journey of God's servant from the sanctified mosque to the mosque at what was called "the remote end." This interpretation identified God's servant with Muhammad, who went from the Kaaba in Mecca to Jerusalem. The Muslim tradition also sees Jerusalem as the place to which Muhammad went on his wondrous horse Burak. It seems that this interpretation is based on the Talmudic tale (Sanhedrin 98) about the horse ("Susia Burka") which the King of Persia offers for the Messiah to ride. That is, the night journey to the Temple Mount is the journey of the successor religion (Islam succeeding Judaism and Christianity), where Muhammad is the rider of the Messiah's horse, which is contrasted with the donkey of Jesus, the poor Messiah.

At any rate, Saladin's counter-crusade, his holy war, or jihad, to liberate Jerusalem, required a great deal of propaganda on behalf of Jerusalem. The old ambivalence was suppressed, and Saladin—not unlike Yitzhak Shamir—wrote to Richard Lion-Heart, "Let the King not imagine that such a concession [handing over the city to the Crusaders] is possible." (Forty years after that letter was written the Muslim governor in fact handed the city over to the Crusaders.)

Jerusalem also served as a holy city for Islam in its claim to be the successor of Judaism and the rival of Christianity. Jerusalem was an important city for religious studies and contained large seminaries—it was a holy city in the sense that Qum is a holy city for the Shiites in Iran. Jerusalem was also a city that attracted many mystics, "holy men," apparently under the influence of the Christian monks who lived in and around it. They saw Jerusalem as a place for the purification of the soul and, above all, as the city of the resurrection.

This picture of the three religions wrestling over God's little acre in Jerusalem obscures the infighting that goes on within the various sects of each religion. Jerusalem is the scene of a huge Monopoly game played not only in church courtyards, monastery towers, and grave plots but also in the "holiest places," where a struggle goes on over each floor tile, each column, each window. A visitor in the nineteenth century observed that each Christian pilgrim sees the pilgrims from countries other than his own as heretics and scoundrels who have left the true God and betrayed the true church; Muslims and Jews were at least brought up in ignorance, while the rival contesting Christians are liars, since they were brought up on the true Bible. Anyone who has seen riots among the people wearing black robes in the Church of the Holy Sepulcher, as I once did, realizes that the situation has not improved since the nineteenth century. Once the mediator between monks and nuns was the sultan's representative; now it is Mayor Teddy Kollek. An old Arab proverb says that no people are more corrupt than the residents of holy cities; certainly no people are more fanatic.

The Turkish regime in Jerusalem must be credited with the construction of the city's magnificent walls, but during the Turkish period Jerusalem became a degenerate and dirty provincial town. When Napoleon fought the Turks in Palestine he besieged Acre—then an important naval city—and did not bother to go to Jerusalem. The desire to clean up the city seized many Protestant visitors in the nineteenth century, and Theodor Herzl, the visionary of Zionism, wrote in his diary, "If one day Jerusalem will be ours, then the first thing we must do is clean the city of its filth." Teddy Kollek, who was born in Vienna, Herzl's city, can be seen as the Jewish broom Herzl envisioned.

At the end of the Ottoman Turkish period—during the nineteenth and early twentieth centuries—a new, imperial competition for Jerusalem took place. Although it was ruled by a Turkish pasha who often acted arbitrarily toward its residents (the pasha Abdullah forced Christian women to wear only black and Jewish women to wear only red), the city nevertheless reverted to the political arrangement that had begun in the sixteenth century but became more important than ever when the Ottoman Empire was crumbling. Special privileges— "capitulations"—were granted to the residents who were citizens of the great powers, exempting them from the jurisdiction of the Ottoman Empire and placing them under the authority of the consuls of their own powers. Citizens with capitulations had a personal status comparable to diplomatic immunity today. The foreign consuls of Russia, France, England, Prussia, and Italy were, in effect, local governors. Jews who were citizens of any of these countries were granted capitulations when they came to Jerusalem, and, as a result, their numbers in the city began to increase. By the middle of the nineteenth century they had become a majority. At the same time the European powers competed with one another to build up the sites of the holy places as well as to construct hospitals and hostels for pilgrims. This was the first period in which there was an active, energetic Protestant presence in the city.

Though the Ottoman Empire contributed very little to the city's physical development, its political conceptions have had a far-reaching effect on the Middle East in general and particularly on today's Israel and Jerusalem. The Ottomans conceived of society as composed of religious or ethnic communities rather than individuals. Among these communities, in the Ottoman view, there is one reigning community, and the government exists mainly for its sake; the other communities have the status of minorities. For the Israelis of today as well as the Ottomans of the past, it is very important to show, through acts of government, who is the ruling community and who is the government. If, for example, in present-day Israel Druses and Circassians, unlike Israeli Arabs, serve in the army, then they deserve more rights than Arabs, because they are loyal to the state. The government allows the minorities broad legal autonomy in matters of personal law: marriages are thought to take place within a community rather than between communities, and intermarriages have no legal status. In general the Israeli government, like the Ottomans in the past, does little to interfere in religious matters, which are very important to these smaller communities.

At the same time, members of minority communities are, in a serious sense, second-class citizens, and their status is derived from their communities' secondary, if not marginal, status. In most of the West the notion has taken hold that the state defines one's nationality and that, whatever religious or ethnic community a person might belong to, he is nevertheless, for example, an American or a Canadian citizen. That political conception is not accepted in the Middle East, including Israel. There the state belongs to the nation that makes up the ruling majority. What is so confusing about Israel is that on the one hand the rhetoric used by its leaders is the American-style rhetoric used in Western countries, while on the other hand the dominant Israeli views about rights of minorities, majorities, religion, state, and government are mainly Ottoman. The British Mandate, which replaced the Turkish regime after World War I, did not change the basic Ottoman conception.

The prevailing Israeli view concerning Jerusalem is still essentially Ottoman. Of the 504,000 residents of Jerusalem (1988 figures), 361,000 are Jews, part of the nation that rules Jerusalem. The rest of the residents—173,000—are non-Jews, and they are divided into communities, mainly according to their religion. The communities are tolerated, or not tolerated, according to the Israeli government's judgment of the degree of threat that they pose.

THE NATIONAL MOVEMENT of the Jewish people—Zionism—displayed from the outset a deeply ambivalent attitude toward Jerusalem. On the one hand, the movement's name is derived from the word "Zion," which was originally the name of a fortress (and range of hills) in Jerusalem. From this it became an alternative name for Jerusalem as a whole and even for the whole Land of Israel. Zionism also took from the holy geography of Judaism the notion that Jerusalem is the highest of all places. Thus immigration to Israel is *aliyah* (literally, ascending), while emigration from it is *yerida* (literally, descending). The movement translated into political action the yearnings of generations of Jews for Jerusalem which were expressed in the prayers and customs mourning Jerusalem's destruction.

On the other hand, Zionism had ambitions to create a new Jewish society that would be wholly different from Jewish life in the Diaspora. But Jerusalem was the least appropriate place for the founding of such a new society. Not only was it full of aliens, but it was inhabited by the "old Jewish Yishuv," or settlement, whose members were in an even deeper state of exile than the Jews in the Diaspora which the Zionists had left. Most of the Jerusalem Jews were part of an ultra-Orthodox community of the sort that Zionists were rebelling against—a community that lived on donations and did not have the kind of productive life that the Zionist revolution aspired to. There was thus a tension between the desire to return to the nation's historic capital and the need for a tabula rasa, a clean slate. It is no wonder, then, that the Zionists preferred to build the new Hebrew city in the golden sands of Tel Aviv.

In Jerusalem itself a compromise solution was found between the tabula rasa and the historic homeland: the pioneers settled just outside the historic city and built a new Jerusalem there, including the first Jewish university—the Hebrew University. The Zionist leaders of Palestine continued to swear by the name of Jerusalem, but they did not live there, and used it only for their official activities. Most of the immigrants to Israel, about 80 percent, settled along the Mediterranean coast, a region that had never been the historic homeland of the Jewish people. Even the Zionists' speeches about the land of our "forefathers" were not to be taken literally. The early pioneers, particularly the second President of the state of Israel, Itzhak Ben-Zvi, were still capable of considering the Arabs living in Palestine as descendants of the Jews who had lived there during the period of the Second Temple, beginning around the fifth century B.C.

This belief was not merely a romantic fantasy. The claim that a Palestinian Arab descended from the early Jews—say, one living in Anta, which is perhaps the Anatot where the prophet Jeremiah lived—is no less probable than that of, say, Menachem Begin or Golda Meir. In the popular and ahistoric version of Jewish history, the destruction of the Second Temple is linked with the exile from the land. But a considerable part, perhaps even a majority, of the Jewish people already lived in the Diaspora before the Temple was destroyed, and after it was destroyed the size of this Diaspora did not increase very greatly. Most of the Jews who survived the Romans' destruction of the country remained in Palestine. It is not particularly far-fetched to conjecture that they were the ancestors of those inhabitants who accepted Islam many generations later.

Israel's astounding victory in the Six-Day War created a sense of triumphalist history among the Jews in Israel and in the Diaspora. History, after many centuries, seemed "on our side," and many nonbelievers saw the liberation of Jerusalem as a "sign from Heaven."

This feeling brought to prominence fundamentalist Zionism, a branch of Zionism that is interested in the ancestral homeland but has very little interest in the creation of a new society. Zionism for fundamentalists has become extremely literal; its followers are no longer content to dwell next to the ancestral city but insist on dwelling within it; they insist on living in the Old City, in the very heart of the Arab quarter.

Zionist leaders of the Jewish community at the time of the British Mandate preferred to live in Tel Aviv rather than in Jerusalem; all but a few of their rival leaders in the Palestinian movement lived in Jerusalem. This fact, too, affects what is happening today. One recurring obstacle to negotiations between Israel and the Palestinians has been Israel's demand that the Jordanian-Palestinian delegation to any peace conference should not include Arab representatives from East Jerusalem. The Shamir government claims that all of Jerusalem is part of the state of Israel and that allowing Palestinians from Jerusalem to take part will undermine the legitimacy of Israel's annexation of the eastern part of the city. Israel has long claimed that residents of East Jerusalem are Jordanian citizens tolerated by Israel; now it is not willing to accept them even in a Jordanian delegation to the conference.

Israel's argument against the participation of East Jerusalem representatives is a matter of principle, but it is also an attempt to prevent Faisal Husseini, the leader who represents the mainstream of the PLO on the West Bank, from taking part in talks. Husseini is the scion of a family whose members have been Arab leaders since the middle of the seventeenth century. His great-grandfather, Salim Effendi, was mayor of Jerusalem under the Turkish regime, while his grandfather, Musa Kazim, was its mayor under the British Mandate. While Musa Kazim was mayor, the members of the great Jerusalem families became the Arab spokesmen for all of Palestine.

The great Jerusalem families take pride in descending from the family of the Prophet, but in fact they became rich and politically strong mainly under the Turkish regime in the nineteenth century. Some of them acquired both their riches and their power from being tax collectors and officials throughout the Ottoman Empire. Husseini's grandfather was one of the first to state the Arab position against the Zionist settlement of Palestine, but he was willing to speak to the Zionists, and all the more so to the British. The radicals in the Husseini family were Kazim's cousin, the notorious Grand Mufti of Jerusalem, and Kazim's son—Faisal's father—Abd el-Kader el-Husseini. The Grand Mufti, Haj Amin el-Husseini, was mainly responsible for changing the Palestinian position from one that relied on the British for help in opposing the Jewish community to one relying on Hitler's Germany.

This turn toward Nazi Germany was a fateful political and moral mistake for the Palestinians, and Arafat's recent support for Saddam Hussein reminds one of it. But other nationalist movements turned to Hitler in the hope that he would secure them national independence. A faction of the Jewish underground, one of whose commanders was Yitzhak Shamir, tried, at the beginning of the war, to make a deal in which Jews would acquire a state, which would then support Germany. However, Shamir's underground group was on the fringe of the Jewish community, and the Nazis were not interested in it. The Mufti, on the other hand, was the dominant Palestinian leader, and the Nazis were very interested in making a deal with him.

Faisal Husseini's father, Abd el-Kader el-Husseini, was the greatly admired commander of the armed Palestinian Arabs, apparently the only leader capable of organizing their war effort in 1948. He was killed in a battle on the road to Jerusalem in April of that year, and his death was an important factor in the disintegration of the Palestinian military opposition. Faisal Husseini inherited his grandfather's politics—combining antagonism to Zionists with attempts to speak to the Americans (heirs to the British in the region) and to the Israelis. Other members of the great Jerusalem families lost some of their standing among the Palestinian public; and some of the Hebron families who moved to Jerusalem during the twentieth century have become more important to the economic life of the city. But Faisal Husseini, as the son of a national hero and the member of a family strongly identified with Jerusalem, is a symbol no less important in Shamir's eyes than in the eyes of the Palestinians. And Shamir, in addition to his fear of speaking to the Palestinians at all, does not want any Palestinian at the negotiating table who symbolizes Jerusalem.

Still, while Husseini was not at the negotiating table at the Madrid talks, he is a member of the PLO-sponsored committee advising the Palestinian negotiators, who respect him as a natural leader of Palestinians now under Israeli occupation. If they do discuss Jerusalem, what specifically will they be talking about?

One solution, which is little discussed, but is actually being carried out, is that of Ariel Sharon. He wants to push the Arabs out of Jerusalem by taking over buildings and land, mainly in the Muslim quarter (where Sharon himself has moved) and in the area near the Mount of Olives. Such a policy has paradoxically become easier to put into effect since the *intifada*. After the misfortune that befell the Palestinians when they abandoned their villages in 1948 and became refugees, they adopted a strategy of clinging to their land (*sumud*), which involved a considerable degree of collaboration with the Israeli government, a government that has often been willing to buy a degree of calm at the price of leaving things more or less as they are. The *intifada* is partly a revolt against any sort of collaboration with the Israeli government.* This leads to a weakening of the Palestinians' ability to hold on to their land, since they cannot, for example, get building permits or work permits and in general are less able to pull strings with Israeli authorities.

Another solution is Teddy Kollek's "Ottoman" solution, which Israel can be expected to put forward in any negotiations about Jerusalem, if they ever take place. All of Jerusalem would remain under absolute Israeli sovereignty. The municipality and the central government would guarantee to provide services to all parts of the city, Jewish and non-Jewish, without discriminating against the Arabs. Non-Jewish residents would be given broad autonomy in cultural and religious affairs, and perhaps even a special status in the places holy

---

*Useful information and analysis on how this collaboration worked in Jerusalem can be found in Michael Romann and Alex Weingrod, *Living Together Separately* (Princeton, N.J., 1991). Of special interest is the account of how Arab headmen acted as mediators between the city's Arab population and the political and municipal authorities.

to Islam. Israel would guarantee that their life in the Arab parts of the city would go on undisturbed.

As for Palestinians who follow the main political tendency represented by Husseini, they will demand a return to the 1967 borders, even in Jerusalem, with the parts of the city that were under Jordanian control on June 4, 1967, returned to Arab hands. This means that East Jerusalem would be under Palestinian sovereignty. Some Palestinians, of course, reject any division of sovereignty over Jerusalem, and some reject any division of sovereignty over Palestine as a whole, while a good many reject any negotiations with the Israelis. But among Palestinians who have a plausible claim to representing the majority, some seem willing to accept the idea of one city within which there is a divided sovereignty.

Finally, there is the solution that I am advocating—joint sovereignty over Jerusalem, with Jerusalem remaining one city that is the home of two capitals, that of Israel and that of Palestine. The apparent simplicity of this formulation clearly contains hidden dangers, but it seems to me workable. As far as I know, it has no precedent, however. There are cities with a special territorial status, such as the Vatican, and in modern history there have been free cities such as Danzig; but no city I know of has had joint sovereignty.

What sort of legal system would the city have? Let's say two robbers, one Israeli and one Palestinian, are caught breaking into a local bank in Jerusalem. Would they be brought before the same or different judges, and would the same law be applied to each of them? To whom could they bring their appeal and who could pardon them?

Such questions suggest that the solution of one city with divided sovereignty is much simpler than the notion of one city with joint sovereignty. Under divided sovereignty, if the bank robbery took place on the Israeli side of the city then both suspects would be tried according to Israeli law; if on the Palestinian side, they would both be tried under Palestinian law. For municipal matters, on the other hand, there would be a joint city council, and the city's administrative laws would be those drawn up and accepted by this council. Why not accept the simple solution of divided sovereignty over the city rather than the complex solution of joint sovereignty?

Joint sovereignty is preferable, however, because it provides the strongest guarantee that the city will not once more be divided. In the case of divided sovereignty a conflict in the city is more likely to deteriorate into the city's physical separation into two parts, much as Berlin was divided. An agreement on joint sovereignty would explicitly exclude such redivision. It is well to remember, moreover, that in East Jerusalem—the part which was under Arab sovereignty until 1967—there are now 120,000 Jews, who will not accept Palestinian sovereignty and a Palestinian legal system. Even an Israeli government willing to freeze settlements and discourage further settlements on the West Bank would not force them out.*

What of the inevitable conflict between different legal systems that would arise under joint sovereignty? A breach of contract between two people belonging to two different legal systems (say, British and French) poses the problem of who should try the case and according to which law. This is a relatively simple matter, and international contracts usually include paragraphs determining what should be done in such cases. The problems that might arise with respect to conflicts of law in a Jerusalem under joint sovereignty are obviously extremely complicated, but they do not seem to be beyond solution. For example, one should distinguish between the question of which court would try offenders in Jerusalem and the question of which legal system would be used for the trial. It is entirely possible that the same court with the same judges could try cases using different legal systems when appropriate.

Judges from the British House of Lords under the Empire served as the supreme court of appeals for the crimes committed, say, in

*In their thoughtful new book *No Trumpets, No Drums* (New York, 1992), Mark Heller and Sari Nusseibeh put forward a proposal for Jerusalem's future that is similar to the one I advocate here. The one matter on which we differ might turn out to be crucial, however. They too envisage Jerusalem as one city with a municipal government elected jointly by Jews and Arabs. But they also envisage it demarcated by "imaginary sovereignty lines." They speak of "Israel's" Jerusalem and "Palestine's" Jerusalem. By imaginary lines they presumably mean boundaries that would have no effect on the city's daily life; but to have sovereignty lines, even imaginary ones, means that each party can in principle impose its will in times of tension, and thus turn imaginary lines into solid walls. Imaginary sovereignty lines could be used as exit lines. My suggestion of shared sovereignty is intended to block that exit.

Australia or Palestine. As such they were required to consider each case according to the laws prevailing in each of the countries of the Empire. The flexibility of the House of Lords depended on affinities among the legal systems prevailing throughout the Empire. In Jerusalem as well, the possibility of settling difficulties would depend in part on the affinities between the Israeli and the Palestinian legal systems.

The problem of the conflict of law might be eased if each resident were to be tried according to his or her personal status within the system he or she belongs to. The idea of personal status would continue with respect to marital law among Israel and its neighbors as an inheritance from the Turkish Empire. An Israeli Muslim would be tried in matters of marriage and divorce in a Muslim court according to Muslim law, while a religious Jew would be tried by a rabbinical court according to Jewish law. This idea of personal status could be adapted for the residents of Jerusalem, although I would hope that it would not be applied along the lines of the religious communities, as is now the case in Israel.

It is very likely that a solution of the sort I am suggesting would require, in the last analysis, granting Jerusalem special status, so that it would have its own laws, which would be agreed upon by the parliaments of the two states and would be part of the laws of each one of them. But far more difficult to solve than such legal problems are the political and psychological ones. How can you expect, I am asked, that after all the intense hatred, suspicion, and rivalry that has existed between Jews and Arabs in Jerusalem, they will be able to live within a political system that requires such complex cooperation? One step that might make this cooperation easier is the old idea of governing the city by boroughs. Each borough would be largely autonomous in determining its character and its leaders. This would protect the national and religious communities in the city. Such an arrangement could be important for the Christian communities and the ultra-Orthodox Jewish communities as well as for the Muslim Arabs. Thus the solution I suggest for Jerusalem is built upon legitimate separation no less than general cooperation under joint sovereignty.

The psychological problem is how to turn the burning hatred of today into "Platonic hatred"—that is, into an idea of hatred emptied of its emotion. The principle that should be kept in mind is that political steps must lead to psychological reconciliation, rather than vice versa. When, as a result of the Madrid conference, the stone-throwing youth of the *intifada* felt there was some political hope, they approached Israeli soldiers and offered them olive branches of peace. If political negotiations had been delayed until such a gesture had been made, they might never have taken place.

The Jerusalem of today, under Israeli rule, is practically speaking a divided city. Since the *intifada* began, the city has been divided by boundaries of fear. Jews simply do not enter some districts and Arabs are wary about entering others. Joint sovereignty might be able truly to unite Jerusalem for the first time. The removal of the boundaries of fear is a condition for the real unification of the city.

I am a Jerusalemite. I grew up in Jerusalem, and the city has grown on me. Most Israelis have a strong symbolic bond to Jerusalem, but very few have a concrete attachment to the place. Many Israelis, in fact, cannot bear the "earthly Jerusalem," which I love. They stay away from the city. Indeed, some parents will do their utmost not to allow their children to go on a one-day school trip to Jerusalem if they can help it. They see Jerusalem as a kind of Belfast.

I have a symbolic bond to Jerusalem, too—that is, to the section of the city that has "symbolic and historic significance." But that part of Jerusalem constitutes less than 1 percent of the total municipal area. The Jews' symbolic bond to Jerusalem is constantly exploited to sanction Israel's unilateral annexation of parts of the West Bank under the magical name "Jerusalem." In Israeli rhetoric, Jerusalem has the divine attributes of being one, indivisible, and eternal. This is a cynical ploy to allow the city an ever-expanding universe. In 1993, for example— two years after I wrote my essay—Jerusalem grew from 108,000 to 123,000 dunams (4 dunams = 1 acre), and that was not the end.

What is on the minds of many Jews in Jerusalem and elsewhere nowadays is not the conflict between Jews and Arabs over the city, but the fear that the ultra-Orthodox community will "take over" Jerusalem.

They already account for 57 percent of the city's nursery school children. Informed guesses—and secularist fears—suggest that the ultra-Orthodox community will double itself by the year 2010 and will reach 38 percent of the total Jewish population of Jerusalem (26 percent of the total general population). This fear, which is not free of anti-Semitic undertones, is genuine and strong, and will cause many Jews to leave Jerusalem.

Most Jews tend to forget, however, that by the year 2010 the Arab community in Jerusalem will also have grown considerably. Estimates are that it will constitute 31 percent of the city's total population. And the Arabs want a political solution to their plight, not merely a "municipal" solution. So I stick to my guns, and I continue to maintain that the best solution to the complexity of this promised-punished city is to make it one, the capital of two states.

But this is a solution not easily agreed on. The initial publication of this essay prompted a response from the mayor of Jerusalem at the time, Teddy Kollek, who wrote as follows:

> *Avishai Margalit is a Jerusalemite I hold in high regard. I enjoyed reading his concise and elegant history of this city, which he so rightly says has "more history than geography." However, I strongly disagree with his conclusions.*
>
> *Before discussing that, however, I must comment that, in the age of television with its attendant erosion of historical memory, I am not comfortable if someone merely says, "In 1967 Israel conquered East Jerusalem. . . ." Twenty-five years later, I feel it is important to state that this was the result not of a war of Israel's choosing but of a war of aggression initiated by all our Arab neighbors that, had our enemies had their way, would have been a war of extermination. Let me add that though I am in favor of territorial compromise, I protest the assumption hidden behind much Arab argumentation that there need be no penalty for attacking Israel repeatedly.*
>
> *I agree wholeheartedly with Professor Margalit that Jerusalem must remain one undivided city, and I believe this is the true desire of virtually all Jerusalemites, no matter what their persuasion.*

Like Professor Margalit, I also feel that the currently touted Palestinian proposal for divided sovereignty is, despite the intention of most of its supporters, a recipe for redividing the city. I have thus argued since the idea of divided sovereignty was first put to me by the late President Sadat during his historic visit to Jerusalem.

Unfortunately, I find Margalit's proposal, joint sovereignty, to be no less dangerous. City government, especially in a heterogeneous city like Jerusalem, is a political system that must balance an endless array of competing claims, put forth by history and geography no less than by culture at every level, by progress, by the course of events in the world at large, and by the desires and actions of groups and individuals. Margalit's concept of joint sovereignty hatches an unworkable system, where even the smallest matters would require complex adjudication and where decision making and spontaneous acts of leadership could be interfered with endlessly. The examples, criminal and personal legal issues, which he frankly presents as being intricate and complex are still easier to regulate a priori than mundane and crucial municipal issues. Municipal government must be able to be flexible and responsive to a host of questions like town planning and provision of services, not to mention unexpected problems or issues imposed by national policy like taxation, customs, immigration, and the like.

Professor Margalit suggests returning to "the old idea of governing the city by boroughs." In fact, an evolution of this idea is already in place in eleven neighborhoods in Jerusalem, eight Jewish and three Arab. As budget and local willingness permit, I would be happy to see this program of neighborhood administration councils cover the whole city. The idea is to devolve a considerable amount of municipal power to smaller and more homogenous units, to involve people in decision making for their immediate surroundings and to teach them that democracy is not just going to the polls every four or five years, but also the give-and-take of identifying and resolving problems and goals.

One point must be added to the summary of my "Ottoman solution" for Jerusalem's governance: Palestinian citizens of Jerusalem—though they are good taxpayers and were voting in in-

creasing numbers in municipal elections until the last round (held February 1989, when the intifada was a year old) and though many hold responsible jobs as municipal employees—have never been willing to serve on the City Council—that is, fully to join the political game. When, for the first time, before the last elections, a leading Palestinian announced his candidacy, the Arab response was the firebombing of his family's two cars, with no public condemnation of the violence by his community. He got the message and withdrew. It is my expectation that once there is an overall settlement, one that I believe must leave Jerusalem under Israel's sole sovereignty, the Palestinians here will realize that there is no longer any point in fighting for turf. Then, it is my hope, they will rise to the challenge I have offered them for twenty-five years and organize themselves as an effective political lobby, electing representatives to fight for the rights of their constituents. The Palestinians would thus have a say in all matters that affect their lives as residents of Jerusalem. Democracy is a game that works well for the people who play.

It is no secret that I find much to criticize in my government's policies in Jerusalem and elsewhere. And yet, all our faults are not to be compared to the viciousness of Arab internal terrorism, the terrorism they have directed against Jews and others, and the unabated aggression of the Arab states. Therefore, I reject and consider absolutely immoral the current tendency to give equal weight to Jewish and Arab political claims in Jerusalem and greater censure to bad behavior on the part of Jews. The world has no right to this leveling, just as biased criticism from without does not excuse us from honest evaluation of our own behavior.

Returning to Professor Margalit, I don't know of any philosopher who is a mayor nor any mayor who is a philosopher. There are good reasons for that.

I replied to the mayor, as follows:

The mayor of my city, in his response to my essay on Jerusalem, ends with the punch line: "I don't know of any philosopher who is *a mayor nor any mayor who is a philosopher. There are good reasons for that."*

The philosopher Michel de Montaigne served very successfully in a position equivalent to mayor of Bordeaux from 1581 to 1585. There were good reasons then for appointing a philosopher as mayor: war, danger of plague, and a severe outbreak of religious fanaticism. When such things happen, conventional wisdom doesn't work; something else must be tried.

In 1714 another great philosopher, Montesquieu, was appointed to a position equivalent to deputy president of the Bordeaux City Council. Montesquieu ran on a platform declaring: "If I knew something that could serve my nation better but would ruin another, I would not propose it to my prince, for I am first a human being and only then a Frenchman." I'm sure Mr. Kollek would not disqualify this position just because it came from a philosopher and is therefore not "practical."

Perhaps all Mr. Kollek wanted to say in his punch line was that I wouldn't be a suitable mayor of Jerusalem. If so, he's right. Yet it would be equally right to say that I can't be compared with Montaigne or Montesquieu. So perhaps there's still a place for a good philosopher to be mayor of Jerusalem.

Mayor Kollek brings two arguments against my suggestion for joint Israeli-Palestinian sovereignty over Jerusalem—one moral, one practical. The moral argument seems to be that Israeli Jews have the exclusive right to Jerusalem because the Arabs attacked Israel in 1967 and could have destroyed it, therefore must pay for their aggression. Mr. Kollek adds that the Arabs' "political claims in Jerusalem" must be judged with respect to the fact that their terror is more despicable than anything Israel has done to them. The practical argument is that joint sovereignty simply won't work.

Mr. Kollek's moral principle is the punitive one that guided the authors of the Treaty of Versailles. A very high price in human lives was paid in our century for that principle. To the best of my knowledge, Mr. Kollek has been an ardent supporter of Israel's peace treaty with Egypt, whose actions led to the war. Yet this treaty was possible only because the Versailles principle was not applied and Egypt got all its territory back.

I fought in Jerusalem in that June of 1967, and I, too, was shelled by the Jordanian Legion. Yet I don't recall any Palestinians fighting us—only the Jordanian Army. The Palestinians were, at most, cheerleaders. If Mr. Kollek must have someone pay the price of sovereignty, let him send the bill to King Hussein.

But Mr. Kollek can relax. The Palestinians have paid in very hard currency for that war. Who knows better than he that 150,000 Jews (the number is his own) have been settled on the other side of the Green Line, on Palestinian land? Mr. Kollek can also breathe easy about the balance of terror between us and the Palestinians. We are doing pretty well. We have, in fact, killed many times more of them than they have of us (or of themselves). And this is without counting the thousands of Palestinians sitting in our detention camps without trial, those whose houses have been blown up, those who have been exiled, and those who are tortured while under arrest. In the balance of terror the Palestinians are clearly on the lighter side of the scales. Indeed, Mayor Kollek ought to be careful with the principle that terror should be paid for with sovereignty. He's liable to lose a lot of sovereignty over that principle.

Now for the practical argument. Mr. Kollek presents matters as if we are faced for the first time with three options, and he as an experienced mayor is telling us that only one of these options works. The options are: (1) full Israeli sovereignty, including coexistence with the Arab residents, who are supposed to accept our sovereignty; (2) divided sovereignty; (3) (my suggestion) joint sovereignty. There is, of course, a fourth option, which seems to have become one preferred by the Israeli government: full Israeli sovereignty without any Arabs in the city.

Mr. Kollek forgets to mention that the only option that has been tried so far is his own. It has been tried for more than twenty years, with an enlightened mayor full of goodwill. And it has failed disastrously. The Arabs have not made peace with the Israeli sovereignty that was declared immediately after the 1967 war. And after twenty years of Mayor Kollek's regime they rebelled. Every Israeli government has supported Mr. Kollek, including the Likud government (which never, in a city with a clear majority of Likud voters, ran a substantial rival against him for the mayoralty). Every mayor has complaints against the central government, including Mr. Kollek. But he has been given the opportunity to carry out his option, and it has failed. Not because Mr. Kollek isn't a good mayor—he's the best—but because his option doesn't work.

Mayor Kollek doesn't tell us exactly what would be hard about running a city under joint sovereignty. He just makes the general statement that running a city is a very difficult and complicated matter, involving "town planning and provision of services." I believe him. I also believe that if the Palestinians were prepared, as part of a peace agreement, to accept exclusive Israeli sovereignty over the city, running the city would be much easier than under joint sovereignty. In fact, if the Palestinians would agree to leave the city altogether, it would be even easier to run.

But the question is whether the Palestinians will agree to accept Mr. Kollek's solution. Even though they are making every effort now to leave the discussion on Jerusalem for last, there is no sign that they would be willing to accept exclusive Israeli sovereignty over the entire city. All the signs suggest that they would not. Mr. Kollek could argue that his own solution—Israeli sovereignty plus coexistence—has not yet been tried because Israel has not yet reached an agreement with the Arabs. If such an agreement is reached, he expects the solution will succeed. I don't believe that his solution can be the basis for an agreement; but if the Arabs agree to Mr. Kollek's formula of their own free will, I can assure him that neither I nor my colleagues will insist on our own solution, even if we are convinced it is more just.

There are good reasons to be skeptical about my own option. Amos Elon, in his book on Jerusalem, says that it's hard to believe that Israelis and Palestinians will be the first to put into effect the only reasonable solution for the city—peace with the removal of rigid borders of sovereignty. But, in contrast to Mr. Kollek's option, which we know for certain has been tried and hasn't worked, at least my option hasn't yet been tried.

10

THE KITSCH OF
ISRAEL

NOVEMBER 1988

A BIZARRE CONTROVERSY TOOK PLACE IN ISRAEL RECENTLY OVER the question: should soldiers be allowed to cry at the funerals of their comrades? The chief of the Northern Command favored allowing tears; the chief of staff was against them. The background of this exchange was a report in the Israeli press that paratroopers were seen weeping at the funeral of three friends who had been killed in an incident at the northern border. The question posed was whether an army proud of its fighters can afford to have them seen weeping in public.

The general who opposed crying—or, more exactly, being seen crying—was a Sabra born on a kibbutz; the one in favor of showing soldiers crying was a Polish-born survivor of the Holocaust. The Sabra officer is generally considered a rational and reasonable person, anti-melodramatic but not antiheroic. The officer born in Poland is considered a tough, able, and obstinate disciplinarian. The first officer is the archetype of the Sabra fighter; the Polish-born officer, for Israelis, is in some sense his opposite.

The argument about the soldiers' tears goes to the heart of a fundamental issue about sentimentality in the Zionist revolution, the revolution that took it upon itself to mold a "New Jew," and that saw wet eyes as the hallmark of the sentimental old-type exilic Jew. The New Jew was not supposed to shed tears. When Menachem Begin came to power in 1977, tears regained their legitimacy. Begin, appealing to the more recent immigrants, wanted to discredit the Sabra as the model of the New Jew and he succeeded in doing so. But even before Begin, Golda Meir prepared the way. Her contribution to Israeli political culture was a particularly confident form of self-righteousness. Begin added to it his own brand of sentimentality. The sentimental revolution of the righteous that was heralded by Mrs. Meir and cemented by Begin turned the two of them into model Israeli Jews in the eyes of Diaspora Jews as well as of many new immigrants and their children in Israel itself. The Israeli Sabras, even those who were sympathetic to their politics, were often disgusted.

The motif of crying paratroopers is not new. In "hours of greatness" the Israeli public expects its soldiers to cry. Countless printed words and photographs were dedicated to the famous weeping paratroopers at the Wailing Wall when it was first taken on the fourth day of the Six-Day War. This crying was perceived as testimony to the greatness of the hour. Fighters with "hearts of stone melting away in tears, by the Wall of stones with human heart," to quote one of the heroic pop songs of those days. I remember a wedding immediately after that war when, upon inspecting the wedding gifts, the groom discovered with amazement no fewer than three garish, expensive paintings depicting weeping paratroopers at the Wailing Wall. But even then tears were not the only or the most forceful symbol of the paratroopers "returning" to the wall. The quasi-official symbol became the photograph by the veteran *Time* photographer David Rubinger which shows a group of unshaven helmeted paratroopers at the wall, in the middle of which one sees—*ecce homo*—a young, blond, clean-featured fighter with his eyes lifted upward and holding his helmet next to his heart. This altogether non-Jewish gesture of taking off one's hat at a holy place became the symbol of the return of the New Jew to the site of his holy temple.

Not long after the pictures of the weeping fighters at the wall were circulated there appeared a more sophisticated but no less ideological kind of publication, known in Israel as "shooting and crying" literature. Its principal text, which made a great impression at the time, was a book called *Siach Lochamim*, which contained conversations with soldiers, mainly kibbutzniks, after the Six-Day War.* The book's clear but unstated message was one of rueful moral self-congratulation: we are beautiful, but we must shoot to kill—though not before we go through an agonizing search of our tormented soul. For the sake of the record it must be said that in the same book Amos Oz came down hard on the jingoistic euphoria of the time, but his was not the prevailing tone. A more recent criticism of the same sentiment is to be heard in "Shooting and Crying," a pop song written by a young Israeli rock singer named Sy Hyman, whose explosive energy reminds her fans of Janis Joplin. Her song is banned by Israeli radio. (With the uprising in the territories, the latest twist given to Hyman's phrase is "beating and crying.")

The blond innocence of the New Jew has long been part of the Zionist fantasy that underlies the myth of the Sabra. This myth at the same time seeks to protect the Sabra from the image of the "yellow beast." His toughness and coarseness are popularly understood as merely superficial qualities, for inside every coarse Sabra, the myth has it, hides a sensitive youth struggling to come out. The tourist guidebook cliché according to which the Sabra is so called after the fruit that is prickly outside but soft and sweet inside is meant to give a succinct and saccharine expression to this myth, and much effort has been invested in nurturing it, notably through the thriving industry of books dedicated to the memory of fallen soldiers. It is almost invariably pointed out that they secretly read the poetry of Rachel

*The Seventh Day: Soldiers' Talk about the Six-Day War, recorded and edited by a group of young kibbutz members (London, 1970).

("the Israeli Anna Akhmatova") or Alterman ("the Israeli Gumilov"). These soldiers never got much credit for their love of poetry while alive, only after their premature deaths.

The mythical Sabra, forever young, has somewhat aged. In the Israel of today he is best epitomized by Defense Minister Yitzhak Rabin. Much can be said about the nervous brutality of the aging Sabra Rabin, but he is certainly true to the myth in at least one respect: he is not sentimental. And certainly the tears shed by fighters over their fallen comrades are not necessarily an expression of sentimentality. Sentimentality is not shown by the first tear, the tear of sorrow for the loss of somebody one has known. Rather, sentimentality, along with its artistic embodiment in kitsch, is expressed by what Milan Kundera—a shrewd connoisseur of kitsch—calls the "second tear."

According to Kundera's distinction between the first and second tear in *The Unbearable Lightness of Being*, the second tear is a "meta-tear," the tear we shed from solidarity with the collective feelings of the group we belong to at the sight of the first tear. It is a manifestation of a vicarious sentiment: it does not come out of the person's direct involvement with the object of feeling but rather comes out of a derivative excitement that accompanies reflection. It is a passive emotion that replaces direct emotional involvement. Kundera paid no attention to the further twist in kitsch: when the second tear comes without the first one's ever occurring. This is kitsch in its pure form: the presence of the first tear serves only to dim it.

The "New Jews" of the Ben-Gurion years were afraid of tears. Tears are an expression of helplessness. They come about, for example, when someone close is irrevocably lost, or with deep frustration. Tears can be an expression of happiness, too, but even then there is an element of helplessness, for these tears usually express relief following anxiety or tension, often in a situation in which we find ourselves helpless.* The objection, in Ben-Gurion's Israel, to what Kundera later called second tears had to do both with their expressing passivity and acquiescence and with the fact that they spring from vicarious feelings. In any case tears were perceived as a substitute for action. Instead

*See the excellent book by Nico H. Frijda, *The Emotions* (Cambridge, Eng., 1986).

of whining for the Jewish fate, the demand of the early Israel was for action to change it.

THE IMMIGRANT PARENTS of Israeli Sabras were ambivalent about eliminating tears from their children's experience. On the one hand they were proud of the "goys" they had reared, but on the other hand they felt that with the abolition of tears there disappeared also a certain ideal that to them was not only important but also part of the Jewish experience: the ideal of being a *mensch* in the sense of being sensitive to the suffering of others. The *mensch*-ideal of this parent generation has always been ambiguous. Sometimes it referred to those sensitive to any human suffering and sometimes to those sensitive to the suffering of Jews only. This ambiguity with regard to the "other" permeates Jewish culture in general. Thus "man" in the biblical "when a man dieth in a tent" (Numbers 19:14) is taken by the Talmud to refer to Jews only, while man in "Ye shall therefore keep my statutes, and my judgments: which if a man do he shall live in them" (Leviticus 18:5) is taken to refer to any human being. This thoroughgoing ambiguity in the entire Jewish tradition could nourish universalistic tendencies just as it could also, obviously, nourish particularistic and tribal ones.

The wave of sentimentality that surged when Begin came to power had none of the universal sense of *mensch*—notwithstanding Begin's gesture, never repeated, of allowing some Vietnamese boat people into the country. The sentiment was exclusively of the "love of Israel" kind—that is to say of tribal sentimentalism: "The whole world is against us," as one Israeli popular song has it, and we are against the world. Of course, the notion of a diffuse "human brotherhood" which has us all belonging to the "family of man" is also fraught with sentimental kitsch, but the kitsch of "love of Israel" is of the tribe and of the tribe alone.

In Israeli cultural criticism the discussion of kitsch in this sense has recently become widespread in daily conversation as well as in writing. The Arab-Israeli writer Anton Shammas has written on the subject (in the French magazine *Levant*, under the title "Kitsch 22," and translated into English in *Tikkun*, September–October 1987); a special issue of *Koteret Rashit*, a magazine reflecting the mood of the Israeli intelligentsia, was devoted to kitsch in June. The concept of kitsch in these works mostly has to do with manifestations of vulgarity and bad taste, and not, at least not overtly, with criticism of the political culture of Israel. But one must ask why there is such a high concentration of kitsch in Israel, and the reasons are not far to seek. To begin with, Israel has a state ideology. Second, Israel is constantly preoccupied with marketing an image: to the world in general and to the Jewish Diaspora in particular. Third, Israel is a new country with no established tradition. Fourth, it is a country that by history and by nature combines the sublime with the trivial: supermarkets and gas stations spring up where once the prophets trod. Fifth, Israel is a country of tourism. Sixth, the occupation of the West Bank and Gaza produced its own culture. And lastly, the state of Israel is a product of a national movement deriving from nineteenth-century European Romanticism.

Not every one of these reasons seems necessarily a source of political kitsch. Countries and cities devoted to promoting tourism, while they generate plenty of kitsch, produce mainly its commercial variety. They mass-produce objects that by their nature should be unique—a multitude of Acropolises in Athens and of Davids in Florence, and a Mozart stamped on every chocolate ball and hotel towel in Salzburg. Art is reproduced on the assembly line with no regard to texture, size, proportion, or original setting. The purpose of these objects is only to remind one of the original article.* The "original article" can also be a story, as in the case of Bethlehem, the tourist town that prides itself on the expertise of its artisans in making little olive-wood mangers.

ON THE FACE of it Jerusalem seems like any other tourist city only more so: it is important to all Christian sects and denominations, holy to Islam, and of course the center for all Jewish "lovers of Zion." But Jerusalem is also a city one-third of whose inhabitants are under an

---

*I learned much on this from a doctoral dissertation (in Hebrew, unpublished) by Tomas Kulka, "Aesthetic Judgment and Border-Line Cases of Art" (The Hebrew University of Jerusalem, 1984).

occupation that is unacceptable to them. Spectacular audiovisual performances have managed, for more than twenty years, to present Jerusalem as a showcase of coexistence, the city of eternal peace—no doubt tourism's phenomenal success. This façade of religious and human brotherhood crumbled with the Palestinian uprising. No aspect of life in Israel remains unpoliticized, tourism included. And if tourism contributes to kitsch in Israel—and in Jerusalem in particular—the kitsch comes with a distinctly political flavor.

The best Israeli kitschmen have made a living out of Jerusalem. To take an example, Israel's former President and the current Minister of Education, Yitzhak Navon, a formidable kitschman, wrote a poem to accompany a short book of photographs of the seven gates of the Old City of Jerusalem, in which each gate implores God to choose it as the one through which the triumphant Israeli Army will march into the city during the Six-Day War. Properly enough, God chooses the humblest gate. In general, Jerusalem kitsch features the exotic combination of "the old and the new." Everybody is familiar with photographs of the New Jew, a sun-tanned athletic youngster invariably seen in contrast with the proverbial old Jew, with his fur cap, walking through narrow alleyways, his eyes shining from his lined face with the "wisdom of the centuries"—while an old Arab sits on a stool sucking on his narghile and a gowned Franciscan monk wearing sunglasses walks between them. The eternal city of three religions.

The main idea is clear. The Jews in Israel have taken literally the Hegelian metaphor of "the return to the world stage"; they have turned the entire country into a stage and its Jewish inhabitants into actors who "face the Diaspora." Jerusalem and Masada are the most important stage sets; Teddy Kollek is the benign stage manager. Even Israel's "wars of survival" sometimes take on the aura of a theatrical production. The Six-Day War was fortunate to have had one of the world's best stage sets, the Old City walls, in the foreground. One of the co-producers of scenes from that war was the present President of Israel, an arch-kitschman, Chaim Herzog. He would probably not have even been considered for the presidency if not for his highly successful performance as a daily commentator on the state radio during the fighting, and as keeper of the national legacy of kitsch.

Tourism and a widely circulated political image are here combined, kitsch being the glue. Kitsch is largely based on a fast and easy identification of the represented object. The emotion supposed to be evoked in the spectator comes merely from a reference to the object. It is thus enough to provide a glimpse of Masada, or the Wall, or the Temple Mount, to move the "Jewish heart." In genuine art there is always some estrangement of the represented object: it is shown in a new way and under a new light. The idea of kitsch is to arouse, through an easy and familiar stimulus, a strong emotion that comes from the spectator's relation to the original object—much like the feeling evoked by a perfumed handkerchief in a nineteenth-century romantic novel. In this respect Israel is ideal as a stage. Everything is so compact. *Nightline*'s helicopter takes off from Jerusalem, reaches Masada in minutes for a discussion on mass Jewish suicide, and we are instantly back in Jerusalem to see the Temple Mount, the Golden Dome, and the Wailing Wall—everything is so clear, Jews and Arabs fighting for the same piece of land. Where else can such a concentrated stage setting be found, with such obvious and accessible symbols?

Because of its political and economic dependence on the United States in general and on American Jews in particular, Israel is much preoccupied with marketing its image. The American Jews indeed sometimes play the role of middlemen with regard to this marketing, but the middleman is in a bind. He himself is an addicted consumer of the image produced by Israel, and at the same time he wants to help to improve the marketing of the image for general consumption. Diaspora Jews have to decide which features of the merchandise are saleable and, more important, which of its faults should be glossed over. The Israeli product nowadays makes life difficult for these middlemen. Its standards are in decline, while its price tag rises. Part of the difficulty is that the middlemen do not entirely control the information the Gentile consumer receives: some information comes from "unwanted sources."

One feature in this marketing—also an important element in the phenomenon of kitsch in general—is the elevation of the trivial, sometimes to the point of making it appear sublime. Practically every Israeli woman soldier is an officer; virtually every desk officer was once an Entebbe hero, the kitschy son of Ari Ben Canaan of *Exodus*. The earnest promotion of the trivial contributes to kitsch because by its nature it drives away the main enemy of kitsch, which is not good taste but humor—not only jokes but ironic distance of any kind.

IN THE KITSCH culture of the Israeli occupation, perhaps most striking to the eye is the architecture of the new settlements in the territories. Cheap land as well as heavy government subsidies were provided to the settlers. People dwelling in tiny flats in Tel Aviv's depressing satellite towns suddenly were able to build their "dream villas," and the settlements, consequently, are laid out like an army encampment but with red-tile roofed houses in the style of a Swiss chalet. This is what the Jerusalem poet Dennis Silk sees in "On the Way to the Territories":

> *We're passing a suburb of redemption on the left, the saved*
> *like these barrack affairs. They have broody rectangular*
> *dreams above which they hang the flag of their disposition.*
> *The more romantic plant Swiss Chalets guarded by a*
> *bemused militia. Here they yodel a psalm, there they*
> *mensurate it in a barrack.*

Switzerland, with its snowcapped Alps, cows in the meadows, and cozy villages with their little churches, has long provided the kitsch image of pastoral innocence; and it is this image of peace that the settlers seek to transplant onto the barren hills of Judea and Samaria: Switzerland in the Holy Land.

Lack of tradition in the new state, on the one hand, and on the other a long tradition of its founders—a tradition also rebelled against—provide fertile ground for kitsch. This kitsch was really the product of the "instant tradition" created in the newly founded state. In this spirit, dances of "biblical" shepherds, in colorfully embroidered "authentic" peasant costumes, were invented in Israel in the 1950s and performed with smiling optimism. At the same time Israel saw a lot of socialist kitsch, the kitsch of the "great march" toward tomorrow's better society. In fact the May Day parades of the Labor movement in the first decade of the state are fixed in my memory as far more impressive than any of the state holidays, Independence Day parades included.

The new immigrants largely from North Africa did not always understand this propaganda. I remember as a child a parade with a huge portrait of Lenin, which the crowds cheered, shouting "Weizmann! Weizmann!" True, Chaim Weizmann, Israel's first President, had a goatee as well as a shining, balding forehead, but he had bulging pockets under his eyes, which were quite unlike Lenin's Mongol eyes; the crowd may have been confused by the kitsch technique of retouching, which erases lines and blurs individual features. Indeed, the new immigrants who at the time mistook Lenin for Weizmann eventually brought about the complete collapse in Israel not only of Weizmann's values but of the socialist "world of tomorrow."

What remains from that period and has become part of the current nostalgia in Israel is the Russian songs sung by the Sabra socialist youth movements. Many of these songs tell of Cossacks of the Dnieper and the Don, who often took part in pogroms and in more than a few cases raped Eastern European Jews. Evening entertainments featuring such songs and devoted to "beautiful Israel" are often organized around the country these days. Among the most enthusiastic participants are the sons and daughters of the new immigrants of the 1950s. Each week hundreds of young people sing through the night at Tel Baruch, near Tel Aviv's famous prostitutes' beach, itself bustling with action.

The Zionist movement that founded the state of Israel was an outgrowth, among other things, of Romantic nationalism in Europe. Hermann Broch was right in observing* that vulgar expressions of Romanticism are an important source of kitsch, and the national mass movements born out of the Romantic movement—Zionism included—owe much of their kitsch to this source. But we owe the political kitsch of present-day Israel also to its having a state ideology.

---

*See his "Notes on the Problem of Kitsch," in G. Dorfles (ed.), *Kitsch: The World of Bad Taste* (New York, 1967), pp. 49–76.

In countries with such an ideology, especially in totalitarian ones like communist Russia, Nazi Germany, or fascist Italy, the state has a monopoly on state popular culture, while in countries with openly competing ideologies there can be found varieties of kitsch—Catholic kitsch, socialist kitsch, American Dream kitsch. In countries with a state ideology, government itself appeals to the masses by producing, with the help of its clerks, the state's mass culture; it is not the case that rulers prefer kitsch art only because it is useful in manipulating people and that for them anything that works on the masses is equally good. Khrushchev disliked modern art, and the Nazi leaders had a genuine predilection for heroic kitsch. The episodes of modernism in postrevolutionary Russia and of futurism in fascist Italy were brief because the rulers disliked them: no one has ever claimed that Stalin preferred Picasso to socialist realism.

In *The Unbearable Lightness of Being* Kundera's heroine, Sabina, maintains that her hatred of communism is based on aesthetics, that it is really a hatred of its "smiling brotherhood" kitsch. But it is wrong in my view to take kitsch to be solely a concept of aesthetic criticism: it has moral connotations, too. Nor is the moral criticism underlying the use of this concept exhausted by the manipulative nature of kitsch. It has much to do with its sentimentality. Sentimentality in my view is a necessary condition for kitsch, and it is what distinguishes kitsch from mere bad taste. Sentimentality in certain situations is more than just vulgar silliness; it can also be evil. Mark Jefferson described the phenomenon well in an article called "What Is Wrong with Sentimentality?" (*Mind*, 1983). One group of emotions, among which are nostalgia, self-righteousness, melodrama, and of course sentimentality, has in common a peculiar kind of distortion of reality that facilitates uninhibited indulgence in a strong feeling. The differences among the emotions in the group have to do more with the way they distort reality than with the quality of the feeling involved in each of them. Nostalgia distorts the past through idealization, in order to indulge in tenderness. Self-righteousness distorts the moral character of others in order to indulge in "holy wrath" against them and in self-pity for having to tolerate such people in the world.

Self-righteousness is accompanied by total blindness to one's own moral defects. Sentimentality distorts reality by turning the object (or event) represented into an object of complete innocence, in order to indulge in feelings of sympathy—easy to do with crying children, smiling beggars, gloomy clowns, sleeping babies, and sad-eyed dogs. Heroic kitsch turns the fighting soldier boy into an object of complete innocence. The sentimental distortion of reality can have cruel results, however, for it implies that the objects of innocence are constantly being menaced. The enemy of total innocence is total evil; the innocent and pure with whom we sympathize have to be relentlessly protected from those plotting their destruction.

STATE KITSCH IN Israel is inextricably tied to the image of the Israeli soldier or settler as an emblem of total innocence; those menacing him are therefore all the more deserving of severe punishment. The leaders seem to have convinced themselves of this. "We shall never forgive the Arabs for having forced our children to kill them," Golda Meir said. The violation of our children's innocence and purity is held to be unforgivable. Israel's shrine of kitsch is not, as may have been expected, the Wailing Wall, but a place that should have been furthest away from any trace of kitsch: Yad Vashem, the memorial for the Holocaust, where a "children's room" has been dedicated recently.

The real significance of this room is not its commemoration of the single most horrible event in the history of mankind—the systematic murder of two million children, Jewish and Gypsies, for being what they were and not for anything they had done. The children's room, rather, is meant to deliver an implicit message to visiting foreign statesmen, who are rushed to Yad Vashem even before they've had time to leave off their luggage at their hotel: that all of us here in Israel are these children and that Hitler-Arafat is after us. This is the message for internal consumption as well. Talking of the PLO in the same tone as one talks of Auschwitz is an important element in turning the Holocaust into kitsch.

At the time of the outbreak of the *intifada*, when official Israel felt the pressure of criticism both from within Israel and from abroad, it pulled out its secret weapon, the Holocaust. In Israel this year we had longer, and more vulgar, memorial services for the Holocaust than any I can remember previously. But the climax was an event that, even in a kitsch-haunted country like this one, many people felt went too far. It was a Holocaust Quiz, shot "on location" in Poland. The quizmaster was Yitzhak Navon, and participating in it were Jewish boys and girls who were asked questions about what took place in the camps, and they were awarded two points for each correct answer. Applause was not allowed because it was judged to be in bad taste and to "desecrate the memory of the victims."

Against the weapon of the Holocaust, the Palestinians are amateurs. True, some of them have adopted their own version of Holocaust kitsch, based on the revolting equation of the Israelis with Nazis and of themselves with Nazis' victims; but as soon as the Israeli authorities put Operation Holocaust Memory into high gear, with full-fledged sound-and-color production, the Palestinians cannot compete. The absence of the main actor and the stage queen, Begin and Golda, is certainly a loss for political kitsch, but a new star has risen, Benjamin Netanyahu ("Arafat is worse than Hitler"), and prospects are now bright—nothing will make us cut the kitsch.

This piece meant trouble. The hate mail I received from the United States after it was first published, in 1988, was astounding. The milder sort of threats took the form of "My wife and I have been long-standing supporters of your university. We did not realize that they keep people like you there. We are reconsidering our contributions." "What did you write that made our relatives in the States go berserk?" asked worried friends.

This reaction taught me an interesting lesson. You can criticize Israel's politics and it leaves Americans relatively indifferent ("It's only politics"), but you can't criticize the political use of symbols. This is taken as a sacrilege—not in Israel, but in the United States.

I have omitted here a sentence in the original essay that had wrong information in it about the children's memorial room at Yad Vashem. I was misled by information received from several sources, including an employee at Yad Vashem itself; given the touchiness of the subject, I should have checked it out further. I am sorry about the original mistake, but I am not sorry in the least about the rest of the article.

11

ARIEL SHARON:
FIGHTING AND
PREPARING TO FIGHT

AFTER THE MASSACRE OF HUNDREDS OF WOMEN AND CHILDREN IN the Sabra and Shatila refugee camps in 1982 during the Lebanon War, a commission of inquiry in Israel found that Ariel Sharon, as Defense Minister, had "indirect responsibility" for the massacre. The massacre was carried out by Maronite Christian units, but Sabra and Shatila were under Israeli control and Israel had responsibility for them. The commission demanded that Sharon be dismissed from his post. A friend of Sharon's said at that time, "Those who didn't want him as chief of staff got him as Defense Minister; those who don't want him as Defense Minister will get him as Prime Minister."

This was not a promise but a threat, and it still hovers over public life in Israel, a sword of Damocles. Damocles, it will be remembered, was invited by the tyrant Dionysus to a sumptuous banquet at which he found himself eating and drinking under a naked sword hung on a thin thread. To give a sumptuous banquet and hang a naked sword from the ceiling over his enemy would not be out of character for Ariel Sharon.

In February 1990, Sharon resigned his position in the cabinet as Minister of Industry and Trade. For months he and his allies had been accusing Prime Minister Yitzhak Shamir of being too "soft" on the *intifada* and even willing to deal indirectly with the Palestine Liberation Organization; following the dissolution of the national-unity coalition government in March, he continues to challenge Shamir for the leadership of the governing Likud Party. Sharon is a man who knows only two states of mind, fighting and preparing for fighting. In his battle with Shamir he has been making alliances on Shamir's political right, including the members of the small parties, such as the Tehiya, that implicitly favor expulsion of Palestinians from the occupied territories; and pressure from these allies of Sharon's was one of the main reasons for Shamir's refusal to deal with the PLO and with his subsequent defeat in the Knesset.

If the current efforts of Shimon Peres to form a government should fail and Sharon were to become Prime Minister, he would first have to win the support of centrist political opinion, which is willing to tolerate implicit recognition of the PLO. "I am Arik De Gaulle and only I can bring about peace with the Palestinians," he likes to suggest. Meanwhile he is trying to put across to American public opinion, and especially the organized Jewish community in America, a message that can be summarized as follows: "I, Sharon, am not the bully that you think I am. I am a sensitive warrior who is fighting hard and strong for God's little acre of Jews in their land, against the Arab scoundrels trying to kill them."

Sharon claims that he is not, as he is often said to be, a master of improvisation, but a careful planner for the future who pays a great deal of attention to details. Indeed, Sharon is a man with a long-standing scheme, and the publication of his autobiography* can be seen as part of his grand design to become Prime Minister of Israel.

---

*Warrior (New York and London, 1989).

The book, which was written with the assistance of David Chanoff, may serve Sharon's purposes. It tells a continuously interesting story of Sharon's rise to power, and in this respect it is very different from the expensive, illustrated books that Israeli leaders often write and get published in English and that are bought mostly as bar mitzvah presents. But an honest bookseller would have difficulty deciding whether he should list Sharon's autobiography as fiction or nonfiction. Questions about truthfulness arise not primarily from what is in the book, but rather from what is not. *Sharon: An Israeli Caesar* by Uzi Benziman* contains at least some of the missing material.

Sharon, who is now sixty-one years old, has held important positions in Israeli politics and military affairs for four decades. During the 1950s, when he was in his twenties, he became a commander of the Israeli Army's paratroopers. In this position he not only carried out raids on Egypt, Syria, and Jordan but also had much to do with their planning, and with deciding when and how they would take place. He successfully advocated increasing the frequency and intensity of such raids, which led to the Sinai War of 1956. During the 1960s, when Sharon was in his thirties, he was chief of staff of the Northern Command, and had considerable influence on the decision to increase the violence of Israeli attacks against Syria; these attacks were among the principal causes of the Six-Day War of 1967. During his forties Sharon had a leading part in the Yom Kippur War of 1973 and in setting up the rightist bloc—headed by Menachem Begin—that in 1977 for the first time in Israeli history took over the government from the Labor Party. At the end of the 1970s, as the government minister with responsibility for settlements, he expanded the Jewish settlement of the occupied territories. During the 1980s, when he was in his fifties, Sharon planned and brought about the Lebanon War while Defense Minister in Begin's government.

Though relatively young compared with other Israeli politicians, Sharon has thus had a central place in Israel's recent history. To understand Sharon's past is to understand something important about the state of Israel; and to understand his future, the future of the

---

*New York, 1989.

state of Israel as well. The differences between the Hebrew and English titles of the books by and about him convey something of the mythology that surrounds him. In Hebrew Sharon's book is called *Halohem*, which should be translated as *The Fighter*. But *Warrior* sounds more patrician, more Roman, like something from Plutarch.

The English title of Uzi Benziman's book, *Sharon: An Israeli Caesar*, refers to Julius Caesar, who crossed the Rubicon and destroyed the Roman republic, suggesting that Sharon threatens to destroy democracy in Israel. The Hebrew title of Benziman's book, *He Does not Stop at Red* (*Lo Otzer Ba-Adam*), is taken from a protest song against Sharon that was popular during the Lebanon War. There is an obvious difference between someone who does not stop at a red light and a leader who crosses the Rubicon, but, as it turns out, Benziman, in many respects a responsible and careful critic of Sharon, also subscribes to the heroic myth prevailing in Israel that Sharon is the best general in the world and one of the best in Israel.

A single motif recurs throughout Sharon's military and political life: "always escalate." He believes that in the muddle resulting from an increase in violence he will always come out the winner. He will know how to create a situation in which people turn to him because he is self-confident and he knows what he wants. This constant desire to raise the level of violence springs partly from Sharon's strategic sense and partly from his character.

SHARON WAS BORN in 1928 in Kfar Malal, a village ten miles north of Tel Aviv. His parents came from Russia. His father was an agronomist named Scheinerman, and his mother had studied medicine but did not finish her education. His father was a stubborn, quarrelsome man, and apparently highly intelligent. The family had strained or hostile relations with their neighbors in the village. When Arik was hurt by a fall and blood was flowing from a deep gash in his chin, his mother did not take him to the village clinic, but, in order to avoid contact with the other villagers, she ran with him through two miles of fields to a clinic in a neighboring community. One must distrust or hate others very much, or be greatly hated, or both, to act in such a way. In any case, Sharon seems early to have acquired a tendency to maintain deep suspicion and vindictiveness toward the people around him for a long time. Benziman's book tells us that as a little boy Sharon walked around with a stick in order to hit the other children in the village.

Kfar Malal was a cooperative village, each of whose families had originally a plot of land of equal size. Sharon's family was the only one in the village that marked off its property with fences and protected it with dogs. From time to time the family took over more land, and the Scheinerman family plot soon became the biggest in the village. Benziman's account of the ways the Scheinermans enlarged and secured their plot of land made me think of studies of animal territoriality, as when a lion marks off his territory with urine. It seems that this sense of territoriality was very strongly imprinted on Sharon's character.

Sharon's account of his childhood is the most interesting part of his autobiography, and one suspects it was written with two audiences in mind. For the American reader the description of Sharon's family evokes a frontier settlement in the Wild West—the rugged individualism of the Scheinermans in contrast to the other settlers and especially to the Indians—that is, the Arabs. Sharon never makes it clear that the village he grew up in was a collective settlement based on ideals of mutual assistance and solidarity.

For the Israeli reader Sharon's account is based on the Zionist myth according to which, once upon a time, everything was chaos, the land was swamp, and there was darkness on the face of the waters. Then the pioneers, the "men of Genesis," arrived from Russia and established civilization—the kibbutz and the *moshav*. These pioneers apparently never did anything trivial in their lives—their every action was exemplary and "larger than life." Sharon is a son of the gods in this Zionist myth; he was born from the salt of the earth, and he has spent much of his life fighting for the basic elements of life—water, land, and security.

During the War of Independence in 1948, Sharon was a company commander in what was for the Israelis the most disastrous battle of the war—the battle of Latrun. Latrun was a police fortress that the

British had built on the road from Tel Aviv to Jerusalem. It was manned by well-trained regular soldiers of the Jordanian Legion, and in their attack on the fortress the Israelis did everything wrong. They started out late on a scorching hot summer day, carrying insufficient water, and were soon discovered. Hundreds of Israeli fighters were killed, among them Holocaust survivors who had been taken to the battle straight from the boats that had brought them to Israel from Europe. Sharon himself was wounded. He claims that the cries of the wounded who had been abandoned in this battle left a deep impression upon him, and because of them he insists on never abandoning his wounded men in the field.

In 1952 Sharon left the army and began to take courses in Middle Eastern studies at the Hebrew University, but he was often called back into the army to carry out retaliatory raids against villages in neighboring Arab countries that were suspected of providing shelter to Palestinian attackers. To make these raids more effective, the army decided to form a special commando unit, and Sharon was asked to lead it. Unit 101 was in fact a collection of about forty wild, daring fighters whose main purpose was to carry out raids across the border. After five months this unit was combined with a battalion of paratroopers, and Sharon became the commander of the battalion (about 300 fighters) and later of a brigade of paratroopers (about 1,200).

Although he was by then no more than a lieutenant colonel, he became an important figure in Israel's defense policies. The explanation he gives for his success at this point seems to me convincing. At the end of the War of Independence, Ben-Gurion broke up Israel's best fighting units, the Palmach (assault companies), whose soldiers had been drawn from socialist youth movements and were influenced mainly by the Marxist Mapam Party, which was to the left of his own Labor Party. Because Ben-Gurion feared Mapam's influence on young people, he dissolved the Palmach. As a result, Israel, during the early 1950s, had no well-trained offensive fighting units. Moreover, the army at that time was drafting young men who had just arrived in mass immigrations, largely from North Africa, and did not speak Hebrew, had little education, and were ill prepared to take part in a modern army. The Israeli Army was then a very ineffectual fighting force, and a battle with the Syrians at Tel Mutila ended in a severe defeat. The army was unable to stop the infiltrators from among the Palestinian refugees, who at first came mainly to steal from the Israeli settlements, but increasingly committed acts of political terror against civilians. The commander in chief, Moshe Dayan, and Sharon, as commander of the paratroopers, did much to raise the standards of fighting in the Israeli Army, especially in improving the army's ability to fight at night.

Sharon was given his first important battle command in 1953 while he was still commander of Unit 101. He was put in charge of an attack against the Jordanian village of Kibbiya, from which infiltrators had been crossing the border. Only a small-scale action had been planned, but Sharon had forty-two houses demolished, some while the families that lived in them were still inside; and he had sixty-nine people killed, mainly women and children. After the attack Ben-Gurion summoned Sharon for questioning. He was concerned that Sharon's commando unit was composed of fighters who had been in Begin's underground, the Irgun, and Shamir's underground, the Lehi, and had carried out indiscriminate slaughter in villages such as the one at the town of Deir Yassin during the War of Independence. When he realized that Sharon's unit consisted of men from the kibbutzim and *moshavim*, and thus qualified as "our own boys" from the Labor movement, he was relieved. To protect Sharon and his men he announced that the killing had been carried out by Israeli vigilantes and not army soldiers.

These events created a strong link between Ben-Gurion and Sharon, one that Sharon would always try to suggest was closer than in fact it was. He would, for example, park his car near Ben-Gurion's office even if he did not have an appointment with him. In *Warrior* Sharon attributes his later troubles with the army command to the fact that Ben-Gurion befriended him and, in promoting him, passed over commanders who were senior to him. He gives an almost biblical picture of Ben-Gurion as the old patriarch Jacob, handing over the coat of many colors to his beloved son Joseph/Sharon, for which his older brothers, out of jealousy and vengefulness, throw him into the pit.

Ben-Gurion obviously liked Sharon and respected him as a daring and inventive commander, but he also had reservations about Sharon's truthfulness. Ben-Gurion put a high value on soldiers telling the truth. For him lying was a privilege of political leaders—that is, a privilege reserved for himself—but Dayan and Sharon, soldier-politicians, thought that they should have this privilege as well.

In one important matter Sharon does tell the truth. He writes that it was the Israeli attacks on the Egyptian Army camps in Gaza in 1955, which he commanded, that caused Nasser to sign an arms treaty with Russia (through a surrogate, Czechoslovakia), which made Egypt a much more formidable enemy of Israel. On the day of the attacks, Ben-Gurion made a speech in the Knesset saying that he was extending his hand in peace to Egypt; during the night he sent Sharon to strike at Nasser's army.

The retaliatory attacks carried out by Sharon in Jordan, Syria, and Egypt were intended to raise the cost to neighboring countries of serving as a base for infiltration into Israel. But Sharon's attacks actually caused infiltration to increase and become more violent. The larger purpose of the attacks was to raise Israeli morale by showing that the government was able to react strongly. Sharon was the first Israeli army commander to work closely with the press, and his success was to a large degree a journalistic one. Even primitive military actions were reported in the Israeli newspapers as if they were strokes of pure military genius.

The Palmach, like the French Resistance, was a great literary success. Both movements produced many writers who described their adventures. The French Resistance was in some cases more successful in producing literary work than in fighting the Nazis, while Sharon's success was not literary but journalistic. The retaliatory attacks were photographed, and Sharon and his fighters made a dramatic impression on the Israeli public, although Dayan, with his eye patch, was perhaps more photogenic.

In the Sinai War of 1956, however, Sharon got into deep trouble. He was sent as head of the paratroopers' brigade far into the Sinai to divert the Egyptians from defending against Israel's real strategy, which was to set up a line of defense nearer to Israel's borders. He was given explicit instructions not to enter the Mitla Pass and not to get involved in a battle. Sharon wanted to be the first to reach the Suez Canal, however, and he sent through the pass an "exploratory force," which the Egyptians ambushed. The paratroopers found themselves fighting a heroic but unnecessary battle, which claimed about forty dead and hundreds of wounded.

After the war, the high command severely criticized Sharon— Dayan accused him of a serious violation of instructions—and so, too, did the paratroop officers, who accused him of faulty leadership and even of cowardice. Other officers who had been under Sharon's direct command for years also expressed bitterness about him after the 1956 war. His deputy, Yitzhak Hoffi, who was to become a general and, later, the head of the Mossad, and is now the administrator of the Israeli Electric Company, once said to the head of intelligence that Sharon needed psychiatric treatment because he was suffering from paranoia. Coming from a stolid officer with highly conventional views, the remark would suggest that Sharon's symptoms were apparently obvious to everyone, even to someone like Hoffi.

The military command decided that Sharon's rise in the army should be stopped. He was sent to the military academy at Camberley, England, for a year, in the hope that he might emerge an officer and a gentleman. If a gentleman is someone who does not inflict pain, as Cardinal Newman once put it, then Camberley certainly failed with Sharon.

When he returned to Israel in 1962 his wife, Margalit, was killed in a traffic accident. Sharon describes this event with honorable restraint—precisely the same restraint with which he later describes the death of his beloved son Gur, who was killed at the age of eleven when another boy shot him unintentionally with a rifle that was in Sharon's house. But touching as these two tales are, even they require the corrections to be found in Benziman's book. Sharon ascribes his wife's accident to the fact that the car she was driving, which they had brought back from England, had right-side drive. But, according to Benziman, many of Sharon's acquaintances believe his wife committed suicide in the accident after discovering that Sharon was conducting an affair with her younger sister, Lily, who, shortly after her death became Sharon's wife and the mother of his children. More-over, after his son's death Sharon was vengeful toward the boy who had shot Gur, accusing him of intentionally killing him. The boy and his mother, the widow of a pilot, were forced to move away from their home, which had been near Sharon's.

Yet the personal life of Sharon, as with other Israeli politicians, is given no importance in Israeli politics. It was because of his record during the 1956 war that Sharon's career remained blocked for seven years; during this time he wandered around the army like an evil spirit, embittered and feeling ill-used, with the soldiers under his command paying the price of his dissatisfaction. Yitzhak Rabin, who had been appointed commander in chief in late 1963, finally promoted him to the significant position of chief of staff of the Northern Command. In order to minimize his obligation to Rabin, Sharon claims that Ben-Gurion forced Rabin to promote him. Perhaps Ben-Gurion asked Rabin to help Sharon, but he certainly didn't oblige him to do so, and Sharon knows this.

Such incidents are important for understanding Israeli politics to-day. Many active political leaders in Israel are former army generals, and among these are some who have been in close touch with Sharon, including Mota Gur, Rafael Eytan, Chaim Bar-Lev, Ezer Weizman, Matti Peled, Meir Pa'il, Rechavam Ze'evi, and of course Yitzhak Rabin. In their politics some of these men, like Matti Peled, who for years has advocated a Palestinian state, are very left-wing, and some, like Rafael Eytan, are very right-wing, but their political positions on the left or right are not necessarily reflected in their relations with one another, and particularly not in their attitudes toward Sharon. More important are often old cliquish affections and hatreds that go back to their army days, and these have been dragged into Israeli politics. One example is Sharon's rivalry with Rabin for the position of Defense Minister, in which he tries to create the impression that he would be much more successful than Rabin in suppressing the *intifada.* This rivalry with Rabin is difficult for him, because he in fact owes Rabin a favor or two. In 1982, during the siege of Beirut, for example, Rabin supported Sharon's use of harsh tactics, such as shutting off the water and food supplies to the city.

The officers of the Northern Command may have respected Sharon as a commander, but most of them hated him personally. He was capricious, insulting, and wild, as Benziman's book shows. To his credit it should be said that he acted that way to everyone and not only to his subordinates. His own commanding officer was Avraham Yoffe, Rabin's brother-in-law, a huge, affable man, nature-loving and Arab-hating. Yoffe is the only man for whom Sharon in his book expresses unambivalent affection. Yoffe gave Sharon freedom to take what military actions he wanted, and within a short time Sharon's skirmishes along the Syrian border, as I have noted, had much to do with bringing about the 1967 war.

In that war Sharon had his finest hour as one of three division commanders on the Egyptian front in the Sinai. His task was to capture a large, fortified Egyptian enclave at Abu Ageila in the central Sinai. Using shrewd and complex tactics, he succeeded in capturing the Egyptian force with few losses. The arrows he drew on the map to plan the attack actually matched what happened in battle—a rare event in war, and one that brought Sharon much favorable publicity. It is often said that this battle is taught as a model of military tactics in military academies throughout the world.

IN VIEW OF such claims, it seems worth asking: How good is Sharon? In other words, what kind of military commander is he, from a purely technical point of view rather than a political or moral one? In my view Sharon's performance has been very uneven. At best he was perhaps the most talented field commander in Israel. He can "read" a battle well; he is imaginative, he is able to keep his soldiers moving according to plan, and he is good at visualizing the topography. But Sharon also has been very unimpressive in some battles. The crossing of the Suez Canal during the Yom Kippur War—in which Sharon, with a bandage on his forehead, was the subject of much publicity— was certainly not well conducted: too many troops were wasted. And if the Lebanon War, in which Sharon failed badly as the overall commander, is taken into account, his record becomes even more doubtful. Sharon's average is above average, but not remarkably so.

While in art one judges peaks, in war one should perhaps judge by averages.

A similar assessment could be made of Sharon's intelligence. Sharon at his best can be brilliant, but he can also be stupid. During the years between 1967 and the Yom Kippur War, and especially during the years of the war of attrition on the banks of the Suez Canal, the Israeli general staff could not decide on the best strategy to defend the southern borders. Sharon was opposed to the Bar-Lev line, a proposed string of fortifications along the eastern side of the Suez Canal. He thought this was a static conception of defense similar to the Maginot line, and he argued instead for a mobile defense. Except for the famous Israeli Army commander Yisrael Tal, most of the general command opposed Sharon's idea. Sharon leaked reports to the newspapers about the controversy, in order to create the impression that he was in favor of something "dynamic" and therefore good, while Bar-Lev's idea was "static" and therefore bad. Since Sharon himself was perceived as dynamic, and the phlegmatic Bar-Lev was perceived as static, Sharon's view seemed plausible.

This widely accepted, simplified description of the static versus the dynamic is not entirely accurate, however, as a meticulous and honest book about the Yom Kippur War by General Avraham Adan ("Bren"), shows.* Still, if the war made it clear that Sharon's criticism of the Bar-Lev line was partly justified, neither the Bar-Lev line nor a failure of military intelligence caused Israel to stumble as badly as it did in the Yom Kippur War. The deeper fault lay with a greater error, in which Sharon was an active participant. The army command and the government believed that Israel's regular army, with three hundred tanks, was sufficient to block the Egyptians on the southern border. They believed that Israel must not create fears about danger on its borders by calling up the reserves, because doing so would endanger the status quo and invite the superpowers to intervene. As a result, Israel simply did not have adequate military forces in place to repel the Egyptians when they attacked. Sharon was lucky: he left the

---

*On Both Banks of the Suez (San Francisco, 1980).

Southern Command and active duty with the army a few weeks before the war broke out.

Sharon had left the army once before, in 1969, when his relations with the entire army command had become intolerable. At that time an election campaign was going on and Sharon joined the right-wing bloc led by Begin. But Pinhas Sapir, then Finance Minister and the kingmaker of the Labor Party, was so afraid of Sharon entering political life that he forced Chief of Staff Bar-Lev to take Sharon back into the army. He then began to lead a double life—in the army overtly and in politics covertly.

In 1970 Defense Minister Dayan appointed Sharon to "impose order" in the Gaza Strip, where the refugee camps were controlled by the Palestinian organizations. What Sharon did then is relevant today, since he claims that by using the same methods now he would succeed in suppressing the *intifada*. He ordered that the parents or relatives of a child caught throwing a stone be expelled from the occupied territories and sent into the desert with a canteen and some pita bread—a fate just like their "ancestors" Hagar and Ishmael in the Bible. Sharon also expelled the Bedouins by stopping up their wells —once again a tactic suggestive of ancient biblical cruelty. Such actions at other times would have made international headlines, but after having been attacked in the 1967 war, Israel had won an exceptional freedom to act. With characteristic hypocrisy, Golda Meir, who was Prime Minister at that time, privately described Sharon's imposition of "law and order" in the Gaza Strip as a danger to democracy, and backed him fully in public.

The *intifada* has radically changed the situation in the Gaza Strip. Palestinian resistance now has broad popular support there, whereas in 1970 it was carried out only by members of a few organizations. A year ago Israel published a list of about seven hundred wanted men from among Palestinian activists; simply to be on the list is to be turned into an outlaw. With nothing to lose, these young men have become "full-time employees" of the *intifada*, fleeing their homes and clustering together in small groups with such revolutionary names as the Red Eagle or the Black Panther. The army pursues them with the help of informers and shoots them on sight. They in turn murder anyone they suspect of being an informer. On a much larger scale, the situation resembles the one Sharon faced in 1970, and the methods used by the army are strikingly similar to those Sharon used to "impose order" in Gaza at that time.

IN 1973 SHARON left, or was asked to leave, the army. With the assistance of some American supporters he bought a ranch—the largest private farm in Israel—and he openly entered politics. In a short time he succeeded in bringing together the coalition of right-wing parties, headed by Menachem Begin, that made up the first Likud bloc. In an episode hilariously described in his book, we are told how the heavyset Sharon raced Shmuel Tamir, a rival political leader who is rather fat, up ten flights of stairs in order to be the first to announce to the press his version of the negotiations. Sharon got there first, entirely out of breath. He soon became head of the Likud's election campaign for the Knesset.

When the Yom Kippur War broke out later that year, Sharon went to the Sinai as the commander of a division in the reserves. But he went not only as a commander but also as a politician campaigning for office. He immediately grasped that if he could be the first to cross the Suez Canal he would be "Arik, King of Israel." To command such a crossing became his primary goal, and he sometimes acted against Israel's military interests in order to achieve it. He shamefully betrayed the soldiers of another officer, General Adan, who were fighting on the same front, by refusing to send them reinforcements when they were in serious trouble. Intense arguments among the generals were frequent during the Sinai War. After the war, unlike most of the others, Sharon circulated his own version of their quarrels to the American press.

In 1977, ten years after Golda Meir called Sharon "a danger to democracy," Begin said that Sharon was capable of surrounding the Knesset with tanks. So the view that Sharon threatens democracy is held not only by the Israeli left; many in Sharon's own party are deeply convinced of it, citing his self-evident demagogic qualities. Sharon presents himself as the "strong man," cursing his superiors and promising to save the people from the dark forces that threaten them, in contrast to the weak and treacherous leaders who can't be counted on. He shows unlimited ambition and disrespect for the law, and he is given to open displays of physical power. But there is also a distinctive protofascist quality in the way Sharon tries to combine the qualities of hero and victim. He attracts the support of the fearful masses in a land of immigrants by complaining that he, like them, is a perennial victim of the "establishment"—yet he also presents himself as the hero who can take on the people in power, and win. He will save the people in their time of danger from all those who threaten their interests. Only he, the victim-hero, knows how to do this.

In 1977 Sharon ran for the Knesset on an independent ticket in the same elections that brought Begin and the Likud to power. His list won two seats and he immediately joined Begin's party and the Likud government as Minister of Agriculture with responsibility for settlement of the territories. Sharon saw Begin as a pompous rhetorician and a legalist who lacked the capacity to get things done, but he respected his hold on the people in the streets. In his book Sharon evidently wants to show that he does not belong to Begin's crowd, that he is in the line of the Labor "aristocracy" deriving from Ben-Gurion. For his part, Begin, a man of exaggerated Central European politeness, was astounded by Sharon's coarseness but fell victim nevertheless to the flattery and charm that Sharon can use when he wants.

Sharon, who came to be called "the bulldozer" because of all the roads and settlements he ordered to be built, did more than any other man to advance Israel's colonization of the territories. But in doing so he abandoned his ministerial responsibilities for agricultural development within Israel proper, which continued to deteriorate while he was in office. Sharon intended to bring an end to Labor's settlement plan, the so-called Allon plan, which called for settlements mainly in the Jordan Valley. Instead he established settlements throughout the territories, especially on the mountain ridges and even among the Arab villages, intending to destroy any chance that Israel would ever give back the territories.

Sharon has for years advocated a political plan based on the idea that Jordan is the Palestinian state. He believes that the PLO must be helped to take control of Jordan, where Palestinians are already a majority. Then it will be possible to arrange a practical compromise with them concerning the West Bank. Israel will have the territories and the Arabs who remain in the territories will be citizens of Jordan-Palestine.

Sharon did much to support the Camp David Accords, and agreed to the removal of the settlements in the Sinai, thus giving Begin a free hand to establish them on the West Bank. But his part in destroying the town of Yamit, the most prominent of the Sinai settlements, aroused suspicions about him among the settlers. They saw him as an opportunist, who, in spite of being their advocate in the government, was capable of changing his spots at any moment.

In the 1981 election Begin won a surprise victory, and he appointed Sharon Defense Minister. From his first day on the job Sharon started preparing for a general war in Lebanon, collaborating with his commander in chief, Rafael Eytan, who had been one of his officers in the paratroopers. The war had three main purposes: to drive the Palestinians out of Lebanon and into Jordan, in the hope that they would bring down King Hussein; to drive the Syrians out of Lebanon; and to establish a Christian government in Beirut that would make peace with Israel. Sharon sought backing for his plan from Reagan's first Secretary of State, Alexander Haig, and it seems clear that Haig gave Sharon much-appreciated support. In his book Sharon first supplies Haig with an alibi, claiming that the latter opposed the Lebanon War, then immediately adds that Haig told Begin during the war, "Once you start it, you have to finish it as fast as possible."

In my view Sharon attacked Lebanon because he wanted to preside over a "perfect war" that would demonstrate his military and political genius. But he failed miserably in every respect, and one reason he did so was his constant need to deceive the government and the public about the aims of the war. To avoid creating the impression that he was going to invade the entire country right away, he said he would stop at forty kilometers; he then went further, using more and more troops and greater violence each day.

A story I was told by a friend who was a paratroop officer under Sharon illustrates how Sharon escalates a conflict. Once, in the early 1950s, Sharon asked his officers what they would do if they wanted to capture hill X, and the government only gave them permission to capture hill Y. Sharon said: You capture hill Y, of course, and then you send a reconnaissance unit from hill Y to hill X, to make sure that "everything is OK." The unit "encounters fire" from hill X, you notify the government that the unit is in danger, and you request authorization to "rescue" it. Afterward you explain that in order to save the unit you had to capture hill X. This formula captures Sharon's logic. His entire career, including the Lebanon War, can be seen in the story of hill X and hill Y.

He will say virtually anything to get his way. For example, he accuses the Labor Party opposition of having joined hands with the Peace Now movement, which opposed the war in Lebanon, to bring about his failure there. This is nonsense, since Sharon himself knows that the Labor Party did its best to avoid cooperating with Peace Now. Only after the Sabra and Shatila massacres did the Labor Party agree to stand on the same platform with Peace Now.

Throughout his book, Benziman accuses Sharon of being a glutton who cannot control his appetite. His tone on this matter is oddly moralistic. However, concerning the one instance in which Sharon's gluttony had political significance, Benziman is silent. Sharon's allies in Lebanon, the Phalangists, were a mafia led by the Bashir Gemayel, who immediately grasped that Sharon loved to eat and supplied him with splendid meals to keep him content. But there is no such thing as a free lunch, and the price of these meals was paid by many who are now dead.

Sharon's dismissal from the Defense Ministry after the Sabra-Shatila commission of inquiry presented its findings only heightened his sense of himself as victim-hero. He claims that Begin handed him over to a foreign power in much the same way that the men of Begin's underground were handed over to the British by Ben-Gurion's Haganah. But the "foreign powers" in Sharon's case are judges of the Israeli Supreme Court. Sharon's description of an episode at the funeral of Begin's wife reveals just how persecuted he felt:

As we walked toward the open grave, I happened to turn my head and saw behind me two men in black hats, black ties, and black overcoats walking together and staring at me with the blackest of looks. The eyes belonged to Judge Kahan and Judge Barak [two members of the commission that condemned him].

Sharon returned to his ranch but he remained a minister without portfolio in the government, and immediately after Begin, in a state of clinical depression, resigned, Sharon staged a comeback. He ran against Shamir for the leadership of the Likud, and lost, joining the cabinet instead. Now, by resigning, he has challenged Shamir again.

Sharon produced his most recent spectacle at the Likud Party convention in mid-February. What happened there was one of the main reasons the Shamir government fell a month later.

With the help of two Likud ministers, David Levi and Yitzhak Modai, Sharon wanted to get a resolution passed that would make it impossible for Shamir to accept the U.S.-sponsored plan for an Israeli-Palestinian meeting in Cairo. This was to have caused Labor to quit the national-unity coalition government, and ultimately Shamir to fall as Prime Minister. Two essential conditions were stipulated in Sharon's resolution. First, East Jerusalem Palestinians would not be allowed to participate in the projected elections on the West Bank, nor would their representatives be allowed to participate in the Palestinian delegation to the talks in Cairo. Second, Palestinians who had been deported from the occupied territories would also be excluded from participation in the delegation. It was patently clear to everyone that these conditions meant not only that there would be no talks in Cairo but also that the national-unity government would come to an end.

The challenge was direct and blatant. There was a general expectation that a showdown would take place from which Shamir would emerge victorious. The irony, of course, was that Shamir's desire for the Cairo meeting to take place, and for that matter the Palestinian elections themselves, was even weaker than that of his three challengers. After all, it is Shamir more than anybody else who is the champion of the Greater Israel. However, Shamir at that point desperately needed space to maneuver, so that he could continue his delicate balancing act of procrastinating over the so-called peace process, while holding his coalition government together and not directly

confronting the United States. Sharon was trying to deprive him of
that space.

SHARON ACTUALLY FORCED the Likud Party to face a central dilemma. Does its future lie in its being a conservative, centrist, establishment party or is it rather to become a right-wing radical party?
So long as Menachem Begin was its leader, the party somehow managed to embrace—or to appear to be embracing—both these choices.
In recent years the rise of the Shas Party among the poor Oriental
Orthodox community on the one hand, and on the other hand the
rise of the ambitious young professionals surrounding Shamir (Dan
Meridor, Ehud Olmert, and Roni Milo), made it more and more difficult for the Likud to continue as both a conservative and a radical
party. The result has been a gradual shift toward the center. Sharon
set out to undermine this shift. He senses that if the Likud were to
become a respectable establishment party, there would be no big role
for him to play.

As chairman of the convention, Sharon began with an explosive
announcement—that he was resigning from the cabinet so as "to be
free to fight for his vision." He had kept his surprise move secret from
his two collaborators, sharing it, as he said, only with his wife. Instantly Sharon became the victim-hero of the convention, which then
continued without any agreed-upon agenda. Shamir proceeded to deliver a lengthy policy statement, planning to put it to a vote of confidence. Sharon had in mind a full policy debate, ending with a list
of resolutions that would be put to a vote. There being no agenda,
however, Shamir tried at that point to "steal" a vote of confidence:
he concluded his speech and asked the delegations then and there to
endorse it.

Sharon was well prepared for such an outcome. He had a second
microphone ready at his seat at the head table, and his followers took
the seats in the front of the hall. Just when Shamir was appealing to
the delegates to raise their hands in a vote of confidence, Sharon stood
up and in a voice louder than Shamir's quickly read out his own
resolutions, asking the delegates to raise their hands in support of

ARIEL SHARON · 237

them. Pandemonium followed. Shamir and his entourage left the hall, to shouts of "Ceauşescu!" Ceauşescu!" by Sharon's supporters, while all of Israel watched what was happening on television.

Sharon certainly managed to cause Shamir considerable political harm. He made it inescapably clear to him that he is a leader of a deeply divided party. The road from the convention to Shamir's rejection of the American peace plan, and to the subsequent toppling of the government in March, was short. But was Sharon the winner? The answer to this is not yet clear. In announcing his resignation, he at least kept his reputation for surprising and daring moves. In Israel, according to conventional wisdom, you don't resign. "You leave the cabinet for five minutes and you find yourself out for the next twenty years."

The political situation in Israel is so much in flux that it is hard as yet to estimate the gains and losses of the different factions. Sharon is perhaps not after all a clear winner. What is clear is that he has managed to upset the status quo. And here we come to the more important question. If Sharon were to become Prime Minister, what then?

Sharon is an opportunist and he will do whatever he thinks will bring him success. If it were clear to him that making peace would transform him into a national hero, he might make peace. But by temperament he is far more at ease with himself, and in control of his destiny, when he is making war. Therefore the chances that he would be drawn to war are considerably greater than the chances that he would be drawn to peace.

Lady Caroline Lamb said of Byron that he was "mad, bad, and dangerous to know." With Sharon one must add an amendment: it is also dangerous not to know him.

Now, in 1998, Sharon is politically very much alive and kicking—especially kicking. He is perhaps the most powerful minister in Benjamin Netanyahu's government. He can block any move of Netanyahu toward the Palestinians if he decides to do so.

The only change in Sharon since 1990, apart from age, is in his attitude toward Jordan. In the old days, he promoted the idea that "Jordan is Palestine"—namely, that with the help of Israel the Palestinians should take over Jordan, thus satisfying their need for a Palestinian state—and that would be the end of it, "it" being the Palestinians' claim on the West Bank. Now Sharon has become a "Hashemite." He works closely with King Hussein, the Hashemite King of Jordan, even making sure that his kingdom gets water from Israel.

It seems that Sharon has given up on the idea that he will be Prime Minister of Israel. But he has not given up on the idea of being the kingmaker.

12

YITZHAK SHAMIR: A MAN
OF THE UNDERGROUND

MAY 1992

IN JULY 1946 BRITISH TROOPS SURROUNDED TEL AVIV IN AN EFFORT
to wipe out the headquarters of the Jewish underground fighters, who
they assumed were somewhere in the city. Yitzhak Yzernitsky, one of
the commanders of the underground group called the Lehi—otherwise known as the Stern gang—happened to be in Tel Aviv that day,
to meet with Menachem Begin, the commander of the other underground group, the Irgun. Yitzhak Yzernitsky was disguised as an Orthodox rabbi in traditional dress, and he used the name Rabbi Shamir.
A British detective officer, John Martin, identified him immediately
in spite of his disguise and ordered his arrest. That he did so cost the
detective his life. Two gunmen from the underground, dressed as
tennis players, waited for Martin at the court of his tennis club on
Mount Carmel, and there they shot him down.

Many years later Yitzhak Hasson, who had been in charge of intelligence for the underground, wrote that Shamir, who knew all the secrets of the underground, was lucky not to have fallen into the hands of security services like the ones he now presides over.* For it never entered the minds of the British to torture Shamir in order to get information out of him. They blindfolded him with a smelly rag and took him to Damascus, where, befitting his status as a dangerous man, they put him on a special plane and sent him to a detention camp in Eritrea. Together with his friend Ben Eliezer, Shamir escaped from the camp in January 1947, to the French colony of Djibouti. The French governor described the two of them as follows: "They brought me these two guys—one with the face of an intellectual [Ben Eliezer] and the other [Shamir], his bodyguard, with the face of a killer."

It is important for members of an underground, like members of the Secret Service—and Shamir was both—to have an appearance that does not attract attention. Shamir, however, has sharp, distinct features. His large head sits on a solid, dwarf-like body. His jaw is square, and his eyebrows are especially bushy. Indeed, the first time Shamir wore a disguise, the uniform of a Polish officer, he was quickly spotted. In 1942, after he had escaped from the British Mazra prison in northern Palestine, and was walking along the road from Haifa to Tel Aviv, a former guard from the prison approached him and asked, "You're in the Polish Army? How did that happen?" Shamir uttered a Polish curse and ran away.

YITZHAK SHAMIR WAS born Yitzhak Yzernitsky in 1915, in the small Polish town of Rzhnoi.† In his family he was known by the nickname "Itzel." The first name Shamir chose for himself in the underground was "Michael"—an interesting choice, for Shamir took the name from the Irish underground fighter Michael Collins, whom he greatly admired. Michael Collins, who had sprung Eamon de Valera from

---

*In *Dvar*, September 2, 1991.
†The only biography of Shamir is in French: Charles Enderlin, *Shamir* (Paris, 1991). It contains useful information.

prison, headed the British list of wanted men. That Shamir identified himself with a professional revolutionary who had fought both the British and his own people—a tough, practical organization man rather than a man of words—is not surprising. But it is worth recalling that Collins was the person largely responsible for signing the 1921 pact with Britain which established the Republic in the southern part of the island and gave up the provinces that are now called Northern Ireland. Shamir should be compared not with Michael Collins but with the revolutionaries who ambushed Collins at Beal na Blath and killed him as a traitor for giving up a part of his ancient homeland.

A friend told me that he once heard Shamir say the biblical figure he most identified with was King Saul. It seems surprising that this melancholy, indecisive, moody king should appeal to Shamir. It may be that Shamir identifies with the Saul who went looking for his father's donkeys and stumbled upon the kingship. Shamir always insists that he is in power not because he has chosen a career as a politician but because he is carrying out a mission. An analyst trying to trace the winding paths of his psyche would not be satisfied with such a simplistic explanation, and might risk a "deeper" one. Saul was the underground name of Eliyahu Giladi, Shamir's friend, who escaped with him from the Mazra prison in 1942. Believing that Giladi was an adventurer who might endanger the underground, Shamir later was responsible for his execution. Yet Shamir named his daughter, who was born in 1949, Gilada, after the same Giladi. Giladi is a skeleton that pops out of Shamir's closet from time to time, and we will return to him later.

The name Shamir, which Yitzhak Yzernitsky later adopted as his civilian name, is also interesting. To an Egyptian journalist Shamir once offered the explanation that *shamir* in Hebrew means a hard rock: the name was intended to show the Arabs whom they were dealing with. This meaning of the word is one that appears in the Bible in Ezekiel 3:9: "I will make your forehead like adamant [*shamir*], harder than flint. Do not fear them, and do not be dismayed by them." Shamir did not mention the other meaning of his name— thorns growing in deserted wastelands: "And I will make it a desolation; it shall not be pruned or hoed, and it shall be overgrown with briers [*shamir*] and thistles" (Isaiah 5:6).

"I'm seventy years old today," Shamir said in 1985. "I've been in the Land of Israel for fifty years and I've been fighting for our principles for sixty years. Do you really think I'll give up these principles for anyone?" Seven years have passed since then. Shamir likes to say that the sea is still the same sea and the Arabs are still the same Arabs. One can just as easily say that Shamir is still the same Shamir: he will not give up the convictions of his youth. Shamir's statement in 1985 is in my opinion the key to understanding the man and especially to understanding his policies. A man who was close to him in the underground but who is very far from him now told me, "It isn't a matter of principles but of something much more animalistic: Shamir is a bulldog that is gripping a bone called the Land of Israel in its jaws and will not let go."

To understand Shamir one must turn to the distant past. The Yzernitsky family were tanners and not poor. Shamir's father was a Zionist, who sent Itzel first to a modern religious Jewish school and then to the Herzliya high school in Bialystok, in eastern Poland. This high school belonged to the distinguished Tarbut Jewish educational network of Eastern Europe. The classes were held in modern Hebrew, and they included studies of the Bible and of Hebrew literature, subjects that were not taught in traditional Jewish schools in Eastern Europe. In comparison to Begin, a powerful public speaker, Shamir is almost inarticulate, but his Hebrew is precise. He also learned French for his work in the Mossad's Paris office, and when he was elected Prime Minister he mastered basic English. "If I had to learn Chinese I would do it," he said, and meant it.

THE FIRST YOUTH movement Shamir joined was the Gordonia, a Tolstoyan Zionist group, and young Itzel soon realized that it was not the place for him. He joined the Betar movement instead. Betar was the youth organization of revisionist Zionism, the movement founded by Ze'ev Jabotinsky, which aimed to revise the official Zionist policy and doctrine of Chaim Weizmann. Revisionist Zionism exploited the disillusionment that arose from the British government's failure to carry out its promise, stated in the Balfour Declaration of 1917, to use its "best endeavours" to establish a national home for the Jews in Palestine. Unlike Weizmann, Jabotinsky believed that only strong pressure—which, he claimed, Weizmann was unwilling to use owing to the "obsequiousness of his Diaspora mentality"—could compel Britain to assist in the fulfillment of the aims of Zionism. These aims, in Jabotinsky's view, were to create a Jewish majority on both sides of the Jordan River and, in consequence, a Jewish state there.

The adult revisionists came from the circles of the "white" Jews in Russia after the 1917 revolution. They were extreme anti-Bolsheviks, but they had liberal politics. By contrast, most of the members of the Betar youth movement came from the Jewish communities of Poland, Lithuania, and Latvia, which were all very much influenced by Polish national and Catholic Romanticism. These trends, in some of their manifestations, came to have fascist overtones, as indeed did the Betar movement itself. Betar members wore neat uniforms with brown shirts and took part in quasi-military drills honoring Jabotinsky as if he were a *Führer*. The central idea of revisionism was the creation of Jewish armies, even in the Diaspora. This was an "orthopedic" thought—to straighten the people's back. But it was also seen as politically necessary—Zionism would be realized in blood and fire. In practice Betar specialized in elaborate martial ceremonies: "Man's superiority over the beast is the ceremony," said Jabotinsky. (Ceremonies, however, have always made Shamir uncomfortable.) Betar's central theme was nationalism mixed with much talk of blood and earth: "With blood and sweat," a Betar anthem ran, "we will create a race, proud and generous and cruel." Many are still waiting for the generous part to emerge.

Two tendencies were in conflict within the revisionist Zionist movement. One was a patriotic liberal nationalism, reminiscent of the spirit of the Risorgimento in Italy. The other was the Italian-style fascism of the 1920s and 1930s. Jabotinsky, at different times, expressed both. Menachem Begin, who was the head of Betar in Poland before he came to Israel, had his own inner conflicts. In the Knesset, he was a liberal; he was against imposing military government on

Arabs inside Israel, and while he was Prime Minister, he stopped systematic torture by the Shin Bet. But when he addressed crowds in the street he revealed himself as a ferocious demagogue.

In Shamir's case, on the other hand, one finds no such conflicts. He's made of different stuff. Although Shamir comes from Betar, from which he absorbed his all-encompassing nationalism, he is not, in contrast to Begin, a Betar type. He was actually shaped more by the "maximalist Zionism" he encountered in Palestine when he first arrived there in 1935, after studying for a year at the Law School of Warsaw University.

The twenty-year-old Yzernitsky came with a student's certificate to study Hebrew literature at the Hebrew University in Jerusalem, but he never studied there. The Hebrew literature he knows he read on his own: the writers who influenced him included Uri Zvi Greenberg (1894–1981), the highly gifted and visionary chauvinist poet and essayist whose work he still knows, and Yonatan Ratosh, whose poems he may not have read but whose militant essay "We Aspire to Power" he read and cherished. Shamir found a place for himself in the fringes of the Yishuv, the organized Jewish community in Palestine, where Ben-Gurion and other Zionist leaders were severely criticized for preaching restraint in the face of the Arab violence that erupted in the pogroms of 1929 and continued from time to time during the 1930s, culminating in the great Arab revolt between 1936 and 1939. The greatest shock was the Arab massacre of Jews in Hebron who had lived there for generations and were in fact not Zionists at all.

The maximalist critics to whom Shamir was drawn included not only Uri Zvi Greenberg but ideologues such as Abba Ahimeir and Yehoshua Yevin. These men felt that the Yishuv's policy of relying on the police force of the British Mandate to protect Jewish fighters was humiliating. They called for retaliatory strikes against the Arabs. They had their differences with the Irgun Zvai Leumi—the National Military Organization—but they approved of its martial strategy. Late in 1937 Shamir joined the Irgun and until 1939 took part in its terrorist activities, which were little different from the ones conducted in present-day Beirut: the Irgun placed bombs in the markets of Arab towns and fired on Arabs in their buses.

This terror was both preceded and accompanied by a dramatic

change in the maximalist Zionists' attitude toward Arabs. Previously they had talked of possible coexistence with Arabs under Zionist rule; now they considered Arabs to be foreigners who were defiling the fatherland: "No peace to the Hebrews and the Arab wolves in Sion," wrote Uri Zvi Greenberg. "But blood will determine who is the ruler here. . . . And I say: The country conquered by blood, and only her conquered by blood, is made holy for a people of holy blood . . ." However embarrassing it is to admit it, Greenberg is a world-class poet—the Ezra Pound of Hebrew poetry.* The maximalists called him a "Poet and Legislator." In 1949, in the only interesting speech he ever gave in his life, Shamir accepted Greenberg as a poet but rejected him as a legislator:

> From him we learned vision and fervor, but when it comes to the realization of the vision I will not accept his advice. I have reached the conclusion, out of past experience, that if we take his advice on how to realize the vision we will damage his vision severely—it will not be fulfilled. After all, our ambition is not only to read poetry, but mainly to realize, to act.†

The maximalist Zionists criticized not only the leadership of the Yishuv under Ben-Gurion but also Jabotinsky himself. A central political question for Zionism was always on which international power Jews should depend in order to carry out the Zionist plan. Jabotinsky's answer, in spite of his criticism of the Zionist leadership, was Britain. Even after the pogroms of 1929 to which the British turned a blind eye, he believed that Britain should be given another chance. The maximalists argued that Britain had no intention of helping the Zionist enterprise and should be considered a foreign power in the land,

---

*Greenberg's work is widely read in Israel. Three volumes of his collected poems, edited by Dan Meron, have been published and six are still to come. Hundreds of his poems were translated into English by Harold Schimmel. The translations have been held by the Institute for the Translation of Hebrew Literature in Israel for some ten years, and are as yet unpublished.

†*Lehi Revealed: Minutes of the Conference of the Fighters for the Freedom of Israel, March 1949* (in Hebrew, Ramat Gan, 1985), p. 91.

and that another powerful country had to be found to support the Zionist cause.

This search for a helpful foreign power underwent many transformations in Shamir's circle, as we shall see; its members turned from their original attachment to the semi-fascist Poland of the colonels, to the fascist Italy of Mussolini, to Hitler's Nazi Germany, and finally to Stalin's Soviet Union. One thing is clear—they considered Britain and the decadent Anglo-Saxon world to be treacherous, and believed it had to be replaced as an ally. This suspicion of the Anglo-Saxon world has remained with Shamir to this day.

The maximalists' criticism of Weizmann and Jabotinsky not only was political but took the form of highly emotional and often bitter rhetorical claims which one can find in the writings of Greenberg, among others: Zionism must not be based on Jewish misery. The Land of Israel is not an orphanage. The justification of Zionism is not anti-Semitism and oppression but the idea of establishing a kingdom by achieving mastery—*Herrschaft*; that is, legitimate repression—over the land. We are masters: the land belongs to "Supermen," children of the Zionist revolution. The concept of mastery remains with Shamir to the present day. As for the other concept, that of "the kingdom," although it is somewhat ridiculous to picture Shamir as a Davidic king, with biblical robes and sandals, one aspect of the idea stuck: that historical Jerusalem is and must be "the heart of the kingdom." Also, a kingdom is not a democratic institution—and for Shamir and his friends, to carry out the Zionist vision does not mean one has an inherent commitment to democracy.

Although many maximalists originally derived from the labor movement, they became its bitter enemies. They hated communism, but they had an immense admiration for revolution and for Lenin. They saw him and his revolution as having set an example for the Zionist revolution: heroic sacrifice, cruelty, asceticism, readiness for radical social change, concentration on a single goal, contempt for the bourgeoisie, and the ability to create myths and symbols that had the emotional intensity of religion. They wanted to transfer all these attributes to the Zionist revolution, while adding a new element of their own: a deep revolutionary contempt for the intelligentsia. According to Shamir, intellectuals lack a sense of timing and they are impatient and stupid about tactics. He considered Uri Zvi Greenberg and his friends to be such intellectuals who are incompetent in practical matters. There is only one thing you can't take away from the intellectuals, in Shamir's opinion: the ability to create myths and symbols and to outline a vision of large goals.*

The myth that meant the most to the maximalists was that of the great Jewish revolt against the Romans in the first century A.D. They identified with the zealots, especially with the sect known as the *sicarii*, named for the short knives (*sica*) they wore in their clothes. The *sicarii* used these knives to spread terror in order to ensure that the revolt would continue without compromise. Shamir once recalled how, after emerging from a British prison, he came to an orchard, where he met a young man whom he described as follows: "Long-bearded, wild, swarthy and thin. He reminded me of an early Hebrew zealot hiding from the Romans and their traitorous allies in a Judean cave." The Jewish revolt against Rome, which caused half the population of Judaea to be killed, made roughly the same amount of sense that a declaration of war by Israel against the United States would make today. But it is precisely considerations of sense and cost that the myth of the revolt is intended to obliterate.

The other myth that inspires Shamir to this day is the myth of the traitor. For Uri Zvi Greenberg, the evils of treachery were personified by Sanballat the Horonite, who in the fifth century B.C. opposed the building of the walls around Jerusalem after the Jews returned there. (See Nehemiah 3–4.) When Shamir's current rivals on the left protest the settlements in the territories, and expose the facts about them, he considers them not merely political rivals in a democratic regime who disagree with his policies, but traitors—Sanballats who act as "informers" to the Americans. In Shamir's world there are three types of people: those who are faithful to the maximalist idea;

Lehi Revealed, p. 98: "When I read, in the literature of the Russian Revolution, words of derision and contempt about intellectuals, I did not at first understand: after all, it was those intellectuals who had laid the foundations for the revolution. But now I understand it, from our own experience. Intellectuals are necessary and important for every political movement, but they are inclined to be detached and to ignore realistic elements in carrying out their ideas. Without their ideas we are nothing, but without an understanding of reality their ideas will remain forever in a world of ideas." —My translation.

people who are not informers even though they are not helpful; and traitors. The last category is the most extensive one for Shamir: once it even included Begin and the Irgun. Shamir is not a religious man, but there are many Orthodox people among his assistants because he believes in believers. They are more likely to be loyal.

Shortly before Jabotinsky died while visiting the United States in 1940, there was a split in the Irgun between the group headed by Irgun commander David Raziel, who remained loyal to Jabotinsky, and those who were loyal to Avraham Stern, known by his underground name of "Yair." There were personal reasons for the split, but the main factors were ideological and political. The central problem facing the underground at the time was what to do during World War II. To the followers of Jabotinsky, it was obvious that the war against Nazi Germany must be supported by the Jewish nation. All attacks against the British must cease, and the Jews must rally to their support. Indeed, Raziel was killed commanding an attack in Iraq that had been coordinated with the British army.* Menachem Begin, who had arrived in Palestine in 1942 with General Anders' Polish army, was appointed to replace him in 1943.

Stern, by contrast, made a distinction between an enemy and a foe. The enemy is the occupier of your homeland—that is, the British— while a foe is anyone with strong anti-Semitic views. Stern recognized no obligation to fight one's foes, and he even believed that it was permissible to enter into agreements with them. According to this view, Hitler was a foe but not an enemy; it was the British who must be fought. Stern's goal was to establish a Jewish kingdom within the borders of the biblical promise—from the Nile to the Euphrates— while deporting the Arabs from this region.

At first Shamir did not join Stern and he was not yet a member of his organization in the summer of 1941 when Stern sent a messenger to Beirut to contact the Nazis and offer them the following

---

*A good biography of David Raziel was written by his nephew, Arye Naor (the secretary of the cabinet under Begin): it contains a detailed account of the split in the Irgun. See Arye Naor, *David Raziel: The Life and Times of the Commander-in-Chief of the "Irgun" Underground in Palestine* (in Hebrew, Tel Aviv, 1990).

proposal: "The establishment of the historical Jewish state, on a nationalist and totalitarian basis, tied by treaty to the German Reich, in accordance with the preservation and strengthening of future German power positions in the Near East."* Through his messenger Stern offered to cooperate with Hitler's forces actively on condition that this effort would be appropriately recognized. The mission failed; the Nazis were simply not interested.

We can reconstruct approximately when Shamir became privy to these dealings with the Nazis.† In the fall of 1941 Stern's underground command group met to discuss a threat—shortly to be carried out—made by two important commanders to leave the group, partly because of the failure of the mission to the Germans. The discussions continued for three days in an atmosphere of crisis. On the third day Shamir joined them—that is, he was immediately included in the command group. Even if Shamir had not previously known about the dealings with the Nazis—which is highly implausible, since he was so quickly admitted to the group of top leaders—he obviously knew about them from that day on. He also knew that Stern was determined to renew his connections with the Nazis, for it was decided to do so during the discussions; in fact, a second and equally futile attempt to contact the Nazis was made later in 1941.‡ It was also decided at that time that Shamir would have a part in planning robberies to provide financing for the underground.

Shamir thus became a partner in an underground movement which was wholly isolated from the Yishuv. Most of the other Jewish leaders rejected its actions, especially after members of the Lehi killed two Jewish police officers while trying to murder several British detectives. In February 1942 the British murdered Stern himself when they discovered his hiding place in Tel Aviv. Most of the members of the

---

*See Joseph Heller, *Lehi: Ideology and Politics 1940–1944* (in Hebrew, Jerusalem, 1989), Vol. I, p. 124.

†See Ada Amichal Yevin, *In Purple: The Life of Yair-Abraham Stern* (in Hebrew, Tel Aviv, 1986), p. 250.

‡The second mission was carried out by Nathan Yelin-Mor in December 1941. A few days before Stern's murder, he was caught and arrested in Syria before making contact with the Nazis.

underground were arrested and put in the Mazra prison. When in August 1942 an opportunity arose for some of them to escape, Shamir was chosen first in the hope that he would put the underground back on its feet. He had to take an assistant with him, and he chose Giladi.

The Giladi affair is still surrounded by mystery. Shamir decided to eliminate him, arguing that he was a dangerous adventurer who planned to assassinate the leaders of the Yishuv. But Giladi was never given a trial by the underground, and his own version of the story is buried in the sands. In any event, after Giladi was killed, Shamir called together thirteen of the underground commanders and demanded their approval of the execution, which he got.

To this day no one knows precisely what Giladi was planning to do or what was the basis for Shamir's claims against him. He is described by his fellow Stern group member Nathan Yelin-Mor as subscribing to the nihilistic credo of the mid-nineteenth-century Russian revolutionary Dmitri Pisarev: "Whatever can be smashed must be smashed. Whoever can withstand the blow is healthy. . . . Hit out hard right and left."* Giladi was apparently a brave man, and by Shamir's standards he was loyal to the Zionist idea. He may also have been a psychopathic revolutionary. But the actual evidence about him is hazy. What is clear from the evidence we have is that it was Shamir who decided that he had to be killed.†

WHAT BEGAN AS Stern's underground was now known as Lehi (*Lohamey Herut Israel*—Fighters for the Freedom of Israel), and it was headed by a three-man command with Shamir in charge of organization and operations. The underground was organized as a revolu-

---

*Nathan Yelin-Mor, *Lohamey Herut Israel* (Fighters for the Freedom of Israel), third edition (in Hebrew, 1975), p. 101.

†There is no controversy over the fact that Shamir made the decision to execute Giladi. See Yelin-Mor's *Lohamey Herut Israel*, p. 102, and J. Banai (Mazal), *Hayyalim Almonim* (in Hebrew, Tel Aviv, 1978), p. 145. A question remains whether Giladi was killed by Shamir himself. The sources are deliberately ambiguous on this point. Yelin-Mor writes that he expected Shamir and Giladi to "come to the drawing of pistols" one day, and warned Shamir to be alert to the danger and make sure that "he drew his pistol first." I read this as suggesting he did so—and so do the Lehi people who have talked to me about it.

tionary conspiracy, not as a quasi-military group like the Irgun. There were no ranks, only "tasks" to be carried out. Against the background of the organized Yishuv, whose Zionism was characterized by the slogan "yet another dunam and yet another goat," Shamir's Zionism was ridiculed by his rivals from the Irgun as adhering to "yet another dead British policeman and yet another one." A circular Lehi put out in 1944 for its members—Shamir most probably took part in drafting it—speaks of three stages of battle: the stage of terror, to educate the people and attract the world's attention; the stage of guerrilla warfare and sabotage, to prepare the general public for revolt; and, finally, the stage of revolt itself—a general revolt of the entire nation. Translated into Arabic, this could be George Habash's plan for revolution.

Lehi's most important action, which Shamir and his colleagues planned at the time of his escape from prison, was an attack on Lord Moyne, the British Minister of State for the Middle East, who was in Cairo during the war. The idea was to demonstrate that, in contrast to the Irgun, Lehi was fighting against British imperialism in general and not just against the British administration in Palestine. When Moyne was assassinated in November 1944 the two Lehi men who killed him were caught, put on trial in Egypt, and executed. They won considerable sympathy from the Egyptian intelligentsia in Cairo.*

The year 1944 also marked a political turning point for Lehi: its

---

*In a speech made in 1949, Shamir gave the following account of the assassination:

Let me tell you the history of one of our peak operations. We once sent comrades abroad to execute an anti-imperialist operation par excellence, an attempt on the life of Lord Moyne. On the face of it, a simple matter—two boys were sent and, as usual, of the very best. They arrived in Cairo, rented two bicycles, and quietly strolled in the luxurious street where the Lord's villa was located. They emptied their magazines, couldn't escape, and were hanged. This is how it was accepted. But what went on before this operation took place? This is how you reach such a peak: already "Yair" [Stern] had talked to one of the boys, who went to those places, about an assault on the Minister of State in Cairo. (At that time someone else served in this role: Lyttelton.)

I heard by accident that such a plan existed, and I heard it spoken about as if it were a fantasy. When I was planning my escape from Mazra I thought that such an organizational goal should be set—that we should be able to reach the possibility of an attempt on the life of the British Governor of the Middle East. *Lehi Revealed*, pp. 97–98.

leaders now saw the Soviet Union as a candidate for an alliance with the Jewish national movement. The idea of turning to the Soviet Union for support became a central issue in 1949, when the underground was transformed into a political party in the new state of Israel. Shamir headed the pro-Soviet faction. Joseph Heller, in *Lehi: Ideology and Politics*, a comprehensive study of Lehi's ideological development, speaks of Lehi as committed to the kind of "national Bolshevism" expounded by extreme nationalists who, during the Weimar period, admired the Bolsheviks for their ruthless political methods.

But was Shamir really a national Bolshevik? I am convinced that the ideology that has always meant the most to him is instead one that can be characterized as national egoism. In other words, the national interest, as defined by a dedicated ascetic revolutionary avant-garde prepared for sacrifice, is the supreme value, and no moral constraints apply to it. National egoism is built upon two strong inclinations: a readiness for sacrifice, which gives the individual an uplifted moral feeling, and a willingness to cast off any moral inhibitions, which allows the collective to do whatever serves its interests.

Shamir was never a Communist, and seems to have no interest in one vision of the social order as preferable to another. But as a national egoist he was attracted by the possibility of a national communism, as in Tito's Yugoslavia, that would have Soviet support but without Soviet rule. From the mid- to the late 1940s Shamir considered this a serious possibility. The proposition that "the end justifies the means" is a ridiculous phrase. "What else could justify the means," the philosopher Sidney Morgenbesser asks, "if not the end?" A Hebrew expression, "The end sanctifies the means," is more precise. Shamir has always believed in this. He is not by any means an ideological communist, but he is a psychological Bolshevik. However, in one important sense, Shamir is a revolutionary of a pre-Bolshevik type. He does not believe in mechanical history. He is a voluntarist; history, in his view, is shaped by strong wills. Hence the Jewish people, if united and resolute, can impose its will against all odds.

IN MAY 1948, when the British left Palestine, Shamir returned, via Paris, from his place of exile in Eritrea. Along with the rest of the

Lehi leaders, he considered Ben-Gurion's government defeatist, since it was prepared to abandon Jerusalem by allowing it to become an international city. They saw Count Bernadotte, the United Nations emissary who had saved many Jews from the Nazis, as a pro-German Swedish aristocrat whose suggestions for internationalizing Jerusalem they suspected Ben-Gurion might accept; and they decided to kill him.

After Bernadotte was assassinated by order of the Lehi command, of which Shamir was one of the three principal leaders, many members of the underground were arrested and Lehi was outlawed by the new Israeli state. Shamir organized the remaining Lehi members into an illegal underground movement but now against the Israeli government. During the first Israeli elections in 1949 there appeared a "Fighters' Party," with Shamir, along with five other Lehi members, among its main leaders. The Lehi soon obtained a state pardon and became a legal party.

It attracted few votes, however, and Shamir found himself with a family to support but no job. He became a bookkeeper in a small official agency. When a government position as an inspector became available, he applied for it. Ben-Gurion said to the Minister of the Interior, "I understand that you intend to employ the terrorist Yzernitsky. I oppose it." That was enough. Shamir went into the movie business and even planned to import art films from France.

In 1956 after Ben-Gurion lifted his ban on employing members of Lehi, Shamir was offered a job by Isser Harel, who was serving at that time as both head of Israel's internal security services and as head of the Mossad, Israel's CIA. The similarity between the two men is striking—both have the same short stature and the same Cheka mentality, which sees the Secret Service as a kind of ascetic order which is absolutely loyal to an idea and is capable of any act of cruelty or terror that is considered to be for the good of the state. When some documents fell out of the car of Foreign Minister Moshe Sharett (who later served as Prime Minister), Harel demanded that Sharett be investigated on suspicion of spying. Paranoiac fantasies were not uncommon in the Mossad: it is the Jesuit order of national egoism; and as such it suited Shamir perfectly. Shamir was directly accountable to Harel, not to the head of a department, and this created the impression that Shamir held a position of high importance. But the jobs he carried out and the numbers of agents assigned him show that he was by no means a central figure in the Mossad organization.

Five of Shamir's Lehi friends were hired by the Mossad along with him, among them an expert in explosives and the inventor of letter bombs. In the late 1950s President Nasser of Egypt undertook an ambitious project of manufacturing missiles under the supervision of German scientists. The Al Kahira missile, Nasser boasted, was capable of reaching Beirut. This was enough for Harel. He proposed that Israel should give the highest priority to the threat of these missiles and should try to kill the German scientists involved. In this he won the support of Foreign Minister Golda Meir; but Ben-Gurion and Shimon Peres, who was then general director of the Defense Ministry, believing that the missiles were not sophisticated enough to threaten Israel seriously, felt it would be more worthwhile to extort considerable military assistance from Germany in compensation, since the embarrassed Germans were still trying to get rid of their Third Reich image.

In the meantime the Mossad went ahead with its campaign, called Operation Damocles, to assassinate the German scientists. Letter bombs were sent to German scientists in Egypt as well as in Europe. Some of them were opened by secretaries or by members of the scientists' families, and several people were killed or injured; some were blinded. Ben-Gurion wanted to stop the campaign against the scientists, and as a result Harel left the Mossad; he was followed shortly by Shamir, who left in March 1963. The fact that Shamir left the Mossad at this time, and that he became Harel's partner in a factory for prefabricated buildings, suggests that he agreed with Harel's position on the operations against the German scientists; but this has yet to be proven. In any event, the hostility and lack of trust Shamir displays toward Peres seem to have originated during this period.

IN 1970, AT the age of fifty-five, Yitzhak Shamir entered politics. Avraham Stern's brother, the contractor David Stern, recommended him to Begin, and Shamir was attracted to Begin's Herut Party as the only one advocating a Greater Israel, the single issue of importance in Israeli politics so far as Shamir is concerned. He was put in charge of organization in Herut, and he became a member of the Knesset in the elections following the 1973 Yom Kippur War. During the election of 1977 he worked in the party's campaign headquarters, which was headed by Ezer Weizman and was highly effective in getting Begin elected Prime Minister. Begin did not ask Shamir to be a minister in his government, but appointed him speaker of the Knesset. "We appointed the head of Lehi to be speaker of the Jewish parliament. What a revenge of history!" he is said to have remarked.

Shamir was openly opposed to the peace treaty with Egypt. He once summed up his attitude toward peace treaties in general by saying, "Peace is an abstract thing. You sign a paper and say, 'Here is peace,' but what if tomorrow you tear up the paper and with one stroke of the pen you abolish the treaty?" The same remarks apply to his views of political agreements in general. During the last Knesset elections Shamir signed an agreement with Tehiya, the extreme right-wing party, promising that Tehiya members would join the government. When he violated the agreement, the head of Tehiya, Yuval Neeman, called Shamir and asked him, "What about the agreement? Should I hang it in the museum?" Shamir answered, "Do whatever you want with it."

No one in Israeli politics has ever broken agreements so blatantly as Shamir. His statement "For the sake of the Land of Israel it's all right to lie" is often quoted in the Israeli press. Israeli politicians caught on to this a long time ago, and none of them believes his promises. Recently, to Shamir's annoyance, President Bush and Secretary of State Baker have caught on as well. Still, both in Israel and abroad the most unreliable Israeli politician is thought to be Shimon Peres, even though Peres, not Shamir, has almost fanatically kept the agreements he has made. He even kept his agreement to rotate as Prime Minister with Shamir in the national-unity coalition government formed after the 1984 elections.

Very few Israeli politicians would have withstood the temptation to violate that agreement, especially since Peres was very successful as Prime Minister. He eliminated the 700 percent inflation of the preceding Shamir government, withdrew the army from Lebanon (a move that Shamir opposed), and for a time was even quite popular.

He kept the agreement with Shamir in order to be seen as trustworthy, but it didn't do him much good. Reliability in Israeli politics does not depend on a commitment to tell the truth and honor agreements. Reliability means having an aura of authenticity, which has much to do with toughness of manner. Shamir and Rabin are perceived as authentic, while Peres is perceived as slick.

Moshe Dayan, one of the negotiators of the peace treaty with Egypt, resigned as Foreign Minister in the Begin government when he realized that Begin in fact regretted having signed the treaty and was trying to avoid keeping his commitments to the Palestinians. Begin did not offer the post to Shamir, but offered it instead to two ministers of another party, both of whom refused. For six months Begin took over the portfolio himself, and only then, partly owing to internal pressure from his own party, did Begin appoint Shamir Foreign Minister. In that capacity Shamir was one of the first people to receive reports about the massacre taking place in the Palestinian refugee camps of Sabra and Shatila in Lebanon. Morally insensitive as usual, he did nothing. The commission of inquiry set up following the massacre clearly blamed him for this. But the one who paid with his job, and was later dropped from the Likud Party list by the party convention, was the minister who told Shamir by telephone about the massacre going on in the refugee camps.

Begin resigned from office in September 1983. Shamir ran for Prime Minister in the Likud central committee and obtained a 60 percent majority. He set up a new government, keeping the portfolio of the Foreign Ministry for himself. The government lasted less than a year, and early elections were held in a situation of economic catastrophe, with the army stuck in Lebanon and soldiers being killed each day. Moreover, the uncharismatic Shamir had to run in the shadow of Begin, who was worshipped by his party and its supporters. Yet he didn't lose. The Likud had established itself as a major party, and people voted for it regardless of its leader. For Likud voters, especially those of Oriental origin, the Likud is not a party but a second home. (Its status as a home is now seriously eroded by the internal power struggle between Shamir and David Levi, the Sephardic Foreign Minister. Levi accuses Shamir and the Likud leadership of treating the Sephardic community with contempt.)

Two major blocs emerged, Likud and Labor, neither of which was able to form a government on its own. Instead, a national-unity government was formed in 1984 with the position of Prime Minister in rotation: first Peres, then Shamir. What happened then might recur in this year's elections, in which Shamir is now running against Yitzhak Rabin. Although it seems possible, as I write in the early spring, that Rabin could defeat Shamir, the popularity of the Labor Party usually peaks too early. The elections are in June, and Shamir, who has held the office of Prime Minister longer than anyone else in Israel since Ben-Gurion, may still recover unless the economic situation worsens before the elections.

This may happen if the United States government continues its policy of withholding loan guarantees, for without the guarantees Shamir will find it more difficult to manipulate the economy to the Likud's advantage during the campaign. Thus his position is not an easy one. The Israeli stock exchange fell sharply when the news arrived that the guarantees would not be forthcoming. Many people who have money invested in stocks are middle-class Likud supporters who understand the gravity of the economic situation. Some of them may prefer to vote for Rabin as a Prime Minister who would freeze the building of Israeli settlements on the West Bank and "bring peace," at least with the United States. If Shamir loses the election and is forced into the opposition, he will probably retire. Aside from the fact that he is seventy-seven years old, parliament is not for him.

In 1988, following the Knesset elections, another national-unity government of Likud and Labor was formed, this time without rotation. Shamir was the sole Prime Minister, and in May 1989 his government authorized an Israeli peace initiative. This was called "the Shamir initiative," a contradiction in terms since Shamir does not initiate anything, certainly not peace. The American pressure on him to do something forced him to accept, as a temporary stalling tactic, what was actually Rabin's initiative in the hope that the Arabs would continue their usual practice of rejecting any Israeli initiative. This did not happen, and to Shamir's great misfortune, Baker and Bush acted as though they were taking him seriously. Thus Shamir finds himself conducting discussions with the Arab states and the Palestinians. Until now he has been successful in making sure that the only thing that happens at the discussions is what Rabin rightly calls "grinding water."

MENACHEM BEGIN DIED in March 1992, and since then Israelis have been asking two questions about him: Why did he retire in 1983? And why did he then become a recluse? One of the answers offered for both questions is that he regretted the Lebanon War and felt guilty about its victims, but this seems to me doubtful. After Begin's resignation there was a hunger strike of Israeli doctors, and Begin met with a group of them which included Jabotinsky's granddaughter. She later said to some of her friends, "I know the signs of clinical depression from my work, and Begin is a textbook case." Begin had previously had severe attacks of depression; and the most convincing explanation for his resignation is that he was suffering from a clinical form of depression. But the true enigma, in my view, is not why he resigned but why he closed himself off from the world for nine years. That he was in a state of depression for all those years does not appear to be a likely explanation. The answer, in my opinion, is pride. Israel is too small to provide any place to retire to—it has no country houses, no Colombey-les-Deux-Eglises. Like God, Begin was forced to preserve his honor by hiding from his believers.

A few days after Begin's resignation, a Knesset member from Shamir's party entered the office of the new Prime Minister. "How good it is to come into the office and not feel that you're in the presence of God," he said. Shamir blew up at the astounded Knesset member. "I'm like Begin! I'm like Begin!" he shouted. This should be interpreted not as an outburst of megalomania, but as an attempt to say, in effect, I intend to assert my authority just as Begin did, and you'd better not feel at ease in my office. But the enigma of Begin seems simple compared with the enigma of Shamir. Two sorts of accounts can be given of Shamir, and it's hard for Shamirologists to decide between them.

Thesis: There is no such man. Shamir is nothing but an incarnation of the status quo. He doesn't take any initiatives. He has no analytical understanding of Israel's situation. He lacks imagination and the capacity to lead. He represents the members of a powerful bureaucracy who preserve their authority by making use of a man as gray as a foggy day, just as the apparatchiks ruled the Soviet Union in the name of Chernenko. He has no distinctive abilities or even an ego that drives him forward; a group of his close associates is effectively running things. It's a waste of time to discuss Shamir and his past because he is a deeply boring man who has never said anything interesting in his life; he is not, in any case, the one who decides things.

Antithesis: Shamir is a cold-blooded man of iron will who cares about one thing only—the Greater Land of Israel. He's not particularly intelligent but he's clever and sly. He feels no need to impress people but he is acutely aware of what is happening around him. He doesn't have his head in the clouds as Begin did. He constantly reads intelligence reports and masters their details. He fudges decisions in matters that seem unimportant. But the so-called status quo has been carefully created by Shamir, and not by an invisible apparat. He is not just passive, he's hyperpassive. He devotes enormous effort to ensuring that nothing will happen, and that Israel will keep the territories.

Synthesis: Shamir is exactly what the thesis claims in all matters he considers of secondary importance, which is almost everything. But he is exactly what the antithesis claims on issues of primary importance to him; and what is most important to him is the power to leave to the next generation the decision to extend Israeli sovereignty to the occupied territories, which are part of the historic Land of Israel. Shamir's success with many American Jews seems based on their confidence that he is essentially a tough bargainer—a Jewish Assad. But Shamir is not a bargainer. Shamir is a two-dimensional man. One dimension is the length of the Land of Israel, the second, its width. Since Shamir's historical vision is measured in inches, he won't give an inch. He will not bargain about the Land of Israel or about any interim agreement that would involve the least risk of losing control over the occupied territories.

How can one tell a hard bargainer from someone who, in the end, won't bargain at all? Looking at Shamir's past record is not always useful. After all, the most important peace agreements in recent world history were achieved by people of integrity who reversed their previous commitments: De Gaulle's agreement on Algeria, Begin's on the Sinai, De Klerk's on apartheid and white control. Why should Shamir be different? Because Shamir, unlike the other people I have mentioned, isn't interested in being "written down in history," as he puts it. De Gaulle, Begin, De Klerk all seemed highly conscious of their place in history. Shamir, from all the evidence we have, does not have any comparable consciousness. His past record, together with the fact that he doesn't care what people think, provides good reason to believe that he is not a bargainer at all—in other words, that he is not open to any sort of compromise.

An ancient Jewish legend tells of a small worm that King Solomon used to break up large rocks for the construction of the Temple. Shamir doesn't want to be considered a bulldozer, like Sharon. His ambition is to be the worm that breaks up the rocks for the Temple; it's enough for him to be a tiny, practically invisible, but inexorable force. Indeed, the Hebrew name for King Solomon's worm is *Shamir*.

"The sea is the same sea and the Arabs are the same Arabs" is a memorable utterance of Shamir's. The truth is that the sea is not the same sea—it is much more polluted than it used to be—and the Arabs have changed, too. But Shamir is still around and he is still the same Shamir. He is against Netanyahu—he does not trust him to keep the territories in Israel's power; in fact, he does not trust him on anything.

There is one accomplishment for which Shamir deserves great credit—keeping Israel out of the Gulf War in 1991. We now know that he was under pressure from within his party to do something, but for once his nerves of steel and his knack of active inaction served Israel well.

13

YITZHAK RABIN:
SOLDIER AND STATESMAN

MAY 1992

ROSA COHEN, YITZHAK RABIN'S MOTHER, WAS A DAUGHTER OF THE Russian Revolution, a non-Zionist socialist. She arrived in Palestine from Odessa having originally hoped to go to Scandinavia, remained there as a member of Kibbutz Kinneret, and took part in its life with immense revolutionary zeal. She had an uncle in Palestine—the distinguished Zionist publicist Mordechai ben Hillel Hacohen (1856–1936), who had given the first speech in Hebrew at the founding Zionist Congress in Basel in 1897—a memorable accomplishment, since Hebrew was not a living, spoken language at the time. If Rabin's great-uncle was capable of reviving a dead language, Rabin himself can cause severe injury to a living one. Rabin was brought up speaking Hebrew, but the Hebrew he speaks is wooden and full of embarrassing errors.

Rabin's father, born in the Ukraine, emigrated to the United States as a young boy. During World War I he came to Palestine to join the Jewish Brigade, which included David Ben-Gurion and Ze'ev Jabotinsky among its famous members. A friendly, tenderhearted man, he married Rosa Cohen in 1921, and their son Yitzhak was born in Jerusalem in 1922. The family moved to the first Jewish city in Palestine, Tel Aviv. There, in the Labor movement school, Rabin was strongly attracted to the idealistic Zionism of his teacher Eliezer Smoli, the author of *Frontiersmen of Israel*, a saga of agrarian Jews working with their hands to create a just, communal farm life out of the hostile Palestinian swampland, and fighting with treacherous Arabs, much as Western frontiersmen once fought with the Indians.

When he was fifteen Rabin was accepted as a student at the Kadoorie agricultural school near Mount Tabor. Just as Wellington claimed that "the battle of Waterloo was won on the playing fields of Eton," the Israeli War of Independence, one could claim, was won on the fields of Kadoorie. The first members of the elite fighting force called the Palmach—an abbreviation of the Hebrew term for "assault companies"—which did much to win the war in 1948, were recruited from the Kadoorie school in 1941. The Palmach was the most effective and professional branch of the Haganah, the Zionist underground military organization. Rabin was invited to join it that year by Yigal Allon, who had been in the first class to graduate from Kadoorie, and went on to become the Palmach's commander in 1945. Rabin acted as Allon's deputy in the War of Independence, and Allon was eventually appointed Foreign Minister in Rabin's government.

Rabin was the outstanding student in his class at Kadoorie—a not inconsiderable achievement—and he won the British High Commissioner's prize for academic excellence, as well as a scholarship to Berkeley to study hydraulic engineering. He might well have had a successful career in many fields, but he was unable to take advantage of the scholarship because of his commitment to the Palmach, and since he is too opinionated to be an autodidact, the result is that he is strangely ignorant and lacking in culture.

In September 1969, Golda Meir offered Rabin the post of Minister of Education in the government she planned to set up following the November elections. In his autobiography he describes his reaction as follows:

> The idea of education was very exciting. I had not aspired to be a professional educator, but I believed that my background in the Palmach and in the army included, in a broad sense, extensive dealings with education for positive values.*

He had, he says, serious criticisms of the educational system because "the official study program allotted more hours to Madame Pompadour than to all the underground fighting units of Israel—the Haganah, Palmach, Irgun, and Lehi." The truth is that Madame Pompadour is allotted not even one minute in the Israel school curriculum. Rabin apparently uses the name "Madame Pompadour" to stand for the entire French Revolution, as well as the *ancien régime*; and the Israeli schools could, in fact, profitably devote more time to the French Revolution than to the study of Zionist underground movements. It is not the excessive interest of teachers in "Madame Pompadour" that poses a problem for Israelis today but the limitations of Rabin's own education, which ended at Kadoorie, and which since then has been concerned only with "positive values."

The first Palmach operation in which Rabin took part, in June 1941, was directed against the Vichy French regimes in Syria and Lebanon. During 1941 and 1942, when Nazi forces were advancing toward Palestine, the Palmach mounted guerrilla attacks that were intended to help the British Army. Moshe Dayan recruited Rabin to take part in the campaign against the Vichy French. (Later the same day, fighting in a village several miles away from Rabin's unit, Dayan lost his left eye.)

In October 1945, Rabin was appointed deputy commander of one of the Palmach's more ambitious and successful missions, an attack

---

*All references are to Rabin's two-volume autobiography, written with (the *Ma'ariv* journalist) Dov Goldstein, under the title *Pinkas Sherut* (*A Record of Service*) (Tel Aviv, 1979). A shorter, one-volume version also appeared, *The Rabin Memoirs* (in English, Boston, 1979).

on a British Army camp at the foot of Mount Carmel, which was intended to liberate hundreds of illegal immigrants, Holocaust survivors whom the British had arrested. This operation had to be conducted with great care, not only to avoid excessive British casualties, but to protect the Holocaust survivors, who refused to be separated from the bundles of possessions they had brought with them.

At the end of June 1946, Rabin, together with his father, was among the many arrested on "Black Saturday," the day that the British rounded up and imprisoned many of the leaders of the Yishuv, the Jewish settlement in Palestine, and members of the Haganah. Rabin himself used the British tactics of "Black Saturday" against the *intifada*, when, as Israel's Defense Minister in 1987, he arrested tens of thousands of *intifada* activists and put them under administrative detention.

The 1948 War of Independence began, before the British left Palestine, on May 15 with a fierce battle against Arab forces for control of the roads, and particularly for the road to Jerusalem, which was under siege. The twenty-six-year-old Rabin, by then the operations officer of the Palmach, was given the extremely difficult task of forcing open the road to the city with two battalions, consisting of some five hundred men. This was the first attempt by Jewish forces to carry out a relatively large attack. It failed, and the number of casualties was very high. Later, after another battalion joined Rabin's forces, he was appointed commander of the Palmach's famous Harel Brigade, which was in charge of defending Jerusalem and the corridor leading to it. Rabin, like the other officers in this war, had to learn how to command in the midst of battle, and the price in casualties was immense: about 70 percent of the Harel fighters were killed or wounded. Whether many of these casualties could have been avoided, as the controversial military historian Uri Milstein has claimed, remains a matter of debate.*

Rabin had an important part in the defense of Jerusalem, particularly because David Shaltiel, the commander of the city, failed to take the initiative when he should have and proved utterly incom-

*The War of Independence: Out of Crisis Came Decision (in Hebrew, Tel Aviv, 1991).

petent. One of Israel's founding fathers, Zalman Aranne, came to see Rabin during one of the most difficult hours of the war, and said, as Rabin recalls in his memoirs, "I've known your parents for years. . . . If the Palmach doesn't enter the battle immediately, the southern part of Jerusalem will be lost." Anyone who grew up in the Yishuv at the time knows that there was no refusing a request by Aranne put in this way. The Palmach forces took over the main burden of defending the city.

Rabin gave up the command of the Harel Brigade in June 1948 and became Yigal Allon's operations officer in the battle for the central part of Palestine. Later he joined the staff of the chief of the Southern Command against the Egyptian Army. People who knew Rabin at the time have told me he was a superior staff officer, methodical and thorough; in fact he rose in the army hierarchy exclusively as a staff officer. His record as a commander of troops in the field was limited to the period when he was in charge of the Harel Brigade, and in that capacity his success is less clear.

By the time the war was over and the truce with Egypt was signed on the island of Rhodes—at which Rabin was present as a technical military adviser—Ben-Gurion was disbanding the Palmach. Although apparently only a routine matter of relieving officers from military service, this was actually one of the most severe traumas of the young state, and its repercussions affected Rabin's subsequent career.

During World War II a split had occurred in Mapai, the Labor Party headed by Ben-Gurion and the leading party in the Yishuv. About a third of its members, most of them from the kibbutzim known collectively as Ha-Kibbutz Ha-Me'uhad, as well as a considerable number from Tel Aviv and other cities, formed a group known as Faction B, which was opposed to Ben-Gurion and his associates, and particularly to Ben-Gurion's "Biltmore plan" of 1942, which stipulated that the Jewish state would be established in only a part of the land of Israel. (This plan, named after New York's Biltmore Hotel, where the plan had been approved, did not set the boundaries of the state, but it implied that the country would be divided.)

The members of Faction B were opposed to dividing the country, and, being Marxists, they were also against the "reformist" socialism of Ben-Gurion and his allies. They saw the Soviet Union as the model of socialism and the victorious Red Army as the model of a socialist army. Most of the Palmach supported Faction B. Ha-Kibbutz Ha-Me'uhad was in effect the Palmach's home base, and nearly all the Palmach's commanders came from there. Many Palmach members supported themselves by working half the time on the kibbutz and spending the other half in training.

In the early 1940s the members of Faction B were arguing that they should not join the British Army but should instead establish a Hebrew defense force that could protect the Yishuv after the war. Ben-Gurion, by contrast, believed that joining the British Army was the best way for young Jews to obtain free, professional training, and that doing so would also improve the Yishuv's international reputation as a community that had taken part in World War II. He also saw the Palmach as a threat to his authority, because it had great influence on many of the most capable and committed young men and women. Rabin, for his part, was not politically active during his days in the Palmach. He accepted Faction B's argument in favor of an independent Jewish force, but so far as we know he never took part in leftist criticism of the Mapai.

Ben-Gurion did everything he could after the War of Independence not only to disband the Palmach but also to get rid of most of its senior commanders, particularly Yigal Allon, the most senior of them all. Rabin, however, who was not clearly identified with any faction, was allowed to stay in the army and make it his career. The feeling among the Palmach people, who had done most of the fighting during the War of Independence, was reminiscent of the famous line from Schiller's play *Fiesco*: "The Moor has done his work, the Moor may go." A final gathering of the Palmach leaders was arranged, which was partly a farewell party, but also partly a protest by people who felt insulted. Ben-Gurion issued an order that anyone still serving in the army was forbidden to appear at this meeting. The night it was to take place Rabin was with Ben-Gurion, and, "sitting on pins and needles," as he puts it, he asked Ben-Gurion in one of the more eloquent of his statements, why he could not attend:

Why are you putting my friends and me, who have remained in the army, in an embarrassing dilemma between our wish to maintain discipline and our debt of friendship, brotherhood in arms and partnership to the people with whom we have walked a long way? Why are you forcing us to choose between two evils: either to participate in the gathering and thus to disobey orders, or not to participate and thus to violate the rules of friendship —to be considered a traitor in our friends' eyes?

Ben-Gurion did not answer, and Rabin went to the meeting. Ben-Gurion did not forget this, but Rabin's friends from Ha-Kibbutz Ha-Me'uhad did not forget it either. During the 1960s Ben-Gurion held up Rabin's appointment as chief of staff, giving as one of his reasons that Rabin had disobeyed an order not to attend the Palmach's farewell party. The people of Ha-Kibbutz Ha-Me'uhad, on the other hand, have always supported Rabin against Peres within the Labor Party as "one of us."

FROM THE BEGINNING, the Israeli Defense Forces (IDF) were divided into two rival factions: people who had been in the British Army on the one hand, and, on the other, former members of the Palmach. The former British Army members were noted for their rigid hierarchy of rank, their discipline, and their "army bullshit," while the youth movements that had made up the Palmach had a looser system of command, more in the style of a guerrilla movement. Rabin was allowed to recruit some former Palmach officers to serve on the teaching staff of the course for battalion commanders, the most advanced course then given. This gesture toward Rabin and other former Palmach members was made by General Hayyim Laskov, whom they considered their principal enemy from the "British school," but who had a reputation for being exceptionally decent and honest. Rabin got along with him well, and served as his deputy when Laskov was chief of staff.

By contrast, Rabin's relationship with Moshe Dayan was cold to the point of hostility, partly because Dayan considered Rabin to be loyal to Allon, Dayan's closest rival. Dayan had upstaged Allon on several occasions—he took over from Allon as chief of the Southern Command when the Palmach was disbanded, and he was appointed Defense Minister instead of Allon on the eve of the 1967 war. The rivalry between Dayan and Allon recalls Plutarch-like clashes between leaders—Dayan and Allon as Marius and Sulla. Both were Sabras and both were commanders of the earliest Palmach companies; in their struggle for power, they neutralized each other, with the result that neither of them ever became Prime Minister of Israel. The rivalry between Rabin and Peres is full of resentment and malice, but they seem no more than pale replicas of Dayan and Allon. They do not have the depth, the charm, the charisma of the originals.

The rivalry between Rabin and Peres is personal, but there is more to it than that. Peres, for years a high bureaucrat in the Ministry of Defense, is the founder of Israel's military-industrial complex, and Rabin, as a general, was in the position of being Peres' customer. Rabin was strongly opposed to the megalomaniacal attempt to produce all of Israel's military equipment within the country so that Israel could be self-sufficient in case of an arms embargo. This notion of self-sufficiency has led to extremely expensive small-scale production lines on the one hand and to the sale of arms to despicable foreign regimes on the other. Rabin was also opposed to Peres' purchases of arms largely from Europe during the 1950s and 1960s: he would have preferred American weapons. Not only militarily but politically, Peres wanted to link Israel with Europe, especially France and Germany, in contrast with Rabin, who did not know much about Europe and had no particular respect for it. For Rabin the outside world has always meant the United States.

But the political and ideological differences between Peres and Rabin should not be exaggerated. Over the years they have agreed on many issues, such as preferring to deal with King Hussein instead of with the Palestinians, and the antipathy between them is in the last analysis much more personal than public. Nahum Barnea, a journalist who is a shrewd observer of the Israeli scene, noted that Rabin, despite the woodenness of his speech, has a talent for nastily labeling his rivals. In his book he calls Peres "an indefatigable underminer," and this phrase has stuck to Peres in the public mind—partly because accusations tend to stick to Peres, who does not have Rabin's "Teflon" qualities, and partly because Peres is in truth indefatigable in undermining his opponents.

During the Suez conflict of 1956, Rabin was the chief of the Northern Command, on the Syrian border, while the main action of the war was directed against Egypt in the Sinai. Rabin's principal activity was to expel Arabs from northern Israel: "I solved one problem in the North," he wrote, "by taking advantage of the fighting in Egypt and in coordination with the United Nations: We transferred about two thousand Arabs—who constituted a serious security problem—from the places where they lived in the central demilitarized zone (south of Lake Huleh) to the eastern side of the Jordan." What he means by "coordination" with the UN is unclear.

In January 1964, Rabin was appointed chief of staff of the Israeli Army, and in 1967 he was military commander of the Six-Day War. He also bears considerable responsibility for the escalation of tensions with Arab nations that led to that war. During a meeting of the Knesset Security and Foreign Affairs Committee that took place during the tense weeks before the war, Dayan, who was not a member of the government at the time, addressed Rabin directly, saying, "You carried out ill-considered operations. You flew over Damascus. You attacked Samoa in broad daylight."

Dayan was referring here to Israeli planes that shot down six Syrian planes in a premeditated aerial ambush in April 1967, and had also flown over Damascus. He was referring as well to the Israeli armored convoy that, in November 1966, entered the village of Samoa on the West Bank, which was under Jordanian rule, and, during a clash with the Jordanian Army, killed scores of Jordanians. This operation, which took place during the day, was described as a reprisal for Jordanian-sponsored attacks, but it was quite different from the nighttime attacks by Israeli commandos that had become customary under Dayan's command. In this case Jordanian sovereignty was openly violated and by large forces.

When Rabin arranged a meeting with Dayan after his testimony, Dayan told him that it was a mistake to put General Nasser's leadership to the test in the Arab world, and that the operations against Syria and Jordan pushed Nasser into a position where he had no choice except to take aggressive action: "Thus we forced him to defend his prestige in his country and in the Arab world and this led to a serious escalation in the Middle East." No doubt Dayan had his own ambitious motives for attacking Rabin, but his criticisms were plausible nonetheless.

The period between mid-May and the outbreak of war on June 6 was called "the waiting period" in Israel. During that time Rabin met not only with Dayan but also with Ben-Gurion, who, making some of the same criticisms as Dayan had, told him: "You have brought the country into a very serious situation. You bear the responsibility." The word "you" referred to Rabin as well as the Prime Minister, Levi Eshkol. Moreover, the Interior Minister, Moshe Shapira of the National Religious Party—at that time one of the moderate parties in Israel—accused Rabin of having caused "Israel's plight." Then, on May 23, Rabin had a nervous breakdown that lasted for two days, which was concealed for years, although he has acknowledged that he had been in a state of "mental and physical exhaustion." He attributed his physical state to nicotine poisoning (he was a compulsive chain smoker) and overwork, but he admits in his memoirs that he had "strong guilt feelings. I couldn't forget Shapira's remarks. I had dragged Israel down into its plight." At the time of his collapse Rabin called Ezer Weizman, then the general in charge of operations, and told him in confidence what had happened. Years later, just before a vote between Peres and Rabin on who would succeed Golda Meir, Weizman, who wanted to help Peres, wrote an article telling the story of Rabin's breakdown.

Although Rabin was partly responsible for the escalation that led to the war, he was also responsible for preparing the army for, and planning, the most brilliant success in its history. Rabin has solid claims to being Israel's best chief of staff. That the photogenic Dayan stole most of the spotlight from him during the war—especially in the foreign press—has obscured the fact that Dayan took command of troops who were ready to fight. In Rabin's opinion Dayan's contribution consisted mainly of raising morale and giving the army and the Israeli public a sense of confidence. But that public, as opposed to the foreign correspondents who were drawn to Dayan, saw Rabin as the hero of the war.

Rabin's most popular moment came just after the Six-Day War when he gave a speech at the newly liberated Hebrew University campus on Mount Scopus. "I worked for two weeks preparing the speech," he wrote. "After consolidating the central ideas and the structure of the speech, I was assisted in its formulation by several people, especially my aide at that time, Rafael Efrat." Rabin has many faults, but lying is not one of them. In this case, however, Rabin is simply not telling the truth. The speech was written for him from beginning to end by Mordechai Bar-On, the IDF's chief education officer at that time. Rabin merely changed a few expressions because he was afraid no one would believe he had written them.

It's too bad he didn't keep this in mind when he hired Dov Goldstein to write his autobiography, since Goldstein produces the kind of kitsch of which Rabin himself has never been guilty; Goldstein puts words into Rabin's mouth that Rabin could not possibly have written:

We arrived at the Wailing Wall. The stones tell a story. A long story of suffering and pain, of exile and persecution. As if the historical memory of the Jewish people were entirely concentrated in the cracks between the stones of this holy Wall. As if all the tears are trying to burst out while all the hopes are proclaiming that this is not a time for crying. An hour of redemption. An hour of hope. An hour of Jewish unity. An hour of ascension of the soul.

Rabin, in my view, would have to admit that he did not write this passage. Yet he insists that he wrote the Mount Scopus speech, which, in the heady atmosphere following the victory, sounded modest and humane, with its talk of the army's need for "moral values," and, for this reason, had a strong effect. He said, for instance, that Ben-Gurion wrote to him saying, "I am proud of your speech. You have been privileged to be chief of staff in the finest hour of our glorious army—and you are indeed worthy of this." After all that, it would have been hard for Rabin to admit he didn't write the speech.

RABIN WAS APPOINTED Israel's ambassador to the Washington of Nixon and Kissinger. When Nixon had visited Israel in 1966 and 1967, accompanied by Pat Buchanan, he was thought to have no political future, but Rabin somehow understood that he intended to run again for President and he gave him—in his own words—"the red-carpet treatment." Nixon was grateful, and he remembered Rabin and the carpet. As a successful general in Washington, while Americans were unable to boast of any victories in Vietnam, Rabin had everything going for him. It's true that he is extremely shy, socially awkward, unable to make small talk, and uncouth—in short, the opposite of a diplomat—but in the social atmosphere of Washington at the time a general ranked higher than a diplomat.

While Rabin was serving in Washington, a war of attrition consisting of cross-border raids and artillery attacks was going on between Israeli forces in Sinai and the Egyptians on the other side of the canal. After the sweeping victory of the Six-Day War, this war of attrition was, for the Israelis, a very wearying anticlimax. From Washington, Rabin pressed for an escalation of the war through bombing deep inside Egypt. A telegram from Rabin to the Israeli government stated: "We have achieved a noticeable improvement in the United States position. Continued improvement depends first and foremost upon us—through persistence in aerial bombing of the heart of Egypt."

The bombings Rabin recommended took place and led to an unprecedented Soviet involvement on Egypt's behalf: the Soviet Union supplied Egypt with SAM-3 missiles that Israel (as well as the United States at that time) was unable to respond to, and that shot down Israeli Phantom jets and caused Israel serious damage.

Rabin was in a bizarre position as ambassador. A few days after the Six-Day War, the Israeli government headed by Golda Meir, of which Menachem Begin was a member, had passed a resolution that is now hard to believe: in return for peace, Israel would be prepared to retreat completely to its prewar borders with Syria and with

Egypt—in other words, to evacuate the Golan Heights and Sinai. But Meir's government later regretted this decision and quietly rescinded it without telling the Americans or even their own ambassador in Washington. During Rabin's entire term of office the Nixon administration was trying without success to figure out the Meir government's policy toward Israel's borders. Rabin himself did not understand the policy and said so. Finally the Prime Minister cabled him an explanation: "The policy of the Israeli government is striving toward a significant change in the border with Egypt, which means a change in sovereignty and not merely an Israeli presence. We are not using the word "annexation" because of the negative connotations of the term."

Here, in my view, lies a key to the 1973 Yom Kippur War, for this determination to expand Israel's borders would have become apparent to Sadat. One person who understood the disastrous implications of this policy was George Meany, head of the AFL-CIO and a close friend of Golda Meir. "I know what negotiation is," he said to Rabin. "I know the rules very well. . . . I consider the Egyptian position constructive. I cannot understand your position."

Rabin was the liaison between Golda Meir and the American government, especially Nixon and Kissinger, and also Attorney General John Mitchell, with whom he became well acquainted. Abba Eban, who was then Foreign Minister, was disregarded and not consulted. Rabin and Eban despise each other. Eban, the eternal outsider of Israeli politics, ironic (though without self-irony), worldly, intelligent, cultivated, and unwilling to take a stand when it mattered, could hardly be more different from Rabin, who is sarcastic but not ironic, a provincial Sabra, uncouth, and suspicious.

Rabin writes that his mentor in those years was Henry Kissinger: "With his characteristic Kissingerian broadness of view he painted before my eyes a picture of international dimensions," says the excited Kadoorie pupil after his first tutorial with the master. By contrast: "As is well known, it is difficult to have a dialogue with Abba Eban. Anyone who tries to have a 'discussion' with him ends up a listener." Rabin "learned" from Kissinger that one should enter into negotiations only from a position of strength. This is the magic formula of realpolitik. But it is just about as "realistic" as the formula "Sell stocks only at their highest price, not when the price is going down." Even when the price is going down, one may have to sell stocks, either because they may go down even further or because one needs money immediately. The same holds for the relationship between power and negotiations.

Rabin adopted what he took to be Kissinger's conception of the relationship between the United States and the Soviet Union and applied it to the relations between Israel and the Arab world. According to this view, there is no chance of peace. The only thing one can hope for is a state of nonbelligerency, anchored in interim agreements made "from a position of power." In view of the strategic stalemate in the balance of power between Israel and its neighbors, one can only make arrangements to ensure that the present situation will not deteriorate into actual war. Détente, not peace, is all one can realistically hope for. Kissinger, for his part, was able to negotiate unexpected agreements with both the Soviet Union and China. Rabin, it seems clear, since he saw peace with Egypt as an "unrealistic" aspiration, would not have been able to negotiate the peace treaty with Sadat as Begin did. Like many proponents of realpolitik, Rabin commits the fallacy of identifying an optimistic view of a possible solution with an optimistic view of the chances of achieving it. Some of those who criticize current international arrangements while hoping for a better world have an optimistic view. But this does not mean that they are necessarily optimistic about the chances of achieving a better world; they only believe that it is important to try.

For Rabin, the person who presents an optimistic alternative lacks seriousness and is likely to be a dangerous dreamer. Even now he talks only about an "interim agreement" with the Palestinians, nothing more. He claims that if elected he will reach an interim agreement on autonomy for the Palestinians within six months to a year. I will presently examine what he means by autonomy, but on the whole I believe him. Rabin likes to talk about "marching with two feet," the military foot and the political foot. This implies the brutal use of force in order to arrive at negotiations from a "position of power." Rabin's current popularity with Israeli voters—he leads in all the polls—is based on the fact that he expresses the ambivalence of most of them: they favor his "two feet" policy—brutality toward the Arabs as well as negotiations.

RABIN RETURNED TO Israel from Washington after openly trying to help Nixon win the election against Senator George McGovern in 1972. He correctly perceived that a Republican administration would be less likely than a Democratic administration to interfere with Israel's policy on developing nuclear arms. After the Yom Kippur War, when Golda Meir and Moshe Dayan were forced to resign because of public protest over their responsibility for Israel's failures, Rabin was elected to the Knesset and found himself a candidate for Prime Minister, with Shimon Peres as the rival candidate.

Peres invited Rabin for lunch and, according to Rabin's account, suggested they arrive at an understanding:

Let's try to learn something from the experience of our senior colleagues: Allon and Dayan fought each other and tired themselves out—and neither of them became Prime Minister. Let's make a gentlemen's agreement to run a fair race. (A little later I found out what constitutes a fair race for Peres and how much value his word has. . . .) Whoever wins, the other will accept the decision and act accordingly.

The kingmaker of the Labor Party, Pinhas Sapir, who was then Finance Minister, made sure that Rabin would win. This, however, did not ensure that Peres, as Defense Minister, would obey Rabin.

Gush Emunim was founded after Rabin took office in 1974, and toward the end of 1975 its members settled in the West Bank district of Sebastia in defiance of government policy against settlements in Samaria. Rabin writes that he "considered Gush Emunim a very serious phenomenon—a cancer in the body of democratic Israel." However, Rabin claims, it was impossible to prevent Gush Emunim from starting settlements, since Peres supported its members as "true idealists"—and Peres was not the only one in the Labor Party to do so. Rabin, to his credit, never called the settlers pioneers or said their settlements were a contribution to national security. He considered them a heavy burden on the state.

For Rabin the issue of the settlers was a repeat of the story of the *Altalena*, the ship that arrived in Israel in June 1948 carrying arms that had been bought in Europe for the Irgun. Its members, except for those in Jerusalem, had already been drafted into the IDF, and Ben-Gurion considered the shipment of arms an act of rebellion against the central government he headed. He assigned Rabin to sink the ship, and he did so. The lesson Rabin learned from this event was the need for "one central authority. No more splits, no more civil war between Jews." Sebastia was Rabin's *Altalena*, but he failed to impose the central authority he once claimed was necessary. His authority was seriously undermined as a result. Rabin had been chosen as Prime Minister by Sapir, not by the people.

Rabin was the first Sabra to become Prime Minister, and, as such, he raised high expectations that he would move away from Golda Meir's political immobilism with respect to the Arabs. This hope was dashed. He did not do so partly because Meir, though not officially in power, still was held in awe in the Labor Party. But there was a deeper, "psychological" reason why Rabin deferred to Golda's will. Many Sabra generals of his generation had formidable pioneering mothers, of whom Golda Meir was an archetype. Among them were Dvora Dayan, the mother of Moshe Dayan; Haya Slutsky, the mother of Meir Amit, who was Rabin's rival for the post of chief of staff; Yehudit Simhoni, the mother of Asaf Simhoni, who was chief of the Southern Command in the Sinai campaign; and Rosa Cohen, Yitzhak Rabin's larger-than-life mother. These were strong-willed and spartan women, highly ideological and active in public affairs. They devoted very little time to their home and children, and raised sons who made careers as warriors yet were ready to yield to the will of Israel's founding fathers and mothers.

Lacking in political experience, with the embittered Golda Meir breathing down his neck, he was a mediocre Prime Minister. His principal failure was his inability to come to an agreement with Sadat, leaving this to Begin. He was also unable to come to an agreement with King Hussein, who demanded a corridor near Jericho as a condition for an interim agreement. He was, however, able partly to rehabilitate the economy, which had been ruined by the Yom Kippur War. He also wisely preserved Israel's neutrality during the civil war in Lebanon, authorized the Entebbe operation, and relaxed the government's control over state television and official information available to the press.

In fact, Rabin permitted more severe criticism of himself and his government than any other Prime Minister had done, either before him or after him. He and his government paid a very high price for this tolerant policy, for it allowed a positively suicidal degree of exposure of government corruption. (Rabin's Housing Minister committed suicide as a result.) The impression was created that the Israeli government had become more corrupt than ever, while it was actually at its least corrupt during this period. Finally the press revealed that Rabin's wife had a bank account in the United States—which is against the law in Israel—and he resigned. Peres ran at the head of the Labor Party slate in the 1977 elections, lost, and Begin came to power.

Rabin now became a member of the opposition in the Knesset, but during the 1982 Lebanon War Ariel Sharon, then Minister of Defense, called upon him to act as an "adviser." Rabin advised Sharon to "tighten up" the siege of Beirut, which in effect meant entirely cutting off the supply of food and water to the city, while at the same time subjecting it to heavy aerial bombing. "I can live with a twenty-four-hour bombardment of Beirut," he is notoriously remembered to have said. He said nothing about those residents of Beirut who could not live with a twenty-four-hour bombardment of their city.

IN THE NATIONAL-UNITY government that was formed in 1984 Rabin was Defense Minister, and he held that post again in the 1988 national-unity government. Rabin cooperated fully with Shamir, preferring to work with him rather than with Peres, who was subjected to an astonishing campaign of character assassination by the Likud. At the same time, the Likud was characterizing Rabin as the good guy of the Labor Party. Rabin thus gained a great deal of popularity among Likud voters. (In a survey published in *Yediot Aharonot* on May 1, 1992, about a third of Likud voters said they favored Rabin as Prime Minister.) Now that Rabin has defeated Peres in the Labor Party's internal elections, and is running against the Likud, it will be hard for the Likud to do to him what Begin and his cronies did so successfully to Peres.

Rabin, like many other Sabras, can be embarrassed by intimacy and often behaves badly toward people who come in direct contact with him. When he was visiting Washington as Prime Minister, President Jimmy Carter once invited him, as a gesture of friendship, to come to his daughter Amy's room to say good night to her. Rabin just stood there, unable to utter a friendly word. His social nervousness makes people around him cringe, but the voters do not see him close up and so his roughness seems to radiate authenticity. Before the Labor Party elections both Peres and Rabin were asked, "What was the saddest day of your life?" Rabin replied, "The day my mother died." Peres answered, "The day I heard that Yoni Netanyahu was killed at Entebbe." Peres' answer was so phony, so clearly intended to remind the public that Peres had been the Defense Minister at the time of the Entebbe operation, that it is no wonder he is widely seen as inauthentic, or, in Israeli jargon, "unreliable."

The day after the *intifada* began, on December 10, 1987, Rabin went to the United States on an official visit as Israeli Defense Minister. Not only had he failed to anticipate the Palestinian uprising, he did not recognize how serious it was, and it took him ten days to return to Israel. As soon as he landed at the airport he made the outlandish and unsupported statement that Syria and Iran were behind the disturbances. Shamir announced, as usual, that the PLO was behind them, although the PLO was no less surprised by the uprising than Shamir and Rabin. Rabin argued soon afterward that the *intifada* could not be put down by force and that the "political foot" must be used as well. What he actually did, however, was especially brutal; he said that Israeli soldiers should use their batons to "break the arms and legs" of Palestinians. He then seemed to retract this advice. "But you gave us sticks!" exclaimed one of the soldiers to Rabin. "What did you expect us to do with them?" Rabin seemed truly surprised by criticism throughout the world of what he had said. After all, he implied, breaking arms and legs is not as terrible as killing.

During the current election campaign Rabin's views have been considerably transformed partly because the Labor Party has become more dovish. From his recent pronouncements the following picture emerges. He is willing to offer the Palestinians "autonomy-plus"— the "plus" referring to his readiness to reach an accommodation on the critical issues of water and land, although it is still unclear to what degree Palestinians would have a say over the large proportion of the land that has been acquired by either settlers or the government. Moreover, Rabin distinguishes between "political" settlements, which mostly turn out to have been built by, or under, the Likud and which are not needed for Israel's security, and "security" settlements —that is, those built by Labor. However, Rabin has also said, "The security value of Bet Shan"—a small border town inside Israel's 1967 border—"is many times more than that of Ariel and Emanuel," the largest towns built in the occupied territories.

Such statements suggest that Rabin also regards as "political" the settlements built within areas that are densely populated by Arabs, which the Palestinians would insist on controlling under any peace agreement. "Security" settlements, on the other hand, are those in areas with relatively few Arab villages, which raises the possibility that in future negotiations the Palestinians would let Israel maintain sovereignty over them. Rabin is ready to freeze all settlement activity immediately, and to channel the huge sums that would thus be saved to absorbing immigrants.

In addition, Rabin, reversing Shamir's policy, is ready to consider East Jerusalem's Palestinians as full partners in the peace talks. As for the Golan Heights, his position is that it is possible to reach a compromise on them without wholly abandoning them. Since the Heights are some forty kilometers wide, Israel, in exchange for demilitarization, could withdraw some twenty to thirty kilometers, and still have a presence on the slopes.

Rabin has also changed the political strategy of the Labor Party. Peres never stopped hoping that the religious parties would join a coalition government headed by Labor, and his efforts to win them over were shamelessly corrupt. Rabin, by contrast, assumes that the religious parties belong to the right-wing coalition. If, however, Labor can put together a so-called "blocking bloc," composed of Labor, the unified small liberal-left parties, and the Arabs, this would prevent Shamir from forming his own coalition government; then and only then, Rabin believes, would the religious parties be willing to join a government under his leadership. (They would do so for the same reason given by Jesse James when he was asked why he robbed banks: that's where the money is.)

The Israeli Knesset has 120 members. If the Arab parties win seven instead of six seats (which is possible), if the unified list of the liberal left maintains its bloc of ten members (also possible), and if the number of Labor representatives increases from thirty-nine to forty-three (seemingly possible, as I write in early May), Rabin will have his blocking bloc. It is even conceivable that he will end up with a tiny majority of one or more. This would mean accepting as legitimate a government that relies on the votes of the Arab parties to form a majority. Such a majority was unacceptable to Labor in the past, but it is acceptable to Rabin today. Should he achieve it, he would face such fierce opposition to any serious peace initiative that he might well have to resort to a national referendum to approve, for example, a partial withdrawal from the West Bank.

Elections are scheduled for June 23. Israeli voters, writes the journalist Nahum Barnea, tell the truth in opinion polls but lie at the ballot box—that is, they succumb, when they vote, to pressure from their peers. In the opinion polls Rabin is clearly preferred over Shamir, but voters are liable to cling to the more aggressive party when they cast their ballots. And this time the choice is between Shamir, who would have Israel replace South Africa as an apartheid state—he is hardly willing to offer the Palestinians even a Bantustan—and the Labor Party, which is willing to reach some sort of interim agreement. The chances are that Israelis will be faced with a paralyzed and paralyzing national-unity government. There is also the frightening prospect that the elections will lead to negotiations among the political parties lasting for many months, during which

Shamir will head a transition government. It has been said about Rabin's candidacy for Prime Minister what Samuel Johnson said about marriage: "It is the triumph of hope over experience." But a hope it is.

Yitzhak Rabin was murdered by a Yemenite Jew during the electoral campaign in 1995. The ending of his funeral, like the burial of Caesar, had a Shakespearean twist. Rabin's close aide Ethan Haber displayed a bloodstained piece of paper on which "The Song of Peace" was printed. It was the sheet of paper Rabin had been holding to help him with the words as he sang this song, along with tens of thousands of participants in the rally in Tel Aviv supporting his peace policy where he met his death. Rabin was shot just after he stepped down from the podium, and his blood soaked the neatly folded sheet of paper he had put in his breast pocket moments before. Rabin had a resonant, deep bass-baritone with which, plainly out of tune, he had tried to sing this last song of his life. Unlike Rabin, the crowd did not need help with the words: "The Song of Peace" had been the anthem of the Peace Now movement for years, ever since its first peace rally in that same square in Tel Aviv in 1978.

"Raise your eyes with hope, not through rifle sights," says the song. (This is not quite what it sounds like.) The line is an allusion to a famous remark made by Rabin's brother-in-law, General Abraham Jaffe, who had once been asked, "How do you view the Arab problem?" and had answered, "Through a rifle sight."

It was Rabin, who had finally raised his eyes from the rifle sights after so many years, whom the Peace Now crowd was cheering at that rally. For a long time he had been ambivalent about the peace promoters who had organized the demonstration. He was just as ambivalent about his own first steps toward reconciliation with the Palestinians. It was this very ambivalence, which resonated so perfectly with the gut feelings of Israel's political center, that allowed him to persuade Israelis that his agreement with the Palestinians was the right thing, that the Oslo Accords were their best hope. The center did not want a happy agreement with lots of goodwill, only the logic of the inevitable. For them, as for

Rabin, Peace Now reeked of too much goodwill. And Rabin's eschato-logical handshake with Yasir Arafat on the White House lawn in that distant September 1993, which to Israelis and perhaps to Rabin himself conveyed the feeling that he was grasping an eel in his hand, was just fine.

Rabin did not fake his ambivalence in order to "sell" his policy; he was constitutionally incapable of faking anything. He was ambivalent, pure and simple. Paradoxically, the virulent rightist attacks on him resolved his ambivalence and enabled him to come to terms with his own policy of making peace with the Palestinians, not just in his head but also in his heart. Commentators on the peace rally in Tel Aviv were off the mark when they attributed its significance to Rabin's act of making peace with the Palestinians. In fact, it was the peace Rabin made with the Accords' supporters and with himself that was of the greatest import. For the first time he looked happy—and just at that moment he was gunned down.

Rabin's assassination was a political assassination. This is not so banal as it sounds. Not every assassination of a political figure is a political act. Kennedy's assassination, for example, was not political. But Yigal Amir was trying to change Israeli policy by murdering Rabin, and he pretty much succeeded.

Indeed, Rabin's assassination was political in more than the obvious sense that the assassin aimed to achieve a political goal through murder. It was political in the sense that the murder of Jean Jaurès or Walther Rathenau was a political murder by the right. The Israeli right wing —including Netanyahu's "respectable" right—with its menacing dem-onstrations on the streets of Jerusalem, with its display of overt death symbols (a coffin, a hanging rope) along with a poster of Rabin in an SS uniform, created a climate that made the question of who would do Rabin in a merely statistical one.

The Israeli left nourishes a deep resentment of Netanyahu, in part for his allowing or condoning the demonstrations that made Rabin's murder a serious possibility. Many Israeli cars sported a bumper sticker reading, "We shall never forget, we shall never forgive." There are many conflicts in Israeli society, but Rabin's violent death defined a major rift like no other rift in Israel.

I remember a tense meeting with Rabin. I was part of a delegation representing many of the Peace Now people who were in the square at that fateful rally, and we were visiting Rabin as Defense Minister; we had come to ask permission to have a demonstration in Hebron. At one point Rabin asked me, "How many voters do you have?" I have no idea where I got the presence of mind and audacity to reply, "I don't know how many voters we have, but I do know that the historians of the future will come from our group." I can only wish I really knew where the future historians will come from. But any historian worth his or her salt must recognize that Rabin was a serious statesman. This is a very rare commodity in Israel.

14

SHIMON PERES:
AN UNPAID DREAMER

APRIL 1996

SHIMON PERES FIRST MET DAVID BEN-GURION IN 1946, WHEN PERES had just been nominated secretary of the Labor movement's youth movement; he was, in his own words, "the young unknown." Ben-Gurion was chairman of the Jewish Agency, already "a legend." Peres had to get to Haifa. There weren't many cars in Palestine at the time, so it had been arranged that Peres would drive to Haifa with Ben-Gurion. Ben-Gurion was silent throughout the journey. On the out-skirts of Haifa, Ben-Gurion suddenly turned to Peres and said, "You know, Trotsky was no statesman." Peres asked why. "Because of his concept of no-peace-no-war," Ben-Gurion said.

That's not statesmanship. That's some sort of Jewish invention. A statesman has to decide one way or the other: to go for peace and pay the price or to make war, knowing what the risks and dangers are. Lenin was Trotsky's inferior in terms of intellect, but he became the leader of Russia because he was decisive. He decided on peace and paid the heavy price that peace required.

Ben-Gurion was alluding to the 1917 peace treaty of Brest-Litovsk between revolutionary Russia and Germany. Bukharin urged that the Russian revolutionaries go on with war and die "sword in hand." Lenin was for peace at any price. Ben-Gurion could sympathize with either man, but not with Trotsky, who wanted neither war nor peace. This, for Ben-Gurion, was a "Jewish invention."

The bitter historical irony is that the legacy of Ben-Gurion himself to Israel was the "Jewish invention" of neither war nor peace with its neighboring Arab countries. He was able only to arrange cease-fire and armistice agreements which erupted every decade into wars—in 1948, 1956, 1967, 1973, and 1982.

Yitzhak Rabin and Shimon Peres attempted to extract Israel from the state of no-peace-no-war. They were both ready to pay a heavy personal price for doing so. Rabin lost his life, and Peres has tied his political future to carrying out the peace agreement with the Palestinians. He may soon pay the price on election day.

Peres describes his relations with Ben-Gurion in *Battling for Peace*, his recently published autobiography. But we get a fuller account of his early years in the authorized biography written by Matti Golan and published in Hebrew in 1984.* What is clear from both books is that, for Peres, Ben-Gurion set the standard for what counts as a "historical achievement" in Israel. He also did so for his disciples Moshe Dayan and Rabin, and for his adversaries—notably Menachem Begin. To "make history"—that is, to do something that will be remembered as having secured Israel's future—has been a conscious concern of Israel's leaders; and to do so, a leader must compete with Ben-Gurion's greatest accomplishment, the founding of the state itself. To make history now would be to finish Ben-Gurion's unfinished

---

*I rely on the original, Hebrew version. Golan's *The Road to Peace: A Biography of Shimon Peres* subsequently appeared, a shorter English version, translated by Akiva Ron (New York, 1989).

business, settling Israel's relations with the Arabs. Begin, for his part, wanted to make peace where Ben-Gurion failed to make peace, and he also wanted not simply to defend Israel but to take the military initiative and win a more decisive victory than Ben-Gurion ever did. He made peace with Egypt and started a disastrous war in Lebanon. Dayan, as Begin's Foreign Minister, wanted to atone for his own failure to prevent the war of October 1973; he knew that only peace with Egypt might earn him a place in the history books.

Rabin and Peres had their first chance to "make history" in the 1970s. When Rabin succeeded Golda Meir as Israel's Prime Minister in 1974, after the October War, Peres was his Minister of Defense. Instead of making peace with the Arabs, they were at war with each other. The suspicious Rabin believed that Peres, the "indefatigable underminer," was constantly plotting against him. In June 1992, with Labor's first election victory in fifteen years, they got their second chance. They were by then both in their early seventies. They had come to conceive of peace, in William James's phrase, as "a moral equivalent" of war. There is nothing self-evident about this equivalence, certainly not in Israel. While Rabin was forming his new cabinet, his predecessor, Yitzhak Shamir, said, "We still need this truth today, the truth of the power of war, or at least we need to accept war as inescapable because without this, the life of the individual has no purpose and the nation has no chance of survival."*

In 1991 Shamir's government had been dragged by Secretary of State James Baker to the Madrid peace conference. This was followed by bilateral talks between Israel and a delegation of Palestinians from the occupied territories, including, among others, Hanan Ashrawi and Faisal Husseini. When Rabin came to power in 1992 he assumed personal responsibility for these bilateral talks and kept Peres at a distance from them. However, Rabin came in for severe criticism both from Western governments and from his supporters in Israel's civil rights movement when he expelled 415 Hamas activists to Lebanon in December 1992. He suddenly needed Peres' support within the Labor Party, and Peres became his partner in negotiations with the Palestinians.

*Yediot Aharonot, June 22, 1992.

Both Rabin and Peres were thinking of an accommodation with the Arabs that would take place in two phases. In the first phase, during their first term of office, they would make an "interim agreement" with the Palestinians from the occupied territories, and possibly a joint declaration with the Syrians of the principles for a future peace arrangement, while also negotiating for mutual recognition with Jordan. The interim agreement would give the Palestinians control of most of Gaza and local authority in the West Bank. For the second phase, which was to take place during their second term of office— that is, after the 1996 elections—they projected several new agreements. One would replace the interim agreement with a "permanent" arrangement that would be negotiated with the elected Palestinian authorities. It was presumed that the Palestinians would achieve sovereignty, or something close to it, over much of the West Bank and Gaza. Ever cautious, Rabin wanted to test the good faith of the Palestinians at each step. He and Peres also hoped to implement the declaration with Syria, and make a peace agreement with Jordan.

One part of this plan worked out more successfully than anticipated when a peace treaty was signed with Jordan in July 1994. Another turned out less well: the talks with the Syrians have come to a standstill. An interim agreement turned out to be feasible, but instead of dealing with the Palestinians from the territories, Israel made a deal with the PLO leaders who had been based in Tunisia.

This was possible because Yossi Beilin, then Deputy Foreign Minister, and Peres' confidant, had set up a secret negotiating channel in Oslo, using two Israeli academics as intermediaries. The Israeli professors were not themselves politically influential. But their Palestinian counterpart, Abu Ala'a, turned out to be very important indeed. Although the Israelis were quite unaware of it at the time—Israeli intelligence reports contained fewer than five pages about him*—he was in charge of the PLO's finances. More than anyone else, he knew how close to bankruptcy the PLO had become, owing to its disastrous backing of Saddam Hussein during the Gulf War. Its usual sources of money, particularly in the Gulf states, had dried up.

By May 1993, Peres had become confident that the Oslo talks could

*See David Makovsky, *Making Peace with the PLO* (Boulder, 1996), p. 23, n. 15.

lead to a deal. He asked Rabin's permission to take them over himself and Rabin refused. But Rabin agreed that an ally of Peres', the director general of the Foreign Ministry, Uri Savir, would head the negotiations; the Oslo talks were upgraded still further when Rabin assigned one of his confidants, the lawyer Yoel Singer, to join them. But Rabin remained skeptical. When asked about the talks by Secretary of State Warren Christopher, only a few weeks before an agreement was reached, Rabin dismissed them with a wave of his hand. Rabin was never an articulate man but was highly expressive in his body language. Christopher concluded that the Oslo track was not serious.

But the PLO and Israel soon signed an interim agreement to be carried out in two stages. The first stage, which came to be known as "Gaza and Jericho first," called for Israeli withdrawal from most of the Gaza Strip and from the township of Jericho, and for the establishment of a Palestinian authority in these two places; at the same time Israel was to recognize the PLO. In the autumn of 1995, some two years later, the second stage, known as Oslo II, was put into effect when Israeli forces withdrew from all the major cities of the West Bank except Hebron, as well as from hundreds of villages, and the first Palestinian elections took place. Israel remains in control of most of the rest of the occupied territory and also of its main water supplies. Still to be negotiated is the "permanent" arrangement with the Palestinians that will replace the interim agreement.

The four recent suicide bombings by members of Hamas, in which sixty-two people have been killed, have now put Labor's second term of office in jeopardy. It is still not clear whether the Oslo Accords will lead to a historical change or whether they will amount to merely another episode—interesting but ultimately insignificant—in the hostile relations between Israel and the Arabs.

PERES STARTED THINKING about his place in history at a young age. In 1958, as the thirty-five-year-old director general of Ben-Gurion's Ministry of Defense, he became friends with France's Socialist Prime Minister, Guy Mollet. In one of their conversations—reported by his biographer but not by Peres in *Battling for Peace*—Mollet wanted to know whether Peres approved of his having helped De Gaulle regain power. He told Mollet:

A man in power lives under stress. One event comes after another, here he is summoned on the telephone and there he speeds in a car, and then, after a while, he wakes up one morning and asks himself, "What have I achieved in my life?" I believe that the truly great men can free themselves, at the right moments, from the world of drama and reach the world of history, enter the memory of the people. If the people remember you for many generations—this is history.

If the Likud comes to power on May 29, will the Oslo agreements be forgotten by the next generation or will they be remembered as the beginning of the historical reconciliation between the two peoples? Certainly Rabin's assassination will not be forgotten. But the future of the peace between Israel and the Palestinians may entirely depend on Labor's attaining a second term of office. This means that a handful of Hamas suicide bombers, if they succeed in depriving Labor of victory, will have wiped out a political development that looked for a while as if it might change history.

Zhou Enlai was once asked whether the French Revolution was a good thing. "Too early to tell," he said, and this must for now be the answer to the question whether the Oslo agreements are of historical significance.

Several quite different outcomes are worth considering. The first is that the Oslo agreements created irreversible political facts. After all, if the Likud candidate, Benjamin Netanyahu, is elected, what can he do? Could he, realistically, reconquer Gaza, reoccupy the West Bank towns, and restore the military administration that formerly ruled them, along with the military detention centers in which many thousands of Palestinians were held? This would be an immensely expensive and dangerous undertaking, all the more so now that twenty thousand Palestinian police in Gaza and the West Bank have arms. Still, while Netanyahu may be unable to annul the agreements, he could freeze them. That is to say, he could decide not to move ahead with their next stages, and would only refuse to negotiate "permanent" status on any terms the Palestinians could possibly accept. He would drag on the negotiations forever.

At the same time, however, Netanyahu would be aware that many of his supporters want both revenge for the bombings and the complete separation of Israel from the Arabs. The current vision of many Likud voters is one of tangible, physical isolation from the Palestinians, preferably on the model of the Berlin Wall—including electrified wires, mine fields, and heavily guarded checkpoints. If the Likud, once in power, cannot annul the Oslo Accords, and if Hamas terror activities continue to exert pressure on Likud leaders to separate Israelis from the Arabs physically, one likely consequence will be that the old Likud fantasy of an undivided Greater Israel has no future.

But there is a more chilling possibility: if Hamas terrorism continues, a Likud government will be constrained neither politically nor militarily from annulling the Oslo agreements and returning to the old system of direct Israeli occupation. This is the outcome that the Hamas militants prefer, since it would effectively bring to an end the rule of Yasir Arafat—not just in practice but officially as well—and would deliver many of his supporters to the Hamas. This is also what some Israelis to the right of Likud would prefer. They would like to be able to say of the Palestinians—whether in Israel or in the occupied territories—that "they are all Hamas," and await an opportunity to expel as many of them as possible into Jordan so as to fulfill at last the vision of the Greater Israel, cleansed of Arabs.

Benjamin Netanyahu and some key Likud ministers he would appoint, Dan Meridor and Benjamin Begin, would probably not push for the annulment of the Oslo Accords; nor would they necessarily want to get rid of Arafat, at least not right away. They would be quite satisfied to deprive the accords of any remaining significance. They would probably do so, first, by reviving the old Likud policy of settlement in the West Bank, filling the territory with Jewish settlements so that the Palestinians cannot control any continuous strip of land linking the towns and villages. In such a case Israel would remain de facto sovereign over the entire West Bank; the Palestinians would, at best, be relegated to Bantustans. This is the practical meaning of the Likud platform of the Greater Israel, and nothing that has happened on the West Bank thus far as a result of the Oslo agreements precludes its being fulfilled.

After the four suicide bombings, Peres imposed a policy of prolonged closure in the territories. All movements of people and goods from Gaza and the West Bank to Israel were banned, as were movements among the Palestinian towns on the West Bank. Some restrictions have since been relaxed, but the result is an economic siege which has taken its toll on the Palestinian economy. Palestinians who work in Israel, estimated at sixty thousand, provide the territories with a vital source of income. Ironically, when closure was previously applied, before the Oslo agreement, Israel channeled modest amounts of money to the territories in order to alleviate the Palestinians' economic plight, but after the agreement, Israel sees itself as exempt from any responsibility for the consequences of closure.

The closure policy is also extremely dangerous to Arafat's authority. When he recently visited Nablus, he was almost chased out of Al-najah University by angry students. Arafat is also under heavy pressure from the Israelis to capture Mohammed Dayf, the current leader of the Hamas military units, as a condition for lifting the closure.

The leaders of the ideological right wing in Israel were always of two minds about closures. They supported them because closures meant being tough with the Arabs. At the same time, they were afraid that imposing closure along the Green Line—the pre-1967 border of Israel—would resurrect the very frontier they tried so hard to erase. The right-wing parties, however, sense that most Israelis now favor separation between Israelis and Palestinians. Separation could mean two sovereign states, with elaborate physical barriers between them, or it could mean a separation between the Israeli and the Palestinian communities within a Greater Israel. The latter is an apartheid notion of separation, in which Palestinian enclaves would be controlled by carrot-and-stick policies of closure. Following Rabin's views, some important ministers in Peres' government, notably Ehud Barak and Chaim Ramon, advocate physical separation. The Likud leans toward the second, apartheid notion of separation. Peres, for his part, has rejected both notions of separation. He writes that he is for "soft borders, not rigid, impermeable ones. Borders are not walls."*

If the Likud wins, then, the Oslo Accords may well turn out to be a mere episode, a footnote to history. The accords may be deprived of any meaning, and—if terror resumes—the Likud could well annul them altogether. Peres needs another term of office in order to make the Oslo Accords a historical fact.

IN THE EVENT that Peres does not win the election, then his most enduring and highly problematic accomplishment will have taken place some four decades ago, when he almost single-handedly initiated and then carried out Israel's nuclear program. In *Battling for Peace* he describes how Ben-Gurion supported him while many other Labor leaders agreed with Abba Eban, who described the nuclear reactor as "an enormous alligator stranded on dry land." Israel's nuclear capacity undoubtedly had a huge impact on the history of the state of Israel and of the entire region, but Peres cannot claim credit for it since it is an unmentionable subject in Israel's politics.

Still, those like myself who oppose nuclear deterrence on moral grounds have to admit that nuclear deterrence has worked so far. According to the Arab leaders themselves, Israel's nuclear capacity is the single most important element in the Arab perception of Israel's military might. An Egyptian former general told me, for example, that the Egyptian Army's plans for the opening stages of the 1973 October War were confined to the Suez Canal zone from fear that if they penetrated Israel further, the Israeli leaders might have felt sufficiently threatened to use nuclear weapons. Israel's nuclear power, it also could be argued, was decisive in convincing the Arab states that Israel could not be annihilated and that negotiations were preferable. At the same time, a nuclear capacity, with its potential for deadly accidents, makes tiny and overpopulated Israel dangerous not just to its neighbors but to itself as well.

In the 1950s Peres was ostensibly no more than a civil servant,

---

*Shimon Peres with Aryeh Naor, *The New Middle East* (New York, 1993), p. 171.

deputy to the director general of the Ministry of Defense, and then, after 1952, director general. But the Minister of Defense was the all-powerful Ben-Gurion, and Ben-Gurion backed Peres. In later years, Peres himself became Minister of Defense during Rabin's first term as Prime Minister, and between 1984 and 1986 he was Prime Minister. But I doubt he ever had more power than he did in the 1950s when he was a civil servant under Ben-Gurion. Indeed, Peres had a crucial part in all the major decisions of the 1950s, including establishing Israel's close relations with France, organizing the Suez campaign with France and Great Britain in 1956, and in working out the secret military understanding with France and West Germany that they would support Israel if it was attacked.

During Israel's first decade, foreign policy meant, above all, a policy to acquire arms. The Soviet Union was supplying Egypt with heavy weapons by way of Czechoslovakia—under the Czech-Egyptian pact of 1955—while Great Britain and the United States imposed a general arms embargo on the Middle East. Israel's only hope to acquire weapons that would outmatch Egypt's was to work out deals with West Germany and France. Relations with post-Holocaust Germany were still difficult, however, in spite of the reparations agreement signed by Chancellor Konrad Adenauer and Ben-Gurion in 1952. It was Peres who negotiated Israel's armament deals with Franz Josef Strauss, Germany's Defense Minister, and with Guy Mollet and Maurice Bourgès-Maunoury, France's Prime Ministers.

Israel's Foreign Minister at the time was Golda Meir. Peres recalls Teddy Kollek's view that she didn't "so much conduct a foreign policy as maintain a hate list." In that sense, Golda Meir's foreign policy included Abba Eban and Shimon Peres, both of whom she hated. But Kollek's description is only partially true. Meir was eager to improve Israel's image among the nations of the Third World, which saw Israel as an agent of imperialism. She therefore devoted much energy to establishing close ties with many African nations. Peres, by contrast, viewed Israel's relations with foreign countries mainly with regard to their ability to help Israel get arms. The African nations could not provide arms; they needed them themselves.

Peres also was largely responsible for organizing the Israeli military-industrial complex, with a particular emphasis on the aircraft industry. Israel's defense industry introduced advanced technology into its economy, and Peres can take most of the credit for this. Undoubtedly, however, his greatest accomplishment was building the 24,000-kilowatt nuclear reactor in Dimona, with technological help from France. From Peres' book, we get a clear account of what has long been rumored: the prospect of obtaining that technology was Peres' main reason for volunteering Israel's participation in the Suez campaign. The agreement between Great Britain, France, and Israel to attack Egypt was signed in Sèvres in October 1956. Peres recalls, "Before the final signing, I asked Ben-Gurion for a brief adjournment, during which I met with Mollet and Bourgès-Maunoury alone. It was here that I finalized with these two leaders an agreement for the building of a nuclear reactor at Dimona, in southern Israel."

Peres was involved in every stage of the building of the nuclear complex, from recruiting scientists to designing the buildings. But impressive and significant as this achievement may have been, it will always be seen as ambiguous, the creation of a terrible weapon to avoid a terrible outcome. Peres badly needs a "moral equivalent" to the nuclear bomb. In today's Israel he is seen as a visionary, partly because of his hopes that peace will result in a regional common market as well as an aid program, comparable to the Marshall Plan, supported by the United States, Japan, and Europe. "Visionary" has for many Israelis a double edge. In the 1950s it was Ben-Gurion who was credited with having vision. Peres was seen as a doer, so much so that he was derided as a man whose ideology was simply "doism," regardless of content.

Peres' image as a visionary now and as a doer then does not do him justice. He is more intelligent and more imaginative than Ben-Gurion ever was. Many of Ben-Gurion's visions in the 1950s were not his own; they were ideas Peres managed to sell him on. Using his mentor's immense authority, Peres was able to carry some of them out, particularly the creation of a modern industrial establishment. Ben-Gurion was willing to consider even some of Peres' wildest ideas, such as leasing the French colony Guyana in South America so that Israel could use it for agricultural development. This idea was described by Pinhas Sapir, the Labor Party boss of the 1960s, as "a catastrophe, the sort of colonialism and imperialism which will be resented in South America and will be disastrous for us in Africa."

In the years following the Suez campaign Peres was drunk with power—his own as well as his country's. "I propose that in our national thinking we should recognize the centrality of the idea that changes in the Middle East might present us with the necessity, or perhaps the opportunity, to rethink our national borders." This statement, delivered by Peres to the Security and Foreign Relations Committee of the Knesset, could only be interpreted as suggesting the possibility of territorial expansion. Perhaps the greatest change Peres has undergone over the years is that today he recognizes the limits of power, both his own and his country's.

IN THE 1950S Israel was ruled by three strong men: Ben-Gurion as Prime Minister and Minister of Defense, Moshe Dayan as army chief of staff, and Shimon Peres as director general of the Ministry of Defense. For a short period, when Ben-Gurion retreated to his "ashram" at the Sde Boker kibbutz in the Negev desert, Peres and Dayan were joined by Pinhas Lavon, who was appointed Minister of Defense. Sapir warned Lavon about Dayan and Peres: "They will take your socks off while your shoes are on, and you won't even notice." In effect they did. In *Battling for Peace* Peres calls Lavon's appointment a "ghastly mistake," and writes of his "disastrous decisions," including a 1953 reprisal action by the Israeli Army in which sixty-nine civilians were killed in the Jordanian town of Kibbiya. (Peres does not say that Ben-Gurion approved this raid.)

In July 1954 Israel embarked upon a series of undercover operations in Egypt, including a plan to bomb American libraries there, whose aim was to drive a wedge between Nasser's Egypt and the United States. One member of the Israeli cell was caught by the Egyptians in Alexandria, bomb in hand. Later the entire cell was arrested, and two of its members were subsequently hanged. Although efforts were made to keep the plot secret, a political scandal emerged. Within the government and among the Mapai politicians, the question was posed:

Who gave the order to carry out the plan? Forged documents were circulated to pin the blame on Lavon, who resigned in 1955. Peres writes at length about the Lavon affair, never quite saying who was responsible for what, as in the following passage about the strategy meetings he attended with Lavon:

No order was ever issued in my presence to actually carry out any such action, but certainly there was discussion of what action Israel could take against U.S. interests or facilities in Egypt that would create tension and alienation between the two countries. I expressed reservations about the idea. But it did not surprise me, later, that some of the men who had heard Lavon at such meetings came to believe that a covert operation would accord with the minister's new *Weltanschauung*. I cannot say—and I want to make this totally clear—that I ever heard a specific order from Lavon's mouth, but the general policy direction was there; it was present in the air at those meetings.

Peres and Dayan may not have been part of the conspiracy against Lavon, but, as Lavon claimed, "they jumped on the bandwagon" with the others who wanted to bring him down. In the early 1960s Lavon started a campaign to rehabilitate his name, accusing Ben-Gurion of plotting to destroy him and he got the support of some of the Mapai leaders who resented Ben-Gurion and his autocratic ways. The political upheaval that followed led to a split in the Mapai Party, and then to Ben-Gurion's impulsive decision to form his own new party, Rafi. Against his better judgment, Peres joined Ben-Gurion out of loyalty. Dayan joined too.

Peres admired Ben-Gurion and Dayan; Ben-Gurion he both feared and revered, Dayan he adored. Peres considered himself a friend of Dayan's, although it is not clear that Dayan thought he was a friend of Peres'. But then it is not clear that Dayan was anybody's friend. Peres was much concerned to protect Dayan's reputation. ("I don't care about prestige—other people's prestige," Dayan said.) Peres' admiration for Ben-Gurion and for Dayan had much to do with their being ruthless and inconsiderate in the extreme, and also with their being utterly unconventional. To him they both radiated with the inner freedom and spontaneity that he himself, ever self-controlled and calculating, lacked and envied.

Peres had to persuade Ben-Gurion to appoint Dayan chief of staff of the Israeli Army; Dayan's reputation for being anarchic made him an unlikely commander of a military machine based on discipline and order. One day, shortly thereafter, Peres received a telephone call from Ben-Gurion: "Shimon, come immediately."

I ran up the stairs and into Ben-Gurion's room. "That Moshe of yours," he spat at me as I entered, "is standing on the balcony of the IDF headquarters with a rifle and firing at random."

I mumbled something to the effect that this was impossible, that there must be a mistake, and rushed over to the two-story General Staff building next door. Sure enough, Dayan was there, on the balcony, with a shotgun. I flew up the stairs and burst in. "Have you gone mad?" I began. He turned calmly around. "Have you received an invitation to dinner at my house to-night?" he asked. I confirmed that I had. "Do you know what the occasion is?" I admitted I did not. "It's my thirty-ninth birth-day," he explained sweetly. "I've decided to invite thirty-nine guests. The main course will be roast pigeon—and now I'm bagging the pigeons."

Peres, to his credit, admired not only Dayan's rowdiness but also his Hebrew, which indeed was simple, fresh, and finely phrased. Peres' Hebrew is rich and elaborate, with a compulsive tendency toward overcleverness. If at some military ceremony a speaker were to refer to the iron will of the young officers, Peres would respond that the issue is not iron will so much as the will to use iron. He has by now acquired a genuine taste for literature.

Peres was born Shimon Persky in 1923 in Vishneva, a small Jewish shtetl in Poland, now Belarus. He studied Hebrew at school there, his teacher being Yehoshua Rabinowitz, who was to serve as an austere and effective Finance Minister in Rabin's first government in 1974–77, in which Peres served as Defense Minister. Peres' family emi-grated to Palestine when he was ten. It was a petit bourgeois family, and Peres was sent to a commercial school in Tel Aviv. However, in those years education was acquired more in youth movements than in schools, and Peres joined the socialist youth movement, which shaped his future. He transferred to the agricultural school at Ben-Shemen, and there Peres tried to establish a new identity by changing his name, Persky, to a Hebrew name. He first chose Ben-Amoz, after the prophet Isaiah, son of Amoz, but later decided that this was too pretentious and changed it to Peres, meaning vulture.

Curiously, another Polish boy at the same school took the name Ben-Amoz for himself. Dan Ben-Amoz became eventually one of Israel's cultural heroes, a satirical writer, editor, and performer who, more than anyone else, contributed to, indeed shaped, the myth of the Sabra, the tough, shaggy product of the Jewish frontier settlements, the Israeli new man. (Even the Sabra, then, is a Polish invention.) But Peres never became a Sabra. Whether in his hairstyle or dress or in his accent or in his behavior, he could be a cultivated European. Dayan remained for him the quintessential Sabra.

While in school Peres fell in love with Sonia, his carpentry teacher's daughter, whom he later married. He recalls, credibly enough, that he would read poetry to her at nights, along with passages from *Das Kapital*. "It was," he writes, "the Soviet Union that held special fascination for us—both as the country of origin of most of the Jews then in Palestine and as the homeland of communism, the ideology that promised to heal all the ills of the world." He was then "discovered" when still in his teens by Berl Katznelson, the educator and theoretician of Israel's labor movement, who had once written a booklet on Zionism with Maxim Gorky and whose analysis of Stalinist betrayal and despotism convinced Peres, he writes, that he had to "fight with all my strength Marxism, communism and the Stalinist dictatorship." If Ben-Gurion was the labor movement's Lenin, Katznelson was its Plekhanov. Katznelson read an article by Peres and invited him for a series of conversations, mainly about modern Hebrew literature; but the sponsorship of Katznelson largely made his political career possible.

The socialist group Peres joined went on to found Kibbutz Poriya at the Sea of Galilee. Later this kibbutz moved to an adjacent hilltop and was renamed Alumot. My two elder sisters belonged to that kibbutz, and as a small child I used to spend much time there. About

"Shimon" I distinctly remember one remark: "This kibbutz is too small for him." After serving as the secretary of labor's youth movement, Peres was in 1947 recruited to the Haganah, the largest underground military organization, and he was made head of personnel.

On May 15, 1948, when the state of Israel came into being, the Haganah became the IDF, the army that was to fight the War of Independence. Peres made a great blunder when he refused the offer made to him by the first chief of staff, General Dori, of a role which, in 1948, was equivalent to that of brigadier general—the same rank held at the time by Dayan and Rabin. He preferred to enlist "as a simple soldier." That he was not an officer in the Israeli Army was to haunt him ever after. Ariel Sharon relentlessly reminds him and the Israeli public of this fact. When the Entebbe operation took place in 1976, Peres, then Minister of Defense, tried hard to claim part of the credit for the operation and to be identified with it; this did not work. It is still Peres' problem today that in opposing terrorism he looks too civilian.

In spite of Peres' education within the social-democratic wing of the labor movement, and in spite of his being deputy chair of the Socialist International, Peres cannot really be described as a socialist. The ideology he inherited from Ben-Gurion was statism (*mamlachtiut*). He defines it as "the doctrine of state interest taking precedence over all party or sectoral interests." Socialism in this perspective was just one more "sectoral interest." The main idea is that the Jewish nation must create a powerful state, one that not only will generate economic growth through science and advanced technology but must also engage in some great national enterprise. Peres' "statist" zeal has calmed down over the years, but he clings to the idea that great enterprises must be accomplished. Right now it is the so-called Cross-Israel, the proposed superhighway cutting down the middle of the entire length of Israel, which will one day link Israel with its neighboring states. It will be a vast ecological disaster—but then this is not unusual with megalomaniac state enterprises.

MUCH HAS BEEN written about the peace rally in Tel Aviv at which Rabin was assassinated in the fall of 1995. It was not, as most accounts have assumed, a rally celebrating peace with the Arabs; it was, in fact, a rally celebrating Rabin's peace with himself and with the Israeli peace camp. But another gesture took place on the podium, one even more astonishing to Israelis than the earlier handshake in Washington between Rabin and Arafat: it was Rabin's near-friendly gesture of putting his arm around Peres.

The relationship between Rabin and Peres may be likened to an intimate, bad marriage. They went through many years of hostility and resentment toward each other, as they fought for power within the Labor Alliance. But their being thrown together year after year transformed their relationship from active hate to a more abstract, almost platonic, hate, and eventually to something like friendship. Eulogizing Rabin at a gathering of the Labor Party, Peres said, "Just as I had unparalleled rivalry with him, I had in the past three years unparalleled friendship with him. I was astounded by the extent of this friendship." This almost rings true. Rabin and Peres did not think of their mutual political life as a marriage; they saw each other as the only heavyweights left to fight in the Israeli political ring. The others, and especially the leader of the opposition, Benjamin Netanyahu, they both considered to be lightweights. The ability of Rabin and Peres to work together between 1992 and 1995 made them politically formidable. They complemented each other's advantages, and offset each other's flaws—Peres' sometimes flighty imaginative impulses were moderated by Rabin's plodding respect for details. But now Peres has to face elections on his own.

During Israel's general elections of 1984, Peres was head of the Labor Party, Shamir the head of the Likud. The years of Likud rule had brought about an unprecedented three-digit inflation, and the debacle of the Lebanon invasion. The Likud no longer had the charismatic Begin as its leader. Peres had everything going for him, and he was the clear favorite in all the polls. Yet the elections resulted in a tie between the Likud and Labor, which led to a national-unity government with a "rotation agreement": first Peres would serve as Prime Minister for two years, and Shamir for the remaining two years.

During Peres' term of office he was arguably the best Prime Minister Israel ever had. He got Israel out of Lebanon, and he reduced the inflation rate, which had reached more than 700 percent a year, to less than 20 percent, two highly impressive achievements. Textbooks in economics now refer to the methods Peres used to conquer hyperinflation. But that is not the sort of accomplishment people remember.

If Peres can make peace with the Palestinians, he will certainly be remembered. Yossi Beilin, the most thoughtful among the next generation of leaders of the Israeli Labor Party, has already worked out with the Palestinians the basic outline of the "permanent status" agreement. The secret Memorandum of Understanding he negotiated with the Palestinians was signed three days before Rabin's assassination. The plan's basic premise is that there will be a Palestinian state. It envisages the annexation by Israel of about 6 percent of the occupied territories, where roughly 75 percent of the Jewish settlers reside, in exchange for a highway connecting the West Bank with the Gaza Strip. It also foresees, within twelve years, the transfer to the Palestinians of large parts of the Jordan Valley now occupied by Israel. So far, however, this is Beilin's plan, not yet endorsed by Peres. Beilin is for Peres what Peres used to be for Ben-Gurion. In his book, Peres writes that he has long believed that "genuine implementation" of the Camp David agreements "would mean in practice negotiating the handover of the West Bank and Gaza to Palestinian rule, for which we were not ready."

Beilin's plan, or some variation of it, assumes that Israelis are ready; it stands a chance of being carried out if Peres wins the elections. If he does so, he is betting that the same voters will eventually approve Beilin's plan in the referendum Peres proposed in March to undercut the Likud's prediction that he would make a deal Israelis would regret. Two weeks after the last of the four suicide bomb attacks, the polls gave Peres a slight edge (50 percent) over Netanyahu (47 percent). A week before, the polls gave Netanyahu 49 percent and Peres 46 percent, with 3 percent saying they would not vote. If there are no further terrorist attacks between now and election day, I take Peres to have perhaps a slight edge over Netanyahu. The "Rabin effect" which worked for Peres has been offset by the "terror effect" which works for Netanyahu. If Peres wins, this will signify a serious change in the preferences of the Israeli citizens—in contrast to their divided view in 1984. In spite of the enormity of terrorism, the majority of Israelis will be saying that they see no real alternative to making peace with the Palestinians.

If Peres loses, he may blame his failure on a bad error of judgment on his part, namely his decision to authorize the killing—by means of a booby-trapped cellular phone—of Yahya Ayyash, the so-called engineer who personally masterminded the Hamas suicide terrorist attacks against Israelis for many years. In early January, Peres faced a difficult decision. The Israeli General Security Services—Shabak— presented Peres with an opportunity to kill, neatly, a highly dangerous killer. In addition to dealing out rough justice, this operation would boost the morale of the security service, of which Peres is directly in charge and whose reputation was badly tarnished by its failure to protect Rabin. Moreover, the head of the Shabak, who was about to be ousted precisely because of this failure, badly wanted to preside over an action that would enable him to depart with some glory. If Peres had decided to oppose it, his decision might well have leaked to the press, and this would surely have cost him popularity. On the other hand, if (as I believe) the likelihood of terrorist attack by Hamas before the elections was very sharply increased by the assassination of Ayyash, then for Peres to have given the green light to the killing of "the engineer" was a great mistake, one that may turn out to be the greatest mistake of his political life.

In the epilogue to his book, Peres writes:

> Now, in my seventies, as I look back over my life, a phrase comes to mind that was coined by Gabriel García Márquez in one of his stories: "an unpaid dreamer."
>
> My life's work is not yet done. The final, crowning chapters of my biography are still being written at this time. They deal with the subject closest to my heart—peace. We are ending a decades-long history dominated by war and embarking on an era in which the guns will stay silent while dreams flourish. I feel I have earned the right to dream.

Peres' "unpaid dream" is what is at stake in the May elections.

The week Peres lost the election to Benjamin Netanyahu in June 1996, two months after I wrote this essay, a headline in one of the satiric pages of an Israeli newspaper blared, "Peres still leads in the polls." Peres always led in the polls yet lost on election day. Such was the case in 1977, 1981, 1984, 1988, and, of course, 1996. In 1992 it was Rabin who was the head of the Labor Party, and he won.

Napoleon, it is said, used to dismiss those generals whom he deemed unlucky. He found no fault with their conduct; he just considered them "accident-prone." Peres seems to be like one of these unlucky generals of Napoleon's. But is Peres merely unlucky? No. He lost the last election through irresponsibility.

For instance, he went to what was the crucial television debate with Netanyahu arrogantly unprepared, unfocused, and dismissive—in short, he was a disaster. But the debate pumped adrenaline into Netanyahu's veins and, more important, into his campaign. The debate itself was merely the tip of the iceberg; the stupendous stupidity of Peres' campaign could have capsized not only Peres but the Titanic *itself.*

But this is all style. Peres was and still is on a "redeemer" trip, bringing peace to a "new" Middle East through economic prosperity, which is supposed to make all national and religious conflicts obsolete. Given the debris created by Hamas bombs, this "vision" was and is seriously out of touch with most Israelis and with the reality in the Middle East in general. Now that he is out of office, Peres has thus become like Gorbachev—highly respected, especially abroad, but so far irrelevant.

Yet even now Peres may still be able to bounce back. How this might happen I don't know, and neither does he, but by sheer induction from the past I claim that it is possible. And that in itself is a great tribute to the man.

15

BIBI NETANYAHU: THE TERROR MASTER

OCTOBER 1995

"IF DIRECT ELECTIONS FOR PRIME MINISTER WERE HELD TODAY, and the candidates were Yitzhak Rabin and Benjamin Netanyahu, whom would you vote for?" This question was asked of a sample of 501 Israelis in early August 1995. The answers were: Rabin, 41 percent; Netanyahu, 41 percent; undecided, 10 percent; do not intend to vote, 8 percent.*

The question itself is new in Israel. In the next elections, scheduled for the fall of 1996, the political system will have changed, and voters for the first time will directly elect the Prime Minister as well as the parliament. At the same time, in contrast to the American system, in Israel the Prime Minister will continue to be part of the parliament.

---

*Yediot Aharonot, August 11, 1995.

The arrangement is unprecedented in Israel and, so far as I know, anywhere else, and no one is certain whether it will work. Rabin and Netanyahu both support the idea of direct elections for Prime Minister. Each is sure it will work in his favor. Both cannot be right.

These recent polls are important not so much for what they say about future elections as for what they tell us about current Israeli politics. And what they say about Benjamin Netanyahu, whom Israelis call Bibi, is that he could be their next Prime Minister. The polls have forced even people who refuse to take Bibi seriously as a person to take him seriously as a candidate.

The Oslo Accords that were signed in September 1993 by the PLO and the Israeli government stipulated that peace would be made in two stages. In the first, Israel was to withdraw from the Gaza Strip and the town of Jericho in the West Bank, and a Palestinian authority was to be set up in both places. While not all the provisions of the accords concerning this stage have been carried out, Israel has indeed withdrawn from Gaza and Jericho. Most of the details of the second stage have now been worked out, following an agreement on its basic outline reached on July 4. If this agreement is carried out, Israel's security forces will withdraw from six towns of the West Bank, and free elections for the Palestinian authority will be held.

When the Oslo Accords were signed on the White House lawn, they had widespread support from Israelis. Polls showed that 61 percent of those surveyed favored them, with only 31 percent opposed. But support for the accords, as well as for Rabin's government, has eroded with the terrorist attacks by Hamas and Jihad. Even late in 1994, before the murderous suicide bombing on Dizengoff Street in Tel Aviv (Israel's Broadway), which killed twenty-two bus passengers, 60 percent of Israelis expressed their support of the accords. But after a second suicide bombing, at the Beit Lid bus terminal some thirty miles north of Tel Aviv in January 1995, which killed twenty-two Israeli soldiers, support for the accords fell to 35 percent. Polls conducted in early February showed 52 percent for Netanyahu, while only 38 percent favored Rabin.* After a month in which the occupied

*Yediot Aharonot, February 3, 1995.

territories were closed off, terrorist attacks were less frequent, and support for the accords increased once more, although it was not as strong as before.

The general pattern is clear: after every terrorist attack there is a vehement public reaction which is expressed in decreased support for Rabin and his government; but this reaction becomes weaker with time. The outcome of the next Israeli elections will depend largely on whether or not there will be successful terrorist attacks close to the time of the elections. Netanyahu's future is thus heavily dependent on terror.

How much do the terrorist attacks actually hurt Israel? During the eighteen months between the Oslo Accords and March 1995, forty-nine civilians and twenty-two soldiers have been killed in such attacks in Israel, as defined by its pre-1967 borders. During the previous eighteen months, fourteen civilians and six soldiers were killed within the same borders. By contrast, 750 Israelis were killed in traffic accidents during the eighteen months before the accords, and approximately the same number in the eighteen months that followed. But very few Israelis are much concerned about the rate of traffic accidents, while many Israelis are haunted by terrorist attacks.

To some extent the intensity of Israelis' obsession can be traced to the ferocious competition between the two main daily papers, *Yediot Aharonot* and *Ma'ariv*, which together account for about 75 percent of the country's newspaper readers, and which devote many of their pages to each attack. Of course, the press and television did not create the public's preoccupation with terror, but they have greatly magnified it.

Yet there is another, more rational side to the extreme reaction to terrorist attacks since the Oslo Accords. Most Israelis are not interested in the complex details of their government's dealings with the Palestinians. For them the issues can be reduced to a single proposition: the Palestinians want independence and we want personal security. While the accords have brought the Palestinians closer to independence since they were signed, they have brought us less personal security, for terrorist attacks have increased. This view still prevails among Israelis, and, quite apart from Netanyahu's personal qualifications to be Prime Minister, each terrorist attack works in his favor.

When it comes to the more personal reasons for Netanyahu's success in becoming a serious candidate for Prime Minister, they can be formulated as a thesis, an antithesis, and a synthesis.

Thesis: Netanyahu is something like the hero of Jerzy Kosinski's novel *Being There.* His main advantage is, simply, that he is the official head of the Likud and therefore the only alternative to Rabin. No matter who led the Likud, the outcome would not be dramatically different. On this view, Netanyahu has not become more popular than Rabin. According to a poll assessing Rabin's and Netanyahu's particular abilities, Rabin is seen as superior to Netanyahu in every respect: in persuasive ability, 42 percent to 28 percent; in personal integrity, 43 percent to 26 percent; in stamina under pressure, 41 percent to 34 percent.* Since the same poll also shows they would divide the popular vote equally, this must mean decreased support for Rabin's policies, not a preference for Netanyahu as a person.

Antithesis: Bibi Netanyahu is a one-man antiterrorist unit, a sort of Israeli Rambo. If the next Prime Minister of Israel is elected mainly on the terrorism issue, that is itself a sign of Netanyahu's success. While he was still in the army, Netanyahu became identified in several ways with the war against terror. He was himself a fighter in an elite unit (the unit that rescued the hostages from the Sabena aircraft hijacking in May 1972, in which he took an active part). He is also the brother of Jonathan "Yoni" Netanyahu, who was killed commanding the inspiring rescue of the Entebbe hostages on July 4, 1976. Bibi has set up the Jonathan Institute in his honor to mobilize public opinion in the West against terrorism.

Synthesis: The thesis is correct. Netanyahu is not perceived in Israel as having anything particularly interesting or authoritative to say about terror, or anything else. Even his service in an elite unit in the army is marginal to his success and certainly does not make him an authority on security. But although there is no direct connection between his career as an opponent of terror and his political career in Israel, there is an indirect link. Netanyahu is successful in Israel be-

---

*Israel television, Channel One, June 20, 1995.

cause he is perceived as successful. He is famous for having been famous, not for any special traits of character or achievement. And his image as a success, which led Likud voters to elect him as head of their party and as the person most likely to return the Likud to power, is a United States import. As a diplomat in Washington and as Israeli ambassador to the UN during the 1980s, he built a successful career in the United States as a regular and articulate participant in television talk shows, much sought after because of his reputation s a leading expert in "the war against terror."

The synthesis is close to the truth, while the Rambo antithesis is far from it. But it is clear that Netanyahu sees himself mainly as a leader in the antiterrorist cause, and so his record in opposing terrorism should help us to understand him better.

WHEN NETANYAHU WAS drafted into the Israeli Army in August 1967, he joined a prestigious elite unit involved with secret intelligence operations and guerrilla warfare. At the end of five years of service he had reached the rank of captain. In Israel, being an officer in that unit is an impressive achievement, and Bibi was considered a good officer, although not a brilliant one. Rabin has just appointed as Minister of the Interior Ehud Barak, the former army chief of staff who had been Bibi's superior, and the brilliant commander of his unit. Rabin may have decided to appoint Barak in order to diminish Netanyahu's image, for, as a man of action, Bibi, who greatly admires his former commanding officer, can only suffer by comparison.

At any rate, Netanyahu's decision to concentrate his public statements on the war against terror—on micro-security rather than macro-security, one might say—was politically astute. He is well aware that to be recognized as a military expert on the macro level in Israel one must be an army general. For example, Rabin, who was chief of staff at the time of Israel's greatest victory in the Six-Day War, is known as "Mr. Security." But to have been an officer in a highly praised commando unit is to be a certified expert in micro-security. Since in Israel the issue of security is still central to politics, to have experience in security matters is a great advantage for anyone who aspires to be a national leader. In Bibi's case, he and his younger brother, Iddo, did much to make the eldest brother, Yoni, into a heroic national symbol of the fight against terror.

The three Netanyahu brothers—Yoni, Bibi, and Iddo—all served in the same elite force, called The Unit by its members. Bibi brought Yoni into The Unit after Yoni had finished his army service as an officer in the paratroopers, and had just entered Harvard. Yoni, whom I knew and liked, was a fighter possessed of a rare courage under fire. No one doubts that Bibi had deep feelings about Yoni, but these feelings went beyond the intimate sphere of the family. In publishing his brother's personal letters, setting up an institute in his name, and publicizing his story, Bibi made Yoni's experience into a national saga. He had an excellent starting point: Yoni was the only person killed in an antiterrorist operation whose purpose was the rescue of hostages.

The third aspect of Netanyahu's fight against terror—his position as the leading ideologue of this struggle—is even more important than his record as a commando fighter or as creator of a symbol. One of the people "educated" by Netanyahu's Jonathan Institute was Ronald Reagan. The institute organized two conferences on terrorism, one in 1979 and one in 1985. Netanyahu edited the proceedings of the 1985 conference, which appeared under the title *Terrorism and How the West Can Win* (1986), and included two essays by Netanyahu himself on the need to oppose terror. In his own book published in 1993, Netanyahu claims that Reagan read excerpts from the conference record which appeared in *Time* magazine—and shortly afterward the Americans attacked Libya.

Netanyahu does not conceal his pride that the Arab press blamed him for the attack. The irony is that the attack on Qaddafi's house, in which his wife was injured and his adopted child killed, was a typical act of terrorism according to the definition Netanyahu gives in the book: "Terrorism is the deliberate and systematic assault on civilians to inspire fear for political ends."

No less ironic is the fact that Netanyahu is now head of a party formerly headed by Menachem Begin and Yitzhak Shamir, who both ran organizations that clearly were terrorist by his definition. This is not to say that his definition of terrorism is a bad one. The problem is that it does not cover everything that Israelis, and particularly Netanyahu himself, call "terror." It does not, for example, describe the acts of the construction worker from Hebron who came to my neighborhood in October 1991 and, while shouting "Allahu Akhbar," slaughtered three people near my house. This man had no apparent political motives; he simply wanted revenge for an incident on the Temple Mount in which Israeli border police shot seventeen Palestinians. Yet Israelis consider this an act of terror.

Terror, according to Netanyahu, is a matter of harming the innocent. He is right. The problem is that identifying the innocent is a highly contestable matter. My son had left the soldiers' bus terminal at Beit Lid just two minutes before a Hamas suicide bomber blew himself up there. He and his young paratrooper friends had been returning to the army after a few days of home leave. To me, no one could be more innocent. Nevertheless, I can see how the suicide bomber and those who sent him believed that they were killing fighters who were not innocent.

It is interesting that it was the Islamic terrorist organizations, rather than the secular ones, which for some years restricted the targets of their attacks to soldiers, in order, they said, to avoid harming civilians. Only after Baruch Goldstein's massacre of Muslims at prayer in the mosque in the Cave of the Patriarchs in 1994 did Hamas announce that, in spite of its general policy against such measures, it would take revenge in five separate acts and would not confine them to soldiers.

The political aims of the Islamic terrorist attacks are not always clear. In some cases, the suicide bombers may not have specific aims at all—they may view their acts just as a supreme manifestation of religious sacrificial devotion. Hamas as an organization, however, does have a definite political goal—the creation of an Islamic society that will not be corrupt and will be guided by Islamic law (the Sharia). The terrorist actions are meant to show that Hamas has not abandoned the struggle against Israel in order to establish a different kind of Palestinian society—as opposed to Arafat and his Fatah organization, who are portrayed as corrupt collaborators with Israel. Islamic terrorism is intended more to impress the Palestinians than to accomplish a particular political result, at least so far as Israel is concerned.

Terror against Israel is the vehicle for Hamas' struggle to determine the character of Palestinian society.

My use of the word "terror," however, is different from Netanyahu's. In a struggle that is at least partly ideological, terror occurs when the weak group uses violence against the strong one, and does so in circumstances other than battlefield conditions. When the strong group uses violence against the weak one, it is repression. Here a comparison of deaths caused respectively by Palestinian terror and Israeli repression is telling. Between the beginning of the *intifada* in December 1987 and the end of July 1995, Palestinian terror killed 297 Israelis, whereas during the same period 1,418 Palestinians died as the result of Israeli repression, including 260 people under the age of sixteen.

In Netanyahu's view, terror is not what weak groups do to strong ones, but what dictatorships do to democracies. He considers Islamic terror the instrument of a sort of Islamic Comintern whose center is the Teheran dictatorship. In the past he saw the PLO terrorists as a branch of international communism; now he sees them as an arm of international Islam.

But as Olivier Roy argued in his instructive book *The Failure of Political Islam* (1994), there is no Islamic Comintern, no authoritarian center that determines global strategies for Islam and uses its obedient branches to further these aims. Hamas and Islamic Jihad, the two radical Islamic movements in the occupied territories, are only weakly connected to outside organizations. And according to a poll of Palestinian public opinion, Hamas is supported by only 18 percent of Palestinians, and the Jihad by 4 percent.*

The results of such surveys are hardly reflected in Netanyahu's views. He is essentially a Cold War ideologue, and this in large part accounts for his tendency to turn the Israel-Arab conflict into a struggle against international Islam. When the Soviet Union still existed, Netanyahu as a diplomat in Washington argued that Israel was a strategic Middle Eastern asset in the struggle against world commu-

---

*This poll was conducted in the West Bank and the Gaza Strip in June 1995 by the Jerusalem Media and Communication Center.

nism and its terrorist offshoots. Now he agrees that it is an asset to the West on the front line of the war against international Islam.

Indeed, following the Oklahoma bombing and the sarin gas attack in Japan, Netanyahu feels that terror has again become a problem of immense urgency. "Terrorism is back—with a vengeance," is the opening line of his new book, *Fighting Terrorism.*

"Admittedly," he writes, "the *modus operandi* of this new wave of terrorism is usually different from that of the earlier terrorism that afflicted the world for two decades beginning in the 1960s." By a change in the mode of operation, he means that both hostage taking and hijacking have become rare, while bombing has become more precisely targeted.

The new wave of terrorism Netanyahu refers to is mainly home-made terrorism with no international backing. It calls into question the picture of terror he gives in his previous book as a product of grand international conspiracies, promoted by totalitarian regimes, to undermine "the West" by manipulating internal terrorist groups. With the end of the Soviet Union, however, Netanyahu finds that terrorist domestic groups are also totalitarian, implying that such groups as the Idaho militias today practice a totalitarianism more or less comparable to that of the U.S.S.R. Terror has changed mainly in its *modus operandi.*

However, the horrifying events in Oklahoma City and in Tokyo suggest again the inadequacy of the definition of terror that Netanyahu repeats in his new book: *"Terrorism is a deliberate and systematic assault on civilians to inspire fear for political ends"* (author's italics). What is particularly maddening about the acts of terror in Oklahoma and Japan, as well as in other places, is that they lack clearly defined political ends. They belong to what one might call expressive politics rather than to instrumental politics. They give vent to rage against state power and to feelings of revenge (for the "victims of Waco") or else they are extreme manifestations of religious devotion. One goal, however, is shared by more than a few terrorist groups, particularly in the Middle East: that of freeing their members from jail. For many groups this becomes an end in itself.

There is a conspicuous omission in Netanyahu's books on terror.

He makes no estimates of the actual casualties of terrorism throughout the world. In fact, the number worldwide is smaller than the total number of traffic accidents in Israel during the last few years. The effects are terrible, and inexcusable, but they do not pose a major world problem, or even a major problem for "the West." They remain, however, a problem for Israel, where more acts of terror are expected from Hamas.

STILL, WHAT BIBI thinks about Hamas will not affect his own chances in the upcoming elections. What will matter is what Hamas thinks about Bibi. The Hamas leadership wants to sabotage the accord between Rabin and Arafat, and Netanyahu wants to annul it. If he comes to power in the next election, that will mean the end of the Oslo agreements. Precisely this fact led Rabin to announce, "Bibi Netanyahu is a Hamas collaborator. . . . Hamas and the Likud have the same political goal."

But Hamas also has to take into account the public mood among the Palestinians, who are afraid of a new Likud government. In a poll conducted among Palestinians in the territories, 73 percent responded that the Likud has bad intentions toward them, and, even more important, 57 percent of those who said they trusted Hamas also said they wanted the talks with Israel to continue in order to expand Palestinian autonomy to the entire West Bank. The Hamas leaders likely fear that the Palestinians will blame them for helping Netanyahu come to power; and this may prevent the organization from carrying out terrorist acts before the Israeli elections. I say "may" because while the Hamas political leaders seem to be capable of understanding this, I'm not sure that the terrorist squads themselves share their view.

Hezbollah ("the party of God") is the radical Shiite group that wants to establish an Iranian-style Islamic regime in Lebanon and is currently fighting a war with Israel in South Lebanon. When Israel withdrew from most of Lebanon in 1985 it kept a strip of South Lebanon, called the "security zone," in which it maintains troops and strongholds in order to keep the guerrilla forces away from its northern border. The continual war between Israel and Hezbollah in this zone is not terror, in my view, because it takes place under battlefield conditions. Still, Hezbollah fits Netanyahu's image of an Islamic group dependent on Iran more closely than Hamas does. There are close religious ties between Shiite Hezbollah and Shiite Iran—Hezbollah's religious leaders studied in Iran—whereas Hamas is a Sunni Muslim organization. Iran clearly supports Hezbollah with money and arms. But in the last analysis, even though Hezbollah is influenced and aided by Iran, the Iranians do not run it.

The war in South Lebanon has been very costly for Israel. The new commander who was recently put in charge of the front there —General Amiram Levin, who was Bibi's commanding officer in The Unit—has changed Israel's strategy, taking the initiative and chasing the Hezbollah squads northward, past the border of the security zone. Levin, who is perhaps the best field commander in Israel today, has had a number of impressive successes in South Lebanon. Yet it is clear—and no one knows this better than Rabin—that the war there can have no military solution. Rabin rightly believes that a peace agreement with Syria is the only solution. Lebanon has long been a Syrian protectorate, and Lebanese Hezbollah still serves Syrian interests. But if there is a peace accord between Syria and Lebanon in which Israel officially recognizes Syria's "special status" in Lebanon as part of a general agreement, then Syria will be able to eliminate, or at least severely curtail, Hezbollah's activity against Israel.*

IN JUNE 1995 IT looked as if Assad and Rabin were on the verge of reaching an Israeli-Syrian accord. Things look less hopeful now. While the timetable is uncertain, the basic provisions of the proposed treaty are clear. The accord will roughly duplicate the one between Israel and Egypt, an accord stipulating Israeli withdrawal from territories captured in the Six-Day War, which means the Golan Heights. Israel is holding out for withdrawal to the internationally recognized border, while Syria is insisting on Israeli withdrawal to the 1948 cease-fire line. Between the two lines, there is a difference of some 15,000 acres.

*See Peter Partner, "The Rebirth of Beirut," *The New York Review*, June 22, 1995, p. 38.

Immediately after the agreement is signed a process of "normalization" is to begin, including the exchange of ambassadors, while the withdrawal itself will take place three years later. The security arrangements, including the demilitarization of the Golan, have not been agreed on; nor have many other details of the accord. But the direction in which the talks are heading seems clear.

The right wing headed by Netanyahu is bitterly opposed to what it has heard of the treaty. It accuses Rabin of deceiving the voters who elected him, since Rabin, campaigning before the last elections, said that the country would never withdraw from the Golan, not even for peace. Rabin changed his position, but there is plenty of precedent for his doing so. Many important steps in world politics have been taken by conservative leaders who, in the name of the reality principle, "betrayed" the voters who elected them: De Klerk in South Africa, De Gaulle in Algeria, Nixon in China, Begin with the Camp David Agreement, and now perhaps Rabin.

Rabin has promised to hold a referendum on any accord with Syria, a move without precedent in Israel. He believes that he will be able to get popular approval when the details of the accord, particularly the security arrangements, are worked out. He needs the support of only 40 percent of the Jewish voters, since Israeli Arabs will obviously support the accord, and they make up 14 percent of the voters. Reports by Israeli intelligence have convinced Rabin that Assad has changed his strategic approach to Israel and now really wants a deal.

An accord with Syria would mean neutralizing the last front where an army with an offensive capacity still poses a military threat to Israel. Peace with Syria would consolidate the peace achieved with Egypt and Jordan and dramatically reduce the chances of future wars. Rabin wants to conclude the agreement while Israel still holds a nuclear monopoly in the Middle East. He is afraid of an alliance between Syria and Iran that would accelerate the nuclear arms race with Israel, a race in which Syria might get aid from Pakistan. Having lost the support of the Soviet Union, Syria, if the conflict with Israel continues, would be likely to try to acquire nuclear weapons with the help of Iran. A peace accord should reduce the pressures on Syria to form an alliance with Iran.

Such are the considerations that are apparently central for Rabin.

But all this is high strategy. Most Israelis have a more concrete sense of the Golan: they see it as a plateau from which the Israelis living in the valley below are an easy target. In other words, as in old Westerns, they tend to see the bad guys sitting in ambush at the top of the canyon and shooting at the good guys below. Netanyahu makes the most of this image, especially when talking to American Jewish activists visiting Israel.

There are other reasons for Israel's not wanting to give up the Golan Heights. Its Jewish settlements are flourishing, and the Golan is a popular place to visit for both Israelis and foreign tourists. Moreover, Israelis see it as very different from the West Bank, because they think of it as free of Arabs. This is not exactly the case: there are more Druse, who are still Syrian citizens, than Israelis on the Golan —17,000 as opposed to 13,000. The Golan, moreover, has been quiet since the 1973 war; since many Israelis believe that Syria could not mount an attack without support from the Soviet Union, they can't see any reason to give up the Golan.

Of all the arguments against an accord with Syria, the one that disturbs me most is the claim that the Syrians cannot use military force against Israel. All of Israel's wars began with a situation in which the Arabs were assumed to have "no military option." In 1967 it was said that Nasser was deeply involved in a war with Yemen and could not afford to start a war with Israel. But then it turned out that Nasser's way of getting out of Yemen was precisely by opening up a front with Israel. When Nasser was defeated in that war, we were told that it would be many years before he could rebuild his army, and so he would not again resort to military force. But Nasser didn't wait for years—he immediately began a war of attrition with Israel. In 1973 it was said that Egypt and Syria had no military option because Israel's military superiority was so great that they wouldn't dare start a war. The worst war of all then broke out on both fronts. Peace with Syria will not mean the end of the conflict with the Palestinians or the end of terrorism; but it could well mean an end to any military threat against Israel, and this is what Rabin cares about.

If the Israeli-Syrian accord is concluded just before the next Israeli elections, the referendum will probably not be held. The elections, which would center on the accord with Syria, would then take the place of the referendum.

NETANYAHU'S VIEWS ON the great questions of "war and peace" appeared in his *A Place Among the Nations*, published in English in 1993, which appeared in Israel as *A Place in the Sun*. The journalist Rami Rosen, who helped the Israeli publisher edit the book, introduced sections of it in the daily *Yediot Aharonot*, saying

> More than any other senior politician in Israel, Benjamin Netanyahu has been accused of shallowness and superficiality. Precisely the person who studied at the best universities in the world—Harvard and MIT—is often presented as someone who may be capable of transmitting messages efficiently but simply has nothing to say. Netanyahu's book . . . should explode this myth.

(Rosen also observed that when Netanyahu quotes Kant he has actually read him, and that, moreover, it was Netanyahu himself who wrote his own book and no one else.)

Netanyahu's book has two main themes: the right of Jewish people to the Land of Israel and the way to achieve "real peace" with the Arabs. While Netanyahu may indeed have written the book himself, the presence of his father, the historian Benzion Netanyahu, makes itself felt everywhere in its early pages. The elder Netanyahu, a historian specializing in medieval Spanish Jewry, has long been an advocate of Revisionist Zionism, which demands the establishment "in blood and fire" of a Jewish state on both sides of the Jordan River. In the 1930s Benzion Netanyahu was the editor of the Revisionist newspaper *Jordan* in Palestine.

Bibi's account of the British Mandate reproduces a version of the Revisionist Zionism of the elder Netanyahu's generation. In his version, any eccentric, romantic, minor British officer who had read the Bible and saw the Jews as the children of Israel had clearly seen the light, while British officers who had studied Arabic at Oxford and were attracted to the desert tribes were seen as benighted, anti-Semitic "Arabists." Netanyahu's book has many strange quotations from both types of officers, as if there were some great truth buried in the writings of these imperial eccentrics.

But the young Netanyahu's book has a mission—to establish Israel's absolute claim to the occupied territories. I take very seriously the missionary history in his book. Bibi is not superficial in the sense of a salesman who lacks real convictions. He is the product of one of the true believers of Shamir's generation—in the ideological as well as the biological sense. Like his father, he is ferociously committed to a Greater Israel. His arguments are no different from Shamir's, but while Shamir appeared to Americans like the leader of a Balkan peasant party, Bibi seems more like an American politician, a smooth Republican senator, perhaps. His message, like Shamir's, is simply "not one inch," and it would be a mistake to see either of them as a tough negotiator trying to extract a better price from the Arabs in the Middle Eastern bazaar. Like Shamir, Netanyahu is not interested in negotiating but in playing for time. The difference between him and Shamir lies elsewhere. Bibi is at home in the world of television studios, and he especially loves *Hasbara*.

The term *Hasbara* has no equivalent in English, but it partly overlaps with several similar words: "propaganda," "preaching," "indoctrination," "apologetics," "rhetoric," and even "self-righteousness." The literal meaning of the word is "explanation," and it is the specialty of Israel's professional emissaries and publicists. At whom is the "explanation" directed? The intended audiences are not neatly divided into Gentiles and Jews, as one might think. The *Hasbara* mainly meant for Western audiences is addressed just as much to Diaspora Jews who need to be supported in their belief that Israel has always been right as against the "hypocritical" and "perverse" liberal, leftist arguments made by Arab-loving, self-hating Jews. The assumption of *Hasbara* is that these liberal leftists are now as dangerous to Israel as the medieval Jewish apostates who once made use of their inside knowledge of the Talmud to attack the Jewish religion.

A Place Among the Nations is a work of *Hasbara* par excellence.

In fact it is more than that—it is a work of meta-*Hasbara*, a book of indoctrination for the would-be indoctrinator. In 1981 Moshe Arens, who was then Israel's ambassador to the United States, appointed Benjamin Netanyahu to be his deputy at the embassy. And in 1984 Netanyahu was appointed Israeli ambassador to the United Nations. In both jobs Netanyahu was considered a great success, a master of the art of *Hasbara*, especially among the organized American Jewish community. The trouble is that Netanyahu confuses *Hasbara* with policy, and one sometimes gets the impression that he has no idea of the difference between the two.

What is Netanyahu's policy toward the Palestinians? "We'll tell the Palestinians," he says, " 'Forget about a state.' " He wants the security zones, the borders, and foreign relations all to remain under Israel's control. Gaza will be closed off and surrounded by a security fence. The Israeli Army will retain the right to take what action it wants in Judea, Samaria, and Gaza. The Jewish settlements will remain and even be extended. Bibi's plan is clear: it is to freeze the present situation.

"It's a joke," Rabin remarked. "He proposes perpetuating the present situation in the territories and he calls it a plan." Rabin also mocked the plan as "Bibi's second videotape."

The first videotape has come to haunt Bibi no less than the charge of shallowness. On the evening of January 14, 1994, Israel's television audience was treated to the sight of Netanyahu describing how some unknown person had attempted to blackmail his wife, Sara, over the telephone. The blackmailer had threatened to make public a videotape containing graphic material about Bibi's intimate relationship with another woman unless he abandoned his candidacy for the leadership of the Likud. Bibi admitted that he had had a brief affair, adding, "I know who is behind this ugly scandal—one man, surrounded by a gang of criminals, a senior person in the Likud."

It was obvious whom Netanyahu meant: his rival for the leadership of the Likud, David Levi. As it turned out, however, Bibi's accusation was baseless. No such videotape had ever existed. Yet he tried to link the embarrassing story about a tape with his war against terror.

"A crime unprecedented in the history of democracy has been committed," he declared. "The threat of blackmail has been used in an attempt to prevent a candidate from running for party chairman. When you are faced with blackmail of this sort, when they put a gun to your head, you have two choices: you can run away and hide or you can go out and stand up for yourself. I do not run away and I do not hide."

Levi is a man of honor. He never forgave Netanyahu for this false charge; and, most important, he never accepted Bibi's leadership of the Likud. Bibi, in effect, forced Levi to leave the party, saying that he opposed him as part of his war against blackmail. On June 18, 1995, Levi announced that he would run for Prime Minister as the head of a new party.

Levi comes from a development town of Moroccan immigrants who arrived during the 1950s. For such people, the Likud has always been a home more than a party. Levi's career was a Likud success story. It is hard to assess the significance of his departure for the Likud generally and for Bibi's chances in particular. According to the polls, Levi, running as an independent, could win five Knesset seats out of 120 for his own party, mostly at the expense of the Likud. But Levi's departure has badly shaken the automatic sense of belonging and identification that Jews of Oriental origin have long felt toward the Likud. The affair of the "tape," especially Netanyahu's public admission of marital infidelity, may also hurt his chances among religious voters, even though they are now the most right-wing group in Israel. An admission of this sort is not easily glossed over in the religious community. So the tape that never was has its own existence after all.

Meanwhile David Levi has been raising issues that both parties have so far swept under the carpet, particularly concerning the fast pace of privatization of the state's economic and social agencies, which is the main social process taking place in Israel today. For many years, the Israeli public sector—the government, the Histadrut trade union confederation, and the Jewish Agency—made up more than 50 percent of the country's economy. Today government-owned corporations are being sold, and schools, broadcast stations, and cultural activities are also rapidly being privatized. Privatization is considered a form of

"Americanization" among Israelis, and the American-style Bibi is considered part of this process, which includes the much-publicized opening of McDonald's hamburger restaurants in Israel.

Bibi himself has nothing to do with McDonald's. He claims to prefer yogurt; but he is seen as having introduced American-style campaigning into Israeli politics. When Benny Begin, another rival for the leadership of the Likud, was interviewed on the radio during the campaign for the Likud primaries, the interviewer asked him what he had for breakfast. "Netanyahu said he had a yogurt. What did you eat?" she asked.

"That's exactly what the primaries are doing to the Likud," replied Begin. "Yogurtization. The primaries have made the Likud superficial. I am against this Americanization"—by which he meant that the emphasis on the private lives and habits of leaders was trivializing Israeli politics.

Netanyahu's problem from now until the elections is how to remain "superficial" and avoid mistakes, such as making serious statements and thus becoming vulnerable. He has not so far avoided mistakes. In one instance, he saved Rabin's government from the colossal folly of annexing 140 acres of land belonging to Jerusalem Arabs, a plan that had led to a gratuitous conflict with Egypt, Jordan, and the Palestinians. Netanyahu tried to bring down the government through a vote of no-confidence in which he would have been joined by the Arab parties, who were naturally against the annexation. This gave Rabin and Peres a chance to give up the annexation plan and accuse Netanyahu of disloyalty to Jerusalem.

In the last analysis, however, it is not Netanyahu's mistakes that will prevent him from coming to power. The Hamas military units (Izz el Din al Qassam) have only a few dozen fighters, but they, more than anyone else, will determine who will be the next Prime Minister of Israel.

POSTSCRIPT: ON AUGUST 21, in a suicide attack on a Jerusalem bus, a terrorist blew himself up, killing four Israelis and wounding several dozen. A spokesman for Hamas in Damascus took responsibility for the attack, proclaiming that "the five battalions" of the Izz el Din al Qassam are "stronger than what the crazy old Rabin imagines." As of now, therefore, Hamas seems ready to act in ways that favor Netanyahu in the next Israeli election.

I expected Netanyahu to be an example of the blind leading the blind. I did not expect that he would be so incompetent once in office. He projected the air of an executive who knows his business, even if it may ruin mine. But then he blundered so badly that even the cautious Econ-omist described him on its cover as a "serial bungler."

To list Netanyahu's blunders would be not only tedious but politi-cally irrelevant. For one thing, many Israelis have come to admire his Houdini-like ability to free himself from the chains in which he traps himself. His streak of blunders stopped in early 1998, but even if it resumes it may not affect his chances of being reelected. Netanyahu runs on the politics of resentment, which is quite different from the politics of management. Short of disasters he may go on despite his blunders.

16

ISAIAH BERLIN:
PRINCE OF THE EXILES

FEBRUARY 1995

PEOPLE WHO TALK WITH ISAIAH BERLIN ARE OFTEN STRUCK BY A feeling of regret that he does not write his autobiography. Many have annoyed him with their excited pleas that he should devote himself to this task. The demand is understandable. After all, Berlin was at several "observation posts" from which he could follow closely the unfolding of some of the central events in this century.

In 1915, when Berlin was six, his family moved from Riga, the capital of Latvia, where he was born, and eventually ended up in Petrograd. From a window above a Petrograd shop in Wassily Ostrov, the child Shaya, as he was affectionately called by his parents (a diminutive of the Hebrew for Isaiah), watched the Russian Revolution. In 1920, when he was almost eleven, the family emigrated to England. They landed in March, the young Isaiah wearing a coat with a fur collar and knowing very little English. In July of that same year, he won the Surbiton's Arundel House School's first prize for an English essay.

Later Berlin was posted at still another central event of the century. At the British embassy in Washington, the young don from Oxford served during World War II, in order to report to the British government on American public opinion during the war. The folklore about Berlin in Washington is vast, and it includes the true story of Churchill's being impressed by the reports from Washington and asking after the war to meet "this man Berlin," shortly after which the British Prime Minister found himself entertaining Irving Berlin. The mix-up between Isaiah and Irving was not new. Already in 1932, when Berlin was elected first Jewish Fellow of All Souls College in Oxford, there was much excitement in the Jewish community in England, and the Chief Rabbi is on record in the *Jewish Chronicle* congratulating Irving Berlin for his election.

Another extraordinary perch came Berlin's way in the Soviet Union, during the period between the end of World War II and the return of Stalin to his reign of terror, when he was an attaché in the British embassy in Moscow and met the great, embattled figures of Russian literature. Looking at Berlin's life, indeed, one feels that he has met everyone worth meeting: Freud and Virginia Woolf, Igor Stravinsky, Anna Akhmatova and Boris Pasternak, Nehru, Eliot, Toscanini, Churchill, Auden, Malraux, Edmund Wilson, and Bertrand Russell (Russell: "These characters in the Bible are dreadful people." Berlin: "What have you against Jonathan?" Russell: "Come to think of it, I rather like Jezebel. She reminds me of many modern young women of today"), not to mention the major and minor deities of politics and society.

And so, given his prodigious memory and his narrative gift, the demand for an autobiography is eminently justified. But Berlin rebuffs such pleas. He claims in his defense that he has already written lengthy personal impressions, collected in a book, and that everything he had to tell is there. But it is precisely the existence of *Personal Impressions* that leaves one with a taste for more. One wishes to know more, surely, about the "old Menshevik" Rachmilewitch, of whom

Berlin says that he was the purest intellectual he ever met, and influenced him more than anyone else. He met him in London when he was sixteen, and it was Rachmilewitch who did much to open before him the great panorama of music (Berlin's first published article was about Verdi), Kant, Marx, the radical thought of Russia during the nineteenth century, and philosophies of science: the life of the mind in all its aspects.

Berlin also claims—it is his last line of defense—that he is not sufficiently interested in himself to write his own biography. This is not an affectation; it is sincere, and it cuts deep. But it puts me in mind of Nietzsche's comment that the basic feature of a great psychologist is a lack of curiosity in himself. This, of course, was long before our psychological age. The philosopher was thinking of a person, usually a writer, who has the power of imagination to enter into the minds of other people; and this, too, is one of Berlin's great skills.

Indeed, the problem of empathy has been a lasting preoccupation of Berlin's work. For him, there is an essential difference between scientific understanding and the understanding of human affairs. To understand history, religion, culture, and literature, one needs to understand people. Berlin traces these types of understanding to the writings of the thinkers he has done so much to rescue from oblivion, Giovanni Battista Vico, Johann Gottfried von Herder, and Georg Hamann. Berlin is himself one of the great *Versteheren*, or "understanders." He is a psychologist of ideas as much as a historian of ideas. He is addicted to the observation of people, and paints their portraits in the subtlest and most vivid hues.

Perhaps the most famous of Berlin's discriminations of human character is one that he borrowed from the Greek poet Archilochus, between the hedgehog and the fox. "The fox knows many little things, the hedgehog knows one big thing." Thus Tolstoy is a fox (who vainly tried in old age to become a hedgehog) and Dostoyevsky is a hedgehog. Berlin proceeds usefully to classify other thinkers and writers into foxes and hedgehogs. (The philosopher Nelson Goodman once whimsically asked him what would be the proper animal metaphor for one who spends his life knowing one little thing.)

The Berlin memory bank is capable of cashing in any character description for its gold equivalent—namely, an illustrative story or an unforgettable quotation. In what sense was Chaim Weizmann, the leader of the Zionist movement and Berlin's close friend, an ironic man? Well, Berlin will tell Weizmann's last words. When, on his deathbed, he coughed badly and felt choked, Weizmann's doctor told him to spit. "But there is no one to spit at," he replied in Yiddish, and died. It was also Weizmann who said that it is not necessary to be mad in order to be a Zionist but it helps. Berlin is fond of that latter dictum, but the beautiful profile that he draws of Weizmann emphasizes his hero's normality. He presents him as the perfect non-neurotic Jew, and a great man.

"The great man" is a central category in Berlin's view of history. He is, Berlin believes, someone who is capable of changing our notions of what people can do; someone who, in the public sphere, aims at, and causes, a significant historical change of direction, which would have been regarded as improbable before he acted. Genius, by contrast, is not like greatness. Asked how he managed to leap so high, Nijinsky replied that most people, when they jump, come down at once, "but why not linger in the air a little before coming down?" That is genius, and it shows itself in art, in mathematics, in music, in philosophy, in literature. The action is simple and clear, but the rest of us do not know how to begin to do it. But great men (and women) are doers in the social sphere, and we may follow where they lead. Even monsters such as Stalin or Hitler are, for Berlin, great men; but not Gorbachev, for example, since Gorbachev did not intend the consequences of his actions.

For good or for ill, admirably or contemptibly, a great man may single-handedly affect the shape of major historical events. In Berlin's hands, however, the idea of the great man is not an expression of elitism. He intends with it, rather, to celebrate the role of the individual in history. Also the role of freedom: Berlin is a famous foe of the idea of historical inevitability. Berlin does not believe in laws of history that determine every historical event. A historian is not a scientist. In contrast with the scientist, who endeavors to discover underlying similarities between apparently disparate phenomena, the historian strives to highlight what is unique about an age or an event.

UNLIKE OTHER PHILOSOPHERS, Berlin is concerned not only with the sense of a great idea but also with its sensibility. He studies the systematic connection between an idea and the feelings that are attached to it, such as the connection between the idea of nationalism and the sentiment of belonging. For this reason, Berlin's heroes are not only those who have enriched our thought but also those who have contributed to our culture. His deep interest in the Romantic movement, and especially in the conceptions of will and of genius that are central to it, springs partly from the recognition of their crucial impact on our shared sensibility. To make sense of an idea, one turns to logic and philology. To understand the sensibility of an idea, one turns to empathy, and hence to Berlin.

An intriguing case in point is provided by Berlin's book *The Magus of the North* (1994), which is devoted to the thought of Georg Hamann, "a God-intoxicated" thinker. Hamann was a contemporary of Kant, and a fellow citizen of Königsberg. Spiritually, there can be no doubt that Hamann is very distant from Berlin. Hamann's "sleepwalker's certainty," the mysterious, intuitive method of knowledge that is undisturbed by reality, is the complete opposite of Berlin's skepticism, which prizes a robust sense of reality. And yet Berlin understands Hamann so well that he seems to approve of him implicitly, almost.

In the New Testament, the Magi came from the East, led by the bright star of Bethlehem. Hamann, a self-appointed Magus, was led mostly by a pessimistic Paulinian shadow cast on human nature and human reason. According to Hamann, we do not believe for reasons any more than we taste for reasons or smell for reasons.

The city of Berlin, the Enlightenment city of Lessing and Mendelssohn, was, for Hamann, Babylon. The key to understanding him as a thinker, he declared, was his hatred of Babylon; and the key used by Isaiah Berlin to crack Hamann's enigmatic personality is his penetrating hatred of the Enlightenment. For Berlin, any person who, like Hamann, is nurtured equally by the Bible and by the nonbeliever David Hume deserves cracking. Hamann believed that language is an incarnation of God. I don't know about that; but a reader of *The Magus of the North* will see how ably Berlin has succeeded in fleshing out the life and the thought of Hamann from Hamann's own language, which is notoriously suggestive and obscure. Indeed, the reader of this extraordinary book will come to feel that it is finally impossible to understand someone so different from oneself without to some extent identifying with him.

Berlin is liberal through and through, one of the most important liberal thinkers of our time, but he is a particular kind of liberal. He believes in the morality of liberalism, not in its psychology. The psychology of liberalism, which was inherited from the Enlightenment, strikes him as shallow. It is the Counter-Enlightenment (a term Berlin coined), as it was represented by Hamann and Joseph de Maistre, that does more justice to the complexity of the human psyche. It was a shallow but influential assumption of the Enlightenment that all human beings are, in their nature, seekers of happiness, knowledge, and justice, and that they are capable of objectively recognizing these ends. But Berlin is no worshipper of human nature. God may have created the animals, but man creates himself.

It is not only for a more compelling psychology that Berlin turns to the Counter-Enlightenment. He also finds in the darker thinkers an important warning about the limits of science. Berlin has respect for science, and even for scientists; as the founder and first president of Wolfson College in Oxford, he recruited more scientists, proportionately, than had any of the ancient, illustrious Oxford colleges. But there is a great gulf between respecting science and accepting the ideology of scientism. Scientism hides from us the deep Kantian truth, that "out of timber as crooked as that from which man is made nothing entirely straight can be carved." Within the human sciences, people cannot be expected to be arranged into classifications and patterns governed by natural laws; and certainly they cannot be aligned within a social order built according to a master plan.

I have no doubt that if anyone were to approach Berlin in the ancient rabbinical way, with the request that he should teach all there is to know while standing on one foot, he would receive in reply Kant's adage about the crooked timber. The fact that it is impossible to "straighten" people is, for Berlin, a source of joy, not of gloom. He is happy about human diversity. And so he is skeptical about progress as the march of humanity toward a well-defined goal, and prefers what his contemporary Karl Popper described as piecemeal engineering—that is, mending and improving upon those areas of human activity in which we may be able to predict the outcome of our deeds. Such areas may include health, or education, or the Tennessee Valley project. Berlin was acquainted with, and impressed by, the New Deal and the New Dealers, and counted some of them, notably Felix Frankfurter, among his friends. For Berlin, the America of the New Deal was America at its best; and he never shared the Oxonian suspicion of things American as vulgar.

BERLIN'S SPECIAL SORT of liberalism emerged from his recognition that not all values are commensurable. Not even in utopia can harmony reign among all values. Equality and freedom, for example, are bound to clash. Since no single form of life can give expression to all the values that we respect, it is important that forms of life different from our own flourish. Without diverse forms of life, we will all be poorer. Only a liberal society among all societies can do justice to diversity. In Herder's simile, later perverted by Mao, this is the garden in which the greatest number of flowers will bloom.

Among Berlin's many famous essays, his inaugural lecture at Oxford in 1958 on "Two Concepts of Liberty" is the most famous. In that remarkable discussion, he draws a contrast between negative liberty, which is your liberty from my interference in your actions, and positive liberty, which is your liberty to realize your "real interests." Positive liberty may become positively dangerous when negative liberty is denied in the name of "real interests," which are usually defined by others. This is not to say that Berlin is a libertarian. For libertarians, liberalism is based solely on negative liberty. For Berlin, negative liberty is only one justification for liberalism. Pluralism is the other. And liberty is a necessary condition of pluralism.

Berlin likes to remark upon a curious historical fact. The "pro-phetic" thinkers of the nineteenth century predicted some important developments of our century: revolutions in the Third World (Baku-nin), conformism in democratic societies (Tocqueville), the central role of the military-industrial complex (Burckhardt), the concentration of capital and the effect of technological innovations (Marx). Yet all of them believed that nationalism was on the wane. But Berlin, who shuns prophecy, has always assigned supreme importance to nation-alism, and to the hold of nationalist feelings over people. He prefers to think of nationalism in Herder's terms, as cultural nationalism, based on the idea that one's humanity finds its best expression in one's particular culture. In Berlin's world, there is room for different cultures, and no need for rivalry among them. Herderian nationalism is the embodiment of pluralism among nations. At the same time Berlin does not deny the realities of political nationalism, and the "bad" versions of it that are based on theories of superiority and hatred toward the other. Yet he insists that a worldview that does not heed the intensity of nationalist feelings, good or bad, is bound to be ir-relevant. How to deal with nationalism is, for Berlin, the central ques-tion that liberals should be asking themselves these days.

BERLIN HAS BEEN a Zionist all his life. His father once explained the son's attraction to Zionism as an extension of the Hebrew lessons he received as a child, even after the family moved to England. Zi-onism is the national liberation movement of the Jewish people; and Berlin maintains that it was Zionism that in fact created the Jewish nation. In their two millennia of exile, the Jews lost the crucial fea-tures of a nation. They had neither a territory of their own nor a common spoken language, and—since the French Revolution—they even ceased to be a religious community in the traditional way. And yet, although there is no simple definition for the Jewish people, Berlin sees no difficulty in defining the Jews and in recognizing their right to a homeland and their need for freedom from the domination of others.

One drizzly day in Oxford I was walking with Berlin, when suddenly he stopped, waved his umbrella in the air, and asked, "What do you think is common to all Jews?" He continued to specify, in his customary way: "I mean, to the Jew from San'a, from Marrakesh, from Riga, from Glasgow?" And right away he answered his own question: "A sense of social unease. Nowhere do almost all Jews feel entirely at home." Unlike Herder, Berlin tends to identify the need of belonging to a group with the urge to feel at home; and the absence of such a need results in the life of the stranger. "Home," as he quoted Robert Frost, "is the place where, when you go there, they have to take you in."

In one important sense, Zionism has been, for Berlin, a success story. It succeeded in giving the Jewish inhabitants of Israel a home, and a sense of home. In spite of his criticism of Zionist politics when it unnecessarily deprived Palestinians of their homes, he saw Zionism as a success story.

For Berlin, the Jewish people are an extended family. An interesting, possibly even neurotic, family, but by no means a "chosen" one, and not a spiritual community dedicated to Judaism. His feeling of solidarity with his fellow Jews is basic, spontaneous, and unapologetic. It is a family tie. As in a family, there are black sheep, whom Berlin is good at spotting, and there are always embarrassing and irritating relatives. The concern for the family, however, is first and foremost a concern for the welfare of its members, for preventing the suffering and the persecution that have been their lot for so long just because of their Jewishness. Berlin believes that there is truth in the historian Lewis Namier's dubious remark that "there is no modern Jewish history, only a Jewish martyrology." But Berlin is no romantic of suffering, and he sees no glory in martyrdom, nothing sublime or redemptive in suffering. Suffering could never be a blessing, only a curse.

Berlin is not a religious man, and he shows no trace especially of the religious feeling that the Jews are the chosen people. More interesting, he betrays no secular version of this sentiment. But he does feel strongly that the Jews are an old, interesting, and somewhat neurotic family, and he has no patience for Jews who are estranged from their people. In private conversations he is quite fond of unmasking Jews who deny their identity. For him, even Lenin's maternal grandfather falls under faint suspicion.

Berlin's own family is old and intriguing. He is a direct descendant of Shneor Zalman of Liadi, the founder of the Hasidic dynasty of Lubavitch at the time of the Napoleonic Wars. He is the second cousin of the late Lubavitcher Rabbi Menachem Schneerson, whose followers in Brooklyn and elsewhere declared him to be the Messiah. (Yehudi Menuhin belongs to another branch of the same family tree.) Though proud, privately, of his illustrious Hasidic lineage, he felt acute embarrassment at having a self-proclaimed Messiah in the family. His wife, Aline, too, has an old and no less fascinating pedigree. She was born into the family of the Barons de Ginsbourg, who distinguished themselves for three generations, up until the Russian Revolution, as grand bankers in Russia and in Paris, and were prominent in Jewish diplomacy during the pogroms against the Jews in the days of the Tsars; they were also among the most preeminent philanthropic families in the modern history of the Jews.

One of Berlin's earliest childhood memories is the wedding of his aunt to Isaac Landoberg, who later became Yitzhak Sadeh, a legend in Israel. Like Garibaldi, who founded the Red Shirts, Sadeh founded the Palmach, the strike force of the Haganah, whose units played a decisive role in Israel's War of Independence in 1948. Sadeh was not only a general but also a writer. In his early days in Russia, he had been a boxer, a wrestler, and an avid footballer, as well as a painters' model and an art dealer: a pagan, in sum. During the Russian Revolution he came to Petrograd, as a Social Revolutionary officer, to visit the Berlins. Berlin's mother was so terrified of his huge Mauser pistol that she took it from him and put it away in a bowl of cold water, lest it explode. Eventually Sadeh managed to switch sides in the Revolution, and served with the White Army. But he ended his life, in Israel, as a pro-Soviet romantic socialist. In Berlin's eyes, he remained an enchanting adventurer.

On one of Berlin's visits to Palestine, in late 1947, he met Sadeh again. Those were the last days of the British Mandate in Palestine, days of rampant terror. Sadeh, who was on the British authorities' wanted list, met Berlin at the back of a Tel Aviv café. That visit in Palestine, just like the early memories from the streets of Petrograd, bred in Berlin a profound aversion to terror. Berlin is not a pacifist (he was opposed to the Munich agreement, which was popular in Britain at the time), but he detested the methods of Begin's and Shamir's underground, and his attitude did not change when they became Israeli Prime Ministers.

But it was also that visit to Palestine which strengthened his emotional ties to Sadeh. A strong family feeling is, for Berlin, one of the "primary colors" of human emotion. And Berlin has a deep interest in human emotion, despite the fact that by far the greatest part of his adult life was spent at Oxford, where the the most popular emotion seems to be embarrassment, or the need to avoid it.

BERLIN HAS, CURIOUSLY, very few enemies. For many years he held powerful academic positions, yet people loved to love him. When the *Frankfurter Allgemeine Zeitung* sent him its well-known questionnaire, his answer to the question "What are your faults?" was "I am too anxious to please." (His answer to the question "Who would you like to have been?" was "Alexander Herzen.") In an essay on slavery and the emancipation of the Jews, Berlin ascribes the tendency toward ingratiation to Jews newly out of the ghetto. Being eager to please, however, does not make one universally liked; and so the explanation for the universal admiration of Berlin must be sought elsewhere.

It is not far to seek. Berlin is so beloved because he is slow to judge, so forgiving of faults and foibles, so lacking in malice. Once, at a dinner in Paris, Berlin was seated next to Lauren Bacall. She asked him where he lived. "Oxford," he said. "Then perhaps," she asked, "you know my Oxford friend Isaiah Berlin?" "I am he," he replied. She was not the only one who, upon meeting this unforgettable man, felt instinctively and immediately close.

Three years after this essay was first published, Isaiah Berlin died. I made the following remarks at a memorial for him held at the Sheldonian Theatre in Oxford, March 21, 1998:

"You have beautiful black eyes," Greta Garbo once said to Berlin. His eyes were indeed remarkably expressive. They were full of mis-

chievous cleverness, childish inquisitiveness, and skeptical soberness. Today these eyes appear in framed photographs: glassy and formal. The
spark is gone.

One streak in Judaism which Berlin was definitely very skeptical
about is the idea that we are not here to enjoy ourselves. He enjoyed
his life thoroughly, and made it his business to make others joyous in
his presence. This business, of making others joyous, had its price. Or
so he thought.

There's a wonderful lecture of Berlin's entitled "Jewish Slavery and
Emancipation," in which he spells out a parable for the state of the Jews.
He tells there of "travelers who by some accident find themselves among
a tribe whose customs they are not familiar with. They don't know what
to expect. The strangers, being alien to the tribe's form of life, find little
they can take for granted. They do everything they can to find out how
their hosts function. They must get this right, otherwise they may easily
find themselves in trouble. But then this is precisely the reason for which
they are felt to be outsiders. They are experts on the tribe, not members
of it. They are altogether too anxious to please."

For Berlin, as for Tolstoy, the distinction between being natural and
being artificial and affected is basic. Natasha in love, stung by a nettle
in the field, is for Tolstoy an epiphany of the natural, while Natasha
watching French opera, with a stage setting of a phony moon, is an
emblem of the artificial. (Berlin, an avid opera worshipper, never considered the opera to be artificial.) Being at home for Berlin meant the
possibility of being natural, naive, and socially at ease. Jews had lost
the sense of home by being in exile.

When Berlin gossiped about the family it was social history at its
best, and when he talked about social history it was as intimate as
family gossip. It is this sense of solidarity that shaped him as the tribal
cosmopolitan that he was. He had a vision of a world where all people
would have a sense of belonging and of identity, and by virtue of this
would have a natural sense of home, so that they might express their
own humanity to the full.

If Jews for Isaiah meant family, what was Isaiah for the Jews? For
many Jews he was Resh Galuta, Prince of the Exiles. They wanted to
pay him tribute, which on many occasions meant to visit the great man.

Berlin did not mind that in the least, not even when they were bores. He made room for everyone in his dense little diary, then met them, and enchanted them with his warmth, with his instant sense of familiarity, and above all with his mesmerizing stories.

In October 1997 I had received a letter from Berlin, which I asked his permission to publish in the Israeli press. His permission, contained in a fax from Lady Berlin—"Isaiah says 'yes'"—was given in the morning of November 5, just hours before he died. I do not believe that Berlin meant his letter be a political testament, but the circumstances surrounding it made it into one.

The letter surprised me, not because of its contents, but because it was written at all. Berlin did not believe in expressive politics. He believed that political action should be carried out only when there was a reasonable chance that it would make a difference. Being expressive was, for him, the realm of art; being effective, the realm of politics. What counts in politics is what changes the course of events. Yet suddenly he wrote this letter, which I can only take as an expressive act, as an act of standing to be counted. I believe it expressed his deep concern with the way Israeli politics was going and with the direction it was taking. Here it is:

ISRAEL AND THE PALESTINIANS

Since both sides begin with a claim of total possession of Palestine as their historical right, and since neither claim can be accepted within the realm of realism or without grave injustice, it is plain that compromise, i.e. partition, is the only correct solution, along Oslo lines—for supporting which Rabin was assassinated by a Jewish bigot.

Ideally, what we are calling for is a relationship of good neighbours, but given the number of bigoted, terrorist chauvinists on both sides, this is impracticable.

The solution must lie somewhat along the lines of reluctant toleration, for fear of far worse—i.e., a savage war which could inflict irreparable damage on both sides.

As for Jerusalem, it must remain the capital of Israel, with the Muslim holy places being extraterritorial to a Muslim authority, with a guarantee from the United Nations of preserving that position, by force if necessary.

16 October 1997   ISAIAH BERLIN

To this statement, Berlin appended the following personal note on a separate sheet of paper:

Dear Avishai,

This is my formula: of any use to anyone? If not—waste-paper basket. Yours ever, the still far from well,—hence this superfluous 'advice'—

Isaiah